Mosdos Press Literature

Literature

OPAL

SUNFLOWER
I

Educators transmitting appropriate values and academic excellence

Mosdos
Press

Mosdos Press
CLEVELAND, OHIO

Educators transmitting appropriate values and academic excellence

Mosdos Press

Part One
ISBN–10: 0-9858078-5-7
ISBN–13: 978-0-985-80785-6

Set
ISBN–10: 0-9858078-9-x
ISBN–13: 978-0-985-80789-4

MOSDOS PRESS
Literature

EDITOR-IN-CHIEF
Judith Factor

CREATIVE/ART DIRECTOR
Carla Martin

SENIOR CURRICULUM WRITER
Abigail Rozen

COPY EDITOR
Laya Dewick

WRITERS
Lessons in Literature/Jill's Journals
Jill Brotman

Author Biographies
Aliza B. Ganchrow

TEXT AND CURRICULUM ADVISOR
Rabbi Ahron Dovid Goldberg

MOSDOS PRESS
Literature

ANTHOLOGY SERIES

OPAL

RUBY

CORAL

PEARL

JADE

GOLD

unit 1

all about the story!

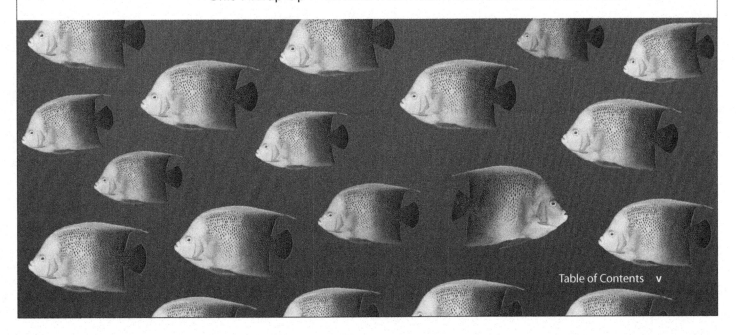

unit 2

all about the plot!

unit 3

all about characters!

For the Teacher

The information below has been provided so that you can fully appreciate the student textbook, the accompanying workbook, and—most particularly—your Teacher's Edition.

The curriculum for each grade level has been developed in such a way that both new and experienced classroom and home school teachers are able to teach effectively and enjoyably. When a teacher is at ease with the material, and well-informed about what is being taught, the teaching that results is vastly superior to what it would be otherwise.

Please read each of the sections below so that you will be familiar with every part of the curriculum. It will be easier to follow the descriptions if you consult your books as you read.

1. **Scope and Sequence:** *Scope and Sequence* is an overview of the curriculum. Unit by unit, *Scope and Sequence* lists the teaching concept of each of the *Lessons in Literature*, the selection target skill, learning strategy, common core curriculum alignment, and genre. *Scope and Sequence* also shows the components of the selection: the tie-in poem and the student workbook activities for that selection. A brief synopsis of the selection is also included. *Scope and Sequence* will enable you to see where you are going—and where you have been—regarding the sequence of skills. You will find the target skill and common core curriculum listings very helpful for lesson plan notations.

2. **Lessons in Literature:** The *Opal* pre-curriculum begins with *Lessons in Literature*. *Lessons in Literature* introduce the literary component, or the language arts skill, that will be taught with the literary work that follows. These lessons are good teaching tools. Use *Lessons in Literature*'s original short selections to give your students initial practice with the targeted literary component or skill.

3. **Reviewing Vocabulary:** Teachers should introduce all vocabulary in the *Word Banks* of the textbook *before* students read the associated piece. In the Teacher's Edition, the *Word Bank* vocabulary is listed on the *Lessons in Literature* pages that precede each selection. Often there are related vocabulary words that are not in the selection. These words are listed separately. Students should complete the Workbook Vocabulary Activity I *prior* to reading the selection.

4. **Getting Started:** *Getting Started* will make it easier for you to begin a dialogue with your students regarding the selection they are about to read. As such, *Getting Started* is a springboard to the selection. It may be an activity, a question, or information that will intrigue students and generate broader interest. Often, *Getting Started* is an aural exercise that will help students hone their listening skills.

5. **Selection Summary:** For each selection, the Teacher's Edition gives a summary of the story—a synopsis that will be a good memory aid when you return to the selection each year.

6. **Blueprint for Reading:**

   • **Into:** Here, the Teacher's Edition parallels the textbook material and both clarifies and elaborates upon the discussion of theme. Theme may be very difficult for many young readers. This fuller explanation enables you to point to specific thematic elements in the selection. *Into* is an invaluable teaching aid.

   • **Eyes On:** This section of the Teacher's Edition focuses on the featured literary component. *Eyes On* also enables you to elaborate on writing style, tone, and language. Here, you will also find insightful teaching hints and thoughtful questions to pose. *Eyes On* helps your students understand the target skill being taught.

7. **Guiding the Reading:** You can guide your students' understanding of the selection with both literal and analytical questions. These questions appear in the Teacher's Edition below the textbook page from which they are drawn. The literal questions are based on the facts of the piece. The answer requires recall only, and can be derived from the page the class has just reviewed. Analytical questions are inferential. Again, the answer can be drawn from the page just read, but the answer is not stated explicitly, as it is with the literal questions. *Guiding the Reading* lists the literal and the analytical questions separately. However, since the questions build on one another, it makes sense to ask the questions in sequential order. Analytical questions build on literal questions, and often, each literal question builds on the one before it.

8. **Literary Components:** *Literary Components* provides a superior lesson tool. They may even be an education for the teacher. Here, numbers in the margins of the selection provide a legend to a list of descriptions of literary components. The numbered, underlined text provides examples of imagery, style, point of view, plot, characterization, setting, foreshadowing, suspense, rising and falling action, climax, resolution, irony, dialogue, figures of speech, and historical or scientific relevance (where appropriate).

   The details of each literary component are not necessarily meant to be shared in their entirety with your class. Their most important function is to ground the educator in the material. Use your judgment, regarding how advanced your learners are, and how many of these insights you think your class will benefit from or appreciate. Often, the *Literary Components* serve as a way to explain a sophisticated point to the educator, so that he or she can, in turn, explain it coherently to the students.

9. **Tie-In Poems:** A majority of the selections have a tie-in poem that follows the selection in the textbook. A brief explanatory statement about the poem appears alongside its image in the Teacher's Edition. These tie-in poems have been provided in the textbook simply to be enjoyed, and often share a thematic or topical link with the prose selection they follow. There is no student curriculum associated with these poems, but, suggested questions are listed in the tie-in poem section to be used at your discretion.

10. **Studying the Selection:**

    - **First Impressions:** The Teacher's Edition *First Impressions* parallels the textbook post-curricular questions, and suggests possible student responses.

    - **Quick Review** and **Focus** provide detailed answers to the questions posed in the parallel sections of the textbook. Additional material has been included for productive classroom discussion.

    - **Creating and Writing** is the final review element in the textbook. The activities in this section are challenging: the first activity requires creative writing grounded in the theme of the selection, and the final activity is non-literate (a work of art, a charitable activity, a fieldwork project, for example). Precise teacher instructions for these projects and activities are provided in the Teacher's Edition.

11. **Jill's Journal:** *Jill's Journal* is a unique literary device that follows five of the prose selections.

    - This is a four-page spread: 3 pages are devoted to *Jill's Journal*; the remaining page describes a power skill for the young reader or writer. Exercises are given for practice.

    - *Jill's Journal* is an "autobiographical," first-person narrative. Jill imagines herself a reporter on assignment. Her journal entries are connected topically with the selection, and place Jill the Journalist back in time or someplace in the world. These pieces are guaranteed to bring students right into the world of the story. Extensive background material is provided in the Teacher's Edition.

12. **Teacher's Answer Guide for the Workbook Activities:** The Workbook Answer Guide is located at the back of each of the two volumes of your Teacher's Edition. Notes To the Teacher has been included with suggestions regarding how best to use the student workbook. Please acquaint yourself with the workbook at the beginning of the semester, *before* you begin using the textbook with your students.

Opal Teacher's Edition

- Scope and Sequence
- Annotated Teacher's Edition
- Workbook Answer Guide

Unit 1: All About the Story!

The elements of a story are introduced in this unit—plot, character, setting, and theme—as well as the basic structure of a story. In each of Unit One's five selections, one of these elements is explored.

SELECTION	CURRICULUM	ABOUT THE STORY	COMMON CORE	WORKBOOK
The Jar of Tassai Grace Moon p. 4 **Genre:** Realistic Fiction **Lesson in Literature:** What Is a Story? *Treasure of the Andes*	**Eyes On:** Story Elements **Skill:** Understanding that a story needs a plot, character, setting, and a theme **Strategy:** Prior knowledge	This is a character-driven story about a Pueblo Indian girl who sacrifices the beautiful jar she had made to save a child from a rattlesnake attack. The stated theme is clear as are the easily recognizable plot and setting.	RL.3.1; RL.3.2; RL.3.3	**Pages:** 2-7 **Vocab. I:** p. 2 **Vocab. II:** p. 3 **MAS:** p. 4 **Lang. Arts:** p. 5 **Graphic Organizer:** pp. 6-7
The Story of the White Sombrero Mariana Prieto p. 20 **Genre:** Folktale **Lesson in Literature:** What Is Plot? *The Three Sisters*	**Eyes On:** Plot **Skill:** Understanding that a plot is what happens in a story **Strategy:** Summarize	Two brothers, one an optimist and the other a pessimist, set out to sell the family-made sombreros at the market. As they encounter various problems along the way, the thematic message of positive thinking and the clear plot are evident to the reader.	RL.3.2; RF.3.4	**Pages:** 8-13 **Vocab. I:** p. 8 **Vocab. II:** p. 9 **MAS:** p. 10 **Lang. Arts:** p. 11 **Graphic Organizer:** pp. 12-13
A Cane in Her Hand Ada B. Litchfield p. 38 **Genre:** Realistic Fiction **Lesson in Literature:** What Are Characters? *The Spanish Ships*	**Eyes On:** Character **Skill:** Understanding that characters are all of the people, animals, robots, etc. found in a story **Strategy:** Making connections	This story about a visually impaired girl provides an excellent lesson in relating to the disabled. The reader learns from the girl's comments about people who talk about her as if she can't hear or is too disabled to understand, just because she can't see.	RL.3.3; RL.3.6	**Pages:** 14-19 **Vocab. I:** p. 14 **Vocab. II:** p. 15 **MAS:** p. 16 **Lang. Arts:** p. 17 **Graphic Organizer:** pp. 18-19
Boom Town Sonia Levitin p. 52 **Genre:** Fiction **Lesson in Literature:** What Is Setting? *The Blue Marble*	**Eyes On:** Setting **Skill:** Understanding that setting means the time or the place that a story takes place **Strategy:** Visualize	A humorous story set during the Gold Rush era builds sequentially as each event unfolds. A town and its workforce grow through the efforts of a feisty young girl who makes pies, sells them, and encourages others to create needed businesses and services.	RL.3.5; RL.3.3	**Pages:** 20-25 **Vocab. I:** p. 20 **Vocab. II:** p. 21 **MAS:** p. 22 **Lang. Arts:** p. 23 **Graphic Organizer:** pp. 24-25
Taro and the Tofu Masako Matsuno p. 74 **Genre:** Fiction **Lesson in Literature:** What Is Theme? *Life on Mars*	**Eyes On:** Theme **Skill:** Understanding that the theme is the story's main idea **Strategy:** Questioning	In this theme-driven story, the main character, a boy named Taro, returns the overpayment of change to the tofu seller. The internal dialogue and moral battle Taro has as he arrives at choosing honesty, poses an interesting and relatable dilemma to think about.	RL.3.2; RL.3.3; W.3.1	**Pages:** 26-31 **Vocab. I:** p. 26 **Vocab. II:** p. 27 **MAS:** p. 28 **Lang. Arts:** p. 29 **Graphic Organizer:** pp. 30-31

Unit 2: All About the Plot!

The elements of plot are introduced in this unit—internal and external conflict, sequence, plot in drama, and main idea—as well as continued curriculum work with the basic structure of the story.

SELECTION	CURRICULUM	ABOUT THE STORY	COMMON CORE	WORKBOOK
Good-Bye, 382 Shin Dang Dong Frances and Ginger Park p. 98 **Genre:** Realistic Fiction **Lesson in Literature:** What Is Internal Conflict? *The Cousin*	**Eyes On:** Internal Conflict **Skill:** Understanding and being able to recognize the internal conflict in a story **Strategy:** Prior knowledge	This realistic story about a girl who moves with her family from Korea to Massachusetts will touch any reader who has experienced moving or going to a new school. As the reader understands the main character's emotions, they will explore their own point of view as they delve into this story's theme and plot.	RL.3.1; RL.3.6	**Pages:** 32-37 **Vocab. I:** p. 32 **Vocab. II:** p. 33 **MAS:** p. 34 **Lang. Arts:** p. 35 **Graphic Organizer:** pp. 36-37
Sybil Rides By Night Drollene P. Brown p. 120 **Genre:** Historical Biography **Lesson in Literature:** What Is External Conflict? *The Underground Road*	**Eyes On:** External Conflict **Skill:** Understanding and being able to recognize the external conflict in a story **Strategy:** Making connections	This is a story of a true event. Sybil Ludington, the daughter of Col. Henry Ludington, was a heroine of the Revolutionary War. She became famous for her night ride on April 26, 1777 to alert American colonial forces to the approach of the British. Her ride was similar to Paul Revere's.	RI.3.2; RL.3.3	**Pages:** 38-43 **Vocab. I:** p. 38 **Vocab. II:** p. 39 **MAS:** p. 40 **Lang. Arts:** p. 41 **Graphic Organizer:** pp. 42-43
Nothing Much Happened Today Mary Blount Christian p. 134 **Genre:** Humorous Fiction **Lesson in Literature:** What Is Sequence? *Mom I Love You*	**Eyes On:** Sequence **Skill:** Understanding what is important about a story and being able to tell about it in sequential order **Strategy:** Summarizing	This is a great comic sequence about all the things that happened while Mother was out shopping.	RL.3.1; RL.3.3	**Pages:** 44-49 **Vocab. I:** p. 44 **Vocab. II:** p. 45 **MAS:** p. 46 **Lang. Arts:** p. 47 **Graphic Organizer:** pp. 48-49
Food's on the Table Sydney Taylor p. 148 **Genre:** Play **Lesson in Literature:** How Is Setting for a Drama Different? *The Driving Test*	**Eyes On:** Drama **Skill:** Make and confirm predictions **Strategy:** Questioning	In this humorous story told as a play, a group of siblings accidentally eat the wrong supper at a stranger's apartment, because they think it is their aunt's new apartment. The play is adapted from an *All-of-a-Kind Family* story, and is an excellent vehicle for practice with predicting.	RL.3.3; RL.3.5	**Pages:** 50-55 **Vocab. I:** p. 50 **Vocab. II:** p. 51 **MAS:** p. 52 **Lang. Arts:** p. 53 **Graphic Organizer:** pp. 54-55
Across the Wide Dark Sea Jean Van Leeuwen p. 162 **Genre:** Historical Fiction **Lesson in Literature:** What Is the Main Idea? *Crossing America*	**Eyes On:** Main Idea **Skill:** Understanding the main idea and recounting details **Strategy:** Inferring	This fictionalized adventure story is about the *Mayflower* voyage. Reading a work of historical fiction about a familiar event enables the young reader to recount the details and demonstrate an understanding of the plot.	RL.3.1; RF.3.3	**Pages:** 56-61 **Vocab. I:** p. 56 **Vocab. II:** p. 57 **MAS:** p. 58 **Lang. Arts:** p. 59 **Graphic Organizer:** pp. 60-61

Unit 3: All About Characters!

The elements of character are introduced in this unit—character attributes, point of view, how characters connect and relate to each other, cause and effect, and biography—as well as continued study of story structure.

SELECTION	CURRICULUM	ABOUT THE STORY	COMMON CORE	WORKBOOK
The Printer Myron Uhlberg p. 192 **Genre:** Realistic Fiction **Lesson in Literature:** What Are Character Traits? *A Different Kind of Hero*	**Eyes On:** Character Attributes **Skill:** Ability to describe a character's physical traits, personality traits, and attributes **Strategy:** Visualizing	The story is based on an event in the life of the author's deaf father, a printer, who saved his fellow workers from a fire in the print room of the newspaper he worked for. Described with clarity, the father's traits and attributes are easily recognizable.	RL.3.3; RL.3.6	**Pages:** 62-67 **Vocab. I:** p. 62 **Vocab. II:** p. 63 **MAS:** p. 64 **Lang. Arts:** p. 65 **Graphic Organizer:** pp. 66-67
Lorenzo & Angelina Eugene Fern p. 212 **Genre:** Fiction **Lesson in Literature:** What Is Point of View? *JoJo and Midnight*	**Eyes On:** Point of View **Skill:** Identifying different points of view **Strategy:** Focusing on story structure	This story is told in alternating sections in both Lorenzo's and Angelina's voices. Angelina wants to climb a dangerous mountain; the stubborn donkey Lorenzo saves her from falling off the edge of the cliff.	RL.3.3; RL.3.5	**Pages:** 68-73 **Vocab. I:** p. 68 **Vocab. II:** p. 69 **MAS:** p. 70 **Lang. Arts:** p. 71 **Graphic Organizer:** pp. 72-73
A Day When Frogs Wear Shoes Ann Cameron p. 234 **Genre:** Realistic Fiction **Lesson in Literature:** Relationships in a Story *When Snow Days Come, Dogs Have Beards*	**Eyes On:** Connections and Relationships **Skill:** Studying the connection and relationships between characters **Strategy:** Questioning	In this story about bored kids on a hot summer day, the reader explores relationships and connections between the characters. A sweet adventure ensues when one of their fathers takes them on an impromptu trip to the lake.	RL.3.3; RL.3.6	**Pages:** 74-79 **Vocab. I:** p. 74 **Vocab. II:** p. 75 **MAS:** p. 76 **Lang. Arts:** p. 77 **Graphic Organizer:** pp. 78-79
The Burning of the Rice Fields Lafcadio Hearn p. 250 **Genre:** Folktale **Lesson in Literature:** Cause and Effect *The Grandmother*	**Eyes On:** Cause and Effect **Skill:** Recognizing that a character's actions influence the events of a story **Strategy:** Questioning and making connections	Realizing there is an approaching tsunami, a wealthy farmer burns his rice fields to attract the villagers who he knows will come to help save his land. This selection is an excellent vehicle for understanding cause and effect in a character-driven selection.	RL.3.3; W.3.1	**Pages:** 80-85 **Vocab. I:** p. 80 **Vocab. II:** p. 81 **MAS:** p. 82 **Lang. Arts:** p. 83 **Graphic Organizer:** pp. 84-85
Mother to Tigers George Ella Lyon p. 264 **Genre:** Biography **Lesson in Literature:** What Is Biography? *Betsy Brotman in Liberia*	**Eyes On:** Biography **Skill:** Understanding that a biography is usually a narrative about a famous or noteworthy person **Strategy:** Evaluating	This biography is about Helen Martini who nursed baby animals for the Bronx Zoo. Done as a narrative poem, this unique form offers drama to this poignant biography.	RL.3.3; RL.3.5	**Pages:** 86-91 **Vocab. I:** p. 86 **Vocab. II:** p. 87 **MAS:** p. 88 **Lang. Arts:** p. 89 **Graphic Organizer:** pp. 90-91

Unit 4: All About Setting!

The elements of setting are introduced in this unit—setting as plot, images, descriptive text, historical setting, and setting as theme—as well as more advanced study of story structure.

SELECTION	CURRICULUM	ABOUT THE STORY	COMMON CORE	WORKBOOK
The Town That Moved Mary Jane Finsand p. 4 **Genre:** Narrative Nonfiction **Lesson in Literature:** More About Setting *Amasina, Doctor of the Amazon*	**Eyes On:** When the Plot is About the Setting **Skill:** Recognizing when the setting is critical to the story **Strategy:** Making connections and description	This is a true narrative of an actual event. A Minnesota town was entirely moved because rich iron ore deposits were discovered under the town. The reader is provided an excellent experience in reading a setting-driven selection told as narrative nonfiction.	RI.3.2; RI.3.7; RL.3.9	**Pages:** 2-7 **Vocab. I:** p. 2 **Vocab. II:** p. 3 **MAS:** p. 4 **Lang. Arts:** p. 5 **Graphic Organizer:** pp. 6-7
Heartland Diane Siebert p. 22 **Genre:** Narrative Poem **Lesson in Literature:** What Are Images? *The Shore*	**Eyes On:** Images **Skill:** Recognizing the images in a narrative poem **Strategy:** Visualizing	This is a beautiful narrative poem praising the attributes of America's heartland. Rich in imagery, the reader can visualize the settings described.	RL.3.4; RL.3.5; RL.3.7	**Pages:** 8-13 **Vocab. I:** p. 8 **Vocab. II:** p. 9 **MAS:** p. 10 **Lang. Arts:** p. 11 **Graphic Organizer:** pp. 12-13
No Laughing Matter Abigail Rozen p. 36 **Genre:** Fiction **Lesson in Literature:** Descriptive Text *Tom and Tola Talk*	**Eyes On:** Descriptive Text **Skill:** Interpreting descriptive text **Strategy:** Visualizing	This story takes the reader back to a time when summers were relaxing and activities were simple. The readers will easily relate to the children in this tale who visit an amusement park and then try to create one of their own.	RL.3.1; RL.3.3	**Pages:** 14-19 **Vocab. I:** p. 14 **Vocab. II:** p. 15 **MAS:** p. 16 **Lang. Arts:** p. 17 **Graphic Organizer:** pp. 18-19
Patrick and the Great Molasses Explosion Marjorie Stover p. 66 **Genre:** Historical Fiction **Lesson in Literature:** Historical Fiction *Sarah and the San Francisco Earthquake*	**Eyes On:** Historical Fiction **Skill:** Understanding and recognizing historical fiction **Strategy:** Story structure and summarizing	A molasses tank exploded, spewing tons of molasses onto the streets. Told as a tall tale about an actual event that happened in 1919 in Boston, MA, the reader experiences nonfiction told as fiction—an interesting learning experience in understanding story structure.	RL.3.5; RI.3.9	**Pages:** 20-25 **Vocab. I:** p. 20 **Vocab. II:** p. 21 **MAS:** p. 22 **Lang. Arts:** p. 23 **Graphic Organizer:** pp. 24-25
Bear Mouse Berniece Freschet p. 96 **Genre:** Animal Fiction **Lesson in Literature:** Creating a Setting *Desert Danger*	**Eyes On:** Setting As the Most Important Element **Skill:** Understanding why the setting is crucial in driving this piece to its conclusion **Strategy:** Visualizing and making connections	This wonderfully told setting-driven selection is about a little mouse who hunts for food in a world fraught with danger, so she can make the milk necessary to feed her young. This story is very well-written and amazingly suspenseful.	RL.3.1; RL.3.3	**Pages:** 26-31 **Vocab. I:** p. 26 **Vocab. II:** p. 27 **MAS:** p. 28 **Lang. Arts:** p. 29 **Graphic Organizer:** pp. 30-31

Unit 5: All About Theme!

The various aspects of theme are introduced in this unit—stated theme, implied theme, drawing conclusions, and comparing and contrasting—as well as continued review of the structure of a story.

SELECTION	CURRICULUM	ABOUT THE STORY	COMMON CORE	WORKBOOK
A Gift for Tía Rosa Karen T. Taha p. 134 **Genre:** Realistic Fiction **Lesson in Literature:** What Is Author's Purpose? *The Children's Home*	**Eyes On:** Author's Purpose **Skill:** Understanding an author's purpose and identifying how we feel when we read a story with a meaningful theme **Strategy:** Inferring, evaluating, and synthesizing	This theme-driven story about the loss of a beloved close family friend, the renewal of birth, and carrying on the tradition of giving, offers an excellent opportunity to develop the comprehension skills of evaluating and synthesizing.	RL.3.2; RL.3.3	**Pages:** 32-37 **Vocab. I:** p. 32 **Vocab. II:** p. 33 **MAS:** p. 34 **Lang. Arts:** p. 35 **Graphic Organizer:** pp. 36-37
Harlequin and the Gift of Many Colors Remy Charlip and Burton Supree p. 158 **Genre:** Fantasy Fiction **Lesson in Literature:** What Is Stated Theme? *Good Neighbors*	**Eyes On:** Stated Theme **Skill:** Identifying the stated theme **Strategy:** Questioning and summarizing	A poignant story with a clear stated theme, this story is about how friends join together, giving a small piece of each of their costumes to a poor friend who doesn't have one of his own.	RL.3.2; RL.3.3	**Pages:** 38-43 **Vocab. I:** p. 38 **Vocab. II:** p. 39 **MAS:** p. 40 **Lang. Arts:** p. 41 **Graphic Organizer:** pp. 42-43
Claw Foot Evelyn Witter p. 174 **Genre:** Fiction **Lesson in Literature:** What Is Implied Theme? *A New Girl in Town*	**Eyes On:** Implied Theme **Skill:** Identifying the implied theme **Strategy:** Making connections and evaluating	This selection, with its implied theme, is about an Indian boy, Claw Foot, who learns to use his talents to save his people from starvation, instead of dwelling on his handicap. He earns a new name—*He Who Thinks*.	RL.3.2; RL.3.3	**Pages:** 44-49 **Vocab. I:** p. 44 **Vocab. II:** p. 45 **MAS:** p. 46 **Lang. Arts:** p. 47 **Graphic Organizer:** pp. 48-49
Beatrice's Goat Page McBrier p. 194 **Genre:** Narrative Nonfiction **Lesson in Literature:** Drawing Conclusions *The Fresh Air Fund*	**Eyes On:** Drawing Conclusions **Skill:** Thinking about the details and the facts in a selection to reach a decision about what the selection is about **Strategy:** Questioning and synthesizing	In this narrative nonfiction piece about how a goat donated through an international charity helps a girl from Uganda fulfill her dream of going to school, the reader will practice questioning and predicting to understand the underlying theme.	RL.3.2; RL.3.3; W.3.1	**Pages:** 50-55 **Vocab. I:** p. 50 **Vocab. II:** p. 51 **MAS:** p. 52 **Lang. Arts:** p. 53 **Graphic Organizer:** pp. 54-55
The Gardener Sarah Stewart p. 212 **Genre:** Realistic Fiction **Lesson in Literature:** Compare and Contrast *Letters to a Friend*	**Eyes On:** Compare and Contrast **Skill:** Recognize similarities and differences between the characters and reviewing the tools used to compare and contrast **Strategy:** Making connections and prior knowledge	This selection is done in letter form. During the Depression a young farm girl goes to live in the city with her grumpy uncle, a baker. Through the optimistic letters she writes home she keeps her family apprised of her life in the city.	RL.3.2; RL.3.5	**Pages:** 56-61 **Vocab. I:** p. 56 **Vocab. II:** p. 57 **MAS:** p. 58 **Lang. Arts:** p. 59 **Graphic Organizer:** pp. 60-61

Unit 6: The Grand Finalé!

All of the story elements taught are reviewed in this final unit. We explore the purpose of biography, differentiating between fantasy and reality, and the importance of dialogue as the student solidifies the study of all of the story elements.

SELECTION	CURRICULUM	ABOUT THE STORY	COMMON CORE	WORKBOOK
Rocks in His Head Carol Otis Hurst p. 262 **Genre:** Biography **Lesson in Literature:** The Purpose of Biography *The Right to Be Treated Well*	**Eyes On:** The Purpose of Biography **Skill:** Understanding that a biography is a true story about a real person's life and it has been written to enable the reader to learn about this person **Strategy:** Evaluating	This biography is about the author's unassuming father, an avid rock collector. He is a simple man, who pursues his interests and achieves unexpected recognition. The reader understands that a biographer's purpose can be just to tell a true story about a regular person.	RL.3.1; RL.3.3	**Pages:** 62-67 **Vocab. I:** p. 62 **Vocab. II:** p. 63 **MAS:** p. 64 **Lang. Arts:** p. 65 **Graphic Organizer:** pp. 66-67
The Naming of Olga da Polga Michael Bond p. 274 **Genre:** Realistic Fiction with Fantasy **Lesson in Literature:** Reality and Fantasy *Pico Goes Home*	**Eyes On:** Fantasy **Skill:** Differentiating between reality and fantasy **Strategy:** Inferring and evaluating	This story is an excellent mix of reality and fantasy. A young girl gets a pet guinea pig and ponders over a name for her. The reader will be challenged to identify the reality from the fantasy as the story unfolds.	RL.3.3; RL.3.5	**Pages:** 68-73 **Vocab. I:** p. 68 **Vocab. II:** p. 69 **MAS:** p. 70 **Lang. Arts:** p. 71 **Graphic Organizer:** pp. 72-73
A Toad for Tuesday Russell E. Erickson p. 290 **Genre:** Novella **Lesson in Literature:** Using Dialogue *Helpful Little Bears*	**Eyes On:** Dialogue **Skill:** Understanding that dialogue tells the reader about the characters and about what is happening in the story **Strategy:** Visualizing and evaluating	Challenging the reader's ability to identify all of the story elements, this fine story has it all—plot, character, setting, and theme. The novella tells the tale of a wise toad, and his developing friendship with his captor, a grumpy, hungry owl.	RL.3.2; RL.3.3; RL.3.5; RL.3.10	**Pages:** 74-91 **Vocab. I:** p. 74/80/86 **Vocab. II:** p. 75/81/87 **MAS:** p. 76/82/88 **Lang. Arts:** p. 77/83/89 **Graphic Organizer:** pp. 78-79/84-85/90-91

Unit 1

unit 1

PEOPLE

PLACES

BRIGHT IDEAS

all about
the story!

FEELINGS

The Jar of Tassai

Lesson in Literature

What Is a Story?

Treasure of the Andes

1. Carlos tripped and fell over the urn.
2. The characters are: Carlos, Papa, Mama, Tomie, and Tomie's Mama.
3. The setting of the story is in Bolivia in the Andes Mountains near Lake Titicaca.

Selection Summary

Tassai is a young Pueblo girl who lives on a mesa overlooking the Painted Desert in Arizona. She works in the fields, grinds the corn, and helps her mother weave baskets. She is quite content, enjoying the simple pleasures of life in an agricultural society. While working outdoors, Tassai has discovered some beautiful clay and secretly made a jar out of it. She has learned to make jars from her mother, and takes enormous pleasure in forming the silky clay into a fine jar. When the jar is painted and baked, Tassai wraps it in a blanket and hides it.

Not long before, the Governor of the Pueblo had announced that a "feast," or what we might call a fair, would be held for the three towns in the area. Every person attending the fair was requested to bring something he or she had made. Prizes would be awarded for the best items.

The day of the fair dawns clear and bright. Tassai is excited, but cannot leave until she has helped her mother all day in the fields. Finally, she hurriedly grabs the blanket that holds her jar and runs to the fair. The Governor and some others are judging the entries. As they approach Tassai, she nervously starts to open her blanket, only to discover that the jar is not in it. She had taken a different blanket, which contains a corncob doll. Crestfallen, she turns to run home to get the jar. Unbeknownst to her, a little girl who saw the corncob doll follows her home. As she is coming out of her house, jar in hand, the girl cries out, for she sees a rattlesnake coming towards her. Tassai raises the jar and shatters it on the head of the snake, killing it.

The girl's father thanks Tassai and tells her that, from what he can see of the pieces, the jar would have won a prize. The Governor does award Tassai a prize, not for her jar, but for her good deed. Tassai is happy. It does not matter that her jar was broken; she can always make another.

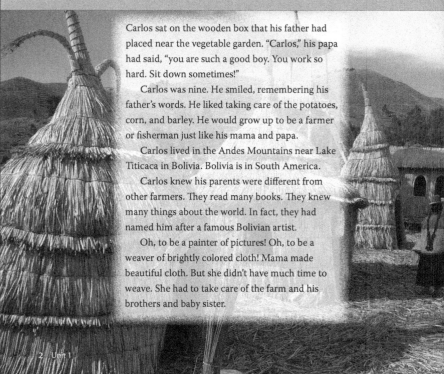

Lesson in Literature...
TREASURE OF THE ANDES

WHAT IS A STORY?

- A **story** is about something that *happens* at a certain *time* in a certain *place*.
- What *happens* in the story is called the **plot**.
- The *people* or *animals* in the story are called the **characters**.
- The *time* and *place* in which the events happen are called the **setting**.

THINK ABOUT IT!

1. How do the boys discover the silver urn?
2. Who are the five characters in the story?
3. Where does the story take place? Name the country the boys live in, and the mountains and the lake that are near their farm.

Carlos sat on the wooden box that his father had placed near the vegetable garden. "Carlos," his papa had said, "you are such a good boy. You work so hard. Sit down sometimes!"

Carlos was nine. He smiled, remembering his father's words. He liked taking care of the potatoes, corn, and barley. He would grow up to be a farmer or fisherman just like his mama and papa.

Carlos lived in the Andes Mountains near Lake Titicaca in Bolivia. Bolivia is in South America.

Carlos knew his parents were different from other farmers. They read many books. They knew many things about the world. In fact, they had named him after a famous Bolivian artist.

Oh, to be a painter of pictures! Oh, to be a weaver of brightly colored cloth! Mama made beautiful cloth. But she didn't have much time to weave. She had to take care of the farm and his brothers and baby sister.

2 Unit 1

Getting Started

The first discussion of the year should be about stories in general. Ask your students what some of their favorite stories are. They may name some books they have read that are familiar to most of the class. Ask them what makes them like one story more than another. Is it the action? Do they like some character that is funny? Does it have a really good ending? Ask them if they prefer serious stories to funny ones, happy ones to sad ones, action-filled ones to more thoughtful ones. Ask each student who answers why they prefer one type of story to another. Lead up to the question: What elements must every story have? The answer is, of course, that every story needs a plot, characters, setting, and theme. But don't use those terms. See if you can elicit these story elements from them in their own words.

After this discussion, read two paragraphs to them. One will be a "non-story," because it will lack some story elements, the other will be a mini-story. We provide you with a sample of each, though you may prefer to make up your own.

"Carlos! How are you?" It was his friend, Tomie, calling. "Want to search for buried treasure?"

"Sure," Carlos shouted back. Their favorite game was hunting for treasure. They had always heard stories that something valuable was buried in the Andes. They imagined finding treasure and being heroes. Then they could both go to art school. They would be famous artists! They had talked about this many times.

"You know, Tomie, I've been thinking. The legend says the treasure is where the earth is like a mirror or a sheet of glass. Well, Lake Titicaca is so calm. It really looks like a sheet of glass!"

They headed for the lake with their llama, Isabella. She wore her bright pink collar and ear tassels. Their spades were set in the pack that she wore.

Carlos and Tomie were near the edge of the lake. Suddenly, Carlos tripped on a rock and fell. "Are you all right?" cried Tomie.

"My hands are scraped, but I'm okay. It was just a big rock!"

"Hey, wait," Tomie exclaimed, as he helped his friend to his feet. "Look at that!" he said. "That's no rock. See, it's shiny—just the way the lake is shiny." They set to digging with their spades, excited. But Carlos worried.

What if it were nothing special? Then there would be no art school.

Little by little they uncovered an old and heavy silver urn. "It's just like what we saw at the museum in the city," Tomie said. They attached the urn to Isabella's pack with rope. They wanted to get home quickly, but Isabella had a heavy load.

Soon they saw their mamas working in the field. The boys untied the urn. Together, they held it up for their mamas to see. "Look!" the boys exclaimed. "We found the treasure of the Andes!"

At first their mothers laughed. "Are you certain it belongs to no one else?"

"Mama," Carlos cried. "How could something so old belong to someone else?"

The two women looked at each other. "Do you know what this means for our families?" Tomie's mama said to the boys.

Carlos' mama nodded. "We have not told either of you how Tomie's little sister needs medicine, or how little food we have had to get by on. We save the food for the children."

"Thank you so much," Tomie's mama said quietly. "You are both heroes."

The Jar of Tassai 5

Non-Story

Our beach is a wonderful place to be. The sand is clean, the water is clear, there are seagulls flying above, and the skies are usually blue and bright. The beach is open during the summer months and is usually crowded, unless you come early in the morning. There are stands where you can buy ice cream and rent umbrellas. There are a couple of brick buildings where you can change into your swimsuit. The bus goes right to the beach, so it is convenient and easy to reach.

Story

Brian and Joseph loved the beach because the sand was clean, the water was clear, and the skies above it were usually sunny. Unfortunately, today was not one of those bright days. When they got there, the seagulls were circling and crying their loud cries. The wind was gusting and sand was blowing into everyone's eyes. "Look!" said Brian, "A funnel cloud is coming our way! We've got to find shelter." Everyone was crowding down the steps of one of the buildings that were usually used for changing. Just as the boys got to the building, they heard a huge crash, as a tree blew down. "Whew," they said. "We're glad we got off the beach."

Discussion

Ask your class which of the two paragraphs is a little story. When they choose the second paragraph, ask them how it is different from the first. The second paragraph has characters. The first does not. The second paragraph has a plot—something changes, a problem arises and is solved—the first does not. Both paragraphs have a setting, but a setting alone does not make a story. Do not accept "action" or the lack thereof as a story element. Action that is not part of a problem and resolution, or action that does not lead to change, is not a story element. One can describe an auto race or a rodeo, but those would simply be descriptions of action, not stories.

Target Skill:	Understanding that a story needs a plot, character, setting, and a theme
Learning Strategy:	Prior knowledge
Common Core Curriculum:	RL.3.1; RL.3.2; RL.3.3
Genre:	Realistic Fiction

Related Vocabulary

agriculture (AG ruh KUL chur) *n.*: farming

arid (AIR id) *adj.*: dry and desert-like

compete (kum PEET) *v.*: to try to be the winner in a contest

craft (KRAFT) *n.*: work that requires special skill, like weaving or pottery making

feast (FEEST) *n.*: a rich, joyous meal for many guests

kiln (KILL) *n.*: an oven for baking clay pottery

pottery (POT uh ree) *n.*: bowls and other vessels made of clay that is shaped, then baked

rural (RUH rul) *adj.*: areas where there are farms and fields, not streets and buildings

Workbook

Related Pages:	2-7
Answer Key Pages:	2-3

The Jar of Tassai

Into . . . *The Jar of Tassai*

The theme of *The Jar of Tassai* is sacrifice and making choices. Tassai must sacrifice her cherished jar to save another human being. And she must decide to do so in a split second. These ideas can only be discussed after the children have read the story, since the whole question of sacrifice does not appear until near the very end of the story. To discuss it beforehand would ruin the surprise climax.

Before reading the story, however, several peripheral ideas may be introduced. Tassai is a Pueblo Indian. She lives a simple life, working all day and having few possessions. Yet, she is happy and contented. Spend some time describing what Tassai's life was like. Explain that her house probably had only one or two rooms. She probably had none of our modern conveniences. Most of her day was spent out of doors working in the fields. Ask your students if they think they would enjoy that kind of a life. It will be interesting to see their varying responses.

Another topic you may wish to explore with your class is designing and crafting. Ask your students whether they have ever done anything like making pottery, painting, woodworking, or the like. Tassai loved every moment spent working on her jar. Understanding the thrill of creating something beautiful is key to appreciating how hard it was for her to sacrifice her jar.

A third topic is "secrets." When should secrets be kept and when should they not? Tell your students that if a secret is something of which their parents would disapprove, it should not be kept a secret. If the secret is something their parents would like, but they want to surprise them, like a birthday present or teaching the dog a trick, they may keep the secret. If they are not sure, they should tell their parents, even if it might spoil a surprise. That is always the safest bet.

Eyes On: Story Elements

In *Getting Started*, we asked you to encourage the students to talk about literary elements in their own words. It is now time to identify these elements with the proper terms. Tassai is a character, as are the Governor, the little girl, and her father. As you read the story, repeat the term so that the children become familiar with it. The mesa, the open area for the feast, and Tassai's house are all settings. Use the term when referring to them.

Identifying plot and theme are more difficult. Here is where the learning strategy, *using prior*

knowledge, comes in. Every child knows instinctively that a story has a plot. Verbalizing what constitutes a plot, though, is something even most adults could not readily do. The easiest way to start teaching about plot is by saying that a story has a beginning, a middle, and an end. Ask your students to think of some story they know. Ask them to tell you how it began and how it ended. Then, ask them what changed in the story between the beginning and the end. A character may have changed, a situation may have changed, or a setting may have changed. If nothing has changed, the piece of writing is not a story. As the students read *The Jar of Tassai*, keep a list of changes. At the beginning, Tassai is making the jar. In the middle, Tassai has finished the jar. At the end, the jar is broken. A somewhat more sophisticated discussion would be: At the beginning Tassai is a sweet girl with a secret; in the middle, she is mature enough to compete at the feast with adults; at the end she is a heroine who has saved a life.

Theme is the hardest element to identify. Drawing on our strategy of *using prior knowledge*, ask your students to identify the theme of a story known to all of them. Here's a simple example: In the book *If You Give a*

The Jar of Tassai

Grace Moon

Tassai[1] lived on the top of a mesa[2] that looked far out over the Painted Desert.[3] The air was as clear as thin ice. It even made the faraway mountains and blue hills look nearer than they really were. <u>Tassai was a</u> **1** <u>Pueblo Indian</u>[4] <u>girl.</u> <u>She was as brown</u> **2** <u>as a nut that has dried in the sun.</u> She liked to lie on the edge of the mesa. She would look over the desert and <u>dream long dreams.</u> **3**

But Tassai did not often have time for dreams. There was too much work for her to do. Tassai worked with her mother in the little fields at the foot of the mesa. It was not hard work, and it had magic in it. It had the magic of watching green things spring up out of the ground where only brown earth had been before.

---

1. *Tassai* (TASS EYE)
2. A *mesa* (MAY suh) is a flat area at the top of steep mountainsides.
3. The *Painted Desert* is a desert in Arizona, east of the Colorado River.
4. The *Pueblo* (PWEB lo) *Indians* are Native Americans who live in the American Southwest. The stone or adobe houses they live in are also called *pueblos*.

Literary Components

1 **Exposition:** The first few sentences introduce us to Tassai. They tell us she is a young Pueblo girl who lives in a rural area.

2 **Simile:** Although it is too early to use terms like *simile*, you may want to talk about how we often compare a new thing to a familiar one to help us picture what the new thing is like.

3 **Characterization:** Tassai is a dreamer. She has ideas about life. As we will see, most of her day is spent doing things; yet, her simple life has not robbed her of imagination.

Guiding the Reading

Literal

Q: Where did Tassai live?
A: Tassai lived on a mesa near the Painted Desert.

Q: What is a mesa?
A: A mesa is a flat area at the top of a steep mountainside.

Q: When Tassai went outdoors each day, what view did she see?
A: She saw faraway mountains and blue hills. The air was clear and the sun was warm. Below the mesa was the desert.

Q: What did Tassai do each day?
A: She worked with her mother in the fields.

Analytical

Q: Did Tassai like living on the mesa? Why or why not?
A: Tassai loved the beautiful area in which she lived. She enjoyed working in the fields and watching things grow.

Mouse a Cookie, the theme is that sometimes, if you do someone one little favor, they will keep asking for more and more. Choose a book or story that has an obvious theme and that is known to most of the students.

In this story, the theme is not really evident until the end. When the children have finished reading the story, ask them what the story's main idea is. You may have to guide them with leading questions. Have them think about the story's climax (don't use the term—it's far too much detail at this point). Discuss how much Tassai loved her jar and yet, how instantly she chose to break it. Ask your class how they know that she made the right choice. Point out that choosing to sacrifice something that is precious for something far more important—in this case, saving a life—is the story's theme. It goes without saying that you must express this in grade-appropriate language.

The Jar of Tassai

Literary Components

4 Sensory Images: Notice how colorful Tassai's world is. The blue hills, her brown skin, the green plants, the brown earth, the red and blue and yellow corn. Soon, we will read of the rich earth tones of her jar.

5 Simile; Sensory Image: Again, the author compares one thing to another: the feel of the clay is as smooth as honey.

6 Exposition: Here is where the story really begins: with Tassai's secret.

Guiding the Reading

Literal

Q: What work did Tassai do in addition to her work in the field?

A: Tassai brought water from the spring. She ground corn. She helped her mother cook and weave baskets.

Q: What was the one thing Tassai did that no one knew about?

A: She was making a jar from clay.

Analytical

Q: What is the one thing that most American children do that Tassai did not do?

A: Tassai did not go to school.

Tassai brought water, too, from the spring at the foot of the mesa. She carried it up the steep trail in jars. For **4** hours each day she ground the red and blue and yellow grains of corn. She cooked when her mother needed her help. She also knew where to find the grass that her mother wove into baskets.

There was one thing Tassai did that no one knew about. This was because she did it only at times when no eyes were watching. She was making a jar from clay that she had found in a secret place. There the earth was **5** smooth as honey to the touch and dark in color. Not even **6** her mother knew that Tassai was working at this jar. It was Tassai's secret.

She shaped it and smoothed it. She knew how to do this from watching her mother. The most beautiful jar of all started to form itself in her hands. She painted fine black lines on it and baked it a golden brown. Tassai thought that there had never been a jar as lovely as this one. She carefully wrapped it in a blanket and put it away in a safe place. **7** **8** **9**

All through the hours while she worked in the fields, Tassai thought of her jar. In her thoughts a little song sang itself over and over again until her feet danced to the music of it: **10**

> It is so beautiful, **11**
> My big, round jar!
> So round and beautiful!
> Only the Moon,
> When it walks on the edge of the world
> Is like my jar.
> Round and smooth it is,
> And has a shine that sings!
> Maybe the Moon has come to me
> To be my jar!

The Jar of Tassai   7

Guiding the Reading

Literal

Q: How did Tassai know how to make a jar?
A: She had watched her mother making jars.

Q: Was Tassai happy with the result of her work on the jar?
A: Yes, she thought it was the most beautiful jar she had ever seen.

Q: What did Tassai do with the finished jar?
A: She wrapped it in a blanket and put it away in a safe place.

Q: Did Tassai forget about her jar after it was completed?
A: No. She thought about it all the time and even made up a little song about it.

Literary Components

7 **Characterization:** We get the sense that Tassai is a good girl who wants to learn everything she can from her mother. The only reason she would keep a secret from her mother is in order to surprise her.

8 **Poetic Language:** When someone is a skilled craftsman, the object being crafted seems to take shape on its own. This is a beautiful way to impart the magical feeling Tassai had as she made her jar.

9 **Foreshadowing:** The reader feels that this blanket-wrapped jar will play a part in the story.

10 **Characterization; Poetic Language:** Once again the author uses the device of things happening on their own. Tassai is portrayed as a sensitive, happy girl who is carefree enough to find herself dancing to a tune without actually intending to do so.

11 **Characterization:** Tassai's world is the great outdoors. The images that fill her thoughts are drawn from the natural world, not the modern technology-filled world in which we live.

Analytical

Q: Why do you think Tassai loved the jar so much?
A: Several answers are possible. She loved it because she herself had made it; because she apparently had very few possessions and each one was precious to her; because she loved having her own secret; because it was a "grown-up" type of object; because it was truly beautiful.

Q: Do you think it was okay to keep this secret from her mother?
A: Yes. Tassai was not keeping the jar a secret because she was afraid her mother would disapprove. She knew her mother would be pleased and wanted to surprise her. That kind of secret is okay to keep.

The Jar of Tassai

Literary Components

12 **Rising Action:** The story is beginning to take shape. A new, important character is introduced and the reader understands that something will soon happen.

13 **Foreshadowing:** The reader knows about Tassai's jar and understands it will be brought to the feast. What will happen to it there?

14 **Sensory Images:** The fair is alive with color. The sights and sounds are dazzling to a girl who is used to silent, open spaces.

Guiding the Reading

Literal

Q: Who called the people of the town together?
A: The Governor of the Pueblo called the people together.

Q: What was his announcement?
A: There would be a feast for the people of three towns.

Q: What did he ask of the people?
A: He asked each person to bring something he or she had made.

Q: What would be done with each of these things?
A: They would be displayed and the best ones would win a prize.

Q: Did the people want to attend the feast?
A: Yes. They were very excited by the prospect.

Q: How did Tassai feel on the day of the feast?
A: She was so excited she could hardly breathe.

Analytical

Q: Do you think the Governor's idea was a good one?
A: Yes. It would give people a chance to mingle and get to know new people. It would encourage trade and business. It gave the people something exciting to which to look forward.

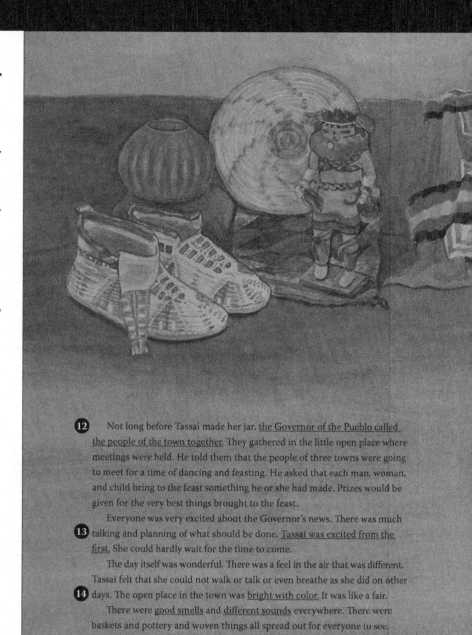

12   Not long before Tassai made her jar, <u>the Governor of the Pueblo called the people of the town together.</u> They gathered in the little open place where meetings were held. He told them that the people of three towns were going to meet for a time of dancing and feasting. He asked that each man, woman, and child bring to the feast something he or she had made. Prizes would be given for the very best things brought to the feast.

Everyone was very excited about the Governor's news. There was much **13** talking and planning of what should be done. <u>Tassai was excited from the first.</u> She could hardly wait for the time to come.

The day itself was wonderful. There was a feel in the air that was different. Tassai felt that she could not walk or talk or even breathe as she did on other **14** days. The open place in the town was <u>bright with color.</u> It was like a fair.

There were <u>good smells</u> and <u>different sounds</u> everywhere. There were baskets and pottery and woven things all spread out for everyone to see.

There were silver bracelets and rings and belts. There were bright blankets and things of leather and wood. There were ears of corn that were bigger than any Tassai had ever seen before. There were beaded shoes and nets for carrying things. There were little cakes made of pine nuts and seeds. There was good food cooking in pots.

Tassai was one of the very last to come into the open place on that big day. She had been busy since sunup, helping her mother. At last she was free. She picked up the blanket in which her jar was wrapped and ran to the open ⑮ place. There she stood, holding the blanket close to her side.

The Governor of the Pueblo moved from place to place with some elderly people. They looked long and closely at each of the many things that had been brought. With them was a visitor from a nearby town. He had come with his little daughter to see the dancing and feasting.

The little girl danced ahead of them as they walked. She looked at ⑯ everything with bright eyes.

The Jar of Tassai   9

Literary Components

⑮ **Rising Action; Foreshadowing:** Tassai is about to enter her precious jar into the competition. As we imagine her holding the blanket, we are edgy. Will the jar drop out of the blanket? Will the blanket hold some surprise? We won't feel safe until we see the jar firmly on the display table.

⑯ **Characterization; Foreshadowing:** This little girl seems a bit too lively. Why is she mentioned? Will something happen?

Guiding the Reading

Literal

Q: Describe what Tassai saw as she entered the area of the feast.
A: There were good smells and nice sounds. There were baskets, pottery, woven things, jewelry, blankets, leather goods, beaded shoes, baked goods, good food, and more.

Q: Why was Tassai late to the feast?
A: She had been helping her mother.

Q: What did she bring with her?
A: She brought the blanket in which her jar was wrapped.

Q: Who was the judge of the competition?
A: The judges were the Governor and some elderly people.

Q: Who walked along with them as they viewed all the objects?
A: A visitor from a nearby town and his little daughter walked along with them.

The Jar of Tassai

Guiding the Reading

Literal

Q: Why was Tassai nervous when the judges started walking towards her?

A: She was afraid they would not like her jar.

When the people had seen everything else, they started walking up to Tassai. She was nervous now. Maybe they would not think her jar was beautiful. Others began to gather around. They had not known that Tassai would have anything to show.

"Maybe it is not very good," she said in a voice that was so low no one heard her. "Maybe it—" Then her words would not come at all.

When she opened the blanket, the beautiful jar was not there. She had not noticed that there were two piles of blankets in the room of her home. The one she had picked up in her hurry held only an old corncob doll.

There was a big laugh from those who stood near. The words of Tassai, explaining what she had done, were lost. Quickly she pushed her way through the laughing people and ran home. She did not know that the little girl had wanted to see that doll again and was following her.

The Jar of Tassai   11

Literary Components

17 **Surprise; Rising Action; Tension Increases:** From being mildly tense that they won't like her jar, Tassai is seriously distressed that she has brought the wrong blanket.

18 **Foreshadowing:** This is a skillful piece of foreshadowing. Although to the reader this small detail goes almost unnoticed, it will play a role in the climax of the story.

19 **Foreshadowing; Action is Approaching Climax:** The little girl innocently follows Tassai home. The reader does not realize how important a detail this is.

Guiding the Reading

Literal

Q: What happened when Tassai opened the blanket?

A: She discovered that all it held was a corncob doll.

Q: What did Tassai do when she saw the corncob doll?

A: She began to run home to get the jar.

Q: Who was the one person who was actually interested in the doll Tassai had brought by mistake?

A: The little girl was interested in the doll.

Q: What did the little girl do?

A: She followed Tassai home, when Tassai went to get the jar.

Analytical

Q: Why do you think Tassai brought the wrong blanket?

A: She had helped her mother all day and in her hurry to come to the feast, had grabbed the wrong blanket.

Q: Do you think it was kind of the people to laugh at her?

A: No, they were unfeeling.

The Jar of Tassai

Guiding the Reading

Literal

Q: Why did the little girl stop suddenly when she got to Tassai's doorway?

A: She saw a rattlesnake pick up its head and begin to slide towards her.

The house of Tassai was the last one in the little town. It was on the very edge of the mesa top. She ran into the door. She did not notice that the little girl who had followed her had stopped suddenly just outside the doorway. The child was watching, with wide eyes full of fear, a snake that picked up its head from behind a big stone. It was a rattlesnake. It moved its flat head

12   Unit 1

closer and closer to the little girl. She gave one loud cry as Tassai came out of the door with the jar in her arms. Tassai had thrown off the blanket and held just the jar in her arms.

There was no time to think. There was no time to call for help. Tassai did the only thing she could do. With all her might she threw the jar at the rattlesnake. It broke into many pieces on the rock, and the snake lay flat and still.

The little girl did not make another sound. Her father, who had heard her first cry, came running. He held her in his arms.

For the first second, Tassai thought only that the rattlesnake was dead. Then she thought of her jar. No one would call it beautiful now. She picked up a little broken piece. As she was looking at it, the father of the little girl took it from her hand.

The Jar of Tassai **13**

Literary Components

20 Turning Point: The story has reached its climax. The reader is suspended in time as the snake, the little girl, Tassai, and the jar are flash-frozen in the moment.

21 Climax; Resolution: The scene unfreezes and in a flash, the snake is dead.

22 Falling Action: Although the snake is dead, the story is not over. There are still a lot of mixed emotions with which to deal.

Guiding the Reading

Literal

Q: What did the little girl do when she saw the snake moving toward her?
A: She gave one loud cry.

Q: By now, what was Tassai holding?
A: She was holding the jar.

Q: What did she do?
A: She threw the jar at the rattlesnake's head with all her might.

Analytical

Q: When Tassai saw the rattlesnake she had no time to think. Do you think that helped her save the girl?
A: Yes. If she had started to think, she might have been too afraid to move, or she might have been too concerned about the jar.

The Jar of Tassai

Literary Components

23 **Theme:** Part of the theme is that deeds are as beautiful as objects.

Guiding the Reading

Literal

Q: What did the girl's father say to Tassai?

A: He said that the jar was beautiful and asked her if she had made it.

Q: What did he say when she said she had made the jar?

A: He thanked her for saving his daughter and said that the jar would have won a prize.

Q: What idea did the Governor have?

A: He said Tassai would win a prize for her beautiful deed.

"That was a beautiful jar," he said slowly. "Did you make it?"

Tassai nodded her head. The man looked at the broken jar again, and said, "I cannot thank you enough for what you have done for my daughter. Your beautiful jar would certainly have won a prize. If only I could think of a way to make up for the lost prize—"

At this point, the Governor, who had been looking on, spoke. "Prizes **23** were to be given for the most beautiful things brought to this feast. Now I would like to give a prize to Tassai who has shown us that a deed can be very beautiful, too." With this he handed her a prize. The elderly people nodded their heads with pride. The children who were gathered around clapped and cheered.

The little girl whom Tassai saved came up and smiled at Tassai. She asked, "Can I see your pretty corncob doll again?" Tassai held out her hand to the little girl and soon they were walking together toward Tassai's house. Now Tassai felt very happy. It did not matter that her jar was broken. She could make another, even more beautiful.

About the Author

Grace Purdie Moon always loved Indians. When she was a little girl, she thought she actually was an Indian since she was born in Indianapolis, Indiana! She and her husband, Carl Moon, who was an artist, spent years traveling in Indian Country, living with different tribes and gathering material for their work. Grace Moon is famous for her paintings of Indian children. She wrote 19 books, and her husband illustrated all of them. They even authored some of these books together.

Literary Components

24 **Characterization; Theme:** Tassai knows her priorities. She is happy about what she has done and has no second thoughts. Practically speaking, she knows she can make a second jar.

Guiding the Reading

Literal

Q: How did Tassai feel about the prize the Governor gave her?

A: She felt very happy.

Analytical

Q: Why do you think Tassai felt happy? After all, her jar was broken.

A: Tassai was old enough to know that saving a person's life is more important than anything else. It helped that she had been given a prize, but even if she hadn't, the enormously good deed that she had done would make her feel happy and proud for the rest of her life.

The Secret

Poem tie-in for *The Jar of Tassai*

In *The Secret*, the narrator takes delight in her secret knowledge of the existence of a robin's nest. Her playful way of not stating the secret injects secrecy right into the lines themselves. There is something about secret knowledge—if it is knowledge of something pleasant and good—that most people relish, and this poem shares that feeling with the reader.

Here are some questions that you may use to discuss *The Secret*.

Q: Do you like secrets?

Q: Do you find it hard to keep a secret? Why or why not?

Q: Some secrets are happy and some are sad. Some are between you and a friend, some are between you and a parent, and some are between you and yourself. Can you give examples of each?

Q: What secret does the poet have here?

A: The poet has seen the robin build a nest and lay four eggs in it.

Q: What does the poet do that makes you feel the secret even more?

A: The poet leaves out the words that tell us what the secret is and makes us guess what they are. By not using the words, she is keeping the secret.

Q: When will the secret be revealed?

A: The secret will be revealed when the baby robins are hatched.

The Secret

Emily Dickinson

We have a secret, just we three,
The robin, and I, and the sweet cherry-tree;
The bird told the tree, and the tree told me,
And nobody knows it but just us three.

But of course the robin knows it best,
Because he built the — I shan't tell the rest;
And laid the four little — something in it —
I'm afraid I shall tell it every minute.

But if the tree and the robin don't peep,
I'll try my best the secret to keep;
Though I know when the little birds fly about
Then the whole secret will be out.

16   Unit 1

Studying the Selection

FIRST IMPRESSIONS
Would you have been able to think as quickly as Tassai did?

QUICK REVIEW

1. What work did Tassai do secretly?
2. What did Tassai hope to do with her jar?
3. Why did Tassai leave the feast and run home?
4. How did Tassai's jar get broken?

FOCUS

5. At the end of the story, Tassai felt very happy, even though her jar was broken. Why did she feel this way?
6. Every story has a plot, characters, a setting, and a theme, or main idea. Copy the chart below onto a piece of paper and fill in the empty boxes.

List three characters	1.
	2.
	3.
List two settings	1.
	2.
List two important things that happen in the story	1.
	2.

CREATING AND WRITING

7. In the story, the Governor gave Tassai a prize for doing a good deed. What do you think it was? Imagine that you are the Governor, and write a letter to Tassai that describes the prize and thanks her for her brave deed.
8. Tassai loved making her jar. At home, find an empty jar. Clean it well and decorate it. Fill it with something you like, such as candy or small pieces of a game.

Studying the Selection

- -

First Impressions

Answers will vary. Some confident students will be sure that they would have acted just as she did. The less confident, or more thoughtful, ones will wonder what they would have done. Some may think they would have frozen in fear, others may feel they would have fled. Some students may offer solutions other than breaking the jar on the snake's head. (These will probably range from the creative to the fantastic!) Point out that it is difficult to know what one will do in a moment of crisis. However, training oneself to think of others, and learning to take action rather than watch passively, are two ways to prepare for a crisis like the one in the story. Ask the students to share some split-second decisions they have made.

Quick Review

1. Tassai was secretly making a jar out of clay.
2. Tassai hoped to bring her jar to the feast and enter it in the competition for a prize.
3. When Tassai opened the blanket in which she thought she had wrapped the jar, she saw that it held a doll, not her jar. She then ran home to get the jar.
4. A little girl had followed Tassai home. Just as Tassai took the jar in her hands, she saw that a rattlesnake was preparing to strike at the little girl. Tassai raised the jar and hurled it down on the snake's head.

Focus

5. Tassai felt happy that she had saved the little girl's life. (Perhaps she felt very happy that she had instinctively done the right thing.)
6. Characters: Tassai, the Governor, the little girl, the little girl's father.

   Settings: the mesa, the fields, Tassai's house, the place where the feast was held.

   Two important events can include the announcing of the feast, Tassai opening the blanket and finding the jar is missing, Tassai running home, the rattlesnake getting ready to strike, Tassai smashing the jar.

Creating and Writing

7. Answers will vary. Encourage the students to think about a prize that would reflect the good deed in some way, like a miniature jar, or a heart necklace. The letter should be written to Tassai and signed by the Governor. If you like, you can have the students design the Governor's seal, or bring in some gold paper and have them cut out a "seal" that they can glue to the letter. They may enjoy "signing" the letter in the handwriting of the Governor.
8. If the children are decorating the jars in school, bring in materials and desert clay-tone colors that were favored by the Pueblo Indians. It would be nice to bring in some photographs of jars that were made by them.

The Story of the White Sombrero

Lesson in Literature

What Is Plot?
The Three Sisters

1. Mom's problem is that the triplets argue all the time.

2. Mom shows them how to plant a garden. She hopes that working together will help them get along.

3. At the end of the story the girls have learned from their plants to help each other.

Selection Summary

Andres and Francisco are two brothers who live in the hills of Mexico. Their mother weaves sombreros, which their father sells at the marketplace. One day the mother decides that the boys are old enough to make the journey to the marketplace on their own. The reaction of each brother is characteristic of their individual personalities. The older brother, Francisco, worries about unknown dangers that may befall them. The younger brother, Andres, is confident and eager to go. The boys load the sombreros onto some burros and start on their journey.

When night falls, the brothers tie their burros to some orange trees and make camp. A wasp flies by and Francisco immediately foresees disaster. The wasps will sting the burros and terrible things will happen, he predicts. Andres views this pessimistic prediction as nonsense and says that even if there are wasps, they will keep thieves away. As it happens, Francisco turns out to be right. The next morning wasps attack the burros in droves, causing them to rear and buck, throwing all the sombreros onto the ground. As if this were not bad enough, some monkeys in the orange trees overhead begin to pelt the two boys with oranges. The monkeys scurry down the trees and put the sombreros on their heads.

While the burros jump into a nearby stream to drown the wasps, the brothers begin to throw pebbles at the monkeys. The monkeys return their fire by throwing oranges at them and grabbing more sombreros. Soon, man, sombrero, and beast are splattered with orange juice. Finally, the monkeys run off, leaving stained sombreros behind. Again, Francisco views everything as hopeless and Andres tries to save the situation. An old man helps them by inviting the brothers to bring their sombreros to his house and wash them in his special bleach.

They do this, take the bleached white sombreros to market, and sell every one of them. Upon their

Lesson in Literature . . .
THE THREE SISTERS

WHAT IS PLOT?
- What happens in a story is called a **plot**. A plot has a beginning, a middle, and an end.
- At the *beginning* of the story, a problem is presented.
- In the *middle* of the story, things happen and changes occur that may solve the problem.
- At the *end* of the story, the problem is solved.

THINK ABOUT IT!
1. What problem does Mom have?
2. What does Mom do that may solve the problem?
3. Why do the girls stop bickering at the end of the story?

The three sisters were triplets. Their names were Annie, Sara, and Dina Smith. They lived with their mom and dad and two younger brothers, Jake and Sam. Their house was on a pretty street with lots of trees.

Not all triplets look alike, but these three girls looked just like each other. And, of course, they were the same age—eight years and four months, to be exact.

It seemed they didn't think the same way about anything. They spent a lot of time bickering. Even when they agreed with each other, they argued about things like who agreed first. Or who looked more like the other. Or who was born a minute or two earlier.

Then their mother would say, "Girls girls girls!"

Once they had a disagreement about who had fallen asleep first the night before. Even Dad said irritably, "How do they know if they were asleep?"

Mom looked for activities that they would like to do *together*. One Sunday afternoon Mom said, "Here's an idea that is just right for you: a vegetable garden called the Three Sisters!"

"Was it named after us?" asked Annie.

"You? Who would name a garden after you?" answered Sara.

Mom said, "This is what the Iroquois Indians did. It is the perfect garden. The three vegetables go together and help each other, just the way you three do."

"Huh?" said the triplets.

18   Unit 1

return home, they tell their parents what happened. The parents decide to bleach all their sombreros in the future. The sombreros are a hit and the family business takes off. The pessimistic Francisco acknowledges that his younger brother is the braver of the two and has the better attitude. He resolves to stop worrying and be more courageous.

Getting Started

When teaching literature, exercises using several modalities should be implemented. Your students will benefit from the variety, which sharpens both skill and interest. Twenty-five percent of the **Getting Started** activities will be in the form of aural exercises. These will help your students develop the ability to listen carefully and answer questions clearly.

The aural comprehension questions will not be graded or handed in to the teacher. Students can mark down which questions they have answered correctly and see for themselves how they are progressing over the course of the year.

"Well, sometimes," sighed Mom.

"So what are these sisters?" asked Dina.

"The Three Sisters," said Mom, "are corn, beans, and squash."

"But we don't like beans or squash," protested Annie.

"I like beans!" exclaimed Sara.

"And I like squash. At least I think I do. Well ..." Dina said, "Mom, what's squash?"

"But why these vegetables?" interrupted Annie.

"The Three Sisters go together because corn is a grain. It's also a carbohydrate. Beans are protein. And squash gives you vitamin A."

"What does that mean?" asked Dina.

"It means you get all the food groups you need. But also the Three Sisters go together because the colors are pretty, and the vines of the beans can grow up the corn stalks. The squash shades the soil. The beans provide nitrogen, which the corn needs. So the Three Sisters take care of each other." Mom sounded like a teacher.

They all went out back to pick a place for the garden. Of course, Sara, Annie, and Dina each pointed in a different direction and shouted, "Here!" "No, there!" "You're both wrong. Right here!" But Mom picked the site. The plants needed sunlight six to eight hours a day.

The next Sunday they dug up the soil. They put something in the earth to help plants grow better. They planted their seeds.

They felt so good after working in the sun. Mom had gotten a tiny picket fence to put around the plot. It looked just right!

Each day after school, the girls went out to look at their garden. They were very excited when little green sprouts began to stick up from the ground.

Two months after the planting, Sara became sick with the flu. Annie and Dina were upset. How would Sara do her share of the gardening?

"Mom," cried Annie and Dina. "What are we going to do? Sara's too sick to do her share! It's not fair."

Mom said, "What is not fair is that Sara feels so sick, and she is worried about her plants. What do you think we should do?"

Annie and Dina looked puzzled. Suddenly Annie said, "Hey Dina. I have an idea." She took Dina's hand. They headed for the back door.

An hour later, Mom looked outside. Annie and Dina were checking the plants and weeding in Sara's part of the garden.

When they came back into the house, they brought some of the flowers from Mom's garden. "Is this all right, Mom?" asked Annie.

"We probably should have asked first," said Dina, "but these are for Sara."

Mom almost cried. "You girls are just like your plants. You are the three sisters who can count on each other."

Target Skill: Understanding that a plot is what happens in a story

Learning Strategy: Summarize

Common Core Curriculum: RL.3.2; RF.3.4

Genre: Folktale

Vocabulary

burro (BURR o) *n.*: a small donkey used as a pack animal

brayed *v.*: sounded the harsh cry of the donkey

jauntily (JAWN tih lee) *adv.*: worn easily, happily, and a tiny bit proudly

poncho (PAHN cho) *n.*: a cloak that has an opening in the middle so that it can be pulled over the head and worn around the body

thicket (THIK it) *n.*: a group of bushes or small trees growing closely together

Related Vocabulary

anxiously (AINK shus lee) *adv.*: worriedly

optimist (OP tuh mist) *n.*: one who thinks the best will happen

pessimist (PESS ih mist) *n.*: one who thinks the worst will happen

Workbook

Related Pages: 8-13

Answer Key Page: 3

Read pages 23-24. Be sure to enunciate in a clear and loud voice. Using appropriate expression is also important. After reading the story, read each question aloud twice. Allow enough wait time for your students to record their answers. The correct answers are in bold letters.

Bear in mind that this first aural exercise may be a new experience for your students and they may be unfamiliar with the format.

1. In what country does this story take place?
   a. Spain   **b. Mexico**   c. Venezuela   d. Italy

2. One day the mother asked her two sons to
   a. help her find the burros.   b. help her weave the sombreros.
   c. go with their father to market.   **d. take the sombreros to market.**

3. What did Andres say to their mother's request?
   a. "I do not know where the market is."
   b. "I do not think anyone will want to buy our sombreros."
   c. "I am brave. I know we can make it all right."
   d. "The way is long and many things can happen."

4. When Francisco saw a wasp fly by, what did he say?
   a. "Surely the wasps will sting our burros."
   b. "One wasp cannot harm us."
   c. "Hide the honey so the wasps will not be drawn to us."
   d. "I have read that seeing a wasp on a journey is a bad sign."

5. What did the boys do with the sombreros as they camped for the night?
   a. Left them on the burros and covered them with blankets
   b. Hid them in a nearby cave
   c. Went down to the riverbank and put them next to a big rock
   d. Put them on the ground near the burros

The Story of the White Sombrero

Into . . . The Story of the White Sombrero

This story is about the difference that attitude can make. Each brother represents an attitude: Andres is optimistic and solution-oriented and Francisco is pessimistic and negative. To zero in on this theme, tell your students that you are going to tell them a little story in two different ways. Here is the story:

> One day last week, my alarm clock did not ring and I overslept. When I woke up, I looked at the clock and saw that I had only a few minutes to get ready for school. I started planning right away. I thought to myself, "I was going to cook myself some oatmeal and squeeze some fresh orange juice. Then, I was going to walk to school to get a little exercise. Instead, I'd better grab a breakfast bar and a glass of milk, and drive to school." Now that I had a plan, I jumped out of bed and ran around getting all of this done. I arrived in school just as the bell rang. "I did it!" I thought, and I smiled to myself.

Here is a different version of the same story:

> One day last week, my alarm clock did not ring and I overslept. When I saw that I had only a few minutes to get ready for school, I almost began to cry. "I hate being late," I thought. Then I got angry. "Why didn't that alarm clock go off?" I got out of bed in a terrible mood and thought, "What's the use of rushing? I'll be late no matter what I do." I decided to skip breakfast because I was so upset, and drove to school. Every time there was a red light along the way, I got mad because I was losing time. I took my time parking, because the bell was just about to ring, and I didn't feel like rushing anymore. I walked in late and was hungry and grouchy all morning.

Point out to your class that in each story the problem was the same: the alarm clock didn't ring and the speaker woke up later than planned. Ask your students if they can describe the difference in the way each speaker reacted to the problem. The differences are:

a. The first speaker does not get sad or angry; the second one does.

b. The first speaker does not try to blame anything or anyone; the second one does.

c. The first speaker develops a plan to solve the problem; the second one does not.

d. The first speaker does her best to carry out her plan and thinks she has a chance of being on time; the second speaker does not keep trying to be on time and is sure she will be late.

e. The first speaker is happy she has tried; the second speaker is unhappy all morning and doesn't realize that with a little effort she could have been on time.

Reinforce the idea that a person's attitude can be the determining factor in success or failure. Tell your students that, as they read the story, they should be on the watch for the attitude of each brother. After one or two of the challenges the brothers face, the class will probably be able to predict their respective reactions to each new problem as it arises.

Blueprint for Reading

INTO . . . *The Story of the White Sombrero*

Sombreros, tortillas, ponchos—Mexico! You can almost feel the hot sun as you read this story. Andres and Francisco are two brothers who live in the Mexican hills. One day their mother asks them to go to the marketplace and sell some sombreros she has woven. The brothers agree, but along the way, so many funny things happen that you might wonder if they will ever reach the marketplace. After you have read some of the story, you will see that each brother has his own way of solving a problem. See if you can predict what each brother will say as new problems come up. Were you right?

EYES ON *Plot*

A **plot** is what happens in a story. A good plot has a *beginning*, a *middle*, and an *end*. The beginning introduces the story and makes you want to keep reading. The middle is where exciting or interesting things happen. The end completes the story. Between the beginning and the end, something must change. The change may be that a problem is solved or that a character learns to act differently. As you read *The Story of the White Sombrero*, see if you can spot the place where one of the characters has changed.

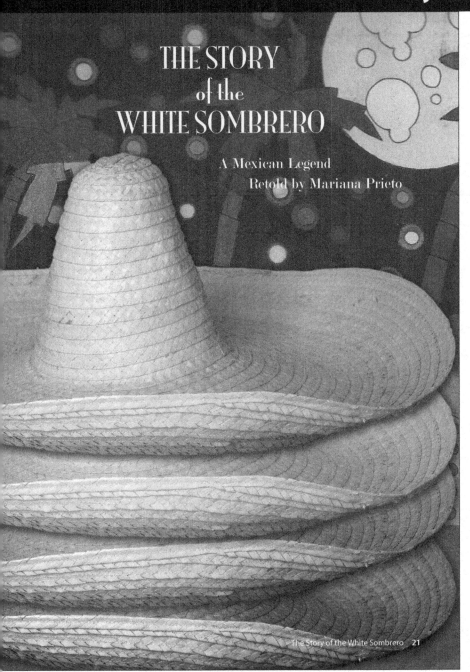

THE STORY
of the
WHITE SOMBRERO

A Mexican Legend
Retold by Mariana Prieto

The Story of the White Sombrero 21

Eyes On: Plot

The Story of the White Sombrero is a good story even without the character development that takes place in it. In discussing the plot of this story, it might be better to deal just with the events, not with Francisco's change of heart. At this early stage of learning about stories, we are stressing the "beginning, middle, and end" that make up every plot. At the beginning, the brothers set out with lots of sombreros to sell at market. In the middle, the sombreros are ruined due to a variety of mishaps. At the end, not only are the sombreros repaired and sold, they become real moneymakers for the family.

This story has a problem and a resolution. When the students have read and enjoyed the story, review it with them by asking what happens at the beginning, in the middle, and at the end. To do this, they will use the learning strategy of *summarizing*. Your students may have some difficulty separating the main points of the plot from the details. While monkeys throwing oranges is really comical—and they will certainly want to include it in their plot outline—it is only a detail of the plot. It will take some practice before your students find summarizing easy. For now, prompt them as they summarize and label the beginning, middle, and end of this story. After a while, they will become more adept at outlining a story's plot. The workbook exercises will be of help in that area, too.

Once long ago, in the hills of Mexico, lived two brothers. One brother was named Andres.[1] He was short and round like a lima bean. The other brother was named Francisco. He was long and thin like a string bean. They lived in the country where wheat is grown.

Their mother, like all the other women, wove broad-brimmed hats, called *sombreros*.[2] She wove them from *paja trigazo*,[3] or wheat straw. She and their father always took the sombreros to the market to sell. But one day she decided the boys should make the journey.

"You are old enough to take the sombreros to market," she told them. "Your father and I have work to do here."

"*Bueno!*"[4] Andres said. "I am brave. I know we can make it all right." His big black eyes were bright and sure.

"I do not know, Mama," Francisco said anxiously. "The way is long and many things can happen." He waved his long, thin arms hopelessly.

"Don't be silly," Andres said. "We can get there all right. If we have trouble, I am sure we will find someone to help us."

So they went and got their little burros and piled the sombreros high on the backs of the animals. When they had tied the sombreros in place, they climbed on their burros and started off for the market.

It was a long, hot ride, but Andres sang as he rode. He might not have, had he known what lay ahead for them.

1. *Andres* (ON dray)
2. *Sombrero* (sahm BRAIR oh)
3. *Paja trigazo* (pah SHAH TRIH GAH SO)
4. *Bueno* (BWAY noh) is Spanish for "good."

> **WORD BANK**
>
> **burro** (BURR oh) *n.*: a small donkey used to carry loads

Literary Components

❶ **Imagery; Simile:** The images of the lima bean and the string bean help us visualize the two main characters. These similes inject both a bit of humor and local color, as one often associates beans with Mexico.

❷ **Characterization:** The mother is described as a typical "hills-of-Mexico" mother, a weaver of sombreros, a hardworking mother and wife.

❸ **Rising Action:** The reader can see that the stage is being set for some action.

❹ **Characterization:** Andres, the lima bean-shaped brother, is brave, confident, and sure.

❺ **Characterization:** Francisco, the string bean brother, is fearful, anxious, and pessimistic.

❻ **Foreshadowing:** The author lets us know that something unexpected is going to happen.

Guiding the Reading

Literal

Q: In what country does the story take place?
A: The story takes place in Mexico.

Q: What were the names of the two brothers?
A: The two brothers are named Andres and Francisco.

Q: What did their mother weave?
A: Their mother wove sombreros.

Q: What is a sombrero?
A: A sombrero is a broad-brimmed hat made of wheat straw.

Q: What did the boys' mother want them to do with the sombreros she had woven?
A: She wanted them to take the sombreros to the market and sell them.

Q: What did Andres say?
A: He said he was brave and that he was sure they'd be all right.

Q: What did Francisco say?
A: He was worried that something might happen along the way.

Q: How were they going to get the piles of sombreros to the marketplace?
A: Their burros would carry them.

Q: What was the weather for the trip?
A: It was hot and uncomfortable.

Analytical

Q: Have you ever seen a sombrero?
A: If somebody has, ask the student to describe how it looked.

The Story of the White Sombrero

Literary Components

7 **Characterization:** Francisco, the pessimistic brother, sees disaster at every turn.

8 **Characterization:** Andres, the optimistic brother, sees the same wasp, but foresees only good coming of it.

Guiding the Reading

Literal

Q: What did the boys do with the burros when night fell?

A: They tied them to some nearby orange trees.

Q: What did Francisco notice?

A: He saw a wasp fly by.

Q: How does Andres answer Francisco? Is he worried, too?

A: Andres is not worried. He actually sees a way the wasps can be helpful. Wasps will frighten away thieves who might steal the sombreros.

Q: What did the boys do with the sombreros for the night?

A: They unloaded them and placed them nearby.

Analytical

Q: Can you compare the two boys' personalities? How are they different?

A: Andres is: confident, brave, optimistic, happy. Francisco is worried, nervous, anxious, unconfident, and fearful. He is sure that bad things will happen. Even though he's only seen one wasp, he already knows there is a whole nest of wasps and that the wasps will sting the burros and that something terrible will happen.

Q: Can you compare the way Francisco felt when he saw the wasps to the way Andres felt?

A: Francisco was a worrier who always predicted that bad things would happen. When he saw one wasp, he predicted that (a) a whole swarm of wasps would come and (b) they would sting the burros. Andres wasn't even sure that any wasps would come, but if they did, he thought they would keep the thieves from stealing their sombreros.

When night came, the boys made camp. They tied the burros to nearby orange trees.

"I saw a wasp fly by," Francisco said. "There **7** must be nests in those trees. Surely the wasps will sting our burros and something terrible will happen."

8 "Nonsense," said Andres. "If there are wasps flying around, they will keep thieves from stealing our sombreros."

The boys untied the mountains of sombreros from the burros and placed them nearby. Then, after feeding their animals, they ate some cold *tortillas*. Finally, they rolled themselves in their ponchos and went to rest on the ground. Soon they were fast asleep.

> **WORD BANK**
>
> **poncho** (PAHN cho) *n.*: a cloak that has an opening in the middle so that it can be pulled over the head and worn around the body

24   Unit 1

Q: Do you know a word that describes people who think like Francisco?
A: Pessimist.

Q: Do you know a word that describes people who think like Andres?
A: Optimist.

They slept until daybreak. The birds calling and singing woke them.

"We must get an early start," Andres said.

So they got up and placed the sombreros on the backs of the little burros.

The Story of the White Sombrero

Literary Components

9 **Simile:** The comparison to wild horses helps us picture how panicked the burros were by the wasps.

10 **Rising Action:** After a quiet night, things are heating up! There are wasps, bucking burros, sombreros all over, and chattering monkeys.

Guiding the Reading

Literal

Q: What did the wasps do? What did the burros do?

A: The wasps stung the burros and the burros brayed and dashed about.

Q: What happened to the sombreros?

A: The sombreros all fell to the ground.

Q: How did the boys try to save the situation?

A: They rushed about picking up the sombreros.

Q: Who were up above them in the orange trees?

A: Monkeys were in the orange trees.

Analytical

Q: Whose prediction turned out to be right, Francisco's or Andres'?

A: Francisco's prediction turned out to be right.

Q: Does that mean that it's better to be a pessimist?

A: It is best to be a realist. That means that you have to hope for the best but prepare for something else. It is not good to expect the worst to happen. If a person is hopeful, even if things don't turn out perfectly, the person can see the good in what did happen. Let's see who turns out to be right in this story; don't forget, the story's not over yet.

They had just tied the piles of sombreros and returned to roll up their ponchos, when the wasps came.

The wasps attacked the burros. The burros brayed in fury and dashed about. The boys wanted to help, but they were afraid of getting stung, so they stayed at a safe distance.

In their panic, the little burros broke the ropes that tied them to the trees. As **9** the wasps stung them, they were like wild bucking horses, not mild little burros. The cords that held the sombreros in place broke, and the sombreros spilled all over the ground, while the boys rushed about picking them up.

Suddenly overhead in the orange trees, a **10** terrible chattering began. The trees were filled with monkeys.

> **WORD BANK**
>
> **brayed** *v.*: sounded the harsh cry of the donkey

26 Unit 1

The Story of the White Sombrero   27

The Story of the White Sombrero

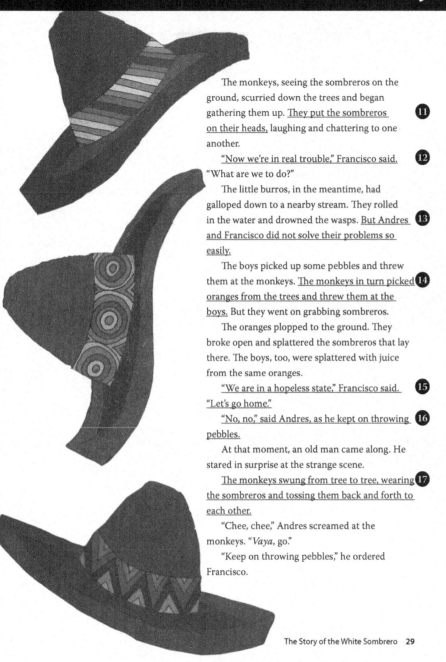

The monkeys, seeing the sombreros on the ground, scurried down the trees and began gathering them up. They put the sombreros on their heads, laughing and chattering to one another. **⑪**

"Now we're in real trouble," Francisco said. **⑫** "What are we to do?"

The little burros, in the meantime, had galloped down to a nearby stream. They rolled in the water and drowned the wasps. But Andres **⑬** and Francisco did not solve their problems so easily.

The boys picked up some pebbles and threw them at the monkeys. The monkeys in turn picked **⑭** oranges from the trees and threw them at the boys. But they went on grabbing sombreros.

The oranges plopped to the ground. They broke open and splattered the sombreros that lay there. The boys, too, were splattered with juice from the same oranges.

"We are in a hopeless state," Francisco said. **⑮** "Let's go home."

"No, no," said Andres, as he kept on throwing **⑯** pebbles.

At that moment, an old man came along. He stared in surprise at the strange scene.

The monkeys swung from tree to tree, wearing **⑰** the sombreros and tossing them back and forth to each other.

"Chee, chee," Andres screamed at the monkeys. "*Vaya*, go."

"Keep on throwing pebbles," he ordered Francisco.

The Story of the White Sombrero   **29**

Literary Components

⑪ Humor; Imagery: The image of the monkeys wearing sombreros makes the reader laugh.

⑫ Characterization; Theme: The contrast between the pessimism of one brother and the optimism of the other brother is emerging as the story's theme. How one *reacts* to life events can determine the outcome of those events.

⑬ Foreshadowing: The author lets us know that more excitement is on the way.

⑭ Humor: Slapstick humor makes us laugh at any age, but is a real favorite of third graders.

⑮ Characterization; Theme: Here is where character causes—or tries to cause—outcome. Had Francisco had his way, the story would have ended here, with the sombreros ruined and the boys going home in defeat.

⑯ Characterization; Theme: Andres' persistence stems from his belief that things will work out in the end. And his persistence *causes* things to work out in the end!

⑰ Humor: The image of the monkeys tossing the sombreros to one another lightens the serious message of the story.

Q: Which boy wanted to give up and leave? Which boy wanted to keep trying?
A: Francisco wanted to go home. Andres kept throwing pebbles.

Q: What did the old man see when he came along?
A: He saw the monkeys swinging from the trees and tossing the sombreros back and forth.

Analytical

Q: Does anyone know the rule about the way monkeys behave?
A: "Monkey see, monkey do."

Q: If you had passed by at that moment, what would you have done?
A: I would probably have laughed and laughed. If I were the helpful type, I might have grabbed some pebbles and thrown them. If I were the bossy type, I probably would have given some useless advice to the boys. (If this were taking place in modern times, I would probably have taken a picture or video of the scene.)

Guiding the Reading

Literal

Q: What did the monkeys do with the sombreros?
A: They put them on their heads.

Q: What were the burros doing in the meantime?
A: The burros went to the stream and rolled in the water to drown the wasps.

Q: What did the boys do to get the monkeys to drop the sombreros?
A: They threw pebbles at the monkeys.

Q: Did that work?
A: No! The monkeys picked oranges and threw them at the boys.

Q: What happened when the monkeys threw the oranges?
A: The oranges plopped to the ground, broke open, and splattered the sombreros and the boys.

The Story of the White Sombrero

Literary Components

18 **Setting:** Here and there the author places details about the setting to help us visualize the scene.

19 **Contrast of Characters; Theme:** Again, the brothers are contrasted. Francisco's pessimism feeds into another negative character trait: giving up too easily.

Guiding the Reading

Literal

Q: What happened when the monkeys tired of the game?

A: Some of them took off the sombreros and tossed them to the ground. Others ran into the bushes, still wearing the hats.

Q: What had happened to the sombreros on the ground?

A: They had gotten all spotted and sticky from the orange juice.

Q: What did Andres suggest they do to clean the sombreros?

A: He suggested they wash the sombreros in the stream.

Q: What did the boys find at the stream?

A: They found the burros at the stream.

Analytical

Q: Can you see a good thing that came of the monkeys throwing oranges?

A: Yes. Because of the oranges, the boys had to wash the sombreros off; when they went to the stream to wash, they found the burros.

Q: Is there a lesson to be learned here?

A: Yes. Sometimes, what looks like a bad thing turns into a good thing. Pessimists like Francisco are not always right.

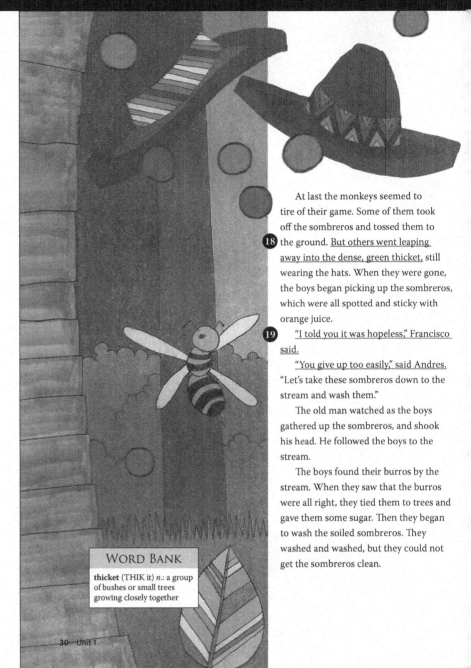

At last the monkeys seemed to tire of their game. Some of them took off the sombreros and tossed them to **18** the ground. But others went leaping away into the dense, green thicket, still wearing the hats. When they were gone, the boys began picking up the sombreros, which were all spotted and sticky with orange juice.

19 "I told you it was hopeless," Francisco said.

"You give up too easily," said Andres. "Let's take these sombreros down to the stream and wash them."

The old man watched as the boys gathered up the sombreros, and shook his head. He followed the boys to the stream.

The boys found their burros by the stream. When they saw that the burros were all right, they tied them to trees and gave them some sugar. Then they began to wash the soiled sombreros. They washed and washed, but they could not get the sombreros clean.

> **WORD BANK**
>
> **thicket** (THIK it) *n.*: a group of bushes or small trees growing closely together

30 Unit 1

"What shall we do?" Francisco asked, half in tears. "Our sombreros are ruined, and Mother and Father will be very angry. I knew something terrible like this would happen."

"Quiet," Andres said. "There must be a way to clean these sombreros. We were told to sell them in the market, so sell them we will."

The old man, who had been sitting silently nearby, spoke at last.

"You boys have had a terrible time and I want to help you. I have some bleach that I made from ground clam shells. Perhaps this will remove the orange juice stains. Come, bring the sombreros to my house and we will try."

So the boys took the wet sombreros to the old man's house. They used bleach on the sombreros and spread them to dry in the sun.

The sun was high now and it was very hot. The sombreros dried quickly. They dried a gleaming white, and the stains were gone.

The Story of the White Sombrero   31

Literary Components

20 **Characterization:** The pessimist always predicts disaster and gets a little satisfaction when his predictions materialize. Some people are never happy unless they're sad!

21 **Characterization; Theme:** Just as Francisco's *trait* of pessimism leads to an *action*: giving up and going home, so Andres' *trait* of optimism leads to an *action*: persisting in finding a way to sell the sombreros.

22 **Turning Point:** The involvement of the old man will change the direction of events. From here on in, things will go better for the boys. But, in keeping with the theme, it is because Andres would not give up that the old man notices and offers to help. Had Francisco had his way, they would have been on their way home by this time.

23 **Setting:** We are reminded that these are the Mexican hills and the setting is hot and dry.

24 **Release of Tension:** The main problem of the story is solved.

Guiding the Reading

Literal

Q: How did Francisco react when the sombreros did not get clean no matter how much they were washed?
A: Francisco decided the sombreros were ruined and that their parents would be angry.

Q: What advice did the old man give?
A: He suggested they wash the sombreros in bleach.

Q: How did he offer to help?
A: He offered to bring the boys to his house and help them wash the sombreros in some of his bleach.

Q: How did the sombreros look after they were washed and dried?
A: They were gleaming white.

Analytical

Q: What was especially useful about the advice the old man gave?
A: He gave the boys a way to use his advice by taking them to his house and giving them bleach. He did not just talk; he actually helped.

The Story of the White Sombrero

Literary Components

25 **Characterization:** This is a boy who can take lemonade and make it into lemons.

26 **Resolution:** This is a nice ending to any story!

Guiding the Reading

Literal

Q: What did Francisco say when he saw the white sombreros?

A: He said that no one would want to buy one.

Q: What did Andres say?

A: He said they would try to sell them anyway.

Q: Who turned out to be right?

A: Andres. The people liked the white sombreros.

Q: What did their parents decide after the boys told them how quickly they had sold the white sombreros?

A: They decided to bleach all of their sombreros.

Q: How did that plan turn out?

A: It was a huge success. They sold them as fast as they could make them and they all became very rich.

Analytical

Q: Why do you think the people liked the white sombreros?

A: Answers will vary. Perhaps they liked something new and different. Perhaps the gleaming white was very attractive.

Q: When the parents decided to bleach all the sombreros, who were they thinking like—Francisco or Andres?

A: They were thinking like Andres because they were being brave, trying something new, and hoping for the best.

"Oh, no," said Francisco. "Look at our sombreros now! They don't look like the sombreros that other **25** people make. Surely, no one will want them."

"We will try to sell them anyway," said Andres. "Come, help me load them on the burros."

So they walked back to the stream with the sombreros and fastened them to the backs of their burros. Then they thanked the old man and went on their way.

At the market, people gathered around the boys when they unloaded their sombreros. No one had seen such white sombreros before. The people liked them and they all wanted to buy them. Almost at once, the boys had sold all of their sombreros.

When the boys were home again, they told their mother and father what had happened to them. Andres told the secret of how they had bleached the sombreros. And Francisco told how quickly they had sold them.

Their parents decided from that day on to bleach all of their sombreros. They sold them as fast **26** as they could make them and they all became very rich.

The Story of the White Sombrero   33

The Story of the White Sombrero

Literary Components

27 **Stated Theme:** If a person has the right attitude, if he has "the courage to keep on trying"—and yes, persistence requires courage—things will come out well in the end.

Guiding the Reading

Literal

Q: What did Francisco admit to Andres?

A: He admitted that Francisco's way of thinking was better than his. He called Andres "brave" and resolved to be brave in the future.

Analytical

Q: What might the old Francisco have said about the plan to make all future sombreros white?

A: He might have said no one would buy the white sombreros, that they would all get poor and starve, and other pessimistic predictions.

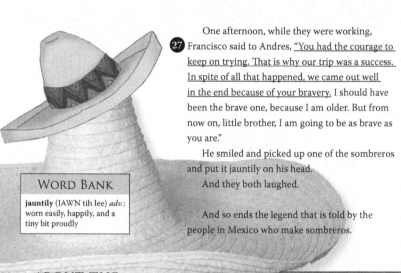

WORD BANK

jauntily (JAWN tih lee) *adv.*: worn easily, happily, and a tiny bit proudly

One afternoon, while they were working,

27 Francisco said to Andres, "You had the courage to keep on trying. That is why our trip was a success. In spite of all that happened, we came out well in the end because of your bravery. I should have been the brave one, because I am older. But from now on, little brother, I am going to be as brave as you are."

He smiled and picked up one of the sombreros and put it jauntily on his head.

And they both laughed.

And so ends the legend that is told by the people in Mexico who make sombreros.

ABOUT THE AUTHOR

Mariana Prieto was born in Cincinnati, Ohio in 1912. She lived and studied in many Spanish-speaking countries and these experiences inspired the settings of many of her books. Mrs. Prieto contributed over 600 articles and short stories to newspapers and magazines. Besides for writing, she worked as a radio broadcaster, librarian, and creative writing teacher. She also taught Spanish to Air Force officers. Mrs. Prieto liked painting, people, cooking, history, and animals.

34   Unit 1

Studying the Selection

FIRST IMPRESSIONS

Have you ever heard the expression "monkey see, monkey do"?

QUICK REVIEW

1. Why were the brothers going to the market?
2. What happened when the wasps stung the burros?
3. What did the monkeys do to the sombreros?
4. How did the old man help the brothers?

FOCUS

5. How was Andres' personality different from Francisco's?
6. What happens in the story is called the plot. A plot can usually be summed up, or *summarized*, in a few sentences. Copy the following chart onto a piece of paper, and, using the helping words, write one sentence next to each word. When you have done so, you will have a summary of the story's plot.

Market	*Example:* Two brothers were sent to the market to sell the sombreros their mother had made.
Wasps, burrows	
Monkeys, oranges	
Old man, bleach	
Sell, money	

CREATING AND WRITING

7. In the story, wasps sting the burros, the burros run away, monkeys grab the sombreros, monkeys throw oranges, and more. Do you think you could write one more episode for this story? It should fit into the story right after the part where the two brothers put the bleached sombreros out to dry. Write about some funny thing that happens to the brothers, the burros, or the sombreros before they reach the marketplace. Ask your teacher if some of the students can read what they have written aloud.
8. Sombreros are big Mexican hats. If you own one, bring one to school for 'Hat Day.' If you don't have a sombrero, bring a hat that is unusual in some way and tell the class why it is special.

The Story of the White Sombrero **35**

3. The monkeys put them on their heads, tossed them back and forth, threw them on the ground, and splattered them with orange juice.
4. The old man helped the brothers bleach the hats clean.

Focus

5. Andres was positive, optimistic, and did not easily give up. He always thought good things would happen. Francisco was negative, pessimistic, and gave up easily. He always anticipated bad things and failure.
6. Sample sentences for the summary:

   Wasps came and stung the burros that were carrying the sombreros, and the sombreros were thrown to the ground.

   Monkeys came and grabbed the sombreros and started to throw oranges at the brothers and the sombreros.

   The boys thought the sombreros were ruined, but an old man came and showed them how to clean the sombreros with bleach.

   The people loved the white sombreros so the family kept bleaching the sombreros and made a lot of money.

Creating and Writing

7. Ask your students to think of a funny "episode." They must have a new problem, like robbers or bears who take the sombreros. They must have a solution for the problem, as well. For example, if they write about how some robbers come and steal the sombreros, they might have the monkeys come while the robbers are sleeping and bring the sombreros back to the brothers, or have the robbers drop the sombreros out of fright when they see some rattlesnakes. Tell your students that before they begin to write, they should decide what the problem will be and what the solution will be. This is actually very good preparation for a skill which will be learned later: outlining.
8. Hat Day can be both fun and educational. Encourage your students to wear hats that have special meaning. Each child should come prepared to tell a story about his or her hat. If there are no hats available at home, have your students make funny ones out of anything that can be found, such as a Styrofoam bowl and some ribbon.

Studying the Selection

First Impressions

Monkeys are lots of fun! You can ask the students if they know any other expressions about monkeys. Examples are "monkey business," "he made a monkey of me," "stop monkeying around." Monkeys are notorious mimics. Although this story has a serious theme to it, let the kids giggle! Sombrero-wearing monkeys throwing oranges is just the recipe for laughs.

Quick Review

1. The brothers were going to sell their mother's homemade sombreros at the marketplace.
2. The burros bucked and threw all the sombreros on the ground. They then ran off to the nearby stream to wash off the wasps.

A Cane in Her Hand

Lesson in Literature

What Are Characters?
The Spanish Ships

1. Jerry stutters.

2. Uncle Jack tells Jerry that many great and famous people stuttered. He says that none of them gave up because of a little stuttering. Also, some of them, like Winston Churchill, taught themselves not to stutter.

3. Jerry is smart; he has a good sense of humor; he seems nice. Jerry sounds pretty grown-up in the way he describes his problem and his feelings. He sounds like he'd be a good friend.

Selection Summary

Valerie Sindoni is a girl who has always needed thick glasses. One day, though, she goes to her cousin's house and finds she is seeing everything through a fog. Frightened, she goes home, where her mother tells her to lie down and rest. That Monday, her parents take her to see Dr. King, who examines her eyes and gives her drops to ease the pain. When Val asks the doctor if she is going to be blind, he tells her that he will do everything in his power to keep that from happening.

Valerie returns to school and struggles just to get around without bumping into things. One day, she is told that a Miss Sousa has come to help her. Miss Sousa tests Valerie and they begin to meet twice a week. Not only does Miss Sousa help Valerie with her schoolwork, she begins to teach her how to use a cane to help her get around. At first Valerie is appalled at using something that blind people use, but the very kind and reassuring Miss Sousa persuades her to use anything that is helpful to her. "A long cane is like a long arm," she says, demystifying and removing the stigma of a cane. Valerie practices walking with the cane, both in and out of the room. Her last fear is that her friends will avoid her if she uses a cane. That fear is soon quieted when her friends let her know the cane makes no difference to them whatsoever.

With this practical, positive approach, Valerie goes on to live a very full life. She participates in sports, dancing, art, music, and crafts, and is well-liked by her friends. Her message is that people must think for themselves—that is, they must do whatever works best and not be concerned about how it looks to others.

Lesson in Literature...
THE SPANISH SHIPS

WHAT ARE CHARACTERS?

- The **characters** are all the people in the story. Some stories have animal characters, or even robot characters.
- The most important characters in the story are called the **main** characters.
- The main characters may change because of what happens in the story.
- An unimportant, or **minor**, character usually remains unchanged throughout the story.

THINK ABOUT IT!

1. What quality does Jerry have that most people notice first?

2. What does Uncle Jack say that makes Jerry feel differently about himself?

3. Jerry has lots of qualities other than stuttering. What do you think some of his other qualities are?

I'm Jerry Gooding. I guess the most important thing about me is that I stutter. I have other qualities, too. But stuttering is the first thing that people learn about me, as soon as I open my mouth.

What does stuttering mean? Well, my dad says there are three types of stuttering. Sometimes I repeat part of a word, like when I asked my brother yesterday, "W– W– W– Where are you going?" I had trouble getting from the *w* to the rest of the word. My brother hates it when I stutter.

The second type of stuttering is sort of like the first but it's more of a hiss. It happened last night. I had to get to basketball practice. "Mom," I said, "SSSSave me ssssome dessert, please." My oldest sister says I sound like a snake when I do that. Of course she never heard a snake speak.

Mom asked when I would be home. This leads me to the third kind of stuttering. It comes in the middle of a sentence. I said, "I'll be back about— *uh hum, uh like*—seven o'clock." I don't know why I said it that way.

Getting Started

This story is about a girl who is visually impaired. In the *Into* and *Eyes On* sections, the curriculum has focused on disabled persons and how they deal with their disabilities. In this section, we will focus on how other people should relate to people with disabilities.

Open the discussion by asking the students if they know of anyone with a disability. Ask them if they have any interaction with a disabled person, and what it is. Interaction could include everything from smiling and saying hello to a student in school, to helping a neighbor at home, to pushing a relative in a wheelchair. Perhaps they have seen their parents helping an elderly person who is disabled. The question you want to focus on is: what is the best thing you can do for a disabled person? The answer you are looking for is: the best thing you can do is to include the disabled person in your daily activities as much as possible. If the disabled person is a student in your school, make sure that student is included at recess, at lunch, and

My doctor says that stuttering runs in families. My father's father—my grandpa—stuttered when he was a kid. He still stutters a little. Nobody can get mad at him for stuttering, because he's Grandpa! What could be more special?

Why do I stutter? I know what I want to say, but I have trouble saying it. People think I'm stupid because I stutter. Tommy at school makes fun of me. That just makes me stutter more. I also stutter when I'm excited or tired.

Mom and Dad say that most kids who stutter get over it. They *outgrow* it. My Uncle Jack says that lots of famous writers stutter. "So what if they stutter?" he declares. "They're geniuses! What about the presidents who stuttered? George Washington! Thomas Jefferson! Theodore Roosevelt!"

The Spanish ships I cannot see since they are not in sight.

Uncle Jack is shouting at this point. "And Thomas Jefferson wrote the Declaration of Independence, practically by himself! And what about Winston Churchill? None of these guys gave up because of a little stuttering!"

When Uncle Jack talks this way, of course it makes me feel good. He is funny, too. He tells me, "Practice saying this. This is what Winston Churchill said over and over to get rid of his stutter. *The Spanish ships I cannot see since they are not in sight. The Spanish ships I cannot see since they are not in sight.*"

I tell Uncle Jack, "None of the kids I know ever heard of Winston Churchill. Who else stuttered?"

"The president of Pepsi Cola. Some famous basketball players."

That sounds pretty weak to me.

Uncle Jack gets serious. "This is not such a bad problem. And, it makes kids tougher. You need to work hard on this. That means ignoring the people who hurt your feelings. You also have to relax and take your time when you speak."

I think about Uncle Jack's words that night. I decide I have to feel good about me. I need to slow down and be more patient with myself. I am going to start practicing with the Spanish ships. I get so much support from Mom, Dad, Uncle Jack, and Grandpa. I am even going to ask my brother and sister to help me help myself.

A Cane in Her Hand   37

Target Skill: Understanding that characters are all of the people, animals, robots, etc. found in a story
Learning Strategy: Making connections
Common Core Curriculum: RL.3.3; RL.3.6
Genre: Realistic Fiction

Related Vocabulary

active (AK tiv) *adj.*: moving around a lot
avoid (uh VOID) *v.*: to keep away from
enable (en AY bl) *v.*: make something possible
gradually (GRAD joo ul) *adv.*: slowly but surely
obstacle (OB stuh kul) *n.*: something that stands in the way of moving forward
physician (fih ZIH shun) *n.*: doctor
stumble (STUM bl) *v.*: trip; almost fall down
vision (VIZH un) *n.*: eyesight

Workbook

Related Pages: 14-19
Answer Key Pages: 3-4

---

at home activities like birthday parties and sleepovers. A helpful guideline is: see the person as a *person* with a disability, not as a disabled person.

You could point out that the best way to help a disabled friend is not very different from helping someone who is not disabled. Going out of your way to say hello, talking to someone who is shy, making sure not to leave anyone out or make them feel unwanted are all things you should be working on.

Into . . . A Cane in Her Hand

A Cane in Her Hand is a perfect vehicle for the discussion of the topic *problem vs. challenge* introduced in the Student Edition. In the story, the heroine, Valerie Sindoni, has a real, clear-cut problem. She is losing her eyesight. Accompanying the primary problem are the secondary problems that so often intensify an already thorny problem. The "side" problems include a social problem (her friends will reject her), an academic problem

(she won't be able to keep up with the class), and the technical difficulty of moving without bumping into things.

As the story opens, Valerie is confronted with the frightening discovery that she is seeing everything through a fog. Her parents, who are portrayed as sensible, practical, and reassuring, take her to a doctor. He is cautiously optimistic and tells her that they will do everything possible to prevent her from going blind. He tells her that he wants her to get all the support she can at school.

At school, Valerie is afraid her friends will desert her if she goes to a special class. Without the special help, though, she cannot keep up with the work in a regular classroom. These two problems are alleviated when her friends stick by her and her new teacher helps her keep up with her schoolwork. Her third problem is solved when the new teacher teaches her to use a cane to avoid injuring herself. All three of her "side issues" are resolved because of the attitude of the people around her. All of them see her handicap as a challenge to be beat. They cannot restore her eyesight, but they can treat her the way they treat anyone else, and they (particularly the teacher) can help her to help herself. The stigma of both the problem and its solutions (the separate class, the cane) is removed, and Valerie finds she is able to do almost anything other kids can do.

Your students should be left with three very important messages from this story. First, look at a problem as a challenge. Think of it as a contest that can be won in some way, even if not in the obvious way. Second, surround yourself with people who are positive and practical. Seek out people who believe in you and believe that you can be helped. Third, eliminate any feelings of self-consciousness, embarrassment, or stigma about your problem or its solution. If Valerie had let herself be ashamed of her eyesight or of her cane, she could not have been such a success at school, with her friends, and in all her activities.

Eyes On: Character

In this story, the literary element we focus on is character. The main character is Valerie Sindoni, the girl who has "a cane in her hand" because she is vision impaired. The only other character that is developed at all is the teacher, Miss Sousa. Because the story is told from the point of view of Valerie, it is rather simple and straightforward. In a way, this is a plus, because you can ask the students to supply the emotions that they think Valerie or any of the other characters may have felt at different points in the story. For example, you could ask them what the parents were feeling when they took Valerie to the doctor. Although the parents were probably full of anxiety, Valerie doesn't mention this at all. Your students, though, can be prompted to contribute this point.

Review with your class the idea that a character is any person or animal that is part of the story. Some characters have a big part in the story and others, only a small part. (The labels of main characters and minor characters will come later in the year.) Ask your students which characters have the biggest parts in this story. The next point to be made concerns point of view, although again, you may not wish to use the term. Most stories are told by a narrator. Ask the class for examples. (The two previous stories

Blueprint for Reading

INTO . . . *A Cane in Her Hand*

What is the difference between a problem and a challenge? A *problem* is a difficulty that a person has. It could be a health problem, a learning problem, or any one of hundreds of other problems. A *challenge* is a difficulty too, but it is a difficulty that is more like a test, or even a dare. In sports, one group will challenge another to a game of soccer. It is as though the first group is saying, "We are hard to beat! Let's see how good you are at this game!"

When people have difficulties in real life, some people call them "problems" and feel very unhappy. They do not feel they can overcome their difficulties. Other people say, "These are not problems, they are challenges!" When you begin to read *A Cane in Her Hand*, you will meet a girl named Valerie Sindoni who has a problem. As you continue reading, you will see her change her problem into a challenge. Ask yourself, "How does she do that?" The answer will be valuable to anyone who has a problem.

EYES ON *Character*

Characters are the people in a story. Sometimes the author tells us what the characters are thinking; other times we have to figure that out ourselves. There are as many types of characters as there are real people. As you read *A Cane in Her Hand*, try to imagine how Valerie feels at different points in the story. Do you know someone who has a challenge like hers? When you think about that person, it will help you understand Valerie. When you read about Valerie, it may help you understand the person you know just a little bit better.

in the textbook are told by a narrator.) This story, however, is told by the main character, Valerie. Therefore, it is told from her point of view; that is to say, everything is described as she experienced it. This is important in this particular story, because Valerie can tell the reader just exactly what it feels like to be vision impaired. When she describes her fears, her hopes, how she feels when people ignore her or say insensitive things to her, we know what she is saying is true because they happened to *her*.

The learning strategy to employ in understanding character is *making connections*. As we read any story, we unconsciously identify its characters with people we know or know of. We also store away these characters as reference points for people or fictional characters we may meet in the future. So, when we read about Valerie, we think of someone we know with a physical challenge. In addition, if we meet a disabled person in the future, we will think of Valerie. As you read the story, or when your class has finished reading it, ask them if they know any physically challenged people. Ask them if they have learned anything new from the story about how to relate to a physically challenged person. In addition to the obvious

My name is Valerie Sindoni, <u>and I don't use my long cane all the time.</u>

Sometimes I don't need it. I don't need it when I go to Roger's house. He's my cousin and lives next door. I've been there so many times, I know every step of the way.

Why do I have a long cane? Because I can't see very well— that's why. But I haven't always had a cane.

I *have* always worn thick glasses to help me see. <u>But one day I found that, even with my glasses, I wasn't seeing well.</u>

I couldn't find my new clothes when I got up. I banged into the door and hurt my knee.

After breakfast, I went outside. I saw something moving in Roger's yard. It was Roger with his little sister Ruthie behind him. <u>They were coming out of a gray fog.</u> "That's strange," I thought. I knew it wasn't a foggy day.

I ran toward them. But I stubbed my toe and fell.

"Hey," Roger yelled. "Look where you're going. <u>You blind or something?</u>"

Ada B. Litchfield

A Cane in Her Hand   39

Literary Components

❶ **Exposition:** One way to draw the reader in is to begin without any introduction whatsoever. The reader immediately wants to know what Valerie's long cane is for and why she doesn't use it all the time.

❷ **Rising Action:** The author takes a step back and begins to explain what the story is about.

❸ **Rising Action; External Conflict:** Do not use the term external conflict in your class, but here is where the story's problem begins to be explained. Valerie is fighting for her sight.

❹ **Foreshadowing:** This line points to the challenge Valerie is about to face: the threat of blindness.

Guiding the Reading

Literal

Q: What is the name of the girl who is telling the story?
A: Her name is Valerie Sindoni.

Q: Why does Valerie have a cane?
A: Because she can't see very well.

Q: When did she start to use a cane?
A: When she couldn't see well enough to find her clothes, even when wearing her glasses.

Q: Who is Roger?
A: He is Valerie's cousin who lives next door.

Q: What happened one day as Valerie ran towards Roger?
A: She tripped and fell.

Q: What did Roger say to her?
A: "You blind or something?"

Analytical

Q: When you see people using a long cane, what do you usually think?
A: I usually think they're blind.

Q: How is Valerie different from a blind person?
A: She can see a little.

Q: Does it sound like Valerie is self-conscious (use "shy about" or "ashamed of" if students don't understand "self-conscious") about using a cane?
A: Answers will vary. To us, it does not sound as though she is, but we will have to read further to see for sure.

lessons learned from this discussion, the literary lesson is that we learn about characters by making connections to real-life situations. In addition, we learn about real-life situations by making connections to characters in stories or books.

A Cane in Her Hand

Literary Components

5 **Characterization:** It should be noted that, with the exception of one minor character, everyone in Valerie's life is kind, considerate, and wise.

Guiding the Reading

Literal

Q: Why was Valerie worried?
A: Because she had a sharp pain in her left eye.

Q: How often did Valerie feel pain in her eye?
A: The pain came and went.

Q: Where did Valerie's parents take her the following Monday?
A: They took her to see Dr. King.

Analytical

Q: Why did Valerie think the day was foggy?
A: Because her eyes were not working properly. The day was actually clear.

Q: Do you think Roger was being mean when he said "You blind or something?"
A: Roger did not intend to be mean. It never occurred to him that Valerie was partially blind.

Q: How do you think Valerie felt as she ran home from Roger's house?
A: She was a little angry and hurt, but she probably realized he had no idea how near the truth he had come. Mostly, she was probably afraid that what he'd said would turn out to be true.

"I guess so," I said, pushing myself up and feeling around for my glasses.

To tell the truth, I *was* having trouble seeing. Everything kept disappearing in a fog.

Ruthie said, "Don't worry, Val. Let's play."

But I was worried. I had a sharp pain in my left eye.

Like the fog, the pain came and went.

"I'm going home," I yelled at Roger.

"Hey, Val!" Roger bellowed, chasing after me. "Come back and play! I didn't mean that about being blind."

"Forget it," I told him and ran into my house and slammed the door.

My mother was worried when I told her about the pain. She made me go to my room and lie down. "Rest your eyes," she said. "I think the pain will stop."

After she helped me to bed, I heard her go downstairs and call my father and the doctor.

I didn't go to school on Monday. Instead, I went with Mom and Dad to see
5 Dr. King. He was glad to see me, and that made me feel better. He took me into a room where he'd tested my eyes before.

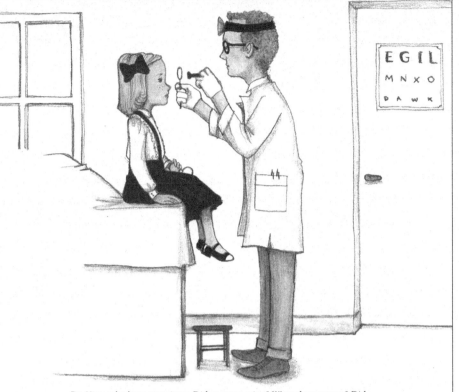

Dr. King asked me questions. Did my eyes sting? Were they watery? Did bright lights make them hurt?

I pointed to my left eye. "This one hurts," I said. "I just can't see through the fog."

Then Dr. King put drops in my eyes. He had me sit in the waiting room while he talked with my parents.

Soon the nurse led me back to Dr. King. He spent some time flashing bright lights in my eyes.

"Am I going to have to go to the hospital?" I asked. I'd had an operation on my right eye when I was little. It hadn't helped much. I still couldn't see very well with that eye.

"I don't think so, Val," the doctor said. "But I will have to check your eyes every few days." I thought he sounded worried. That made me worried too. **6**

"Am I going to be blind, Dr. King?" I asked. I felt like crying. **7**

A Cane in Her Hand **41**

Literary Components

6 **Characterization:** Valerie is very attuned to how people around her feel. When they are optimistic, she is, too. When they worry, she senses it immediately and begins to worry.

7 **Conflict:** The external conflict of the story is Valerie's struggle with the specter of blindness. This struggle, however, is not the story's theme. We have not yet been shown the theme.

Guiding the Reading

Literal

Q: What were some of the questions the doctor asked her?
A: Did her eyes sting? Were they watery? Did bright lights hurt them?

Q: Which eye hurt?
A: The left one.

Analytical

Q: Why do you think the doctor asked Valerie all those questions?
A: He was trying to figure out exactly what was wrong with her eyes.

Q: Was this the first time Valerie had had problems with her eyes?
A: No. She'd had an operation on her right eye when she was little.

Q: What was Valerie most afraid of?
A: She was afraid she was going to be blind.

A Cane in Her Hand

Literary Components

- -

8 Turning Point: Miss Sousa's appearance on the scene is definitely a turning point in Valerie's life.

Guiding the Reading

- -

Literal

Q: What did the doctor tell her when she asked him if she would be blind?

A: He told her he hoped not, and that they would do everything they could to keep that from happening.

Q: How was Valerie's teacher helping her in school?

A: She was letting her go right up to the chalk-board, giving her large print books, and providing her with special paper and pencil.

Q: Who was Miss Sousa?

A: She was the special teacher for students who have trouble seeing.

Q: How could she help Valerie?

A: She could teach her how to travel without getting lost or hurt.

Q: How did Miss Sousa test Valerie?

A: She asked her to read from a book.

Analytical

Q: Sometimes people who have a problem feel very alone. They feel no one is trying to help them. Do you think Valerie felt that way?

A: No, she couldn't possibly. Her parents have brought her to a doctor, the doctor is examining her and helping her, and her teacher in school is helping her in every way she can.

Q: How did Valerie feel about going to Miss Sousa's room?

A: She had a mixture of feelings. She was hopeful that Miss Sousa could help her, but she felt bad leaving her friends, even for a little while.

Q: Have you ever had "mixed feelings"? When?

A: Answers will vary.

"We hope not, Val," he said slowly. "We're going to do all that we can to keep that from happening." Soon Mom was holding my hand. She said, "Dr. King wants us to talk to your teacher, Val. She can help you at school."

"She already does," I said. "She lets me go right up to the chalkboard to see stuff. She gives me books with large print to read. And special paper with black lines and a special pencil too. What else can Mrs. Johnson do?"

"We'll have to find out," my father said.

When Dr. King said it was okay, I went back to school. Mom went with me. She talked to Mrs. Johnson and other people.

It was a bad time. Lessons are hard when you can't see well. And I kept bumping into things, even when I tried my best to see what was in the way.

8 Then one Monday, Mrs. Johnson told me, <u>"Miss Sousa is here. She's the special teacher for children who have trouble seeing.</u> She helps with lessons. She'll also teach you how to travel by yourself so you won't get lost or hurt."

It sounded like it might be all right. But I hated to go to another room and leave my friends, even for a little while.

After Mrs. Johnson went back to the other kids, Miss Sousa gave me a test. She showed me some book pages. I read out loud those I could see.

Then we talked about how people who can't see well get around—by listening carefully, by touching, and by feeling with their hands and with their whole bodies sometimes. These were things I'd been doing for a long time without thinking about it.

I saw Miss Sousa two days a week after that. She helped me with schoolwork. She showed me how to hold my hands and arms so I wouldn't run smack into things I didn't see. I liked Miss Sousa. She's so nice you can't help liking her. I began to think going to her room wasn't so bad.

Then one day Miss Sousa held something out to me. It was a long cane.

"Oh, no!" I shouted. "I don't need that. Only blind people use canes. I'm not blind. I don't want it."

Miss Sousa didn't get mad. She said, "You know, Val, you're getting a lot of bumps lately. It's because you don't see some of the low things in your way. Your hands and arms don't reach far enough."

Well, that was true. It's no fun running into things. It hurts and it makes you feel stupid. I could use some help.

Miss Sousa put the cane in my hand. "A long cane is like a long arm," she said. "With it, you will find the low things before you bump into them."

"A long, skinny arm," I said, and Miss Sousa laughed.

She went on, "I've moved things around in here. I'm going to the other side of the room. I want you to follow me. Use your eyes and ears. Walk slowly. Use the cane as if it were your hand to find anything in your way."

A Cane in Her Hand 43

Guiding the Reading

Literal

Q: What are some ways that people who cannot see get around?
A: They listen carefully, they touch, and they feel with their hands and even their bodies.

Q: What are two ways Miss Sousa helped Valerie?
A: She helped her with her homework and she taught her how to avoid bumping into things.

Q: What did Valerie say when Miss Sousa offered her a long cane?
A: She said, "Oh, no! I don't need that … I'm not blind …"

Q: Did Miss Sousa get angry?
A: No. She explained that a cane can help people who can see.

Q: What would the cane help Valerie with?
A: It would help her avoid bumping into anything her hands and arms didn't reach.

Literary Components

9 **Theme is Introduced:** The story's theme, which is how a person should use every available tool to help him or her succeed, is gradually introduced.

10 **Theme; Conflict:** If the theme is that one should help oneself overcome a disability in every way possible, then the conflict is the resistance one feels when the "help" is somehow embarrassing or uncomfortable. Valerie has a disability: she has poor vision. There is a way she can help herself: by using a cane. Valerie views the cane as embarrassing and frightening; to her it represents blindness.

11 **Theme; Characterization:** Miss Sousa wants to destigmatize the cane. She does so with simple logic. Her philosophy is if it's helpful, use it.

12 **Humor:** Once Val is able to joke about the cane, the battle is almost won.

Q: What did Miss Sousa compare the cane to?
A: She compared it to a long arm.

Q: What did Miss Sousa do to train Valerie how to use the cane?
A: She put things in unexpected places so that Valerie would have to use the cane to keep from bumping into them.

Analytical

Q: From what Valerie said when a cane was offered to her, what do you think was her greatest fear?
A: She was terribly afraid of going blind.

Q: What did she think of the cane?
A: She thought of it as something only a blind person would use.

Q: How did Miss Sousa think of the cane?
A: She thought of it as something anyone who could not see well should use.

Q: What convinced Valerie to try the cane?
A: First of all, Miss Sousa's explanation that using a cane did not mean she was blind relieved her and convinced her to give it a try. Second of all, Miss Sousa's explanation that the cane would keep her from bumping into things convinced her, because she had to admit she was pretty sore from all the times she'd bumped into things.

A Cane in Her Hand

Literary Components

13 **Characterization:** Miss Sousa is not only logical, she is also pleasant and warm.

Guiding the Reading

Literal

Q: What did Valerie do whenever the cane hit something?

A: She walked around it.

Q: How did Valerie do on the first try?

A: She did very well. She didn't bump into anything.

Q: What did Miss Sousa call this way of getting around?

A: Cane traveling.

Q: What did Miss Sousa teach Valerie about cane traveling?

A: She taught her how to do it without making noise.

Analytical

Q: What was Valerie using besides the feel of the cane to guide her?

A: Her hearing. She knew what she was hitting by the sound it made. This probably helped her to know how far she had to move to get around it.

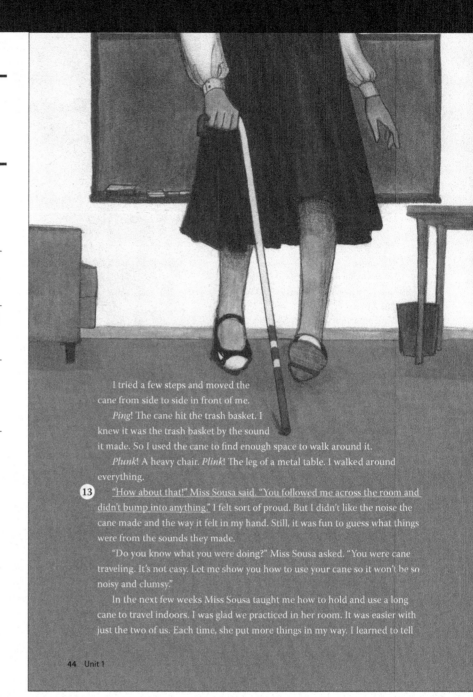

I tried a few steps and moved the cane from side to side in front of me.

Ping! The cane hit the trash basket. I knew it was the trash basket by the sound it made. So I used the cane to find enough space to walk around it.

Plunk! A heavy chair. *Plink*! The leg of a metal table. I walked around everything.

13 "How about that!" Miss Sousa said. "You followed me across the room and didn't bump into anything." I felt sort of proud. But I didn't like the noise the cane made and the way it felt in my hand. Still, it was fun to guess what things were from the sounds they made.

"Do you know what you were doing?" Miss Sousa asked. "You were cane traveling. It's not easy. Let me show you how to use your cane so it won't be so noisy and clumsy."

In the next few weeks Miss Sousa taught me how to hold and use a long cane to travel indoors. I was glad we practiced in her room. It was easier with just the two of us. Each time, she put more things in my way. I learned to tell

44   Unit 1

what was in my way by the sound it made and by how it felt when I touched it with the cane. Then I found how to go around it.

"Val," Miss Sousa said one day, "you're getting to be a very good cane traveler." She made it sound like being a good swimmer or skater. Then she said, "Let me know when you want to practice in the hall."

I wasn't sure I liked that idea. In the room it was okay, but maybe people in the hall wouldn't understand. How about my friends?

Well, they understood! It didn't make any difference to them. Miss Sousa had me practice going from my room to the gym and to the music room. I had my own cane now.

Later, I took my cane outdoors and learned how to find the edge of the walk or a hedge or a fence to help me stay on the path. Miss Sousa stayed right with me.

Now my long cane takes lots of bumps for me. I use it at school, especially going to different rooms. I take it with me when I go places. I don't often go to new places alone. But someday I will, and my cane will keep me from bumping into things or falling when I come to a curb.

Do I mind not being able to see as well as other kids? Yes, I do. But

Literary Components

14 **Characterization; Theme:** Miss Sousa is able to make cane traveling seem like just another type of sport.

15 **Conflict:** The author makes short shrift of this problem. It is raised and settled in two sentences. The friends, who could have presented a grave problem for Valerie, turn out to be supportive and accepting.

16 **Resolution:** The story's conflict is near resolution. Valerie has a practical, matter-of-fact attitude to her cane, which is shared by her friends.

Guiding the Reading

Literal

Q: What did Miss Sousa want to teach Valerie after Valerie got really good at cane traveling in the room?

A: She wanted to teach her how to cane travel in the hall.

Q: How did Valerie feel about this?

A: She wasn't sure. She was afraid people wouldn't understand.

Q: Did Valerie's friends understand when they saw her in the hall with her cane?

A: Yes. It didn't make any difference to them.

Q: What are a few places Valerie takes her cane?

A: School, outdoors, new places.

Analytical

Q: Why do you think Valerie liked Miss Sousa so much?

A: Miss Sousa never scolded Valerie. She always encouraged her. Miss Sousa taught Valerie how to help herself. Most importantly, she taught her that using a cane was nothing to be ashamed of.

A Cane in Her Hand

Guiding the Reading

Literal

Q: What bothered Valerie the most about not being able to see well?

A: When people talked as though she wasn't there it really bothered her.

Q: How did she feel when a lady talked about her right in front of her?

A: She was hurt and angry.

Q: What are some of the many things Valerie can do?

A: Valerie can roller-skate, swim, paint, sculpt, play the organ, and dance.

Analytical

Q: What might Valerie have said to the lady in the store?

A: Valerie could have smiled at her and said "Thank you, that's a nice compliment." The lady would probably have been flustered and embarrassed, but it would have taught her to be more sensitive in the future.

what I mind most is having people talk about me as if I'm not there.

One day I went to the store for Mom. Mrs. Wong, who owns the store, was talking to a woman whose voice I didn't know.

The woman saw my cane and said, "She's such a pretty girl. Too bad she can't see."

That hurt! It made me mad too. Didn't she think I could hear her? Or did she think I was too stupid to understand?

Mrs. Wong understood. It made her mad too. She knows there are lots of things a kid can do without being able to see very well. She knows I can do most things kids in my neighborhood do.

I roller-skate. (Maybe I fall down sometimes, but so does everybody.) I swim. (At camp I won a medal for swimming.) I paint pictures and make things out of clay. I am learning to play the organ. I take dancing lessons.

I have learned to do many things. And like other kids, I'm going to learn a lot more. Miss

Sousa says the most important thing I'm learning is to think for myself.

I wish other people would learn that too. Then they'd know there are lots of ways of seeing. Seeing with your eyes is important, but it isn't everything.

17

About the Author

Ada B. Litchfield was born in 1916 in Harwich, Massachusetts. She worked as an elementary school teacher, editor, and writer of children's books. Mrs. Litchfield wrote 13 children's books, many of them about science or about people with disabilities.

Literary Components
----

17 **Resolution:** The story concludes with Valerie at peace with herself and her life's challenge. She has a healthy, positive attitude to her disability, and has accomplished more than many people without handicaps have.

Guiding the Reading

Literal

Q: According to Miss Sousa, what is the most important thing Valerie has learned?

A: To think for herself.

Analytical

Q: Does it sound to you like Valerie is a confident person?

A: Yes, it does.

Q: How do you think she got that way?

A: Her parents, teachers, and friends all encouraged her to do everything she could to help herself. They didn't make a big deal of the cane, so she could use it freely to get around. They obviously included her in all their activities. Her upbeat personality has helped her achieve a lot.

Q: What are some other ways of "seeing"?

A: Valerie used her hearing, her sense of touch, her cane, and her familiarity with certain places to "see" everything.

A Cane in Her Hand

I Go Forth to Move About the Earth

Poem tie-in for *A Cane in Her Hand*

The poet writes about how he approaches life. He is wise and knowing like the owl, powerful and bold like the eagle, yet peaceful and gentle like the dove.

Here are some questions you may use in your discussion of *I Go Forth to Move About the Earth*.

Q: What are the three birds mentioned in the poem?

A: The owl, the eagle, and the dove are mentioned.

Q: What quality of each of these birds describes one that the writer has?

A: The owl is wise, the eagle is bold, and the dove is peaceful.

Q: Do you think the writer is bragging?

A: The writer is probably expressing his "ideal," the way he would like to be and tries to be.

Q: Why does the poet write about the owl, the eagle, and the dove? Why doesn't he just say he wants to be wise, bold, and peaceful?

A: When you use images (something the reader can picture), the message is much stronger.

I Go Forth to Move About the Earth

Alonzo Lopez

I go forth to move about the earth.
I go forth as the owl, wise and knowing.
I go forth as the eagle, powerful and bold.
I go forth as the dove, peaceful and gentle.
I go forth to move about the earth
    in wisdom, courage, and peace.

48   Unit 1

Studying the Selection

First Impressions

Valerie's success can be attributed to several factors. First and foremost is Valerie herself. She is willing to try new things, she is fairly confident, and she is respectful enough to gain a lot from teachers and parents. She has a lot of good friends, which tells us that she must be a good friend. Secondly, Valerie has a terrific support system. Her parents are strong and supportive, her doctor is wise and helpful, and her school is accommodating. Her teacher, Miss Sousa, is creative, skilled, and warmhearted, and her friends are accepting, generous, and sensitive. It must be noted that Valerie is not severely handicapped. She can see, though not very well. This is immensely different from being blind, and allows her to do almost as many things as a person who can see perfectly. Society deserves some credit as well. In today's world, handicapped people are accepted as never before.

Studying the Selection

FIRST IMPRESSIONS

Why do you think Valerie became so successful at making friends and at activities like swimming, painting, and dancing?

QUICK REVIEW

1. When did Valerie first notice she was seeing things through a fog?

2. What was Miss Sousa's job?

3. What did Valerie say when Miss Sousa offered her a cane?

4. What are four things that Valerie can do just like other kids?

FOCUS

5. What was the most important lesson Miss Sousa taught Valerie?

6. Although this story is mainly about Valerie, it is also about Miss Sousa, Valerie's parents, the doctor, and Valerie's friends. Choose one of these characters and write about three qualities that this character has. For example, you could write that the doctor is friendly, serious, and helpful.

CREATING AND WRITING

7. One day, a lady in Mrs. Wong's store said something that hurt and angered Valerie. Look back at the story and see what that was. Now, imagine that you are Mrs. Wong and that Valerie has just left the store. You want to explain to the lady what she did wrong. Write a paragraph in which you respectfully explain to the lady why her words were hurtful.

8. Vision is not something to take for granted. It is a precious gift that we must guard. Your teacher will divide the class into groups and distribute poster board and markers. Each group will make a sign about protecting their eyesight. The sign should include a list of three rules to follow for strong, healthy eyes and a picture that illustrates each rule.

A disabled child will be integrated as much as possible into a regular class, and aid will be available to make the integration possible. Many laws have been passed to help the disabled function in school and at work and to prevent discrimination against them.

Quick Review

1. Valerie was playing next door at her cousin Roger's house when she first realized she was seeing things through a fog.

2. Miss Sousa was the special teacher for children who had trouble seeing. She helped them with lessons and taught them to get around by themselves.

3. She said, "Oh, no! I don't need that. Only blind people use canes. I'm not blind. I don't want it."

4. Valerie can roller-skate, swim, paint, and make things out of clay. She is learning to play the organ and takes dance lessons.

Focus

5. Miss Sousa taught Valerie to think for herself. She taught her to be unafraid of what people would think and to just go ahead and do whatever it took to live a normal life. She taught her to be positive and confident, and to think of her cane as nothing more than a "long arm."

6. Since the literary skill we are focusing on in this story is recognizing character, this is a good place to see if your students have absorbed the lesson. Make sure the students write in complete sentences about their chosen character, not just compile a list of qualities. You may ask them to back up their statements with examples from the story of how these qualities are revealed. For example, if they write that the parents are caring, tell them to add that they can tell this by the fact that both parents go with her to the doctor and that Valerie's mother goes to school with her on the following Monday.

Creating and Writing

7. Make sure that the paragraph is respectful. Instruct your students to focus more on what the woman should have said than on what she said wrong.

8. Before you start this project, ask the students to think about ways in which they protect their eyes. Some answers would be: they wear sunglasses in the bright sun; they get enough sleep; they see their eye doctor periodically; they get medicine for eye infections; they are careful not to point scissors or knives at their faces; and they keep dirty fingers away from their eyes. You may prefer a slightly different version of this assignment: write a list of these rules on the board (with the help of the students) and have each group choose one rule. Have the groups make illustrated posters of their rules, and hang the whole series of posters around your classroom.

If you wish to expand on this, you can bring in a picture of the eye and teach the students the names of some of the basic parts of the eye. If one of the parents in your school is an eye doctor, you could even have a guest lecturer on care of the eye.

Boom Town

Lesson in Literature

What Is Setting?

Life on Mars

1. The story takes place on the planet Mars. The time is the year 2278.
2. Mars has no atmosphere. It is smaller than Earth. It has two moons.
3. Answers will vary.

Selection Summary

Ma, Pa, their daughter Amanda, her three brothers, and the baby arrive in California after a long journey. It is the era of the Gold Rush, and Pa lives in a tent city while he prospects for gold. But Ma chooses to live with the kids in a cabin in town. The town is really just a few cabins grouped around a stagecoach stop. Amanda feels lonesome and isolated, the brothers are bored, and Pa has no luck in the gold fields.

Looking for something with which to occupy themselves, the brothers plant vegetables and Amanda tries her hand at pie baking. Her first two attempts are failures, but on the third try, she bakes a masterpiece. When Pa comes home on his weekly visit, he showers praise on Amanda and her scrumptious pie. When he goes back to the gold fields, he takes some pie with him.

The next week, Pa returns with coins in his pocket. He has sold Amanda's pie and has lots of customers begging for more. A business is born. Amanda drafts her brothers and soon the foursome are turning out enough pie for the miners. When a peddler visits the town, Amanda suggests that he stay and open a store. When a prospector comes to town in dirty clothes, he asks where he can get his clothes washed. "Why not open a laundry?" suggests Amanda. And so it goes. Wherever Amanda sees a need, she asks someone to fill it. As more people settle in the town, each one contributes his or her talents to the town. In addition, each one provides business for the next. And always, people love to eat. Amanda's pie business expands.

Charlie, an old family friend, needs a place to board his horses. Characteristically, Amanda suggests he open a livery stable. He does, and paves the way for a hotel and cafe to house and feed the farmers who supply the stables. The effect snowballs and soon the town is booming. A banker senses opportunity, and comes to town to open a bank. Amanda asks him to provide sidewalks and streets for the town; he accommodates her. The town now has shops, services, houses, streets,

Lesson in Literature...
LIFE ON MARS

WHAT IS SETTING?

- The *time* and *place* in which the story's events happen are the story's **setting**.
- The *time* includes the time of day and the season of the year. It might include the year in which the story takes place.
- The *place* includes the country, the city, and even the building in which the story happens.

- When you read a story, think of it as a play you are watching. Imagine the scenery that would be on the stage—that is the story's setting.

THINK ABOUT IT!

1. What is the setting of *Life on Mars*? Make sure you include both time and place.
2. What are three ways that Mars is different from Earth?
3. What did you think was going to happen when Jon tasted the bubbling mixture?

The first people who came to Mars were astronauts. After them, regular explorers who walked around and made maps came. Next, people from big corporations like electric companies came. They were going to pay for the colony.

The second round of visitors was mostly scientists. They looked closely at rocks, the rust-colored sand, and the polar icecaps. The scientists wanted to see if human beings could live on Mars. What would colonists do on Mars for food and air?

Mars has no atmosphere. This means nothing holds in the oxygen that we breathe. Also, nothing traps the heat from the sun so it is very cold here. The only way human beings could live on Mars is in a dome, a very high and long and wide plastic dome filled with oxygen. To go outside, people must wear spacesuits. Spacesuits provide oxygen and warmth.

My family and I arrived on Mars in 2275. We were Moonies. My sisters and I were born on the Moon. Only my Mom and Dad had

50   Unit 1

and even a bank. It lacks only a school. That is taken care of when friend Charlie imports Miss Camilla and her husband to teach the children.

The happiest note of all is when Pa abandons prospecting and takes up pie baking. The family business thrives, the children are schooled, and the town booms. All thanks to Amanda.

Getting Started

Ask your students to imagine that your class was going out into "the middle of nowhere" to start a town. (You can even ask them to give it a name.) What will you need? Write a list on the board. A grocery shop? A doctor's office? A hospital? A school? A house of worship? When you have completed the list, ask them which they think are the most important and why. Then say to them, "Okay, now that we know what we need, how do we get people to come to our town and perform these jobs?" Your students may come up with several suggestions, some realistic and some not. They may suggest advertising, paying people to come (ask them where the money been to Earth. They went back home to be trained as food scientists. On Mars, they would ensure that what people ate was safe. They would try to invent new recipes from chemicals, and also from food grown in the fake soil under special lights within the dome.

I was ten when we came here. I hadn't expected Mars to be so beautiful. Outside the dome there is a haze that looks like cinnamon. If you live on Earth you might find it strange here because the mountains are tiny, Mars is only half the size of Earth, and it has *two* moons.

I like Mars, but sometimes I am bored. Even though we have a huge gym, I feel I never get enough exercise. We can't just run around. My sisters and I also complain about the food. There isn't much variety. When my birthday was coming, I thought, *Just one more birthday with no ice cream!* I was going to be thirteen.

It was 2278. My parents' laboratory had grown to include several rooms. They had several assistants. The experiments always looked interesting. My sisters and I would go there when we finished our studies.

Some of the experiments looked like ordinary liquids in glass beakers. The ones that could be tasted were marked with a Y for YES. We liked tasting the liquids and leaving our comments. But I wanted to show my parents that I could be a chemist, too.

I know it was wrong of me. But I wanted to see what would happen if we combined small amounts from two or three separate beakers. There were several liquids that tasted sweet, but they were too watery. So in a separate container, I added thick, almost creamy, goo. This made it sweeter and thicker, but way too sticky.

My younger sister, Bess, said, "Well, how about this one? It is shiny and smooth!"

Caroline, the older of the two, said excitedly, "Yeah! Let's try that!" So we added it to the mix.

There were lots of bubbles, and then some hissing and sizzle. Steam rose from the beaker.

The two girls shouted, "Taste it, Jon. It's *your* experiment!"

I took a tablespoon and helped myself. Ice cream. Plain and simple. Ice cream for birthdays and celebrations. Ice cream we could sell at a stand.

Now we just had to remember how we had made it.

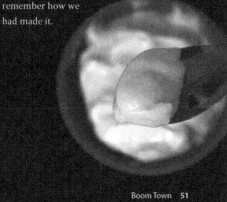

will come from), getting a group of friends together, asking the government to help, and so on.

There was a time that towns were springing up in California like dandelions! What was happening was called the Gold Rush. In 1848 gold was discovered in California. When people heard this, they rushed from all over the United States to California, hoping to be one of the lucky ones to find gold. When they got there, there were few settled places, so people got together and built towns. Everyone had to contribute something. Someone had to be the baker, someone had to be the shoemaker, and someone had to be the schoolteacher. When there was no one to do the job, people would be invited from other places to come to the town and do the needed work. All these services were needed immediately, so the towns grew rapidly. These towns were called boom towns. Soon, people were coming to California not just to dig for gold but to do all sorts of work. People who were creative and hardworking were able to make a lot of money. As they did so, the boom towns grew into cities, and even more people moved out West.

Target Skill:	Understanding that setting means the time or the place that a story takes place
Learning Strategy:	Visualize
Common Core Curriculum:	RL.3.3; RL.3.5
Genre:	Fiction

Vocabulary

furrows (FUR roze) *n.:* narrow grooves made in the ground
cooper (KOO per) *n.:* a person who makes or repairs barrels or tubs
tanner (TAN er) *n.:* a person who makes leather out of animal hides
miller (MILL er) *n.:* a person who grinds grain into flour
blacksmith (BLAK smith) *n.:* a person who makes horseshoes and put them on the horses
prospector (PROSS pek ter) *n.:* a person who searches and digs for gold in certain areas
stagecoach *n.:* a horse-drawn coach that carried passengers, mail, and packages
apothecary (uh PAH thuh keh ree) *n.:* a pharmacy
livery (LIH vuh ree) *n.:* a place where horses are cared for, fed, and stabled for pay
lariat (LARE ee ut) *n.:* lasso; a long, noosed rope used to catch horses, cattle, or other livestock
blossomed (BLAH sumd) *v.:* to flower; to grow and develop tremendously

Workbook

Related Pages:	20-25
Answer Key Page:	4

Boom Town

Into . . . *Boom Town*

There are a few themes in *Boom Town*, and you may choose which you prefer to focus on. The broader theme is the explosive expansion of the West during the Gold Rush years. The land was there, waiting to be settled. It was broad and deep, fertile and lush. The people mistakenly believed that the gold in the mines was where the riches of the land lay. In reality, it was the land itself and the opportunity it afforded the settlers that were its treasures. And, beyond that, it was America and its freedom that was the real gold mine; democracy was more valuable than all the gold and jewels the prospectors could ever dream of.

The more personal theme is tied up with the character of Amanda. She is a composite of all the youthful energy, persistence, and inventiveness that made the West thrive. Her chief quality is her can-do nature. She sees possibilities everywhere and doesn't take "no" for an answer. Adults listen to her because she is so obviously right and they know they stand to benefit from her ideas.

Some minor themes are that hard work (making pies) is a much better bet than hoping to get rich quick (panning for gold). People working together, as they do in this story, benefit themselves and each other. Near the end of the story, Amanda asks the bank to build sidewalks: here we have the notion of corporate responsibility, or, in simpler language, the idea of "giving back."

Eyes On: Setting

The reading skill for *Boom Town* is understanding that setting means the time or place in which a story takes place. The best strategy for achieving this is to *visualize* the story as though it were being presented on a stage. This forces the reader to "see" how people are dressed, what the countryside looks like, and so on. In a story that is dominated by setting, as this one is, the author will give the reader many details about the time and/or place in which the events are happening. This facilitates the visualization that the author hopes will take place.

To help the students visualize the setting of *Boom Town*, bring in some pictures of an actual boom town or any Western town of the mid-19th century. Ask them to describe what they see. In addition, tell them to close their eyes and pretend they are in one of those towns. Ask them what they "hear." Expect answers like "a horse is neighing," "a train whistles," or "some dogs are barking." Tell them to take a deep breath, and then ask them what they smell. Expect answers like "the smell of flowers," "bread baking," or "hay for the horses." Ask them how the air feels on their skin. Expect answers like "warm" or "dry." Tell them to open their eyes. Then explain that all the things they have just pictured in their imaginations are part of setting.

Blueprint for Reading

INTO . . . *Boom Town*

Amanda was a can-do person. When something was needed, she tried to help, and where Amanda lived, *everything* was needed! Out in California in the Gold Rush days, people lived in lonely places that had not much more than a water pump. Except for the few people who found gold, everyone was poor. Amanda, just a young girl, decided to cheer up her family with homemade pies. Then Pa began to sell slices of Amanda's pie, and a business was born. But what about the neighbors? Could Amanda help them?

EYES ON *Setting*

The **setting** is *where* and *when* a story takes place. *Where* might be the African jungle, a busy street in New York, or a space station on Mars. *When* could be 200 years ago or right now or some time in the future. When we read, we use our imaginations. We see the story's setting in our minds. This is called "using our mind's eye." When you read *Boom Town*, imagine a town with rough log cabins, dirt paths, and not much else. Use your mind's eye to picture the town as it changes, and changes, and changes!

BOOM TOWN

Sonia Levitin

It took us twenty-one days on the stagecoach to get to California. When we got there, I thought we'd live with Pa in the gold fields. A whole tent city was built up. But Ma shook her head. "The gold fields are no place for children. We'll get a cabin and live in town."

What town? A stage stop, a pump house, a few log cabins—that was all. It was so wide and lonesome out west, even my shadow ran off.

Ma found a cabin big enough for all of us: Baby Betsy, brothers Billy, Joe, Ted, and me—Amanda. Pa came in from the gold fields every Saturday night, singing:

"So I got me a mule
And some mining tools,
A shovel and a pick and a pan;

But I work all day
Without no pay.
I guess I'm a foolish man."

WORD BANK

stagecoach *n.*: a horse-drawn coach that carried passengers, mail, and packages

Boom Town   53

Literary Components

1 Exposition: This is a wonderful expository sentence. Without a lengthy description, the author puts us right into the Gold Rush experience. We are tired, sore, and grimy after a three-week ride. We don't know what awaits us, but we know the West is new and different.

2 Setting: The students will need an explanation of "a stage stop," which is like a bus stop for a stagecoach. The picture is of a wide, barren place, more like a camp than a town.

3 Setting; Imagery: This sentence describes not the physical setting but the emotion evoked by the physical setting. The speaker feels so alone that it seems she doesn't even have her shadow to keep her company. [Setting evokes mood.]

Guiding the Reading

Literal

Q: What state was the family heading to?
A: They were heading to California.

Q: Where did the men live while they were looking for gold?
A: They lived in tents in the gold fields.

Q: Where did Ma want the rest of the family to live?
A: She wanted them to live in a cabin in town.

Q: What did the town look like?
A: It had a stage stop, a pump house, and a few log cabins.

Q: Who is telling the story?
A: Amanda is telling the story.

Analytical

Q: What clues do you see in the story to help you determine when it takes place?
A: The story talks about stagecoaches, log cabins, and digging for gold. These are hints that the story takes place a long time ago. (Teacher: tell the class that the Gold Rush was from 1848 to 1855, which means this story took place more than 150 years ago.)

Q: What seems to be the thing that Amanda dislikes most about the town?
A: It is so lonesome.

Q: What did Pa do all week long?
A: He worked in the gold fields digging for gold.

Boom Town

Literary Components

4 **Setting:** California seems vast and lonely at first, but Amanda is beginning to feel its beauty, as well. We feel the warm, velvety nighttime skies that are punctuated by points of light, high above the little tin tub.

5 **Poetic Language:** How far is forever?

6 **Colloquial Language:** The use of the colloquialism adds flavor to the setting, placing us smack into rural mid-19th century America.

7 **Rising Action:** The seasoned reader sees signs of rising action in this seemingly random detail.

Guiding the Reading

Literal

Q: Did Pa find any gold?
A: No, he did not find gold.

Q: How did he feel about that?
A: He was always hopeful he would strike gold.

Q: What feeling do the children have, living in the town?
A: They are bored and lonely.

Q: What did the boys do to pass the time?
A: They planted vegetables.

Q: What did Amanda want to do?
A: She wanted to bake pies.

Analytical

Q: How do you think Pa felt when he came home each week without gold?
A: Answers will vary. He may have felt sad, embarrassed, frustrated or philosophical, hopeful, optimistic or have a wait-and-see attitude, and so forth.

Q: What do you think Amanda meant when she said, "The hills spread out as far as forever"?
A: Answers will vary. The line tells you that she felt that the loneliness and isolation of her little town could not be overcome. She felt a million miles away from civilization.

First Ma made him take a **4** bath <u>in a tin tub set out under the stars</u>. Then Pa sang songs and told stories he'd heard from the miners—stories about men finding big nuggets and striking it rich. But poor Pa, he had no luck at all. Still, every Monday morning he'd leave for the gold fields full of hope.

Days were long and lonely.
5 The hills spread out <u>as far as forever.</u> Nights, me and Ma and my brothers and Baby Betsy would sit out and wait for a shooting star to sail across the sky. Once in a while a crow flew by. That's all the excitement there was.

My brothers worked up some furrows. They planted corn and potatoes and beans. Then they ran around climbing trees, skinning their knees. But after all the water was fetched and the wash was done, after the soap was made and the fire laid, after the beds were fixed and the floor was swept clean, I'd sit outside our cabin door with Baby Betsy, so bored I
6 thought I'd die. <u>Also, I hankered</u>
7 <u>for</u> some pie. <u>I loved to bake pie.</u>

> **WORD BANK**
>
> **furrows** *n.*: narrow grooves made in the ground

54 Unit 1

I asked Ma and she said, "Pie would be good, but we have no pie pans and no real oven, just the wood stove. How would you bake pie?"

I poked around in a big box of stuff and found an old iron skillet. I decided to make a pie crust and pick gooseberries to fill it.

Gooseberries grew on the bushes near town. I picked a big pailful and went back home. I made a crust with flour, butter, a little water, and a pinch of salt, and then I rolled it out.

Ma came in and said, "Looks good, Amanda. I knew you could make it. But tell me, how will you bake it?"

I showed Ma the skillet. She shook her head. "I don't think it will work, but you can try."

"It will work," I said. **8**

> ### WORD BANK
> **skillet** *n.:* frying pan

Literary Components

8 **Characterization:** Amanda's confidence and determination are the backbones of the story. [You may compare her to the characters in *The Story of the White Sombrero* and ask which brother she most resembles.]

Guiding the Reading

Literal

Q: What was stopping Amanda from baking pie?
A: They had no pie pans and no real oven.

Q: What did Amanda find that she could make a pie out of?
A: She found a skillet, gooseberries, flour, butter, water, and salt.

Q: Did Ma think Amanda could bake a pie without an oven?
A: No.

Analytical

Q: What ingredient is missing from the list?
A: Sugar is missing.

Boom Town

Literary Components

9 **Simile:** This simile is so much a part of our language that we hardly think of it as a figure of speech.

10 **Characterization:** Amanda is a strong person who is spurred on by failure. She is not weak and hopeless like Francisco (*The Story of the White Sombrero*); she uses her frustration to motivate her to try again.

11 **Simile:** Not only does this simile help us imagine how Betsy sounds when she wails, it also adds color to the setting. It reminds us that out West, coyotes are as common as cowboys.

12 **Characterization:** Amanda keeps trying until she gets it right.

Guiding the Reading

Literal

Q: How did the pie turn out?
A: The pie burned.

Q: Were the brothers disappointed?
A: No. They laughed and used the pie as a ball.

Q: Did Amanda give up?
A: No. She tried again.

Q: Was the next pie good?
A: It was better than the last one, but not good either.

Q: Did Amanda give up after the second try?
A: No, and the third pie was delicious.

Analytical

Q: How would you describe Amanda's brothers?
A: Answers will vary. Some will call them mean, but most will realize they're just good-natured teasers—normal brothers.

Q: What have you learned about Amanda from this part of the story?
A: Amanda does not give up. When she wants to do something, she keeps trying.

Brothers Billy and Joe and Ted stood there laughing. When the wood turned to coals, I pushed my pie inside the old stove. After a while I smelled

9 a bad burning. I pulled out my pie, <u>hard as a rock.</u> Billy, Joe, and Ted whooped and slapped their sides. They snatched up my pie and tossed it high into the air. They ran outside and Billy whacked it hard with a stick. Pie pieces flew all over the place, and my brothers bent over, laughing.

10 <u>I was so mad I went right back in to make another,</u> and I promised none of them would get a bite. I rolled out my crust and filled it with berries, shoved the pie into the oven and soon took it out.

I set the pie down to cool. I went off to do some mending. Next thing I knew, Baby Betsy, just learning to walk, sat there with pie goo all over her

11 face. Too soft, the filling ran down on Betsy, and <u>she wailed like a coyote in the night.</u>

12 <u>It took one more try, but I got it right.</u> That night we ate my gooseberry pie, and it was delicious.

When Pa came home from the gold fields on Saturday night, there was a pie for him, too. "Amanda, you are the queen of the kitchen!" Pa scooped me up and whirled me around. I was proud.

The next week I made an extra pie for Pa to take with him to the gold fields.

Saturday night when he came home singing, <u>coins jangled in his pocket.</u> **13**

We all ran out to ask, "Did you strike gold, Pa?"

"No," he said. "I sold Amanda's pie. The miners loved it. They paid me twenty-five cents a slice!"

After that, Pa took pies to the gold fields every week. <u>And every week he</u> **14** <u>came home with coins in his pockets.</u> Some miners walked right to our door looking for pie. They told Ma, "You should open a bakery."

Ma said, "It's my girl Amanda who is the baker. If she wants to make pies, that's fine. But I have no time."

Ma had a new baby on the way. It was up to me. I figured I could sell pies to the miners and fill up our money jar.

Boom Town **57**

Literary Components

13 **Significant Point:** Although the reader does not realize it, this is really the beginning of success for Amanda, her family, and her town. There is money to be made, but not from gold. It is to be found in Amanda's pie!

14 **Rising Action:** In this one-horse town, people do not realize that there is more money to be made in business than there is in mining.

Guiding the Reading

Literal

Q: What did Pa call Amanda?
A: Pa called Amanda "the queen of the kitchen."

Q: Why did Pa have coins with him when he came home the next week?
A: He had sold Amanda's pie.

Q: How did Pa start to make a little money from that time on?
A: He began to take pies to sell at the gold fields every week.

Q: What did the miners tell Ma?
A: They told her she should open a bakery.

Q: What mistake had they made?
A: They thought Ma had baked the pies. It was really Amanda who had baked them.

Analytical

Q: What do you suppose encouraged Amanda to keep baking pies?
A: First, her father's enthusiasm and the pride he took in her accomplishment encouraged her. Second, the fact that her pies were bringing in money for the family gave her the motivation to keep on making them.

Boom Town

Literary Components

15 Alliteration: The musical language reflects the Western style of speech: rolling and colorful, laced with a dry humor.

16 Theme: The story's theme, interwoven as it is with Amanda's character, is beginning to emerge. Capitalism is smart, and it takes a smart person to realize that.

17 Theme: America was and is the land of opportunity. In the West, the need for any and all businesses was immense. And business was the most surefire way of making money.

Guiding the Reading

Literal

Q: Who helped Amanda bake her pies?
A: Her brothers, Billy, Joe, and Ted, helped her bake the pies.

Q: What is a peddler?
A: A salesman who travels from place to place selling his wares.

Q: What did Peddler Pete sell?
A: He sold pots and pans.

Q: What did Amanda suggest to Peddler Pete?
A: She suggested that he stop peddling his pots and pans and, instead, open a store in their town where he would sell his goods.

Analytical

Q: Amanda says "Anybody can make money out here." Why? What is different about this town?
A: This town had no stores and no services. Anyone willing to work hard could attract customers and sell their product. (In other places, there is a lot of competition, and it's harder to make money.)

But I needed help. I rounded up my brothers and told them, "If you want to eat pie, you've got to work."

15 They grumbled and groaned, but they knew I meant it. So Billy built me a shelf, Joe made a sign, AMANDA'S FINE PIES, and Ted helped pick berries and sour apples.

I needed more pans and another bucket. One day Peddler Pete came by, and with the money I'd made I bought them.

16 "You're a right smart little girl," said the peddler, "being in business like this."

17 I thought fast and told him, "Anybody can make money out here. Folks need things all the time, and there're no stores around. If you were to settle and start one, I'll bet you'd get rich."

58 Unit 1

Peddler Pete scratched his beard. "Not a bad idea," he said. "My feet are sore from roaming. I could use this cart and build my way up to having a store."

So pretty soon we had us a real store called PEDDLER PETE'S TRADING POST. Trappers and traders and travelers appeared. After shopping at Pete's, they were good **18** and hungry.

They came to our cabin, looking for pie. Some liked it here so well they decided to stay. Soon we had a cooper, a **19** tanner, a miller, a blacksmith. A town was starting to grow.

WORD BANK

cooper *n.*: a person who makes or repairs barrels or tubs

tanner *n.*: a person who makes leather out of animal hides

miller *n.*: a person who grinds grain into flour

blacksmith *n.*: a person who makes horseshoes and puts them on the horses

Literary Components

18 **Colorful Language:** The phrase used here, "good and hungry," contributes to the California setting, where we expect to hear expressions like that one.

19 **Detail:** By listing the names of the new businesses, we feel the town's growth is real. This kind of writing is much more powerful than just saying, "and the town grew."

Guiding the Reading

Literal

Q: How did Amanda benefit from Pete's Trading Post?

A: After shopping in Pete's store, people would be hungry and eager to eat a piece of pie.

Boom Town

Literary Components

20 Colorful Language: Again, the Western style that has its own imagery, dry humor, and exaggeration ("even my shadow ran off," "as far as forever," "clear to China,") adds to the story's Western flavor.

21 Theme: Amanda has already learned what her father has yet to discover: there is more money to be made in business than in the mines.

22 Alliteration; Imagery: One does not often think of the smell of leather as sweet, but here, it sounds right.

23 Theme: More of the theme emerges. A town is greater than the sum of its parts. At first there is a bakery, then a tanner, then a laundry, then a cobbler, and then—a town! A town is a win/win situation. People need businesses and services to thrive, and businesses thrive on customers. If people have initiative and energy, they can build.

Guiding the Reading

Literal

Q: Although the town had a cooper, a tanner, a miller, and a blacksmith, what did it still not have?

A: The town did not have a laundry.

Q: What does Amanda suggest to the prospector?

A: She suggested that he start a laundry.

Q: What kind of skilled workers soon set up shop in the little town?

A: A tailor, a cobbler, a barber, and a pharmacist.

Analytical

Q: What is Amanda beginning to understand about how a person probably will make money in her town and how he probably will not make money?

A: Amanda is seeing that most of the prospectors, like her father, are not finding gold. But she sees that if people will open a business, their chances of making money are very good.

A prospector came in on the stage from St. Joe, his clothes covered with dirt. He looked around at the folks eating pie, and he asked, "Is there someone here who does washing?"

I stepped right up and I told him, "What we need is a laundry. Why don't **20** you stay and start one? <u>Why, the miners are sending their shirts clear to</u> **21** <u>China.</u> You'll make more money doing laundry than looking for gold."

The man thought a while, then said with a smile, "You're right, little lady. It's a dandy idea. I'll send for my wife to help."

Soon shirts and sheets fluttered on the line as people brought their washing in. A tailor came to make and mend clothes. A cobbler crafted **22** shoes and boots. We heard the *tap tap* of his hammer <u>and smelled the sweet</u> <u>leather.</u> A barber moved in with shaving mugs, and an apothecary with herbs **23** and healing drugs. <u>So the town grew up all around us.</u>

> **WORD BANK**
>
> **prospector** (PROSS pek ter) *n.:* a person who searches and digs for gold in certain areas
>
> **apothecary** (uh PAH thuh keh ree) *n.:* a pharmacy

Q: Who has more to offer to a growing town—a prospector looking for gold or a skilled worker, like a barber or a cobbler?

A: Although some of the children may say a prospector, because he will have money to spend, the better answer is a skilled worker. The skilled worker fills a need, will spend the money he earns in the town, will settle in the town and raise his children there, will not have as many ups and downs in his income, and so forth.

My pie business blossomed.
Sometimes the line snaked clear around
the house. Baby Betsy entertained the
people while they waited. Billy added
another shelf. Joe and Ted made a bench.
We all picked berries and apples. Even Ma
came to help. We had to get a bigger jar
for all the money coming in.

One day our old friend Cowboy
Charlie rode by. Like everyone else, he
stopped for some pie. "I'd like to rest a
spell," he said. "Where can I leave my
horse for the night?"

WORD BANK

blossomed (BLAH sumd)
v.: grew and developed
tremendously

Boom Town 61

Boom Town

Literary Components

24 **Colloquialism:** The phrase is straight out of the old West.

Guiding the Reading

Literal

Q: How did each member of the family contribute to the pie business?
A: Amanda baked, Baby Betsy entertained the people, Billy added a shelf, and Joe and Ted made a bench. Everyone picked berries, even Ma.

Q: What did Cowboy Charlie need?
A: He needed a place to leave his horse overnight.

Boom Town

Literary Components

25 **Character; Theme:** Amanda's entrepreneurial character and the establishing of a town out West are two strands of the story's theme. Amanda is the cause, the town is the effect.

26 **Theme:** The family is a microcosm of the town. Everyone uses his or her skills to contribute to the growth and running of the business. Everyone is important and everyone stands to benefit from the joint effort.

Guiding the Reading

Literal

Q: What do you call a business that feeds, grooms, and boards horses for pay?

A: A livery.

Q: What did Amanda advise Charlie?

A: She advised him to open a livery stable.

Q: What two new businesses were opened as a result of Charlie's operating a livery stable?

A: A hotel and a cafe were opened to serve all the farmers bringing hay and feed for the horses in Charlie's livery.

Q: How did Amanda benefit from Charlie's stables?

A: The cafe bought Amanda's pies to serve its customers.

Analytical

Q: How does Amanda come up with such good suggestions?

A: She sees what is needed and suggests that someone fill the need.

25 "There's no livery stable," I said. "But why don't you start one? You'd rent out horses, and wagons too. That would be the perfect business for you."

"You're just full of great ideas, little lady," Cowboy Charlie said. He twirled his lariat. "I'd like to settle down. I'll stay here and do just that."

Soon a trail was worn right to Charlie's stable door. All day we heard the snorting of horses. Now Charlie needed hay. Farmers brought wagons and sacks full of feed. With all those people riding in, someone decided to build a hotel and a cafe. The town grew fast all around us.

26 The owner of the cafe bought pies from me, five or six at a time. I taught Billy how to roll the crust. Joe got wood for the stove. Ted washed the fruit, and Baby Betsy tried to stir in the sugar.

> **WORD BANK**
>
> **livery** (LIH vuh ree) *n.*: a place where horses are cared for, fed, and stabled for pay
>
> **lariat** (LARE ee ut) *n.*: lasso; a long, noosed rope used to catch horses, cattle, or other livestock

62   Unit 1

The money jar in our kitchen looked ready to bust. Where could we safely keep all that cash? Lucky us, one day Mr. Hooper, the banker, appeared.

"I'm building a bank," Mr. Hooper said to me. "This is getting to be a boom **27** town."

"We'll use your bank," I told Mr. Hooper, "but the roads are so poor. In winter there's mud, and in summer there's dust. We need some sidewalks and better streets."

"You're a smart little lady," said Mr. Hooper, tipping his hat. "I'll see what I can do about that."

Before we knew it, the bank was built and wooden sidewalks were laid. One street was called Bank Street; the other was Main. Soon every lane and landmark had a name. Pa and my brothers built on a big room for our bakery.

Boom Town **63**

Literary Components

27 **Theme:** The theme is revealed in the series of fictional events that lead to the town's explosive growth. Although no real town was built so spontaneously, the boom towns that dotted the West did grow in a similar, if less spectacular, way.

Guiding the Reading

Literal

Q: Why did Mr. Hooper come to town?
A: He'd heard it was a boom town and he wanted to build a bank that would serve all the businesses.

Q: What would the bank need to provide if people were to use it?
A: The bank would have to provide some sidewalks and better streets.

Q: How did the little empty town change?
A: It had a lot of streets and all of them were given names.

Analytical

Q: How is Mr. Hooper different from all the people who came to the town before him?
A: The other people came to a poor town that had little. They built a store or provided a service and helped the town grow. Mr. Hooper came because he had heard the town was doing well. He hoped to make money from the successful townspeople.

Boom Town

Guiding the Reading

Literal

Q: When the miners saw how much the town had grown, what did they do?

A: They sent for their families, helping the city to grow even bigger.

Q: What was now needed for the children?

A: A school was needed.

Q: What did Pa finally decide to do?

A: He decided to give up looking for gold and help Amanda in the business.

Q: What did Amanda want to do?

A: She wanted to go to school.

Men sent for their families. New houses appeared everywhere. Babies and children filled up the town. We needed a school, and a good schoolmarm.

We knew Miss Camilla from our stagecoach days. She was living up the coast a ways. Cowboy Charlie rode off to fetch her, and she was glad to come.

Miss Camilla, the teacher, had married, and her husband came too. We all got together to build a school. Bells rang out every day of the week. Now this was a real boom town!

One day Pa said to me, "Amanda, I'm through panning for gold. Will you let me be in business with you?"

"Sure!" I said, happily. "I'd love to work with you, Pa, and I'd also like to go to school."

So Pa turned to baking, and we all worked together. Pa sang while he rolled out the dough:

"Amanda found a skillet
And berries to fill it,
Made pies without a pan;

Our pies are the best
In all the West.
I guess I'm a lucky man."

Now Pa is with us every day. There's excitement and bustle all around.
Our house sits in the middle of a boom town!
And to think it all started with me, Amanda, baking pies!   (28)

ABOUT THE AUTHOR

Born in Berlin, Germany, **Sonia Levitin** and her family came to America
when Sonia was four years old. She grew up riding horses, feeding stray cats,
climbing trees, and, of course, reading and writing. When she was eleven
years old, she wrote a letter to author Laura Ingalls Wilder telling her that she
wanted to become a writer. Mrs. Levitin has taught both children and adults,
and her books for children and young adults have won many awards. Her
goal in writing is to connect people. She says writing "must flow, laugh, sing,
and dance with you."

Boom Town   65

Literary Components
- -
28 **Theme:** The various strands of the
theme are knotted and completed. Amanda's
character—dynamic, smart, persistent,
inventive, practical, optimistic, generous, and
forward-looking—is the key that will unlock
the promise of the new land. It will take a joint
effort and the talents of many like her for the
land to flourish, but there is no shortage of
independent spirits and they will leave their
mark on the great and growing country.

Guiding the Reading
- -
Literal

Q: Why was there excitement in the house?
A: Because Pa is working with the family and
because the town is booming.

Q: The town was growing. Who was responsible
for this?
A: Amanda!

Analytical

Q: Was it just the fact that Amanda baked pies
that changed the town?
A: No. It was because Amanda reached out and
kept trying to change things and help people.
Her pie baking alone would not have made
such drastic changes.

General Store

- -

Poem tie-in for *Boom Town*

General stores are fascinating. They hum with activity and boast of innumerable products. Big and little, necessity and luxury, and colorful and dull are crammed into a small but intoxicating space. This poem describes the look and feel of a general store, from the tinkly bell to the kegs of sugar to the rubber boots—all for sale at a good price! The poem's rollicking rhythm and home-spun language add to the old-fashioned flavor of a general store.

Here are some questions you can use to discuss *General Store*.

Q: What is a general store?

A: It is a small store that sells a large variety of products.

Q: When did general stores exist?

A: Every town in America had a general store until supermarkets and bigger specialty stores were built. The change from general stores to supermarkets and department stores took place gradually, probably starting in the early 1900s but lasting long after that in rural areas.

Q: Do you know what bolts of calico are? Tins of tea? Crockery? Sarsaparilla?

A: Calico is a printed cotton fabric that was used for making dresses and shirts. A bolt of calico is a big roll of calico. A "tin" is a can or metal box. Crockery is an old-fashioned word for earthenware dishes. Sarsaparilla is a drink very much like root beer.

Q: The poem has a wonderful rhythm (Teacher: read some lines and emphasize the rhythm.) How does the rhythm help you picture the general store?

A: The rhythm is quick and there are a lot of syllables in each line. This creates the feeling of lots and lots of "items," which is just what a general store has!

Rachel Field

Someday I'm going to have a store
With a tinkly bell hung over the door,
With real glass cases and counters wide
And drawers all spilly with things inside.
There'll be a little of everything:
Bolts of calico; balls of string;
Jars of peppermint; tins of tea;
Pots and kettles and crockery;

Seeds in packets; scissors bright;
Kegs of sugar, brown and white;
Sarsaparilla for picnic lunches,
Bananas and rubber boots in bunches.
I'll fix the window and dust each shelf,
And take the money in all myself,
It will be my store and I will say:
"What can I do for you to-day?"

66   Unit 1

Studying the Selection

FIRST IMPRESSIONS
Can one person really make a difference?

QUICK REVIEW

1. Why had Amanda's family come to California?
2. After weeks of coming home with nothing at all, how did Pa manage to finally bring home a little money?
3. What were some of the businesses that sprung up in the town?
4. What did Pa finally decide to do instead of looking for gold?

FOCUS

5. Amanda was full of ideas and suggestions. How did she know what to suggest to the different people she met?
6. The setting of a story includes the time and place in which the story happens. Imagine that you are Amanda and you have just arrived in the little town. You are taking a walk around. Write at least three sentences describing what you see.

CREATING AND WRITING

7. Amanda built up a business by starting small. First she baked one pie for her family. By the end of the story, her family is running a bakery for an entire town. Can you think of a business that might have started very small? If you know of one, write a paragraph describing how it started and what it grew into. If you don't know of one, you may invent one and write about it.
8. This story describes a lot of old-fashioned businesses, like cobblers, tanners, millers, and blacksmiths. On a sheet of paper, make a small ad for one of those businesses, or others that might have been built in a boom town. Make sure you include the name of your business, its address (make one up), and maybe a sentence describing how good your business is. You may even draw a small picture or logo. Your teacher will collect the sheets of paper and put them together to form a Yellow Pages of all the businesses in town.

Focus

5. When a person needed something that wasn't there, she suggested that he open a business that would fill that need.
6. Walking around town on a summer's morning, Amanda would see a few log cabins, a pump house, perhaps a stagecoach dropping off some people, hills that spread out as far as the eye could see, a big blue sky. She may have seen some little gardens next to the cabins, some gooseberry bushes, and probably grass and trees.

Creating and Writing

7. Many businesses started out as Mom and Pop stores. One famous example is the big corporation American Greeting Cards, whose founder, Jacob Saperstein, started out selling postcards from his pushcart. If you are interested, you can easily find hundreds of similar American success stories.
8. Bring a Yellow Pages to school to show your students what one looks like. Point to the bigger ads and show them what is included in each one. Encourage them to make up addresses that sound appropriate (Main Street; Wild West Avenue; Horseshoe Lane, etc.). Phone numbers are not necessary! Do a little research and give them a list of businesses that thrived during this time period.

Studying the Selection

- -

First Impressions

The answer is, "sometimes." The children will probably be a bit unrealistic and think that the individual always makes a difference. Ask them if they themselves have ever changed something singlehandedly, or if they have any plans to do so. If they have read a story about someone who brought about change, especially a young person, ask them to share it.

Quick Review

1. Amanda's Pa, like many other people who lived in the United States at that time, believed there was a lot of gold in California just waiting to be discovered. He came to dig in the ground, hoping to find gold.
2. Pa made some money selling Amanda's pie.
3. Cooper, miller, tanner, laundry, bakery, livery, etc.
4. He decided to help Amanda bake and sell pies.

Jill's Journal

Jill's Journal

Background Bytes

Towns and cities usually grow over a period of years. But reading about boom towns, we see that gradual growth is not always the case.

What is a boom town? The term *boom town* comes from the word *boom*, which among its many definitions means "the rapid settlement and development of a town or district often through the efforts of promoters."

Regarding boom towns, sometimes the number of people living in a community simply skyrockets overnight. This sort of abrupt and rapid population growth generally occurs when there is some economic boom. What this means is that boom towns spring up at a location where a rare and valuable material has been discovered. In this *Jill's Journal*, the precious resource is coal. It could be gold, silver, diamonds, zinc, lead, or any natural resource. For example, the famous Klondike boom was a gold rush. Boom towns also frequently got their start around sources of energy, such as oil or coal.

Vast stretches of forest, which yield timber for construction, have also been associated with overnight growth of boom towns. In the late 19th century and the early 20th century, because of the sudden expansion of the logging industry, mill towns arose quickly. Since the timber could last only so long in a given location, these boom towns had less than a ten-year lifespan before they became ghost towns or "historic districts" of larger cities.

Other reasons for population booms at particular locations are the proximity of a major waterway, closeness to a major city, major construction projects, and a pleasant climate.

In the United States in the 1800s, boom towns captured the imagination of people across the globe. These were folks who were desperately hoping to "strike it rich" during the U.S. expansion westward. After the 1849 California Gold Rush, new veins of precious metals were found throughout the West—in Colorado, Nevada, Idaho, and Arizona.

A town becomes a ghost town when its source of income vanishes and the people vanish with it. The rapid cycle of life and death for a town is intriguing and sad.

Jill's Journal:
On Assignment in Rhyolite, Nevada

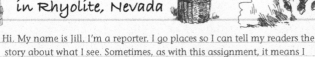

Hi. My name is Jill. I'm a reporter. I go places so I can tell my readers the story about what I see. Sometimes, as with this assignment, it means I have to go back in time.

I am interested in boom towns, how people come and then they go. Old boom towns of the West grew up around mines. They began as little camps with tents. As people in the East or in other countries heard about a new mine—especially a gold mine—more and more people came. They thought they would make lots of money from finding precious metal.

After a while, a general store and other shops would open. There would be a blacksmith to make shoes for horses and a wheelwright to fix wagon wheels. Newcomers also opened restaurants, boarding houses, and hotels. When whole families came, they would build cabins. In many boom towns, most buildings were put up so quickly that they were not sturdy or safe.

Boom towns were not very well-organized. There was no running water, no streetlights, no paved sidewalks, and no rules. Trash was piled up in back of the buildings. Because of this, boom towns were smelly and dirty. Also, they were very noisy. When men returned from the mine at night, there was shouting and there were fights. Sometimes there were gunfights and people got badly hurt.

Boarding houses and hotels were usually small. Hotels were often on the second floor of the restaurants. The general store was a place where people gathered during the day and exchanged news. The merchants who ran the stores, the hotels, and the restaurants made more money selling goods and services to the miners than most of the miners made trying to find gold.

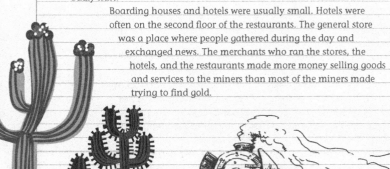

A mine would be worked until it had no more precious metal to mine. No one knew when that would be. But when it occurred, there might be no reason to stay in the town. Many boom towns became deserted.

This is why I am interested in boom towns: One day there are lots of people in the town, and the next day everyone may leave and it becomes a ghost town. *Ghost town* sounds a little scary and very mysterious to me.

Therefore, I have decided to go to the boom town called Rhyolite. Rhyolite is in southwestern Nevada and has an interesting history. By the way, it may be hard to believe, but it is 1908. I went from Los Angeles by train. At Las Vegas I boarded another rail for the 118-mile trip to Rhyolite. This train has only three passenger cars! We have been traveling for five hours. The trip takes six, but I am lucky to have Mrs. Edna Montgomery sitting next to me. She knows I am a reporter from back East, so she is filling me in. I believe she, herself, is a bit of a historian.

Edna has told me that in this part of Nevada, there are several boom towns. She says that in 1904, two men found gold in a hill they called Bullfrog Mountain. This gold was worth a lot of money. As word of their discovery spread, thousands of people came to the region looking for gold.

Now, she says, 5,000 people live in Rhyolite. As we pull into the train depot, I gasp in surprise, "This train station is so beautiful!"

Edna says, "It should be. Why, Mr. Schwab spent $130,000 on it!"

She pats my arm and says proudly, "Jill, there are 19 lodging houses, 24 restaurants, 6 barbers, a public bathhouse, and a daily newspaper in Rhyolite. You may want to take a peek at the new bonnets at Molly's, as well. But I have to be on my way. My husband and children are waiting inside the depot. Why don't you take a walk over to the offices of the *Rhyolite Herald*, our newspaper, and meet one of your fellow reporters? When

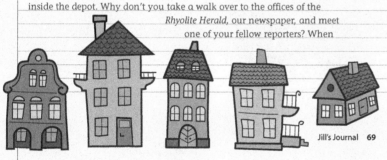

Jill's Journal

Power Skill

1.

Usual Boom Town	Rhyolite
No rules	"Edna said that unlike other boom towns, Rhyolite has laws."
"In many boom towns, most buildings were put up so quickly that they were not sturdy or safe."	Well-constructed buildings
No sidewalks	"I cannot believe it, but right now I am walking on a concrete sidewalk."
"… boom towns were smelly and dirty … When men returned from the mine at night, there was shouting and there were fights. Sometimes there were gunfights and people got badly hurt." Doesn't say specifically, but the description suggests this is not a place where there would be a hospital.	A hospital
"Boom towns were not very well-organized. There was no running water, no streetlights …"	Electricity
Dirty with garbage piled up	"As I begin to walk about, I see that Rhyolite is nothing like the usual dirty and muddy boom towns." As the description continues, it is clear that Rhyolite is a beautiful, clean town.

Cook Bank Building

you've finished looking around town, please join us for tea." This nice woman gives me her address and we part.

As I begin to walk about, I see that Rhyolite is nothing like the usual dirty and muddy boom towns. A very wealthy man whom Edna mentioned, Charles Schwab, bought the mine and spent lots of money here. He had water piped in, paid for an electric line that had to run 100 miles to get to Rhyolite, and even had a train line run to the mine.

I cannot believe it, but right now I am walking on a concrete sidewalk. This place was just desert four years ago. There are electric lights and telephone and telegraph lines! I pass the police and fire departments. Edna said that unlike other boom towns, Rhyolite has laws. I pass a hospital. I am amazed. I wish you could see the Cook Bank Building. It is actually three stories high!

Now I have come to the school. The school has two stories and eight rooms! It is full of children studying and playing. The school also makes room for adults who want to learn how to read and write.

I have walked for several hours and my feet hurt. I stop a passerby and ask for directions to Edna Montgomery's house. The gentleman is dressed like a miner and covered with dust, but he is very helpful. He exclaims, "Ain't this a beautiful town?"

I smile in agreement. When I reach the Montgomerys' house, Edna welcomes me into the cool dining room. She asks me how my sightseeing went.

"I have enjoyed myself," I sigh. "I have been amazed by how busy this town is. Why, it is like a little city."

Edna introduces me to her children, four young ladies that range in age from seven to fifteen. The oldest girl, Dorothy, brings out a plate of muffins. Edna pours the tea into fine china cups that sit on matching saucers.

Two Story Schoolhouse

2. • **General Store:** The general store served the rural populations of small towns and villages and the farmers in the surrounding area. Besides selling food, dry goods, farming equipment and other supplies, they sometimes also served as the local post office and drugstore. A general store needed shelving, barrels, wooden boxes, and crates to store and display the various goods for sale. Store counters held display cases, a coffee grinder, scales, and a cash register.

• **Pharmacy:** Where pharmacists existed, they made those drugs that would have been available in those days. All medicines needed to be compounded (mixed from ingredients) by the pharmacist who used a mortar and pestle, scales or balances, a variety of graduated cylinders, beakers (and other glassware usually connected with chemistry), and the compression device that enabled him to make pills of various colors and sizes. Medications ranged in type from creams, ointments, and powders to medicated lollipops and medicated dog

I think to myself, sadly, that in just two years, in 1910, the mines will dry up. I know this because I have come from many years in the future. Edna and her family do not know this, of course, and I cannot tell them. In 1910, there will be only 675 residents remaining. All the families will have moved away.

All the stores and restaurants will have closed. The banks will shut down. The newspapers, including the *Rhyolite Herald*, will be gone by June 1912. The post office will close in November 1913. The last train will leave Rhyolite Station in July 1914. Since there will be no people left, the Nevada-California Power Company will turn off the electricity and remove its lines in 1916.

After all, by 1916, Rhyolite, Nevada will be a ghost town.

POWER SKILL:
Organizing a Boom Town

1. You are going to compare the usual boom town with Rhyolite. We have given you some hints.

Usual Boom Town	Rhyolite
No rules	
	Well-constructed buildings
No sidewalks	
	A hospital
	Electricity
Dirty with garbage piled up	

2. What would you have done in a boom town? What supplies would you have needed to do this? Choose your business and make a list of what you need. Here are some choices. (You may also come up with your own ideas.)

General Store	**Doctor**
Pharmacy	**Teacher**
Restaurant	**Blacksmith**
Newspaper	**Wheelwright**

3. Make a sign for your business.

chews. Applications included care for the dying, skin conditions, animal diseases, childhood diseases, dental problems, and chronic pain management.

- **Restaurant:** Flour for bread and to make desserts, baking powder, salt, pepper, sugar, honey, molasses, potatoes, rice, butter, jam, whiskey, beer, coffee, milk, eggs, carrots, cheese, some meat. Also chairs, tables, tablecloths, cotton napkins, candles for tables. Plates, glasses, cups, saucers, cutlery. Pots, pans, cooking utensils. An old-fashioned cast-iron stove to cook on. Mops, brooms, dustpans, matches, rags. Ammonia, baking soda for cleaning.

- **Newspaper:** Suitable paper, a printing press, ink, office supplies, tables, and chairs. Old-fashioned typewriters were also used.

- **Doctor:** Actually, doctors were practically nonexistent for early pioneers. Pioneers usually had to treat themselves for injuries and ailments. Settlers used remedies of Native Americans, which often came from local herbs and plants. Pioneer families sterilized their own axe cuts, knife wounds, and barbed wire gashes, which were stitched up by mother, father, or neighbor. If indeed there was a doctor, his most basic necessities were a horse and buggy for making house calls. A doctor's instruments included enamelware pitcher, a blood pressure cuff with a gauge, surgical knives and saws, and a stethoscope. Doctors often doubled as veterinarians.

- **Teacher:** The teacher had a one-room log cabin with a large fireplace. The windows were covered with oiled paper. Chalkboards mounted on the walls consisted of wood planks fastened together and painted black. The erasers were made of sheepskin with the wool side out. Students sat on rough wooden benches with another, higher rough wood bench for their desks. Chalk, quill pens made at home, lead pencils made from lead bullets, small chalkboards. For books, children bring whatever there is at home.

- **Blacksmith:** Blacksmiths shoe horses' hoofs with metal. Probably most importantly, a blacksmith made and fixed tools. The mainstay tools of his practice were a hammer, an anvil, a forge, and tongs. Blacksmith metals were iron and later steel. A blacksmith also needed a solid workbench, chisels, a stout blacksmith's vise, grinding and polishing wheels, measuring tools, saws, and drills.

- **Wheelwright:** Fixed all sorts of wagon wheels and probably did other kinds of wood or iron repair. A wheelwright needed wood for making the wheels and the spokes and iron tires and tire bolts. These last were usually made by the blacksmith.

3. You might want to show your students some pictures of the well-crafted samplers made by young girls. These were hung on the walls of houses and cabins during the Victorian period and the early 1900s. They may also want to see signs that hung outside the various stores and businesses of a Western town during the same periods. This will give them a realistic idea of the styles that were used. Obviously, students' work will vary.

Taro and the Tofu

Lesson in Literature

What Is Theme?
The Blue Marble

1. In the last paragraph, Celi says she should be happy with what she has, and never need something so much she would steal. The theme is how important it is to be satisfied with what one has.

2. Celi's father says, "We have to be happy with what we have," an allusion to the theme.

3. Celi feels jealous but tries hard to be happy with what she has and not to feel jealousy. This conveys the theme of being satisfied with what one has.

Selection Summary

Taro is a young Japanese boy who lives in a small town with his mother and father. The story opens as night is falling. Taro and his mother are waiting for the tofu seller to come along the street as he does every evening, so that they can buy their tofu for supper. When the man does not appear, Taro offers to go to the tofu shop to make their purchase. His mother, knowing that it is cold, dark, and lonely where the tofu shop is, reluctantly agrees to let him go. Taro runs past the bustling, lighted shops to the dim corner store and purchases the tofu. The tofu man tells him that he did not make his usual evening rounds because he had to stay at home with his sick grandson.

Taro's next stop is the candy store. When he reaches into his pocket to pay the candy lady, he discovers that the tofu man has given him a 50-yen coin for change instead of a 10-yen coin. His first thought is to return the coin to the tofu man, but a "little voice" inside his head tries to persuade him that this is not necessary. He (mentally) argues back forcefully, dismayed that any part of his mind could even consider being so dishonest. He pays for the candy and runs back to the tofu store where he returns the money to the tofu man, who hadn't even realized he'd made a mistake. Knowing that his "little voice" had said he should keep the money, Taro feels a bit guilty when the man thanks him. He responds by giving the tofu man half of the chocolate he has just bought as a gift for his sick grandson.

Taro returns home and tells his parents about how he returned the coin to the tofu man. He does not tell them about the internal battle he fought or about giving away half of his chocolate. Taro feels warm and good at the story's conclusion.

Lesson in Literature . . .
THE BLUE MARBLE

WHAT IS THEME?

*   The **theme** of a story is its main idea.
*   Sometimes, the author tells the reader exactly what the theme is. The author may state the theme right at the beginning of the story, somewhere in the middle, or all the way at the end.
*   Other times, the reader must figure out what the theme is by thinking about the story. When that is the case, the theme will probably not be completely clear until the end of the story.
*   All of the story elements—the plot, the characters, and the setting—help build the story's theme.

THINK ABOUT IT!

1. In this story, the author does not tell us what the theme is. However, the theme becomes clear at the very end of the story. Look at the last paragraph of the story and write down the story's theme.

2. In the story, Celi's father says something after a storm destroys their house. What does he say that hints at the theme?

3. The author tells us how Celi feels when she sees Maria's beautiful dress. What are those feelings? How do they hint at the theme?

Nicaragua is a country in Central America. There is a small town in Nicaragua called Bluefields. This is where Celi and Luci and Ada live. The three of them are good friends. They help each other with chores and with taking care of the babies in their families.

There is no road into Bluefields. Visitors either fly in or take a boat from the town of El Rama. Most of the people who live in Bluefields are very poor, but it is very beautiful there. There are 698 fabulous species of birds. The rain forest surrounds the town, except where the River Escondido flows.

Even though they are very poor, the three girls are usually very cheerful. Nicaragua has been badly hurt by hurricanes several times. When Hurricane Mitch came, heavy rains destroyed nearly 24,000 houses and 340 schools. When bad weather comes, Celi's father says, "It can't be helped. We just have to start over again. We are strong people and we will do just fine. We have to be happy with what we have."

Getting Started

Read aloud from the beginning of the story through the middle of page 76 ("I'll get the tofu for you, Mother"). Then read the questions and possible answers. Ask the students to choose the correct answer for each question.

(For more information on aural exercises, see *Getting Started/The Story of the White Sombrero*.)

1. As the story opens, the weather outside is
    a. sunny and warm.
    b. chilly and foggy.
    c. hot and humid.
    d. cold and windy.

2. Tofu is one of the most important foods in
    a. China.
    b. Japan.
    c. Greece.
    d. Italy.

Celi thinks her father is very brave. He is a fisherman and goes out every night in his boat. Her mother is a farmer. Her father has had to rebuild their house two times. She thinks maybe he should be a carpenter.

If they have time to play, the girls and their friends play marbles. A tourist once came to the town on a panga (which is a kind of boat). Before he left, he handed out about 200 marbles to the children. That is when the marble craze started. The children of the town never ask the tourists for anything except marbles.

The girls have no school today. They decide to play a game of marbles with a few friends. One girl, Maria, is wearing her beautiful Sunday dress. Her family has more than the other families. Celi tries hard not to be jealous. She doesn't have a special dress, just a clean old one her mother washed and ironed.

They all sit down on the hard-packed earth in a circle. Maria takes some new marbles out of her little marble pouch.

"Maria, where did you get those?" some of the girls cry. Maria empties the pouch onto a square of cloth. Celi sees a blue one. It looks like it glows. Maria pours out so

many new marbles, she doesn't see that the blue one rolls away. Celi does not say anything. She knows that the blue marble is in the bushes.

Celi stands up, holding her marble bag tightly in her fist. "I'm sorry," she says. "I just remembered I said I would help my mother this afternoon. I can't play right now." She runs towards home.

Celi helps her mother, but all she can think about is the blue marble. She wants it so much. Surely Maria will not miss it. She has so many.

It is early evening. Celi is pretty sure the other girls have gone home. She runs back to the place where they were sitting in a circle. She walks over to the bushes. She crouches down. There is the marble, glowing like a little moon. Oh, how pretty it is!

Celi reaches for it and pricks her finger on a thorn. Her eyes fill with tears. She is about to do a very bad thing. She has never taken something that belonged to someone else. How can she need something so much that she would steal? She feels ashamed. She should be happy with what she has. She grabs the marble and runs to Maria's house.

| **Target Skill:** Understanding that the theme is the story's main idea |
| **Learning Strategy:** Questioning |
| **Common Core Curriculum:** RL.3.2; RL.3.3; W.3.1 |
| **Genre:** Fiction |

Related Vocabulary

delicacy (DELL uh kuh SEE) *n.*: a delicious treat eaten only on special occasions

dim *adj.*: not bright

errand (AIR und) *n.*: a short trip to accomplish something, like buying or delivering something

linger (LING ur) *v.*: spend extra time before leaving a place

respectfully (rih SPEKT full lee) *adv.*: with respect; nicely, not rudely

responsible (ree SPON sih bl) *adj.*: reliable; dependable

struggled (STRUG uld) *v.*: fought to overcome

triumph (TRY umf) *n.*: victory

Workbook

| **Related Pages:** 26-31 |
| **Answer Key Pages:** 4-5 |

3. Where did Taro's mother usually buy tofu?
   a. At the small grocery on the corner.
   b. In the big supermarket.
   c. From her neighbor, who was an expert tofu maker.
   d. From a man who came along the street.

4. What were Taro and his mother waiting for this evening?
   a. They were waiting for the tofu man to come.
   b. They were waiting for Taro's father to come.
   c. They were waiting for their neighbor to bring them some tofu.
   d. They were waiting for the rain to stop so they could go out.

5. What did Taro offer to do?
   a. He offered to cook supper himself.
   b. He offered to run to his father's shop.
   c. He offered to run to the tofu shop.
   d. He offered to run next door and borrow some tofu.

Taro and the Tofu

Into . . . *Taro and the Tofu*

The theme of *Taro and the Tofu*—the choices between right and wrong that we are forced to make as we go through life—is one that is relevant to every age group. In this selection, the theme is presented in a story that a child can relate to. Taro is a good boy who is shocked to find that one part of him wants to do something dishonest. He is confused at first, but because he has a clear idea of right and wrong, he is able to identify one of the choices as absolutely wrong for him. What is especially commendable about this story is how Taro reacts, once he labels the option of not returning the money as "not right": he literally runs to return the money. This gives the young reader a very clear, strong picture of what the right choice is.

Children are very aware of right and wrong. You should be able to have a very meaningful discussion with your class about all the elements of this story. You may ask them about their own experiences with moral "tests" or "challenges" and how they dealt with them. (One cannot call what takes place in this story a moral dilemma: a dilemma implies the inability to choose between two equally valid choices. Once the "voice" suggests keeping the money, there is no dilemma, only a test of Taro's honesty.)

The story ends with Taro feeling happy and warm. This is worth stressing to the children as it is a valuable life lesson. Doing good makes a person feel good.

Eyes On: Theme

What is the theme of *Taro and the Tofu*? As adults, it is easy for us to spot the theme, for it is a very familiar one. It is one person's struggle with and victory over the temptation to do wrong. Theme is the most difficult of all the literary elements to teach, because it is not concrete. One can name a character, describe a setting, or outline a plot, but how does a reader learn to identify a theme?

One learning strategy for identifying theme is *questioning and evaluating*. At this early stage in the semester, we will limit ourselves to questioning. The first question that should be asked is: What is the story *really* about? Which scene or part of the story changed everything? What lines or words can we point to and say "here is where the hero's mind was made up"? Remind your students that in a story, something, usually the main character, has to change or develop. Encourage your students to develop the following three questions: (1) What or who changed?

(Taro changed/developed.) (2) Why did he change? (He was tested by the "little voice" that tried to persuade him to keep money that wasn't his, and he was forced to choose.) (3) What did he change to? (He was now experienced at choosing right over wrong. He was more confident in himself and happy to know he was a good person.) The answers to these questions will have them well on their way to identifying the theme.

Identifying theme is a skill that you will be working on with your students throughout the year. The best way to help them is to teach them by example to ask the right questions.

Taro and the Tofu   Masako Matsuno

It was windy, and the wind was cold. The cold, windy day was growing into a cold, windy night. From the window Taro could see the evening star already shining brightly in the east. Taro was watching for the tofu seller.

Taro and the Tofu   75

Literary Components

1 **Exposition:** The setting is established immediately. The time is evening, the place is a small Japanese town, and the weather is cold and windy.

Guiding the Reading

Literal

Q: What was the weather outside like?
A: It was a cold and windy night.

Q: Who was Taro watching for?
A: He was watching for the tofu seller.

Taro and the Tofu

Literary Components

2 **Setting:** The contrast between the warm house and the cold outdoors will add tension to the action, as the hero, Taro, must brave the cold.

3 **Characterization:** Taro is a respectful boy who wishes to be helpful.

Guiding the Reading

Literal

Q: What is tofu?
A: It is a tasty dish made of bean curd.

Q: Where did Taro's mother buy tofu for the family?
A: She bought it from a man who came along the street every evening.

Q: What were Taro and his mother waiting for?
A: They were waiting for the tofu man.

Q: What did Taro offer to do?
A: He offered to run to the tofu man's shop to find out what had happened to him, and to buy some tofu for supper.

Q: Why was his mother unsure about whether to let Taro go?
A: Because it was getting dark and cold.

Q: What was Taro holding when he left the house?
A: He was holding a small pan for tofu in one hand and a silver coin in the other.

Q: Why was he running?
A: Because it was so cold.

Q: What was the shopping street like?
A: It was crowded and cheerful.

Q: Where was the tofu shop?
A: It was at the end of the street, away from the main shopping place.

Analytical

Q: From what you have read, can you guess how old Taro is?
A: He seems to be young, since his mother is worried about his going out in the dark.

Q: Tofu is one of the most important foods in Japan. What would you say is an important food in America?
A: Answers will vary. They should include bread or meat; the children should understand that tofu was an important part of the family's dinner, not just a side dish.

In Japan *tofu* is what we call "bean curd"—it is very delicious, and it is one of the most important foods of that country.

Taro's mother bought tofu from a man who came along the street every evening. But on this cold, windy evening, the man did not come.

2 In their warm house Taro and his mother waited and waited until finally it was time to cook supper.

"I wonder what has happened to him," said Taro's mother. "This is the first time he hasn't come without letting us know."

"Shall I run to his shop?" asked Taro.

His mother was unsure. "It's getting dark … and cold, too."

"That's all right," said Taro, "it's not so late yet, is

3 it? I'll get the tofu for you, Mother."

From beyond the woods the cold wind blew. Taro, holding a small pan for tofu in one hand and a silver coin in the other, began running as soon as he left the house.

The shopping street was crowded with people buying good food for supper. The shops were light and cheerful.

"Come in and buy, come in and buy! My fish are delicious!" a loud voice called from one of the fish stores.

But Taro didn't stop—this wasn't the place he was looking for. He ran in the direction of the man's shop which was at the end of the street, away from the main shopping place. That was why he went to the houses every evening to sell tofu.

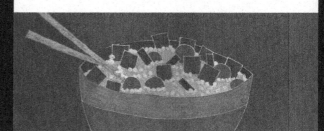

Taro and the Tofu 77

Taro and the Tofu

Taro hurried through the crowd. Beyond the lights and noise of the shops it was cold and dark and lonely; only one dim light showed at the very end of the street. It was the light of the man's shop.

The man was surprised to see Taro. "Are you alone?" he asked. "Did you come here all by yourself?"

"Yes," said Taro. "My mother needs two cakes of tofu. She waited a long time for you to come, but you didn't come. What happened?"

The man took the tofu pan from Taro and said, "I'm sorry, but my grandson doesn't feel well today, so I couldn't leave him alone. But I'll come to your house tomorrow evening," the man added. He handed Taro the filled tofu pan, saying, "Then you won't have to come down in the cold."

"How much?" asked Taro.

"Thirty yen."[1]

Taro handed the coin to the man, who slowly counted out the change under the dim light of the shop.

"Thank you, Taro," he said. "You'd better hurry home, for your mother must be waiting for you."

"Yes—good-by!"

"Don't run, Taro!" the man shouted after him. "My tofu is soft. Carry it carefully so it doesn't break!"

---

1. A *yen* is the smallest coin in Japan, similar to a U.S. penny.

Guiding the Reading

Literal

Q: How was the end of the shopping street different from the main part of it?
A: The main part of the street was bright and cheerful; the end of the street was cold and dark and lonely.

Q: What did the man ask Taro?
A: He asked him if he had come all by himself.

Q: What did Taro ask the man?
A: He asked him what had happened to him.

Q: Why hadn't the tofu man come that evening?
A: His grandson was sick and couldn't be left alone.

Q: What did the tofu man promise Taro?
A: He would come the next evening.

Q: What did the tofu man tell Taro to do after he gave him his change?
A: He told him to hurry home.

Q: Why shouldn't Taro run?
A: If he runs, the soft tofu may break.

Analytical

Q: How do you think Taro felt when he got to the end of the shopping street?
A: He was cold and probably a little frightened.

Q: Do you think Taro knew how lonely a place the tofu shop was?
A: Yes. He had obviously been there before, since he knew just how to get there.

Q: If he did know, what good trait did Taro have?
A: He had courage.

Q: Can you use three words to describe how Taro must have felt when he left the warm tofu shop?
A: Some appropriate answers would be: cold; a little frightened; lonely; happy that he had the tofu; hungry for supper; looking forward to hearing his mother thank him.

Taro and the Tofu

Literary Components

4 **Hyperbole:** The author uses hyperbole to make us notice the strange behavior of the candy lady.

Guiding the Reading

Literal

Q: How did Taro's mother reward him for doing an errand?
A: She let him keep ten yen for himself.

Q: What did Taro plan to spend the yen on?
A: Candy.

Q: What was the owner of the shop usually doing when a customer came in?
A: She was usually reading a newspaper.

Q: What was the most she ever said?
A: "Thank you, good boy" or "good girl."

Q: Did Taro like the fact that the lady never looked up?
A: Yes. It gave him plenty of time to decide what candy to buy.

Q: What did Taro decide to buy?
A: Two boxes of chocolate.

Analytical

Q: Did it surprise you that Taro ran to the candy shop instead of straight home?
A: Answers will vary.

Q: Do you think the shop lady knew who Taro was? Why or why not?
A: Answers will vary. Some may say no, since she never looked up from her newspaper. Others will say yes, as he seemed to come there often and maybe she recognized his voice or movements.

Q: When you shop for candy, does it take you a long time to decide what you want?
A: Answers will vary.

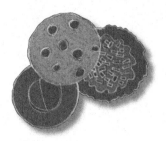

Taro did not run, but he walked fast. Whenever Taro did an errand, his mother let him keep ten yen for himself, so he was in a hurry to get to the little candy store on the main shopping street.

The candy store was run by a lady with big glasses. She always sat in a far corner of the shop, reading a newspaper. She rarely said more than a few words to people. "Thank you, good boy," or "Thank you, good girl," she would say, never looking **4** up from her paper. It was one of the seven wonders to Taro how she knew a boy was a boy—or a girl a girl—without ever looking at them.

And the lady never seemed to care if the children took a long time to decide what to buy with their pocket money. It made Taro feel that all the candies in the store belonged to him until at last he decided just what to buy.

Taro had to decide quickly today so he could hurry home with the tofu.

Two boxes of chocolate, he said to himself, putting his hand in his pocket for the change the man had given him. Taro picked one of the coins to give to the lady.

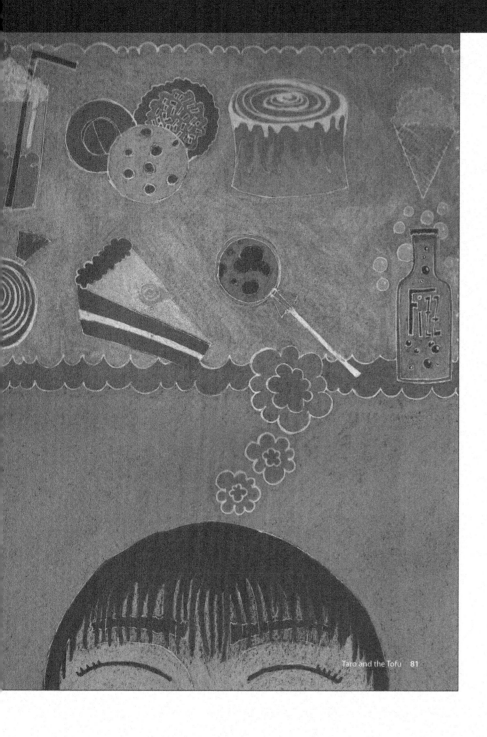

Taro and the Tofu 81

Taro and the Tofu

Literary Components

5 **Rising Action:** From here on in, the story will deal with this issue. As in life, things are going along in their usual bumpy fashion (life is never altogether smooth) when all of a sudden, a major hurdle appears in the road.

6 **Characterization:** It is significant that Taro's immediate reaction is to return the coin right away. This is important, because the internal conflict that is about to arise depends on the fact that Taro is completely honest.

7 **Setting; Conflict; Theme:** A valid obstacle to returning the money immediately is described. The dark and cold are objective facts, not something merely perceived by Taro.

Guiding the Reading

Literal

Q: What did Taro discover in his pocket?
A: A 50-yen coin.

Q: Was it his?
A: No.

Q: What size coin had Taro given the tofu man?
A: He had given him a 100-yen coin.

Q: How much had the tofu cost?
A: Thirty yen.

Q: How much change should Taro have had in his pocket?
A: Seventy yen.

Q: How much change did he have?
A: He had altogether 110 yen: six 10-yen coins and one 50-yen coin.

Q: What was Taro's first thought when he discovered the man had made a mistake?
A: He must return the money immediately.

Analytical

Q: The first thought that came into Taro's head was that he must return the coin right away. What does that tell you about Taro? What kind of boy was he?
A: Taro was honest and responsible.

---

5 But, wait, it was a 50-yen coin!
Where did I get this?
Taro looked at the coin in surprise.
"I thought the man gave me seven 10-yen coins, for the tofu was thirty yen, and I gave him a 100-yen coin," thought Taro. "One, two, three, four, five, six ... Here are six 10-yen coins and a 50-yen ... Then the man made a
6 mistake. I must return the extra forty yen to him right away. He will be sorry if he finds that he lost money."
7 But outside it was already dark and the wind was very cold.

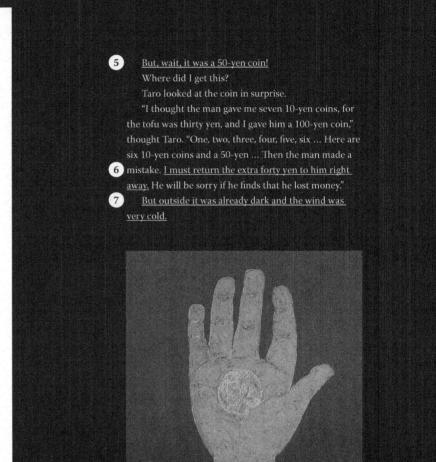

Guiding the Reading (p. 83)

Literal

Q: What did the "little voice" in his head start to whisper?
A: It was cold and late and he could pay the man back tomorrow. If the man worried, it was his own fault for making a mistake.

Q: What are the first two things the "voice" says to Taro?
A: First it says that his mother will be waiting, and then it says that it is just the same if he gives back the money tomorrow.

Q: What is the next thing the "voice" tells him?
A: It tells him that no one knows he has the money. He could spend it on treats for himself.

Q: How does Taro "answer" the "little voice"?
A: He says "No, no, it's not right."

Q: What does Taro decide to do?
A: He decides to return the money right away.

"It's getting late, and very cold ..." a strange little voice whispered inside Taro's head. "Why not tomorrow? Even if the man worries, the mistake is his own fault. It's very cold, and Mother must be waiting," the secret voice said.

Taro looked at the money in his hand and then at the cold outdoors. "It's just the same if you give the money back tomorrow," whispered the voice again. "Besides, who knows that you've got the money? No one need know. Just think, with forty yen to spend, you could buy sweet beans and salted beans and chocolate and even more ... Right?"

"Oh, no—" it was almost a shout inside him—"No, no, it's not right. This is not my money. It belongs to the man, even if it was his fault that he gave me the wrong change. I don't want the candies!" Taro was talking to himself very fast now, as if he were in a hurry to rid himself of the strange, secret voice inside his head. "I will return the money right now."

Taro called to the lady of the candy store, but his voice sounded so dry and cracked that only a little low whisper came out.

"I'll take two boxes of chocolate candy today," he said.

"Thank you, good boy," answered the lady without looking up.

Taro smiled. "And may I leave my tofu pan here for just a little while?" he asked.

"Of course you may, good boy," answered the lady, still looking at her newspaper.

Literary Components

8 **Theme; Characterization:** The theme is introduced here, a bit at a time. What is this "little voice"? Why is it there?

9 **Theme; Conflict:** The "little voice" presents several persuasive reasons to postpone returning the money. Notice that the first argument is disguised as "reasonable"; the second, as "just"; the third, as being considerate of his mother. The "little voice" will use all sorts of approaches to defeat the desire to do the right thing.

10 **Turning Point of the Internal Conflict:** The "little voice" now reveals itself for what it is. It doesn't just want to protect Taro from the cold or keep his mother from worrying, it wants to make him lie and steal.

11 **Theme; Characterization; Climax:** Taro's honest instincts are appalled by his shameful thoughts. His internal voice shouts down the bad idea that has somehow made its way into his brain, and he runs to act against it.

12 **Foreshadowing:** Although the reader wonders briefly why Taro is taking two boxes of chocolate, it doesn't seem terribly significant. We shall soon see that the two boxes of candy present him with an opportunity to do a good deed.

Q: If Taro's "little voice" tells him to do something dishonest, does that mean he is dishonest? [This is a very important question.]
A: No, it does not mean that at all. Our minds have all kinds of thoughts. What we do is what counts, not the individual thoughts. In the story, Taro argues with the "little voice" and does not listen to it. That is what makes him an honest boy.

Q: How do you think Taro felt about the "little voice" that was telling him to keep the money?
A: He was frightened by it. He didn't know he could have such dishonest thoughts. He didn't want to have these thoughts.

Q: What did he do to help himself get away from these thoughts?
A: He decided to give the money back right away.

Q: Do you think this was a good idea? What about the fact that it was cold and dark?
A: It was a very good idea. This way he could prove to himself that he was honest. This way he did not give the "little voice" a chance to persuade him to do anything less than return the money to its owner.

Q: What did Taro ask the lady for?
A: He asked for two boxes of chocolate candy.

Q: What did the lady call him?
A: "Good boy."

Q: What else did Taro ask the lady?
A: He asked her if he could leave his tofu pan in the store for a while.

Analytical

Q: Do you think Taro should listen to the "little voice"? Why or why not?
A: Answers will vary.

Q: Can you explain what the author means when he writes about the "little voice"?
A: The author means Taro's thoughts. There is not really a voice that anyone could hear.

Q: Some of the things the "little voice" says are reasonable. At one point, the "little voice" suggests something that is dishonest. What is that?
A: The "little voice" suggests Taro not tell anyone about the extra money and spend it on treats for himself.

Taro and the Tofu

Literary Components

13 **Characterization; Theme:** Taro does not wait to see if the owner has missed the coin or not. He is thoroughly honest and wants to return the coin regardless. He does not fall for any of the false arguments of the "little voice."

14 **Important Idea:** Even though the man hadn't noticed his error, he surely would have been pained later when he discovered that money was missing. He may also be happy to see that Taro is honest and responsible.

15 **Theme:** Although the story's theme (certainly at the third grade level) is a boy's internal struggle to be honest, there is a sub-theme here, which is whether or not experiencing that conflict is a reason to feel guilty. In this story, the answer is "no." It is human to sometimes have the inclination to do something bad. The important thing is to recognize the inclination for what it is, to fight back with a shouted "No!" as Taro did, and to swiftly do the right thing. How much of this you wish to share with the class depends on their maturity level. It is very important, though, that they not be left with the idea that having a negative thought, or feeling tempted to do wrong, is a blemish. Rather, it is part and parcel of being human.

16 **Theme; Characterization:** One good deed brings on another. "Shy" though Taro may feel about his bad thoughts, now that he has done the right thing, he sees himself as a good person. That self-image leads him to do something else that is kind and generous. It is very important to view oneself as a good person, because good people do good things.

Taro put the tofu pan down carefully beside a 10-yen coin for the candies and ran out of the store. He ran down the cheerful shopping street, through the crowds of people; he was still running when he reached the little shop.

"Back so soon?" said the man, seeing Taro. "Does your mother need more tofu?"

13 "No—I came to give this money back to you," said Taro.

"What money?"

"You gave me the wrong change; you gave me forty extra yen."

"Really? I didn't even see it. Are you sure the money isn't yours?"

"Yes," said Taro, "I'm sure that you gave me a 50-yen coin for a 10-yen coin. I'll put the money here, all right? I must hurry because Mother is waiting for me."

14 "Thank you very much, Taro," said the man with gladness in his face.

15 Taro was happy, but he felt shy too, for he remembered the strange little voice.

16 "Not at all," he said quickly. Before he knew it he found himself taking one of the boxes of chocolate candy from his pocket. "For your grandson," he said.

"Thank you ... thank you ..."

Guiding the Reading

Literal

Q: Where did he go from the candy store?
A: He went back to the tofu shop.

Q: What did he tell the tofu man?
A: He told him that he'd come to return the money.

Q: Had the tofu man been worried about the money?
A: No. He hadn't even realized he had given Taro too much change.

Q: How did the man feel when Taro returned the money?
A: He was very glad that he hadn't lost the money.

Q: How did Taro surprise himself?
A: He found himself taking one box of chocolate out of his pocket and offering it as a gift to the tofu man's grandson.

Analytical

Q: Why do you think Taro ran all the way to the tofu shop?
A: Some will say because it was dark and cold or because his mother was waiting and he didn't want her to worry. Perhaps he was hungry and he wanted his supper. Others will take the thematic approach and say that he wanted to return the money before he could change his mind. Both approaches are valid.

Q: Do you think Taro was surprised that the man hadn't even noticed the money was missing?
A: Taro had considered that possibility so he wasn't altogether surprised.

Taro and the Tofu   85

Taro and the Tofu

The lady in the candy store was still reading her newspaper when Taro stopped to pick up the tofu pan.

"Thank you for keeping it for me," said Taro.

"Not at all, good boy," said the lady, and much to Taro's **17** surprise, she looked up, straight at him.

Taro had never seen her look at anything but her newspaper. What was more, she was smiling at him—it was almost as if she knew what had happened—but, no, it couldn't be!

"You'd better hurry, good boy. It's very late," said the lady.

Taro nodded and went out of the store with his tofu pan. Most of the shops on the shopping street were closed **18** now, and only a few people were still there. The wind was very cold.

Anyway, thought Taro, I don't really care if the lady **19** knows what the voice said, because I gave back the money.

He was so happy that he wanted to run all the way **20** home, but he remembered to walk carefully with the tofu. His hands ached with the cold by the time he got there.

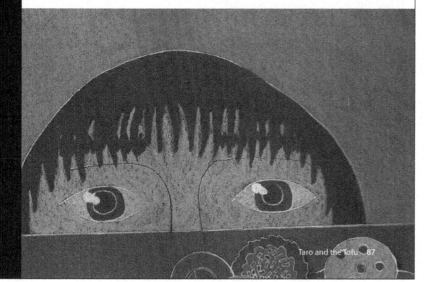

Taro and the Tofu   87

Literary Components

17 **Minor Character:** The candy lady characterization is a bit mysterious. We are left wondering just how much she understands about Taro.

18 **Falling Action:** We are nearing the end of the story. The shops are closing down and it is cold outside as Taro heads for his warm (physically and emotionally) house.

19 **Sub-Theme:** Here might be a good place to discuss the difference between thoughts and deeds. Please see number 15 for discussion.

20 **Theme:** Doing something good, difficult though it may be, gives a person happiness. Doing a good deed might entail discomfort or sacrifice at the moment (for example, here: Taro has to go all the way back to the tofu store in the dark; he has to face the cold; he has to give up dreams of using the coins for more treats), but the resultant happiness is greater than the fleeting reward of doing something wrong.

Guiding the Reading

Literal

Q: When Taro returned to the candy store, what did the lady do that surprised him?

A: She looked up, straight at him.

Q: What did the candy lady do when she looked up?

A: She smiled at Taro and told him to hurry home.

Q: What was the street like at this time of the evening?

A: It was empty and deserted.

Q: What does Taro say to himself?

A: He doesn't care if the lady knows what the "voice" said, since he gave back the money.

Q: How did he feel now?

A: He felt so happy he wanted to run all the way home.

Analytical

Q: Why do you think the candy lady smiled at Taro?

A: Answers will vary. The author does not really answer that question. Perhaps she wishes to convey the idea that when somebody has a moral victory, it is noticed by others in a subconscious way—but that is beyond the vocabulary, if not the comprehension, of a third grader.

Taro and the Tofu

Literary Components

21 **Theme:** Once again, refer to numbers 15 and 19.

22 **Theme; Characterization:** Although he may have felt uncomfortable telling his parents about the secret "voice," he surely would have been proud of giving the candy to the sick child. That he kept both of these secret shows a maturity on Taro's part.

23 **Setting:** The setting is used to tie up the story with the nice contrast between the cold outdoors and the warm feeling of one who has done battle with temptation and won.

Guiding the Reading

Literal

Q: What did Taro tell his parents when he got home?

A: He told them that he had returned the forty yen to the tofu man.

Q: What didn't he tell them?

A: About the "little voice" in his head or about the candy he gave to the grandson.

Q: Why not?

A: He felt like keeping those things to himself.

Q: What did Taro ask his mother?

A: He asked if he could eat some candy.

Analytical

Q: Why do you think Taro kept two things from his parents?

A: He didn't want to brag. He had done two good things: returning the money even though he was tempted not to and giving half of his candy to a sick little boy. (Alternatively, he might have still been uncomfortable about the fact that he'd even thought not to return the money.) One thing is true: when a person does a good deed and does not tell others about it, it is his treasure. He can go back and savor the good feeling he had doing the good deed. Once the event is shared, it loses its "punch." You can compare this good secret with Tassai's good secret—the making of the jar. In both cases, the children were able to savor some good thing that they had done. Point out that, had Taro been troubled about the "voice," he would have been well-advised to discuss it with his parents. At this point in the story, though, Taro seems to have realized himself that doing the right thing was what counted.

At home Taro told his mother and father what had happened to make him so late. He told them about finding the extra forty yen, and he told them about returning to the man's shop. He told them

21 everything—but he didn't tell them about the strange, secret voice

22 in his head, and he did not tell them about giving the candy to the man's sick grandson. Why? Taro just felt like keeping those things to himself.

"May I have a candy now?" he asked.

"Yes, but just one. Supper is almost ready," said his mother.

23 It was still windy outside, and the wind was very cold.

But Taro felt warm. And the chocolate candy was very good.

ABOUT THE AUTHOR

Masako Matsuno grew up in Japan. When she was 23, she came to America to study American children's literature. She has written books in both English and Japanese, translated Japanese books for American children, and translated English books for Japanese children. Mrs. Matsuno wants children all over the world to understand her people. She says, "The Japanese children like playing, eating, singing, and many other things just as foreign children do." Mrs. Matsuno enjoys gardening, reading, music, and taking walks.

Q: Why do you think Taro felt warm even though it was cold outside?

A: He felt very happy that he had done two good things: returned the money and given chocolate to the man's grandson.

Studying the Selection

QUICK REVIEW

1. Why did Taro have to go to the tofu shop?
2. What mistake did the shopkeeper make?
3. What were two good reasons not to return the coin right away?
4. What was one bad reason not to return the coin?

FOCUS

5. Which of the "little voices'" arguments made Taro decide to run back and return the money immediately? Why?
6. Did Taro have to return the money, even though the tofu seller did not realize he had given him too much change? What do you think?

CREATING AND WRITING

7. In the story, the shopkeeper was very impressed by Taro's honesty. Imagine that the shopkeeper wrote Taro a thank you note for returning the money, and enclosed a small gift with the note. On a sheet of paper, write the kind of thank you note that the shopkeeper might have written. At the bottom of the paper, draw a picture of the gift that you think he might have given Taro.
8. Do you know what a diorama is? It is a model of a scene from a story or a real life event. Dioramas are often made by placing miniature dolls, furniture, and other scenery in a shoe box. The story of *Taro and the Tofu* takes place in several different locations. At first, Taro is at home. Then he runs through the streets to the tofu shop. Next, he is inside the tofu shop. Later he goes to the candy store, then back to the tofu shop, and then finally, back home. Bring a shoe box to school and choose one of the scenes in the story for your diorama. Your teacher will provide you with arts and crafts materials to use for your diorama. Design and make the scene, including figures of Taro and another character.

Studying the Selection

First Impressions

No, but if we are really honest with ourselves, it is usually not too hard. In the case of Taro, his "little voice" gave him some valid reasons not to return the money right away. It was cold outside, the area was deserted, and his mother would worry. However, when the "voice" told him that no one would know if he kept the money, all the other reasons were invalidated. He understood that the "voice" was only trying to *delay* his returning the money as a way of getting him to *keep* the money. As soon as he realized this, he ran to return the money, ignoring everything else the "voice" had to say.

There is a profound message here to convey to your students. Here are a few thoughts if you wish to discuss the story at a deeper level. Most of the time, the difference between right and wrong is clear. It is *we* who complicate things because we want to do something wrong without calling it wrong. If we are honest with ourselves, we will run from the wrong choice the way

Taro ran. We will not give our "voice" time to persuade us with false reasoning. We will recognize that we often have to give something up in order to choose what is right. It is well worth it to find the internal happiness that doing the right thing brings. The author hints at this at the end of the story when she writes, "It was still windy outside, and the wind was very cold. But Taro felt warm." These things do not happen overnight. They come of choosing to do the right thing over and over. Each time we ignore the temptation to make the wrong choice, we build confidence in ourselves. Just as Taro went from one good deed to the next—first, offering to help his mother by going to the shop; then, returning the change; then, giving half his candy to a sick boy; then, not bragging to his parents about his good deeds—just so, all of us advance from good deed to good deed.

Quick Review

1. Taro had to go to the shop because the tofu man did not come to their street as he usually did, and they needed tofu for supper.
2. The shopkeeper gave Taro six 10-yen coins and a 50-yen coin instead of seven 10-yen coins.
3. It was very cold outside and his mother would be waiting for him.
4. No one knew that he had the money.

Focus

5. When the "voice" told him that no one knew he had the money and suggested he use it on treats for himself, he shouted back at it.
6. Answers will vary. Most will say it did not matter whether or not the tofu seller knew he'd given too much money to Taro, the money did not belong to Taro. Therefore, Taro was obligated to return the money.

Creating and Writing

7. If you like, you can ask the students to bring some nice stationery or a card to write their notes on. Provide the students with some crayons or markers with which to draw a picture of the gift from the tofu seller.
8. The children should choose one of the following four scenes for their dioramas: Taro running through the store-lined street; Taro at the tofu shop; Taro at the candy store; Taro and his parents eating dinner at home. Provide the students with scissors, paste, construction paper, poster board, and crayons. The more varied the materials you bring, the more interesting the dioramas will be. Glitter, googly-eyes, hair from an old wig, and bits of fabric are a few suggestions.

wrap-up

all about the story!

ACTIVITY ONE

The stories in Unit One take you to many places. *The Jar of Tassai* takes place on a mesa near the Painted Desert in Arizona; *The Story of the White Sombrero* takes you to Mexico; *A Cane in Her Hand* takes you to an unnamed city in America; *Boom Town* takes you to the California of the 1850s; *Taro and the Tofu* takes you to Japan. Your teacher will provide you with some pictures of each location and materials for making a poster. Choose one of the stories in Unit One and design a travel poster for the story's location. Add a slogan like "Come Join Us in Japan!" or "A Golden Opportunity Awaits You in California!" If you wish, your poster can be three-dimensional. For example, you could use little orange balls to paste onto a drawing of an orange tree in Mexico.

90   Unit 1

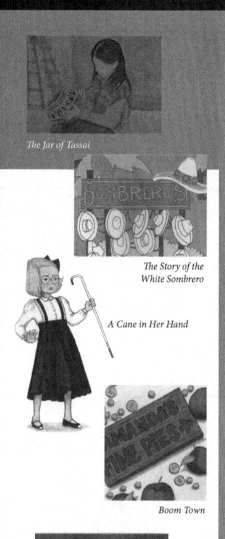

The Jar of Tassai

The Story of the White Sombrero

A Cane in Her Hand

Boom Town

Taro and the Tofu

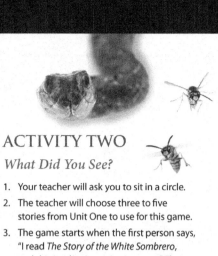

ACTIVITY TWO

What Did You See?

1. Your teacher will ask you to sit in a circle.
2. The teacher will choose three to five stories from Unit One to use for this game.
3. The game starts when the first person says, "I read *The Story of the White Sombrero*, and this is what I saw: I saw *wasps*." The student must name one detail from the story. The next student repeats, "I read *The Story of the White Sombrero* and this is what I saw …" and adds a new thing.
4. Whenever a student cannot think of something else to add, the student must drop out of the circle.
5. The next student starts a new story.
6. The last person to remain in the circle is the winner.

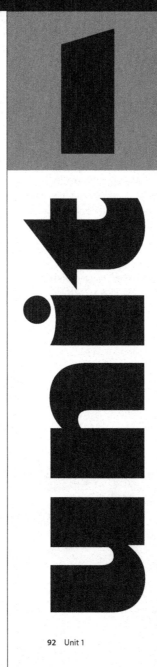

ACTIVITY THREE

Who Am I?

1. Your teacher will choose five students to represent the main character in each of the five stories in Unit One: Tassai, Andres, Valerie, Amanda, and Taro.

2. The five students will be seated in a row in front of the classroom. They will keep which character each is representing a secret.

3. Your teacher will now divide the rest of the class into groups. The groups will take turns asking questions to the students sitting in the front to help uncover their "identities." Each group gets to ask two questions per round.

4. At the end of five rounds, a student from each group will stand up and "identify" each of the five students in the front. Then, the "characters" will stand up and identify themselves. The group with the most correct answers wins.

Here's an example: Mike is playing Andres and Leah is playing Tassai. One student asks: "Mike, do you know how to ride a burro?" Mike answers, "Yes." It looks like Mike might be Andres. A second student asks, "Leah, can you make pottery?" Leah says, "No." Leah is probably not Tassai.

ACTIVITY FOUR

Advice Column

Each of the characters in Unit One has many strong points. For example, Amanda is practical and full of ideas. She is a good baker and knows how to take care of a baby.

1. Choose one character from Unit One and write a list of all the personality traits, talents, and skills this character has.

2. Now, pretend that this character has an advice column.

3. Make up a letter from a person with a problem that this character would be good at solving. It could be a serious problem or a small or even silly problem.

4. Sign the letter with a made-up name.

5. Make up an answer that your story character would write, and sign it with the character's name.

Unit 1 Wrap-Up   93

all about the plot!

THE UNKNOWN

NEW BEGINNINGS

MISUNDERSTANDINGS

SAFARI

ACTION

ADVENTURE

SILLINESS

Good-Bye, 382 Shin Dang Dong

Lesson in Literature

What Is Internal Conflict?

The Cousin

1. At the beginning of the story, Jeremy is lonely because he is an only child.

2. He can be unfriendly to his cousin and let him feel as though he is not wanted or he can be warm and friendly.

3. He decides to be friendly and he is happy with his choice.

Selection Summary

Jangmi is a young Korean girl who lives at 382 Shin Dang Dong. The story opens on a summer's day with rain tapping at the window heralding the approaching monsoon season. Jangmi is sad, because today is her last day at 382 Shin Dang Dong. Her family will be leaving on a plane for the U.S.A. in a few hours. She looks around at her beloved room, bare now, because all her possessions have been packed. As the day wears on, Jangmi becomes sadder and sadder. Her relatives come to share in a farewell meal, her best friend goes to the market with her and shares a last giggle with her, and her trip to the airport is marked with tears.

Jangmi's arrival in the United States is equally glum. She does not think her new Massachusetts house will ever feel like home. When her mother suggests that she might wish to change her name from Jangmi to Rose, which is the English word for Jangmi, she is sure she will never do so.

Soon after the family unpacks their belongings, a stream of neighbors visit with a variety of dishes and treats. A girl Jangmi's age smiles and talks to Jangmi. Suddenly, the world does not look as dark. Jangmi feels she has made a new friend and looks ahead to a good future in which she may, one day, change her name to Rose.

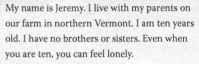

Lesson in Literature...
THE COUSIN

WHAT IS INTERNAL CONFLICT?

- A **conflict** is a struggle. Most stories have a conflict that must be resolved, or settled.

- A conflict can be between two people or between a person and something else, like a fire, or the weather, or a wild animal.

- A conflict can also take place inside a person's own mind. That type of conflict is called an **internal**, or inner, **conflict**.

- Internal conflicts may occur when a character must choose between right and wrong.

THINK ABOUT IT!

1. What problem does Jeremy have at the beginning of the story?

2. Towards the end of the story, Jeremy has an internal conflict. He has to choose between two ways he can treat his cousin. What are the two ways?

3. Which choice does Jeremy make? Is he happy with his choice?

My name is Jeremy. I live with my parents on our farm in northern Vermont. I am ten years old. I have no brothers or sisters. Even when you are ten, you can feel lonely.

A while ago, I asked my mom why I'm an only child. That is what people call it when you have no brothers or sisters: an only child. She sighed, "Jeremy, it is difficult to explain. But *you* make us very happy. It is a blessing just having *you*."

As I said, I have been lonely. But I am used to the way things are.

We have a dog named Lucy. We also have several horses that are good horses for riding. Mine is Patience. When I began riding, I was really clumsy. That was when Patience earned her name. My dad's horse is Jackson, my mom's

96   Unit 2

Getting Started

Leaving home is never easy. Saying goodbye to old friends and places can be a wrenching experience. Ask your students if any of them have ever moved from one house to another, one school to another, one city to another, or one country to another. What was their experience? Was it difficult or easy or a mixture of both? What was the hardest/easiest part of moving?

Ask the entire class how they would feel if they knew they were moving to another country in a few weeks. Discuss what they would do to prepare themselves for the move. What would they pack? To whom would they say goodbye? What measures would they take to stay in touch with their old friends? How would they make new friends? How would they deal with their emotions of sadness, worry, or loneliness? There is much to discuss and, who knows—some of the suggestions may actually help a student who has to move one day!

is Gloria. Their baby is Little Boy. He's too young to ride.

Two weeks ago, my parents said they had something to tell me. It sounded like it was going to be a good thing. Then they said my cousin Will was coming to live with us. "Forever?" I asked. "Where will he sleep?"

Dad said, "Well, we figured you two would share your room. Will's your age. And you had a good time when he visited us from Quebec last January."

"But he came with his own mom and dad then. A visitor is different from a permanent extra person. He is not part of our family."

Mom sort of groaned. "Look, Jeremy. Will's mom is sick. His dad works far away from Quebec in Ontario. Will *is* a family member. His mom is my sister. She needs our help."

I felt miserable. I didn't want to share my mom and dad. I didn't want to share my room or even my horse. I didn't want to share Lucy either. I couldn't remember why I had liked Will.

When my mom and dad went to pick him up at the train station, I said I wasn't going. They both stared at me, like they were shocked. "Look, I have a lot of homework! Isn't it better if I finish it before he gets here?"

Will is here now. He doesn't look happy. I never thought that he might not like this either. But I can't worry about him. I have to worry about me.

My mom shows him the extra dresser in my room. He unpacks. I sit there not speaking.

Then he says, "I brought you a geode. It looks like a rock on the outside, but when you open it, it's purple crystals that sparkle." I think, why do I need an old rock? Will hands it to me, like we're some kind of buddies.

I want to hand it back to him and leave the room, but I can't do that. Mom and Dad would think it was a really ugly thing to do. So, I open it. It is really cool!

It's hard for me to say it, but I ask him which bunk bed he wants, the top or the bottom. He says, "Don't you always sleep on top?"

"Yeah, but you choose. It's probably hard leaving home and all."

"Well, I'll take the bottom. You know, fear of heights." We both laugh at that.

Mom yells from the kitchen. "Hey, I've got apples here. Why don't you two go and give one to each of the horses? And the pony, too—little pieces."

We step outside into the chill October air clutching our apples. "Race you to the barn!" I shout to Will. "Loser is a rotten egg!"

Maybe this isn't going to be so bad after all.

Target Skill: Understanding and being able to recognize the internal conflict in a story

Learning Strategy: Prior knowledge

Common Core Curriculum: RL.3.1; RL.3.6

Genre: Fiction

Vocabulary

enthusiastic (en THOOZ ee AS tik) *adj.*: excited and eager

radiator (RAY dee AY ter) *n.*: a room heater made of pipes through which steam or hot water passes

Related Vocabulary

aroma (uh ROE muh) *n.*: a good smell

correspond (KOR uh SPOND) *v.*: to write letters back and forth

despair (diss PAIR) *n.*: a feeling of hopelessness

farewell (fair WELL) *interj.*: an old-fashioned way of saying goodbye

foreign (FOR un) *adj.*: from another country

suggest (sug JEST) *v.*: to give an idea to someone

Workbook

Related Pages: 32-37

Answer Key Page: 5

Good-Bye, 382 Shin Dang Dong

Into . . . *Good-Bye, 382 Shin Dang Dong*

This story has a simple theme: change. What makes this story different, and far less complex than other stories about change, is that the protagonist, Jangmi, is entirely passive. She does not struggle against her feelings, nor does she struggle against her parents. She simply abandons herself to her sad feelings. When something happens to make her feel better, she feels better. So, as far as any lessons in character (as are found in almost every story in Unit One), there are none to be had here. What this story is a good vehicle for is the recognition, expression, and acceptance of inconvenient emotions.

Jangmi is a Korean girl who now lives in America. The story is a recollection of the powerful emotions she experienced at the time of her move. Discuss emotions your students have had in different circumstances. They have all surely felt fear, anxiety, excitement, happiness, boredom, and sadness. Explain that the first thing to do with an emotion is to accept the fact that it exists. The next step is, if the emotion makes you unhappy, try and discover what can be done to change whatever is causing the sadness, fear, or anxiety. Sometimes those causes cannot be changed. Then, the person either has to change something else—the way Jangmi did when she made a new friend—or change the initial emotional reaction, the way Valerie in *A Cane in Her Hand* did.

Since this story is so much about emotions, the topic of mixed feelings should be discussed as well. By the end of the story, Jangmi, who was completely bleak in Korea, has mixed feelings. She misses the old but is beginning to see value in the new. Explain that people can feel more than one thing at a time, and that this is valid. It is not "mixed up" and it is not hypocritical or dishonest. It is the way people are. Ask your students if they have ever had mixed feelings and to describe the circumstances. This will deepen their insight into themselves and others.

Eyes On: Internal Conflict

Conflict is a very important topic to discuss with your class for two reasons. The literary reason is that a story without conflict is not really a story at all, it is simply a report. The real-life reason is that life is full of conflict, and one of the biggest gifts you can give a child is a healthy, reasoned approach to it.

Blueprint for Reading

INTO . . . *Good-Bye, 382 Shin Dang Dong*

Do you like change or do you like things to stay the same? Some people are adventurers and they love setting out for places they've never seen. Other people love what is familiar and would like it if they never had to leave home for very long. Jangmi is a Korean girl who moved to America when she was eight years old. She remembers how sad and frightened she was of leaving her home, her friends, and her country. Yet, she'd had no choice. As the taxi carried the family to the airport, Jangmi cried. What could you say that would comfort or encourage Jangmi?

EYES ON *Internal Conflict*

Every plot includes at least some conflict. **Conflict** is disagreement of any sort. If you want to go outside and play, but your teacher makes you stay inside, that is a conflict. If you want to go outside and it is raining—that is also a conflict. If you want to go outside and play, but your friend must stay inside and will feel lonely, one part of you may say "don't go." That's a conflict, too. This kind of conflict is all in your mind, and you have to decide what to do. It is called **internal conflict**.

Jangmi faces two conflicts. The first one is easy to spot. She wants to stay in her home in Korea, but she must move with her family to America. The second conflict is inside herself. Should she let herself feel sad for a long time, or should she let go of her sadness and try to find happiness in her new country?

This story is a good vehicle for learning about conflict because it is so simple. Any child can relate to a plot in which adults make a decision that is displeasing to a child. The learning strategy for studying conflict is *prior knowledge*. Relating the story's conflict to your students' prior knowledge of conflict is easy. Just ask them if they have ever had to do something that they didn't want to do. They may even have prior knowledge of the story's conflict: a family moves and the children are unhappy about it. Once you have succeeded in helping your students identify various kinds of external conflict, you can discuss internal conflict. Ask them if they have ever argued with themselves about how they would behave. Have any of them ever felt sad or angry but forced themselves to cheer up?

It is important that a child learns to analyze a conflict by identifying what the two sides of the conflict are and why they exist. This will prevent the child from feeling confused, helpless, and emotional. Even if there is no way for the circumstances to change, the child will be better able to come to terms with a clearly defined and explained situation. In the story,

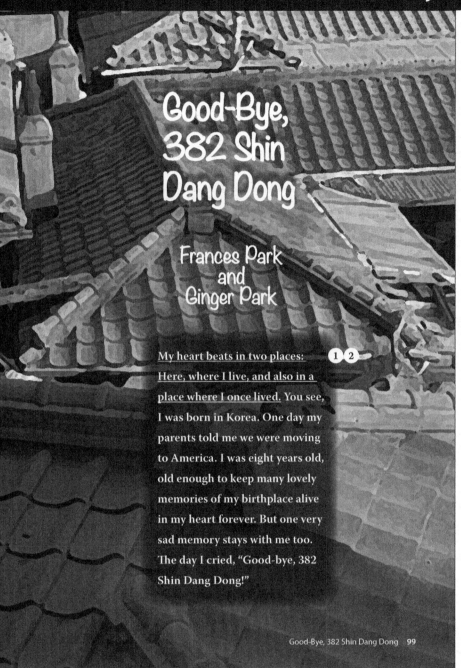

Good-Bye, 382 Shin Dang Dong

Frances Park and Ginger Park

My heart beats in two places: Here, where I live, and also in a place where I once lived. You see, I was born in Korea. One day my parents told me we were moving to America. I was eight years old, old enough to keep many lovely memories of my birthplace alive in my heart forever. But one very sad memory stays with me too. The day I cried, "Good-bye, 382 Shin Dang Dong!"

1 2

Good-Bye, 382 Shin Dang Dong **99**

Jangmi's sadness is hardly addressed by her parents. (Nor, for that matter, is the other side of the conflict: the move and the reason for it.) You can add this missing dimension to the story by asking your students to list the reasons why she felt so sad and what they would say to her to help her. In short, you are asking them how to deal with sadness and disappointment.

Literary Components

1 Exposition: The story opens by presenting the conflict immediately: the narrator is torn between the feelings she has for two places. What those feelings are, why and how she is torn, and how or if the problem will be resolved, remain to be seen.

2 Conflict: The story's conflict is stated in the very first sentence. A young girl is torn away from her home by circumstances she cannot control and is expected to make a new life in a new country.

Guiding the Reading

Literal

Q: What is the narrator remembering?
A: She is remembering the day her family moved from Korea to America.

Q: How old was the narrator when she moved from Korea to America?
A: She was eight years old.

Q: What is 382 Shin Dang Dong?
A: It is the address of her house in Korea.

Analytical

Q: How does the speaker feel when she thinks about the day she moved?
A: She feels very sad.

Q: Do you think this means she dislikes her new home in the United States?
A: It may or may not. Sometimes, when people are unhappy in one place, they remember other places with a lot of fondness. Other times, people may be very happy where they are, but also miss a different place where they were also happy.

Good-Bye, 382 Shin Dang Dong

Literary Components

3 **Setting:** Even before we are given any description of the Korean house in which the narrator lives, a mood is created by the rainy, ominous, pre-monsoon weather.

4 **Rising Tension:** The fact that the move is about to take place adds quite a bit of tension to the story. There is no time for reflection or emotional preparation—the time is now!

5 **Setting:** We get our first glimpse of the Korean home that the narrator is leaving. The delicate and colorful décor of her former bedroom is described. The bare walls that mock her now add to her gloom.

Guiding the Reading

Literal

Q: How did her room look before the family decided to move?

A: There were decorations on the walls and silk cushions and straw mats on the floor.

Q: What kind of weather did the monsoon season bring?

A: The monsoons brought heavy rain.

Q: What state was the girl moving to?

A: She was moving to Massachusetts.

Analytical

Q: The girl had a box marked "Lovely Things." What do you think was in the box? Can you give some examples of what you would put in a box like that?

A: The girl probably put some of her favorite books, toys, school projects, and prizes or gifts into the box. She probably put items that would remind her of happy occasions into the box.

---

3 On that summer day I woke up to the sound of light rain tapping on my window. The monsoon season[1] was coming. I didn't even need to open my eyes to know that. It was that time of year. It was also time to move.

4 In a few hours, I would be on an airplane.

5 When I opened my eyes, my heart sank. My bedroom was so bare! No hand-painted scrolls or colorful fans on my walls. No silk cushions or straw mats on my floor. All my possessions were packed away in a big brown box marked "Lovely Things."

I frowned and listened to the raindrops. One, two, three ... Soon the thick of the monsoon would arrive, and a thousand raindrops would hit our clay-tiled roof all at once. But I wouldn't be here to listen to them. I would be halfway around the world in a strange, foreign place called 112 Foster Terrace, Brighton, Massachusetts, U.S.A.

1. A *monsoon* is a strong wind that blows in from the ocean, bringing heavy rain. The *monsoon season* is the part of the year when it is extremely windy and rainy in certain countries.

100   Unit 2

My parents were very excited.

"Jangmi,[2] you will like America," Dad tried to assure me.

"Are the seasons the same?" I wondered.

"Oh, yes."

"With monsoon rains?"

"No, Jangmi, no monsoon rains."

"No friends either," I moaned.

"You will make many new friends in America," Mom promised me, "in your new home."

But I loved my home right here! I didn't want to go to America and make new friends. I didn't want to leave my best friend, Kisuni.[3]

_____
2. *Jangmi* (JAHNG MEE)
3. *Kisuni* (KEE soo NEE)

Good-Bye, 382 Shin Dang Dong   101

Literary Components

6 **Contrast:** The excitement felt by the parents is incomprehensible to Jangmi. Although she does not question or resent her parents' feelings, she cannot relate to them. She is in her own world of sadness, and their words of encouragement do not seem to have any effect on her.

7 **Theme; Conflict:** The theme is clearly stated here. Jangmi does not want to leave home because she loves her home and because she doesn't want to leave her best friend. People have many other reasons why they don't want to move, but those do not come into play here. Jangmi does not seem to be particularly worried about starting a new school or learning a new language. Her focus is on not wanting to leave behind everything she loves.

Guiding the Reading

Literal

Q: What is the narrator's name?

A: Her name is Jangmi.

Q: Did Jangmi want to move to America?

A: No. She wanted to stay with her friends in Korea.

Analytical

Q: What is the main thing children worry about when they move to a new place?

A: Children, as well as many adults, worry that they will not have any friends.

Q: Do you think Jangmi's parents were right when they said she would make new friends in America?

A: Yes. Most people are able to make new friends when they move. Some are able to make new friends faster than others, but almost anyone can make new friends sooner or later if they reach out to others.

Good-Bye, 382 Shin Dang Dong

Guiding the Reading

Literal

Q: Where did Jangmi and Kisuni go right after breakfast?

A: They ran to the market to buy chummy for the farewell lunch.

After breakfast, Kisuni and I ran out into the rain and to the open market. Monsoon season was also the season for sweet, yellow melons called *chummy*. Kisuni and I would often peel and eat chummy under the willow tree that stood outside my bedroom window. But today, the chummy were for guests who were coming over for a farewell lunch.

At the market we peered into endless baskets and took our time choosing the ripest, plumpest chummy we could find.

"Do they have chummy in America?" Kisuni wondered.

"No," I replied. "But my mom says they have melons called *honeydew*."

"Honeydew," Kisuni giggled. "What a funny name!" ⑧

Good-Bye, 382 Shin Dang Dong **103**

Literary Components

⑧ **Humor; Foreshadowing:** In the midst of all this solemnity, Kisuni is able to giggle. Children the world over laugh at the strange sound of foreign words. There is a hint here about the story's conclusion, in which Mary giggles when she hears the word *chummy*. Both incidents tell the reader that Jangmi will not be sad forever, because as long as children can laugh at funny words, they will doubtless be happy again.

Guiding the Reading

Literal

Q: What American fruit is something like chummy?

A: Honeydew is similar to chummy.

Analytical

Q: Which do you think sounds funnier, "chummy" or "honeydew"?

A: Words in foreign languages often sound funny to the listener. If you speak English, Korean may sound funny. If you speak Korean, English may sound funny!

Good-Bye, 382 Shin Dang Dong

Literary Components

9 Setting; Detail: All the details of a Korean goodbye party add to the picture we have of Jangmi's Korean home and family. We see how steeped in the culture of her country she is and understand why she is so reluctant to leave. The reader understands—even more than Jangmi does—how different life in America will be.

Guiding the Reading

Literal

Q: What did the guests bring?
A: They brought pots and plates of food.

Q: What were the feelings of the people at the party?
A: The people had mixed feelings. They were happy to be together and sad that some were leaving. Love and laughter and tears were shared.

Analytical

Q: Jangmi tells us that there were laughter and tears at the party. How could there be both? Aren't people either happy or sad?
A: People can have mixed feelings. They can feel happy and sad at the same time. For example, if you gave your favorite toy to a sick friend to cheer him up, you might feel happy that your friend is more cheerful, but just a little sad that you are losing your toy.

Soon after we returned, family and friends began to arrive, carrying pots and plates

9 of food. One by one they took off their shoes, then entered the house. Grandmother was dressed in her most special occasion *hanbok*.[4] She set up the long *bap sang*[5] and before I could even blink, on it were a big pot of dumpling soup and the prettiest pastel rice cakes I had ever seen. Kisuni and I peeled and sliced our chummy and carefully arranged the pieces on a plate.

Then everybody ate and sang traditional Korean songs and celebrated in a sad way. Love and laughter and tears rippled through our house. How I wanted to pack these moments into a big brown box and bring them with me to America.

Kisuni and I sneaked outside and sat beneath the willow tree. We watched the rain with glum faces.

---

4. A *hanbok* (HAHN BOK) robe is an outer robe worn in traditional Korean dress.
5. A *bap sang* (BOP SANG) is a table on which a variety of dishes are served, similar to a buffet.

"Kisuni, I wish we never had to move from this spot," I said.

"Me, too," she sighed. "Jangmi, how far away is America?"

"My mom says that it's halfway around the world. And my dad told me that when the moon is shining here, the sun is shining there. That's how far apart we'll be," I moaned.

"That's really far," Kisuni moaned back.

We watched the rain and grew more glum than ever. Then Kisuni perked up.

"So when you're awake, I'll be asleep. And when I'm awake, you'll be asleep," she declared. "At least we'll always know what the other one is doing."

That moment our faces brightened. But a moment later we had to say good-bye. Kisuni held back her tears. "Promise you'll write to me, Jangmi."

"I promise, Kisuni."

Good-Bye, 382 Shin Dang Dong · 105

Guiding the Reading

Literal

Q: What did Jangmi tell Kisuni?

A: She told her that she wished they never had to move from the spot under their favorite willow tree.

Q: When people are halfway around the world from one another, what time is it for one when it is nighttime for the other?

A: When it is night for one, it is day for the other.

Q: What did Jangmi promise to do for her friend Kisuni?

A: She promised to write letters to her.

Analytical

Q: If two people who live half a world apart want to talk on the phone, when would be a good time to call?

A: That's not too difficult to answer. If it is seven thirty in the morning in Massachusetts, it is around seven thirty in the evening in Korea. Most people are awake at both of those times, so that would be a good time to call. However, if Jangmi made a three o'clock P.M. (in the afternoon) call to her friend Kisuni in Korea, she would probably be reaching her at three o'clock A.M. (in the morning)—a time when Kisuni is sure to be fast asleep!

Q: If this story were taking place today, do you think Kisuni would have asked Jangmi to write letters to her?

A: Possibly. People still enjoy writing and receiving letters. In letters, you can enclose pictures, drawings, and other things you might want to share with your friend. On the other hand, most people today would ask that their friend call them on the phone. (Years ago, international telephone calls were very expensive.)

Good-Bye, 382 Shin Dang Dong

Literary Components

10 **Simile:** The simile is supported by the setting. Jangmi's tears echo the rain outside.

Guiding the Reading

Literal

Q: What were Jangmi's feelings as the taxi pulled away from the house?

A: She was so sad that she cried.

Q: What is a row house?

A: As its name tells you, a row house is a house that is attached to another house, which is attached to another house. All the houses form a row of houses.

Analytical

Q: Do you think it was childish of Jangmi to cry when the taxi drove away?

A: Answers will vary. Some might say that a more grown-up person would feel bad but not cry. Others might say that crying is good and very acceptable; even adults cry on certain occasions.

It was time to go to the airport.

"Kimpo Airport," Dad instructed the taxi driver.

10 The taxi slowly pulled away. I looked at our beautiful home one last time. <u>Like rain on the window, tears streaked down my face.</u>

"Good-bye, 382 Shin Dang Dong!" I cried.

On the long ride to the airport, Dad asked me, "Do you want to know what your new home looks like?"

"Okay," I shrugged.

"Let's see," Dad began, "it's a row house."

"A house that's attached to other houses," Mom explained.

"And inside the house are wooden floors," Dad added.

"No *ondal* floors?" I asked him. "How will we keep warm in the winter without ondal floors?"

"There are radiators in every room!" Mom said with an **11** enthusiastic clap. "And a fireplace in the living room! Imagine!"

No, I could not imagine that. In our home we had a fire in the cellar called the *ondal*. It stayed lit all the time. The heat from the ondal traveled through underground pipes and kept our wax-covered floors warm and cozy. A fireplace in the living room sounded peculiar to me.

"And the rooms are separated by wooden doors," Mom added.

"No rice-paper doors?" I wondered.

My parents shook their heads. "No, Jangmi."

My eyes closed with disappointment. I had a hard time picturing this house. Would it ever feel like home? **12**

> ### WORD BANK
>
> **radiator** (RAY dee AY ter) *n.*: a room heater made of pipes through which steam or hot water passes
>
> **enthusiastic** (en THOOZ ee AS tik) *adj.*: excited and eager

Good-Bye, 382 Shin Dang Dong   **107**

Literary Components

11 **Contrast:** Once again, the contrast between the enthusiasm of the parents and the reluctance of the daughter is highlighted. What is notable is the absence of conflict. As bad as Jangmi feels, she does not express any anger or resentment towards her parents.

12 **Turning Point:** Although it may not feel that way, this is actually a turning point. Jangmi has gone from extreme sadness about leaving her home to wondering if there was any hope of being happy in her new home. This is almost the first time she has thought about where she was going as opposed to what she was leaving.

Guiding the Reading

Literal

Q: How were the houses in Korea heated?

A: Each house had a furnace in the basement called an *ondal*. Pipes carried heat from the furnace to the floors of the rooms above the basement.

Q: Why did Jangmi feel disappointment when her parents described the way an American home is built?

A: Jangmi could not picture an American house and wondered if it would ever feel like home.

Analytical

Q: What feeling does an *ondal* floor give to the room in winter?

A: It gives a warm, cozy feeling to be walking on a warm floor.

Q: Have *ondal* floors ever been used in America?

A: Interestingly, although this story was written many years ago when houses were heated with radiators, one of today's most modern methods of heating a home is by running heating elements under the floorboards. As they say, "what's old is new."

Q: Why wouldn't a house such as the one Jangmi's parents described, not feel like home to Jangmi?

A: There is nothing about the house itself that could not feel like a home. It was the fact that that type of house was strange and different to Jangmi that made her unhappy. If an American girl were moving to Korea and told that the houses had no radiators and that the doors were made of rice paper instead of wood, she would feel the same way.

Good-Bye, 382 Shin Dang Dong

Literary Components

13 Turning Point Continued: Jangmi's thoughts continue to focus on the future. She is anxious and pessimistic, but she is beginning to face reality.

Guiding the Reading

Literal

Q: What did the plane have to fly over in order to reach America?

A: It had to fly over the ocean.

On the airplane, I sat by the window. We flew over rice fields and clay-tiled roofs. Already I felt homesick.

The next thing I knew, we were flying over the ocean. At first I could see fishing boats rocking in the waters. As we climbed higher and higher into the clouds, the boats grew smaller and smaller. Suddenly, the world looked very big to me.

"Good-bye, 382 Shin Dang Dong," I cried again.

Dad sat back in his seat and began to read an American newspaper. The words were all foreign.

13 "Dad," I asked, "how will I ever learn to understand English?"

"It's not so hard," he said. "Would you like to learn an English word?"

"Okay," I sighed.

After a pause, Dad came up with—

"Rose."

"Rose?" I repeated. "What does that mean?"

"That's the English translation of your Korean name," Mom said.

"Rose means Jangmi?" I asked.

"Yes," my parents nodded.

"Rose," I said over and over.

"Would you like to adopt Rose as your American name?" Mom asked me. ⑭

"No, I like *my* name," I insisted.

Good-Bye, 382 Shin Dang Dong   109

Literary Components

⑭ **Semi-Symbolism:** Though not true symbolism, this exchange is representative of a struggle. Jangmi's mother is coaxing her to embrace her new life as an American by asking her if she wants an English name. Jangmi is resisting her mother by insisting she prefers her Korean name.

Guiding the Reading

Literal

Q: What does the name Jangmi mean in English?
A: It means "rose."

Q: Did Jangmi want to change her name to "Rose"?
A: No.

Analytical

Q: Do you think Jangmi should have changed her name to Rose?
A: Answers will vary. Some will say that it would have made her transition easier. People would be able to pronounce her name and she would have felt "American" sooner. Others will say she was right to keep her Korean name. It would remind her of who she really was and who she wanted to be.

[Just a note: Times have changed since this story was written. In the past, people with foreign-sounding names frequently "Americanized" their names so as to be accepted in school and the workplace. For the past several decades, however, more and more people have kept their foreign-sounding names. In fact, the pendulum has swung so far in the other direction that it has become very common to give American-born children foreign names.]

Guiding the Reading

Literal

Q: What were some of the new things Jangmi saw on her way to the new house?

A: She saw big, wide roads, rooftops that were shingled, and stores with windows; she did not see rice fields or monsoon rains.

Q: How did the house feel to Jangmi?

A: It felt dark and strange.

Analytical

Q: If you were moving to a new country, do you think your feelings would be the same as Jangmi's when you saw all the different, new things?

A: Answers will vary. Some will say they would feel the same, others would say they would be excited by all the new things. You might wish to add that one way of combating feelings of sadness or anxiety is to try and think of the new situation as an adventure. Jangmi did not do that.

On a foggy morning four days later, we arrived in Massachusetts. After we gathered our luggage, we climbed into an airport taxi.

Even through the fog, I could see that things were very different in America. There were big, wide roads called *highways*. The rooftops were shingled instead of clay-tiled. People shopped in glass-enclosed stores instead of open markets. No rice fields, no monsoon rains. So many foreign faces.

Slowly, the taxi pulled up to a row house on a quiet street. Red brick steps led up to a wooden door.

"Here we are, Jangmi," Dad said, "112 Foster Terrace, Brighton, Massachusetts, U.S.A."

110   Unit 2

Good-Bye, 382 Shin Dang Dong

Literary Components

15 **Semi-Symbolism:** Jangmi is applying Korean manners to American life. She takes off her shoes, but the American floors are not made to be walked on barefoot. Whereas the Korean floors are warm and inviting, the American floors are cold and hard.

Guiding the Reading

Literal

Q: What kind of tree grew in their yard?
A: A maple tree grew there.

The house was just as my parents had described. <u>I took off my shoes and</u> **15** <u>walked on wooden floors. They felt very cold.</u> I opened wooden doors. They felt very heavy. Outside, the fog had lifted. But inside, everything felt dark and strange.

"Look," Dad pointed out the window, "there's a tree just like the one at home."

"No, it's not, Dad. It's not a willow tree," I said.

"No," he agreed. "It's a maple tree. But isn't it beautiful?"

382 Shin Dang Dong, 382 Shin Dang Dong. I wanted to go home to 382 Shin Dang Dong right now. Only a knock at the door saved me from tears.

112   Unit 2

Mom announced, "The movers are here!"

The house quickly filled up with furniture and big brown boxes. The box marked "Lovely Things" was the last to arrive.

I unpacked all my possessions. I hung my hand-painted scrolls and colorful fans on the walls. I placed my silk cushions and straw mats on the floor.

Then came another knock. To our surprise a parade of neighbors waltzed in[6] carrying plates of curious food. There were pink-and-white iced cakes and warm pans containing something called *casseroles*.

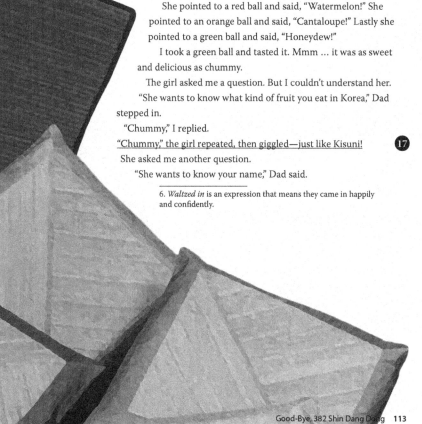

A girl my age wandered up to me with a small glass bowl. Inside the bowl were colorful balls. They smelled fruity.

She pointed to a red ball and said, "Watermelon!" She pointed to an orange ball and said, "Cantaloupe!" Lastly she pointed to a green ball and said, "Honeydew!"

I took a green ball and tasted it. Mmm ... it was as sweet and delicious as chummy.

The girl asked me a question. But I couldn't understand her.

"She wants to know what kind of fruit you eat in Korea," Dad stepped in.

"Chummy," I replied.

"Chummy," the girl repeated, then giggled—just like Kisuni!

She asked me another question.

"She wants to know your name," Dad said.

---

6. *Waltzed in* is an expression that means they came in happily and confidently.

Good-Bye, 382 Shin Dang Dong   113

Literary Components

16 **Resolution:** As the neighbors reach out to the new family, the conflict begins to be resolved. Although it was hard to leave friends, there will be new friends here. Although it was hard to leave a beautiful home and garden, there is a beautiful home and garden here.

17 **Parallelism:** The story is written in parallel lines. The goodbye party at the beginning of the story is repeated as a welcome party at the end. The giggling of Kisuni over the word "honeydew" is repeated as the giggling of Mary over the word "chummy."

Guiding the Reading

Literal

Q: How did Jangmi make her room seem like "home"?

A: She put her "favorite things" all around the room.

Q: What happened to make the family feel welcome?

A: The neighbors came with lots of delicious food. A girl Jangmi's age talked to her and asked her about Korea.

Analytical

Q: What is one thing you could do to feel less alone in a new place?

A: You could put objects you love or photographs of family and friends in your home or school.

Q: What is one thing you could do to help new people feel less lonely?

A: Like the neighbors in this story, you could introduce yourself to the new people, welcome them, engage them in conversation, and, if possible, bring them food or a small gift.

Good-Bye, 382 Shin Dang Dong

Literary Components

18 **Theme; Conclusion:** Jangmi found it difficult to leave her home and she has not forgotten that. Now, however, she realizes that her new home is good, too, and she will slowly embrace it.

Guiding the Reading

Literal

Q: What was the new girl's name?

A: Her name was Mary.

Q: How did Jangmi feel once Mary smiled at her in a friendly way?

A: She was no longer sad. She began to look ahead at having a new friend and enjoying her new life.

Analytical

Q: What very precious gift did Mary give to Jangmi?

A: She gave her the gift of friendship. She reached out to her and gave her hope of a bright future.

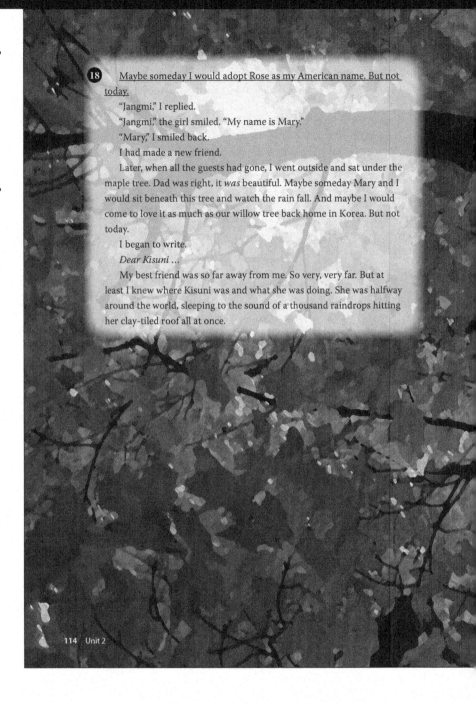

18 Maybe someday I would adopt Rose as my American name. But not today.

"Jangmi," I replied.

"Jangmi," the girl smiled. "My name is Mary."

"Mary," I smiled back.

I had made a new friend.

Later, when all the guests had gone, I went outside and sat under the maple tree. Dad was right, it *was* beautiful. Maybe someday Mary and I would sit beneath this tree and watch the rain fall. And maybe I would come to love it as much as our willow tree back home in Korea. But not today.

I began to write.

Dear Kisuni …

My best friend was so far away from me. So very, very far. But at least I knew where Kisuni was and what she was doing. She was halfway around the world, sleeping to the sound of a thousand raindrops hitting her clay-tiled roof all at once.

About the Authors

Frances and Ginger Park are sisters who grew up in Virginia. They were the only Korean-American family they knew in their town. Writing books about children emigrating from Korea has helped Frances and Ginger connect to the country their parents left. Frances and Ginger Park both love tennis and chocolate. In addition to writing books together, the sisters own a chocolate store in Washington, D.C. They say that the store is a very fun place to be when they are not writing.

Good-Bye, 382 Shin Dang Dong

New Kid at School

Poem tie-in for *Good-Bye, 382 Shin Dang Dong*

This terse poem duplicates the shy questions and answers of a new kid and the kindhearted boy who befriends him. It is a dialogue that is played and replayed wherever there are children. Besides being a delightful poem, it is an instructive one. Anyone reading it gets some very helpful ideas about what to say to the new kid on the block.

Here are some questions you can use to discuss *New Kid at School*.

Q: Have you ever been "the new kid"?

Q: How did it feel? Were people nice or not? Did they know what to say to make you feel comfortable? Did you know what to say to "break into" the group? What advice do you have for both new kids and kids who want to welcome others?

Q: Look at the questions the "old kid" asks. Do you think they are good questions to ask when you want to get to know someone? Why or why not? Do you have some other questions that would be useful? What are they?

Q: Why do you think the questions and answers are so short?

A: They are short because the two boys don't know each other yet, and they're both a little shy and unsure of themselves. Once they know they are friends, they will probably say more.

New Kid at School

Betsy Franco

Where did you come from?
Far away.
Miss your friends?
Every day.
Where do you live?
Maple Street.
What's your name?
Call me Pete.

How old are you?
Just turned eight.
You like hoops?
Yeah, great.
Got any friends?
Nope, not yet.
Wanna play?
You bet!

116   Unit 2

Studying the Selection

FIRST IMPRESSIONS
Jangmi has to leave her house, her friends, and her country. Will anywhere else ever feel like home?

QUICK REVIEW

1. What is Shin Dang Dong?
2. What season was it when Jangmi left Korea?
3. What does the name Jangmi mean?
4. What happened in Massachusetts to make Jangmi feel much less lonely?

FOCUS

5. Explain how the weather conditions may have added to Jangmi's emotions as she left Korea.
6. At the end of the story, Jangmi's feelings have changed. Compare how she felt when she was in the taxi on the way to the airport to the way she felt after Mary introduced herself.

CREATING AND WRITING

7. The days following Jangmi's arrival in Massachusetts were filled with activity. She had to unpack, register at her new school, and meet many new people, both children and adults. Imagine that you are Jangmi and that you are writing a letter to your friend Kisuni in Korea. In your letter, describe everything that has happened in the last few days, including how you've been feeling and how much you've missed her.
8. Jangmi packed a box of "Lovely Things" to take with her to America. Everyone has some treasured items. Choose three or four things that are very special to you and put them in a box. Prepare to show the objects to your class and explain why they are meaningful to you.

Studying the Selection

First Impressions

Young people live very much in the present. Jangmi, never having experienced any real change, is sure she will never adjust to her new life. Your students may agree. Adults know that, at eight years old, Jangmi will be integrated into her new world rapidly. As she grows, the memory of her old life will fade. It will be interesting to hear from children in your class who have moved or changed schools. They may have some useful advice or positive or negative experience to report.

It is useless to tell a child like Jangmi that she should not feel sad. What is useful is to encourage her to try new things and look ahead to new experiences. Some people feel "traitorous" if they enjoy a new life away from their old friends. This is wrong, of course. Making new friends does not have to mean the old ones are forgotten. Jangmi can keep her friendship with Kisuni alive and still make new friends in America.

Quick Review

1. Shin Dang Dong is the name of the street on which Jangmi lived.
2. Jangmi was leaving just as the monsoon season was beginning.
3. Jangmi means "rose."
4. The new neighbors came with gifts of food to welcome Jangmi's family. A girl named Mary introduced herself to Jangmi in a very friendly way.

Focus

5. Jangmi was sad and tearful as she left. The gray skies and rainy weather probably made her feel even gloomier. Also, she knew that monsoons did not exist in Massachusetts. She had already begun to feel sentimental about anything Korean, so leaving the monsoon weather added to her longing for anything Korean.
6. In the taxi, Jangmi was very sad to the point of hopelessness. She did not have mixed emotions—*everything* looked dark to her. At the end of the story, Jangmi is not so sure about how she feels. She sees that her new city has beauty to it. She sees that the people are friendly and that she already has a friend. She has not given up her feelings of sadness, but they are now mixed with lightness that she did not feel while still in Korea.

Creating and Writing

7. If you like, you can give the children stationery and envelopes. Now may be a good time to review how an envelope is addressed. Call the post office and find out how much it costs to mail a letter to Korea and have the children design or copy a stamp of that denomination and draw it on the envelope.
8. Offer some suggestions to the students about what to put in their boxes. Tell them that an item may appear simple to everyone else, but if it has a story to tell, it can be put in their boxes. Allow some class time for the students to "show and tell" the objects they have put in their boxes.

Sybil Rides By Night

Lesson in Literature

What Is External Conflict?
The Underground Road

1. Tice Davids is struggling against his enslavement. He does not want to be a slave.
2. Joseph helps Tice by telling him how to escape to Ohio.
3. The struggle is resolved when Tice follows Joseph's advice and crosses the Ohio River to Ohio.

Selection Summary

It is a momentous year in American history: 1777. Independence has been declared, but that was on paper. Now, independence must be won on the battlefield from the British, who will not easily give up the lucrative colonies across the Atlantic. As the story opens, the British have just marched on Danbury, Connecticut, and burned it to the ground. A rider gallops up to the home of Colonel Ludington to tell him what has happened. Night is falling and there is no one to ride through the countryside and gather the soldiers for battle. Time is of the essence.

The colonel's sixteen-year-old daughter, Sybil, volunteers to ride her horse Star and round up the battalion. The colonel agrees with both reluctance and pride to send his daughter on the dangerous ride. He warns her to beware of strange voices or hoofbeats, and dispatches her with the message, "The British have burned Danbury—gather at Ludingtons'." Sybil sets out on Star for the thirty mile ride in the dark and the rain, whispering, "This ride is for freedom."

Sybil rides from farm to farm and from town to town. Along the way some Redcoats pass her, but she is able to hide from them. Her horse slips in the mud and she loses her voice from shouting her message, but by daybreak she has completed her mission and returned home, wet and exhausted. She has succeeded in gathering four hundred soldiers who, together with other militias, rout the British at Ridgefield, about ten miles from Danbury.

Sybil grows up, marries, and has children and grandchildren who love to hear the story of her midnight ride and how later, George Washington himself came to thank her for her courageous act of patriotism.

Lesson in Literature...
THE UNDERGROUND ROAD

WHAT IS EXTERNAL CONFLICT?
- **External** means outside.
- When the conflict in a story is between a character and something outside the character, it is called an **external conflict**.
- What is *outside* the character? It could be anything with which a character struggles. A storm, an enemy, or a rattlesnake are some examples.
- An external conflict is not necessarily a struggle between right and wrong. It is simply a struggle. For example, a story's external conflict could be about a man trying to keep his ship from sinking during a storm.

THINK ABOUT IT!
1. What is Tice Davids struggling against?
2. Who offers to help Tice with his struggle?
3. How is the struggle—the external conflict—resolved?

118 Unit 2

Getting Started

Communication has always been critical in times of war. Ask your class why this is so. Explain that armies must work together to win. First and foremost, they must know when and where to gather. Once the battle has started, they must know where the others are on the battlefield. They must coordinate attacks and defenses. If they are planning an ambush, they must keep track of where everyone is.

Over the centuries, armies have devised different ways of communicating. Ask your students if they know of any. A few methods they may have heard of are: smoke signals used by the Indians; bonfires lit on hilltops, used in ancient times; carrier pigeons used in ancient and modern times; telegraphs, Morse code, and walkie-talkies in more modern times; and always, human messengers running, riding, climbing, and even swimming.

Sybil Rides By Night

The year was 1831. A young man was on his knees, digging in the dirt. He was planting some seeds in the dry soil. It was midday. He was hot and thirsty.

His name was Tice Davids. He worked and lived on a plantation in Kentucky near the Ohio River. Tice had been born a slave.

He didn't know how old he was. He didn't even know the month or day he was born. He couldn't remember his momma. She had been sold to a slaveholder in Alabama when he was a baby, so he couldn't ask her how old he was.

Tice had no family. His brother and sister had been sold. So had Robert, his best friend when he was seven. He missed his grandma. About a year before, she had been given as a present to an old white woman. The old white woman needed a companion.

The work in the fields was very hard. He toiled and sweated in the sun from early morning until the sun went down. His clothes were like rags. He slept on the floor of a tiny hut. Even though he was young, he felt so tired.

Always, he tried to do what he was told. He didn't want to be hurt.

What would it be like not to be owned? Sometimes he could feel how odd it was—that a person could be bought or sold. Other times it just seemed this was the way life was.

Some days he felt he just couldn't stand to be a slave. He had thoughts that were dangerous thoughts. He could never say what he was thinking to anyone.

But he kept on having the same thoughts. He listened to the other slaves when they whispered. How did they know which way

to go? He didn't have a map to tell him. He wasn't sure he knew what a map was. He had never seen one. Besides, he couldn't read. Slaves weren't allowed to learn to read.

Tice didn't own anything except a smooth pebble he had found. Was there anything he would need to bring with him? He didn't have anything to bring. What would he eat? How far could he go? Would someone help him?

Then Joseph, the wrinkled old man with white hair, spoke softly to Tice one night. "Boy," he sighed, "you got that look on you. What you do, you cross the river. Then run up that hill. You be in Ripley. Ripley hates slavery. The house on the hilltop belongs to the Reverend and Mrs. Rankin. A lantern shines from the window. That be your first stop." Then he walked away. Joseph didn't speak to him again.

Tice waited for a night when there was no moon. Then he slipped away quietly. He ran like crazy through the chill night air. He tripped on a rock and nearly fell, and slid into the icy waters of the Ohio. He could hear the men and the dogs after him. He could hear his heart beating madly as he swam for his life. He reached the Ohio shore.

His white master wasn't far behind. He rowed furiously across the river that separated the free state of Ohio from the slave state of Kentucky. He searched the banks of the Ohio for a long time. Tice had vanished.

His owner returned empty-handed to Kentucky. He was very angry. It is said that he muttered, "It's like he disappeared. That boy must have gone on some underground road."

Sybil Rides By Night **119**

Target Skill: Understanding and being able to recognize the external conflict in a story

Learning Strategy: Making connections

Common Core Curriculum: RI.3.2; RL.3.3

Genre: Historical Biography

Vocabulary

coaxed (KOKST) *v.*: gently tried to get someone to do something

independence (IN dih PEN dunce) *n.*: freedom; the right to think and act for oneself

strained *v.*: tried to make them work even better than they usually did

Related Vocabulary

volunteer (VAHL un TEER) *v.*: to offer to do something without being told

alert (uh LERT) *v.*: warn

route (ROWT or ROOT) *n.*: a certain way travelled from one place to another

halted (HALL ted) *v.*: stopped

liberty (LIB er tee) *n.*: freedom

Workbook

Related Pages: 38-43

Answer Key Page: 6

Of course, today, communications are unbelievably swift and accurate with the advent of the cell phone and the entire spectrum of related gadgets.

Sybil volunteered for an urgent mission: she had to inform all the soldiers within a thirty mile radius to gather at her father's farm. Her ride, like the famous ride of Paul Revere, was both fraught with danger and of critical importance to the war effort. Thanks to her, the colonists mobilized against the British and held their ground.

Explain that Sybil was every bit as much a hero as a soldier who carried a gun. This story describes her heroic deeds.

Sybil Rides By Night

Into . . . *Sybil Rides By Night*

This is a straightforward story of one girl's courageous deed. It is easy to teach, as there are no complex emotions to define or analyze. The setting is classic: the colonies during the Revolutionary War. If you are so inclined, you can build a fine history lesson around the story. It would be good to review the historical facts and relate them to what the class already knows about the American Revolution. Among the basic facts that should be reviewed are: the date of the Declaration of Independence (July 4, 1776); the thirteen colonies that made up the United States (among them, New York and Connecticut, which are the setting of this story); the ruthlessness of the British Redcoats in trying to put down the Revolution; the grassroots character of the Colonial army (explain that the "soldiers" were just the farmers and townspeople who gathered to fight the British); and the strong desire of the Americans for freedom (as Sybil says, "this ride is for freedom").

The theme of the story is courage. To the extent that Sybil is described, it is in terms of her courage and persistence. Throughout the story, she never wavers, never gives in to her fear or exhaustion, and never doubts the significance of what she is doing. The conflict is entirely external. Ask your students why Sybil volunteered for this dangerous job. The answers should include not only her love of country but also her desire .to help her father. She clearly admires him and wants to be a part of his important work. Some of the students may focus on her relationship with Star and her feeling that the two of them can do great things.

It would be interesting to see what responses you get when you ask your students if they think they could do something this courageous. Ask them to share other stories of courageous youth that they have been told. How does one become courageous? This, too, should produce some interesting responses. Some may say you are just born that way, some may say you just make up your mind to be courageous. Point out that sometimes circumstance makes heroes out of ordinary people. Believing strongly in something can give a person courage. In this case, Sybil believed in freedom. She believed more concretely that if she did not warn the men, the British would burn another town. That strong belief mingled with fear gave her courage.

Blueprint for Reading

INTO . . . *Sybil Rides By Night*

Sybil was a teenager whose father was a colonel in the American Army during the Revolutionary War. One night, when most teenagers were sleeping soundly in their beds, Sybil mounted her horse, Star, and took off into the night to warn the men in the neighboring towns that the British were coming. It was dark, it was rainy, it was cold, and it was scary. Would you want to be in her shoes? As you ride with Sybil, ask yourself: Would I, *could* I, do what she did?

EYES ON *External Conflict*

In *Good-Bye, 382 Shin Dang Dong* we learned about *internal conflict*, which is a struggle that takes place inside a person's mind. *Sybil Rides By Night* has a conflict, too, but this time it is between the main character and something *outside* of her. There is Sybil, on one side, and the dangers of the nighttime ride, on the other side. The struggle between the two sides is called **external conflict**. As you read, see if you can guess which side—Sybil or the dangers she faces—will come out the winner.

Eyes On: External Conflict

Identifying the external conflict in this story should be easy for your class. In fact, this story is an excellent tool for teaching about conflict because the two "sides" of the conflict are so clear-cut. To help your students pinpoint the elements of the conflict, draw a vertical line on the board, creating two columns. At the top of the first column write: *For Sybil.* At the top of the other column write: *Against Sybil.* Ask your students to help you fill out the columns. Your chart should look like this:

For Sybil	*Against Sybil*
Colonel Ludington	The Redcoats
Star	The mud
The soldiers	The rain
The townspeople	Exhaustion
George Washington	Sybil's loss of her voice

Sybil Rides By Night

From *Sybil Rides for Independence*

Drollene P. Brown

A young girl named Sybil turned sixteen as the American colonies struggled for independence. Although girls her age were expected to bake, sew, and keep house, Sybil preferred to ride her horse, Star, and to hear about the colonial soldiers and their battles. Sybil's father, Henry Ludington, was a commander in the colonial army. On the night of April 26, 1777, Colonel Ludington got a message: The British had marched to a nearby town, Danbury, and set it afire. If no one stopped them, they would continue marching from town to town, destroying everything in their path. American soldiers had to be rounded up from their farms to fight the British. Who would take that dangerous job? Who knew where each of the farmers lived and was courageous enough to ride through the dark, cold, rainy night? Who would dare to go where British soldiers and outlaws roamed?

Colonel Ludington knew of one such person: his daughter, Sybil. Excited and frightened, Sybil agreed to ride by night.

Sybil Rides By Night   121

Remind your students that in an external conflict, some of the elements in the conflict may not be people. They can be forces of nature, time that is going too fast or too slow, animals, health—any number of things that can work against the protagonist.

Ask your students why conflict makes a story exciting. The answer is that the reader is not sure which side of the conflict will win, and the suspense generated by that doubt keeps the reader interested. The more evenly balanced the two sides in a conflict are, the greater the suspense and the stronger the interest. Ask your students for a show of hands: who likes a story that is full of suspense? Can they name some suspense-filled stories? Can they identify the conflict in those stories? The learning strategy of *making connections* comes into play here because without even realizing it your students will be calling upon prior reading experiences that they have found suspenseful.

Sybil Rides By Night

Literary Components

❶ Exposition: The narrator lays out the story's fundamentals immediately. We are introduced to Sybil, Star, and the belief that carries her through the dangerous night.

❷ Conflict; Foreshadowing: We see that the ride is dangerous by the fact that the colonel is warning his daughter to hide if she hears voices.

❸ Exposition: We now know what the purpose of the ride is.

❹ Minor Theme: A minor theme is the dual relationship Sybil has with her father. She loves and respects him as her father, and she respects and loves him as her colonel. She is a daughter and a patriot.

Guiding the Reading

Literal

Q: Who was Star?
A: Star was Sybil's horse.

Q: What did Sybil whisper to Star?
A: She whispered, "This ride is for freedom."

Q: Why must Sybil ride all over the countryside on a dark and rainy night?
A: She must tell the soldiers who have gone home that Danbury is burning and that they must gather at Ludingtons' immediately.

Q: What rank did Sybil's father hold in the army?
A: Her father was a colonel.

Analytical

Q: In what year did the Americans declare their independence from the British?
A: The Declaration of Independence was signed in the year 1776.

Q: What did the British do when the Americans declared independence?
A: They went to war with America. (Explain that this story takes place during that war.) They sent armies to America to fight the Americans and force them to be ruled by England.

Q: Can you explain why Danbury was burning? What did that tell the colonists?
A: The British had set Danbury on fire to show they would destroy everybody's property if they did not give up their idea of independence from England. The colonists knew that if they did not fight back, the British would march from town to town and burn and destroy everything they could.

❶ Sybil swung up on Star. She patted his neck and leaned toward his ear. "This ride is for freedom," she whispered.

The colonel[1] looked up at his daughter. He handed her a big stick. "Listen **❷** for others on the path," he warned. "Pull off and hide if you hear hoofbeats or footsteps or voices.

❸ "You know where to go. Tell our men that Danbury's burning. Tell them **❹** to gather at Ludingtons'." Sybil listened to her orders. She saluted her father, her colonel. He stepped back and returned the salute.

1. A *colonel* is an officer in the U.S. Army, Air Force, or Marine Corps, ranking above lieutenant colonel.

Sybil thought of what might happen. There were more than thirty miles to cover in the dark and rain. She could be lost or hurt or caught by Redcoats![2] But she did not let these black thoughts scare her. I will do it for the colonies,[3] she vowed. **⑤**

She turned Star south on a line with the river. There would be several lone farmhouses to alert before they reached Shaw's Pond.

It was almost eight o'clock when she reached the first farmhouse. Doors flew open at the sound of Star's hoofbeats.

Sybil shouted her message. She did not stop, but hurried on to the farmhouses that were along Horse Pound Road. It was about ten o'clock when Sybil reached Shaw's Pond.

The houses beside the water were dark for the night. Sybil hadn't thought of this. She had been so excited she had forgotten people would be sleeping.

---

2. Before and during the War for Independence, the British soldiers were called *Redcoats*, for the simple reason that their uniform jackets were red.
3. Before the United States gained their independence from Great Britain, they were called *the colonies*. The thirteen colonies were the first thirteen states.

Literary Components

⑤ **Characterization:** Sybil is courageous. She is aware of the danger but will not be deterred.

Guiding the Reading

Literal

Q: How far would Sybil have to ride?
A: She would have to cover thirty miles.

Q: What dangers would she face during the ride?
A: She would face the dark, the rain, and the Redcoats.

Q: What did Sybil do to save time, yet deliver her message?
A: Sybil shouted her message but did not stop.

Q: What did Sybil find when she reached Shaw's Pond that she had not expected?
A: She found a dark house with the people sleeping inside.

Analytical

Q: Sybil had two feelings as she prepared to leave. What were they?
A: Sybil was frightened of the dark, the rain, and the British. But she was also determined to ride and spread the word to the soldiers.

Q: Which side were most of the people on—America's or England's? How can you tell from the story?
A: Most were on America's side. You can tell from the line, "Doors flew open at the sound of Star's hoofbeats." It seems as though everyone was waiting for word from the colonel. It does not appear that Sybil had to skip any houses for fear they would be on the British side.

Sybil Rides By Night

Literary Components

6 **External Conflict:** All these difficulties are part of the external conflict—the things that are working against Sybil's goal of alerting the soldiers to gather at Ludingtons'.

Guiding the Reading

Literal

Q: How was an entire town alerted?

A: Someone would ring the town bell to alert everyone.

Q: After riding from town to town, how did Sybil feel?

A: Sybil's throat hurt, her heart pounded, her eyes burned. She was wet and muddy.

Analytical

Q: Do you know of some other famous rider who rode from town to town to alert the soldiers that the British were coming?

A: Paul Revere, whose midnight ride was made famous by the poem *The Midnight Ride of Paul Revere*, was another famous rider.

Sybil stopped for only a moment. She coaxed Star up to the door and pounded with her stick.

A window opened. A head poked out. "Look to the east!" Sybil shouted. "Danbury's burning! Gather at Ludingtons'!"

She did not beat on every door. She did not shout at every house. Neighbors called to each other; and in the little hamlets along her way, one of the first ones awakened rushed out to ring the town bell.

When the alarm began to sound, Sybil would stop her shouting and ride on into the darkness.

6 Her throat hurt from calling out her message. Her heart beat wildly, and her tired eyes burned. Her skirt seemed to be filled with heavy weights, for

> ### WORD BANK
> **coaxed** (KOKST) *v.:* gently tried to get someone to do something

it was wet and caked with mud. She pulled her mother's cloak closer against the cold and rain that would not stop.

Sybil would not stop, either. All the soldiers in the regiment must be told. She urged Star on.

Outside the village at Mahopac⁴ Pond, Star slipped in the mud. He got up right away, but Sybil's eyes stung with tears. She would have to be more careful!

If Star were hurt, she would blame herself. She must walk Star over loose **7** rocks and pick through the underbrush where there was no path.

Again and again, Sybil woke up sleeping soldiers. Nearing Red Mills, Star stumbled and almost fell. He was breathing heavily. "You are fine, Star," Sybil whispered.

_____
4. *Mahopac* (mah HO puk)

Sybil Rides By Night **125**

Literary Components

7 **Characterization:** Sybil is a person who takes responsibility upon herself. She does not look for excuses or something to blame when things go wrong.

Guiding the Reading

Literal

Q: Who besides Sybil was exhausted?
A: Star was exhausted.

Analytical

Q: Was Sybil angry when Star slipped in the mud?
A: No, not at all! She was concerned that she was not taking good enough care of him, and resolved to be more careful, even though she was only a girl and he was a big, strong horse.

Sybil Rides By Night

Literary Components

8 **Suspense:** We were warned at the beginning of the story about the danger of hearing hoofbeats.

Guiding the Reading

Literal

Q: What time was it when Sybil heard hoofbeats behind her?

A: It was well past midnight.

Sybil looked at the sky. The moon was half-risen. That meant it was well past midnight. She guessed they were halfway through, but the long ride to Stormville still lay ahead.

8 More slowly now, they started on their way. Then—hoofbeats on the path! Quickly Sybil reined Star to a halt. She jumped down and pulled him toward the trees.

She held her breath and strained her eyes. Men passed so close she could have touched them. They looked like British soldiers, but sometimes

> **WORD BANK**
>
> **strained** v.: tried to make them work even better than they usually did

126   Unit 2

Sybil Rides By Night

skinners[5] dressed like soldiers of one army or the other to fool the people they robbed.

Soon the hoofbeats died away. Sybil's hands and knees trembled as she guided Star back to the path.

"We'll make it," she softly promised him. Star pricked up his ears and started off again. He was weary, but he trusted Sybil.

When they reached Stormville, the alarm had already begun to sound. Someone from another village had come with the news. Sybil was glad, for she could only whisper. She had shouted away her voice.

---

5. During the Revolutionary War, groups of bandits roamed the countryside and robbed both the British and the Americans. They were called *skinners*.

Sybil Rides By Night   127

Literary Components

9 **Characterization:** Sybil has the courage to believe she will complete her mission.

Guiding the Reading

Literal

Q: Who were the riders that passed her?
A: They may have been British soldiers or they may have been skinners dressed like soldiers.

Q: How did Star feel about Sybil?
A: Star trusted Sybil.

Q: What condition was Sybil in when she reached Stormville?
A: She couldn't shout; she'd lost her voice.

Analytical

Q: Why do you think the soldiers did not notice Sybil?
A: The soldiers weren't on the lookout for anyone. The dark and the rain helped Sybil hide from them.

Sybil Rides By Night

Literary Components

10 **Characterization:** Sybil does not view herself as a hero. She just did what she felt had to be done.

Guiding the Reading

Literal

Q: How many soldiers had gathered by the time Sybil returned to her home?
A: Four hundred soldiers had gathered.

Q: What time was it when Sybil reached home?
A: It was sunrise.

Analytical

Q: What qualities do you think Sybil had that enabled her to ride all through the night even though she was tired and afraid?
A: Sybil had courage and determination. Sybil was persistent, which means she stuck to the job and did not give up even when things got very rough. Sybil believed in the cause of freedom. Also, deep down she believed she could do the job—she believed in herself.

Covered with mud, horse and rider turned home. When Sybil rode into her yard, more than four hundred men were ready to march. She looked at the eastern sky. It was red.

"Is Danbury still burning?" she asked and tumbled into Father's arms.

"No, my brave soldier. It is the sunrise. You have ridden all night."

10 "I do not feel like a brave soldier," Sybil whispered. "I feel like a very tired girl. Star needs care," she murmured sleepily as she was carried to her bed.

Early that morning, while that very tired girl slept, her father's men joined soldiers from Connecticut. They met the British at Ridgefield, about ten miles from Danbury.

The soldiers from New York and Connecticut battled with the Redcoats. Most of the British escaped to their ships in Long Island Sound, but they did no further damage.

People spread the word of Sybil's ride. Soon General Washington came to her house to thank her for her courage. Statesman Alexander Hamilton wrote to her, praising her deed.

America was soon a growing, changing nation, and Sybil's life changed, too. At twenty-three she married Edmond Ogden. They had six children, and she kept house. She baked, she mended, and she washed the dishes.

Guiding the Reading

Literal

Q: Who fought the British at Ridgefield?

A: Soldiers from Connecticut and from New York fought the British (Colonel Ludington's men were from New York).

Q: What happened to the British after the battle at Ridgefield?

A: Most of them escaped to their ships in Long Island Sound.

Q: Would you call that a victory for the colonists?

A: Definitely. The British went back to their ships and did no further damage.

Q: What great person came to thank Sybil personally?

A: General George Washington came to thank Sybil.

Sybil Rides By Night

Literary Components

11 **Conclusion:** Sybil's ride is in the past. She is proud of what she has done and remains a patriot.

Guiding the Reading

Literal

Q: What did Sybil do when she grew up?

A: She married and had six children. She raised them and lived to tell the story of her ride to her children and grandchildren.

But sometimes she would stop in the middle of a chore. Remembering that cold, wet night in 1777, she would shiver again. Then warm feelings of **11** pride would fill her as she thought, "Once I was brave for my country."

Sybil lived to be seventy-eight years old. Her children and her children's children loved to hear the story of a young girl's ride for independence.

> **WORD BANK**
>
> **independence** (IN dih PEN dunce) *n.*: freedom; the right to think and act for oneself

ABOUT THE AUTHOR

Drollene P. Brown has been writing ever since she was a child. When she was in school, she would write papers for fun and give them to her teachers to grade. When she got older, she went through many careers, including college professor, banker, editor, writer, book store manager, and business consultant. Mrs. Brown wants to make a difference to people and she loves visiting schools to talk about writing and about her books.

Studying the Selection

FIRST IMPRESSIONS

If there was no adult available to do a dangerous job, would you have the confidence and the courage to do it?

QUICK REVIEW

1. What message was Sybil supposed to deliver to the soldiers?
2. What happened at Shaw Pond that Sybil had not expected?
3. Some riders passed Sybil and Star. Who could they have been?
4. What happened in the battle at Ridgefield?

FOCUS

5. Sybil had powerful feelings that gave her the courage to ride through the night. List three strong beliefs or feelings Sybil had that gave her the strength to keep going.
6. In a conflict, one or more things are working against the main character. List at least three things with which Sybil had to struggle during her ride.

CREATING AND WRITING

7. Pretend that you are a neighbor of the Ludingtons and the *Colonial Gazette* has asked you to write a news item about Sybil's ride. They would like an article that includes details like what snacks Mrs. Ludington sent with Sybil, how Sybil's dog howled for an hour after she left, and so on. Write a long paragraph that includes a lot of interesting (made-up) details. Make sure you have an exciting headline, too.
8. People want to honor the heroes who helped our country win its independence. One way to do that is by putting their names and faces on coins or bills. Another way to remember them is by putting their names, faces, or some symbol of their deeds on a stamp. Using the materials provided by your teacher, design a 99 cent coin or a 50 cent stamp to honor Sybil Ludington.

Studying the Selection

- -

First Impressions

There is no clear-cut answer to this question, as much of it depends on what the job is. In some cases, the best decision would be to do nothing, as a child could make matters worse or put himself in needless danger. In Sybil's case, she was taking the job with her parents' consent and their belief that she could do the job. It is important that you stress to your students how much a part of this decision Sybil's parents were. In fact, one of her motives was to obey and please her father.

It is true that Colonial children were thrust into adult roles at far earlier ages than their modern counterparts. Children were given much responsibility and hard work. Sybil is able to do the adult job because she has the physical strength and the skill to do it as, perhaps, many girls of her age at the time had. The point is that her courage was founded on the knowledge that she had a good chance of completing her mission. Riding the thirty miles would take courage, persistence, and skill—but it would not take a miracle. Courage does not mean attempting the impossible. It means taking on a challenge where the odds are against you but there is a chance you can succeed.

Quick Review

1. The message was to tell the soldiers that the British had set fire to Danbury and that they should gather at Ludingtons'.
2. Everybody was sleeping at Shaw Pond and Sybil had to pound on their door to wake them.
3. The riders were probably Redcoats, but they may have been skinners.
4. The British were forced to retreat to their ships on Long Island Sound. They did no further damage.

Focus

5. Sybil was motivated by at least three strong feelings: her love of freedom; her desire to help her father; and her fear that the British would continue to burn towns if they were not stopped.
6. The rain, the mud, the Redcoats, and Sybil's and Star's exhaustion were working against Sybil.

Creating and Writing

7. Encourage your students to think creatively. They can write gossipy articles and use phrases like "Old Uncle Jed tells us he was looking out his window having his evening cocoa when he saw young Sybil 'take off like lightning on that there steed of her'n ...'" Encourage your students to add details like what clothing Sybil wore, people she met along the way, and perhaps what she was thinking as she rode.
8. Provide your students with paper and colored pencils or markers. For the coin, you should give them a large piece of paper with two circles on it for the two sides of the coin. Bring a few larger size coins to class to give the students an idea of what should be placed on each side of the coin. For the stamp, provide them with a large sheet of paper with the outer edges of a stamp drawn onto it. They will draw their stamps in color on the paper. Remind them to put the denomination of the stamp and possibly US Postal Service, or even the word Forever on the stamp.

Nothing Much Happened Today

Lesson in Literature

What Is Sequence?

Mom I Love You

1. Charlie wrote on the wall four days before Mother's Day.

2. Mom saw the writing the night Charlie wrote on the wall—Wednesday night.

3. d.; e.; b.; c.; a.

Selection Summary

Mother is on her way home from the grocery. She is excited because she has just seen a policeman chasing a robber and wants to tell her children all about it. As she approaches her house, she sees millions of bubbles drifting out of the front window. When she asks her son what is happening, he reveals, one step at a time, a whole series of events that have taken place during the twenty minutes Mother has been at the store. The events, which are revealed in the story starting with the last one and progressing to the first, are listed here in their proper order. The robber that Mother had seen ran into the house, followed by a policeman. As the policeman chased the robber around the table, he knocked over the cake Mother had baked for the bake sale. The children baked another cake, but the batter spilled over in the oven, causing the oven to smoke. The children opened the window to let the smoke out, and a cat ran in through the window. When the family dog began to chase the cat around the room, he knocked over the bag of sugar and got all sticky, thus requiring a bath. When the children bathed the dog, they put in too much soap, which created the millions of bubbles the Mother has just seen.

The story is told one piece at a time by the children in a calm, matter-of-fact way. The mother reacts to each additional piece of information with astonishment and dismay. The children conclude their narrative by saying, "nothing much happened today," as the mother sinks into a half faint.

Getting Started

Read the story aloud until page 139 and the words "Mother grabbed her forehead." Then read the following questions to your students.

(For more information on aural exercises, see *Getting Started/The Story of the White Sombrero*.)

Lesson in Literature . . .

WHAT IS SEQUENCE?

- **Sequence** means order. For example, to list the days of the week in their proper sequence, you would say, "Sunday, Monday, Tuesday," and so on.

- In most stories, the events are described in sequence, the order in which they happened.

- At times, a story will have a flashback, or jump ahead into the future. These events are out of sequence.

- Sequence is especially important in lists, recipes, and instructions.

THINK ABOUT IT!

1. How many days before Mother's Day did Charlie write on the wall?

2. On which day did Mom see the writing on the wall?

3. Put the following events in their proper sequence:
   a. Mother's Day
   b. Charlie writes a note to his mother and makes her a snack.
   c. Charlie sees his mother packing his clothes.
   d. Eleanor sees the writing on the wall.
   e. There is screaming and crying.

Charlie and Eleanor were brother and sister. They were also good friends. Usually, Charlie and Eleanor agreed about things. But when Mother's Day was just around the corner, Charlie had a great idea that he did not share with Eleanor. He did not know where or how he got this idea. It just came over him like a thunderbolt.

Mother's Day was on Sunday. The Wednesday before Mother's Day, he wrote in large letters on his wall,

MOM I LOVE YOU!

This wall had recently been wallpapered. Yet Charlie proceeded, without giving this any thought. He wanted his mother to know how much he loved her, so he wrote with a wide-tipped, black permanent marker. He didn't want the giant words to ever be washed away.

When Eleanor got home, he shouted down to her excitedly, "I'm up here! Wait till you see this!"

Eleanor came running up the stairs and burst into Charlie's room. "Oh my heavens!" she gasped. "Charlie!" She covered her face with her hands. "What are we going to do?!"

"Oh, Eleanor," he said. "Don't worry. I'll tell Mom you helped, too."

"Charlie," Eleanor whispered, "the walls were just done. I know you meant to do something nice, but this is really dreadful."

1. Where was the mother returning from?
   a. a doctor's appointment
   b. a department store
   c. walking the dog
   d. the grocery store

2. What did Mother want to tell the children?
   a. not to spill batter in the oven
   b. not to let any cats in the house
   c. that she had seen a policeman chase a robber
   d. that she had seen the dog chase a robber

3. What did she notice as she got close to her house?
   a. a robber running down the sidewalk
   b. bubbles coming out of the window
   c. a policeman giving tickets
   d. Popsicle chasing a cat

"Gosh, I thought Mom would be so pleased." Charlie looked a little confused. "Maybe you're wrong, El, maybe Mom will think it's very … special."

"Charlie, we need to see if we can get this off the wall. I can't even imagine what Mom and Dad will say."

When they tried to remove the writing, the wallpaper got wet and crumbly. "I don't know why I was so stupid," Charlie muttered. "I've done something terrible." Then Charlie got into bed. He didn't know what else to do.

Mom came home and made dinner. Dad got home at 6:00. Eleanor silently did her homework. Mom said, "Where's Charlie?"

Eleanor spoke with a sort of moan. "Mom, Charlie isn't feeling well. He went to bed."

"To bed?" Mom asked. "I better go up and check on him."

Eleanor waited and then she heard a shriek. There was screaming and crying. Dad looked over to her. "What's all that about, kiddo?" Eleanor felt she couldn't speak. Poor Charlie! Poor Mom!

Mom marched down the stairs. "What has happened to that boy?"

"Mom," Eleanor cried, "he just wanted to tell you he loves you."

"A fine way he has to show it!"

That night his mom didn't come and kiss him good night.

The next day at breakfast, Charlie couldn't look at his mom. He didn't know how to apologize for such a horrible mistake. After school, Eleanor tried to comfort him.

"Charlie, you will see. Everything will get worked out."

Charlie blurted, "I think they hate me now!"

Still, Charlie wrote his mother a note all in capital letters. This note was written on a piece of paper:

MOM, PLEASE FORGIVE ME. I'LL DO 100 CHORES FOR FREE.

I'LL GIVE UP MY ALLOWANCE AND TRY TO PAY YOU BACK.

Charlie made his mom a snack for when she got home: graham crackers with cream cheese and iced tea. He placed the note between the two small stacks of graham crackers. Then he went up to his room and did his homework.

At dinner Mom seemed a little cheerier. She thanked him for the snack and the note. But later on before bed, he saw his mom packing a suitcase with his fall clothes. Why would she be packing his clothes? Were they going to send him away to boarding school to live? He couldn't stand that—to be away from his family.

When his mom came into his room to kiss him good night, she sat down on the bed. She said, "We need to talk."

Charlie said, "You're going to tell me that you and Dad are going to send me away to boarding school!" Then he burst into tears.

His mom put her arms around him and held him in a strong hug. "Oh, you foolish boy. We would never send you away! How could we, when you are going to help us repaper the wall?"

Target Skill: Understanding what is important about a story and being able to tell about it in sequential order
Learning Strategy: Summarizing
Common Core Curriculum: RL.3.1; RL.3.3
Genre: Humorous Fiction

Related Vocabulary

astounded (uh STOWN dud) *v.*: greatly surprised
chaos (KAY oss) *n.*: total confusion and disorganization
drifting (DRIFT ing) *v.*: moving gently down or away
gasped (GASPT) *v.*: took in a sudden short breath because of surprise or shock
intended (in TEN did) *v.*: meant; planned
pandemonium (pan dih MO nee um) *n.*: a wild, disorganized, noisy scene
remarked (ree MARKED) *v.*: commented; said
revived (ree VIVED) *v.*: brought back to life or to action

Workbook

Related Pages: 44-49
Answer Key Page: 6

4. What did Mother do when Elizabeth said they'd bathed the dog?
   a. She laughed.
   b. She cried.
   c. She screamed.
   d. She fainted.

5. How did sugar get all over the dog?
   a. The robber spilled it on him while he was running.
   b. The dog knocked over the sugar bag.
   c. The policeman tripped over the sugar bag and spilled it on the dog.
   d. The cat bit open the sack and the dog crawled into it.

6. What did Mother say when they told her about the cat?
   a. She said they didn't own a cat.
   b. She said the cat was not allowed in the house.
   c. She said that cat was always trouble.
   d. She said the cat had just had kittens.

7. How did the cat get into the house?
   a. It broke the window and climbed through.
   b. It ran in with the police officer.
   c. It was hiding in the sack of sugar.
   d. It came in through the open window.

8. Why was there smoke in the house?
   a. Mother had burned the cake for the bake sale.
   b. The children had spilled the batter in the oven.
   c. The robber started a fire.
   d. The logs in the fireplace were wet.

Nothing Much Happened Today

Into . . . *Nothing Much Happened Today*

This piece is lots of fun. Many of your students will know songs or games that work in a similar fashion. Some of them will be cause and effect, like the children's story about the bee that stung the cow that knocked over the bucket which got the farmer's wife angry, etc. Others will just be sequential like "Old MacDonald."

The story is entertaining for a few reasons. First of all, the slapstick imagery: policeman chasing robber, dog chasing cat, robber banging forehead, and so on, is humorous. Second of all, the contrast between the mother's rising hysteria and the reasoned explanations of the children make us smile. Perhaps it's the contrast between the two, perhaps it's the role reversal in which the parent is the one on the verge of a tantrum—either way there's a nice humor about the children's matter-of-fact description of the havoc that has been wrought.

Eyes On: Sequence

The literary skill for this story is sequence and the learning strategy your students will use is *summarizing*. In the *Guiding the Reading* section of the Teacher's Edition, we have instructed the teacher to stop at various points in the story and review the events. Note that when this is done during the story, the events are given in reverse order, because the story starts with the last event. Near the end of the story, however, the events are summarized by the mother in their correct order. Learning to follow the sequence of events in a story is an excellent method to sharpen a student's memory, to help a student notice and retain details and differences; and, eventually, to help the student learn to outline and summarize.

A concept closely connected with sequence is cause and effect. In this story, each cause has an effect which becomes a cause for the next effect. In the Student Edition we refer to this as "a chain reaction." Chain reactions can be discussed at many levels. You can show the class a picture of the workings of a steam engine or a pulley or any of the many gadgets and machines that work by chain reaction. You can describe a "pileup" of cars in an accident, where the first car's dead stop causes the next car to run into it which causes the next car to skid and so on. There are a lot of funny or slapstick stories that involve chain

Blueprint for Reading

INTO . . . *Nothing Much Happened Today*

Nothing much happens in this story except for ... a policeman chasing a robber, a dog chasing a cat, a room filling with smoke, a million bubbles floating into the sky—and a few other little things. But don't worry, there's a good explanation for everything; read on and you'll see!

EYES ON *Sequence*

Have you ever seen a bowling ball hit one pin, which falls and hits another, which knocks over a few more, and results in a strike for the lucky bowler? If you have, then you have seen a *chain reaction*. Chain reactions can be funny or serious, helpful or destructive. Many gadgets and machines depend on chain reactions to make them work. But one thing that is shared by all chain reactions is that the events take place in a certain order, or **sequence**. The first event causes the second and the second causes the third, just the way the first bowling pin knocks over the second and the second one knocks over the third. As you read *Nothing Much Happened Today*, exercise your mind. Try to remember everything that happened in the story—*in order*!

reactions. After the class has read the story you could play a memory game where you call out one event and ask for its "cause" or its "effect." The first student to answer gets a point.

Nothing Much Happened Today

Mrs. Maeberry held her groceries tightly. She scurried home to tell her children about seeing the police chase a robber. **1** But when she turned down her sidewalk, her mouth flew open. Soap bubbles—hundreds, thousands, maybe millions of soap bubbles—were drifting from her front window. She ran inside. "What's happened?" she demanded. "What's happened here?"

Mary Blount Christian

Nothing Much Happened Today **135**

Literary Components

- -

1 **Exposition; Foreshadowing:** The story opens. We immediately know what kind of a story it will be. There is Mother, there are groceries, there is the word "scurried"; all of those are signals that this story is not heavy, serious, foreign, mysterious, or educational. It sounds everyday, light, and perhaps—though we don't know yet—funny.

Guiding the Reading

- -

Literal

Q: What had Mrs. Maeberry just seen?
A: She had just seen the police chase a robber.

Q: What did she see when she turned down her sidewalk?
A: She saw hundreds of soap bubbles drifting from her front window.

Nothing Much Happened Today

Literary Components

2 **Characterization; Understatement:** Stephen is characterized through his words and his motions. He "shrugs," and everything he says is understated. This is in contrast to the mother, who "demands," and "yells."

3 **Characterization; Humor:** Taking a cue from her brother, Elizabeth "mumbles," and continues the understated manner of describing unusual events. The name "Popsicle" fits the light tone of the story.

4 **Characterization; Rising Tension:** The Mother/children dialogue adds to the humor of the story.

Guiding the Reading

Literal

Q: What did Stephen say when she asked him what was happening?
A: He said nothing much was happening.

Q: Who is Popsicle?
A: Popsicle is the dog.

Q: Why did the children bathe the dog?
A: They bathed him because he'd gotten sugar stuck all over his fur.

Analytical

Q: If you had to guess, what would you say this story was going to be: serious, sad, suspenseful, or funny?
A: The answer is funny, but some children may guess suspenseful.

2 Stephen shrugged. "Nothing much, really."
"But the bubbles!" she yelled. "Look at those bubbles!"
Stephen shrugged again.
3 Elizabeth mumbled, "I guess maybe we did use too many suds when we bathed Popsicle."
4 "The dog? You bathed the dog?" Mother screamed. "Why did you bathe the dog?"
"He got sugar stuck all over his fur," Alan, the youngest, said.
Mother set her groceries down. "I was gone five minutes. How could Popsicle get sugar in his fur?"

136   Unit 2

"He got sugar in his fur when he knocked over the sugar sack. That was when he was chasing the cat through the kitchen," Stephen added.

Mother gasped. "Cat? Cat? We don't *have* a cat."

"I guess you could say it was a visiting cat," Stephen explained. "It came through the window."

"The window?" Mother shrieked. "That cat broke the glass?"

Stephen shook his head. "Nope. The window was open. We had to let the smoke out."

Nothing Much Happened Today   137

Guiding the Reading

Literal

Q: What did Mother say when they told her Popsicle had knocked over the sugar when he was chasing the cat?
A: She said they didn't own a cat.

Q: How did the cat get in?
A: The cat got in through the window.

Q: Why was the window open?
A: It was open to let the smoke out.

Analytical

Q: Do you know what a "chain reaction" is?
A: A chain reaction is when one event causes another, which causes another, and so forth.

Q: Can you remember the links in the chain, so far?
A: So far, the links are, working backwards: the bubbles, the dog, sugar, and the cat.

Nothing Much Happened Today

Nothing Much Happened Today

Mother grabbed her forehead. "Smoke! What smoke?"

"The smoke from the oven when the cake batter spilled over," Elizabeth volunteered.

Mother waved her arms. "Why were you baking a cake?"

"For the school bake sale," Alan reminded her.

"But," Mother protested. "But I baked that before I went to the store."

"We know," Stephen said, "but that one got ruined."

"Ruined?" Mother repeated. "How could my beautiful cake get ruined? I was gone ten minutes, only ten minutes."

"The cake was knocked onto the floor, and it's a good thing it was, too," Elizabeth said.

"I don't understand this. I don't understand this at all," Mother said.

"It's not so bad," Stephen said. **5** "We used too many soap suds on Popsicle because he was covered with sugar. He knocked the sugar over chasing the cat. The cat came through the window when we let out the smoke. The smoke is from the spilled cake batter in the oven. We were replacing the cake you baked because that one got knocked off by the police officer."

Literary Components

5 **Theme:** The story's theme is that things are as good or as bad as you consider them to be. The very same events that are no big deal to the children are disasters to the mother.

Guiding the Reading

Literal

Q: Why was there smoke in the room?
A: There was smoke from the oven when the cake batter spilled over.

Q: Why were they baking a cake?
A: They were baking for the school bake sale.

Q: What happened to the cake Mother had baked for the bake sale?
A: The cake was knocked to the floor.

Q: Who knocked it down?
A: The police officer knocked it down.

Analytical

Q: Can you list the next set of links in the chain reaction?
A: The next set of links, working backwards, are: the window, the smoke, and the cake batter.

Q: Would you call these children "naughty"?
A: No. They have been trying to do the right thing; things just haven't gone as planned.

Q: Can you compare the mother's tone of voice to the children's? How do you know how each sounded?
A: The mother's tone of voice was high, loud, and excited. The children's tone of voice was ordinary and calm. The story says the mother "shrieked," she "grabbed her forehead," and she "waved her arms." The words describing the way the children talked are: "explained," "volunteered," and "reminded." All these words describe a calm way of talking.

Nothing Much Happened Today

Mother's eyebrows shot up. "Police officer! What police officer?"

"The police officer that ran in after the robber," Alan told her.

"MY robber?" Mother gasped. "I—I mean the ❻ grocery robber?" She sank into a chair. "But tell me, please. Tell me how a robber and a police officer ruined my cake."

Stephen smiled. "That's easy. The robber ran around and around our kitchen table. The police officer went around and around after him. The police officer accidentally knocked the cake to the floor. The robber skidded in the icing."

Literary Components

❻ **The Story Comes Full Circle:** The punch lines of many jokes and humorous stories depend on the story coming full circle. That is what the author has done here.

Guiding the Reading

Literal

Q: Why did the police officer run into the house?

A: He was chasing the grocery robber.

Q: How did the cake get ruined?

A: It was knocked over as the police officer chased the robber around the table.

Analytical

Q: What sort of personality would you say Stephen had?

A: Stephen seems calm, mature, and reasonable.

Nothing Much Happened Today

Guiding the Reading

Literal

Q: How did the robber get hurt?

A: He skidded on the icing and hit his head on Alan's head.

Q: The mother lists the sequence of events that caused the chain reaction. Can you?

A: This time, the events will be listed forward, not backwards. The robber is chased by the policeman who ruins the cake so they bake another which causes smoke so they open the window which lets the cat in who is chased by the dog who knocks over the sugar bag and gets all sticky so they bathe him in lots of suds.

Elizabeth interrupted. "And when the robber fell, he hit his head on Alan's head. And you know how hard Alan's head is."

"I know. I know," Mother said. "Let me see now. The robber ran into here and the police officer chased him. They ruined the cake. When you baked a new one you made the oven smokey. Then you opened the window to let the smoke out and the cat came in. Popsicle chased the cat and knocked the sack of sugar on himself. And that's when you bathed him with too many suds?"

142   Unit 2

"That's right," the three children said together. "And that's when you came home."

"Twenty minutes at the most," Mother said. "I *know* I couldn't have been gone more than twenty minutes, anyway."

"We *told* you nothing much happened today," Stephen said. "How was your day?"

"Nothing much," Mother said, sliding further back into the chair. "Nothing much." The last soap bubble floated gently to the end of her nose where it rested, then popped, and was gone.

About the Author

An only child, **Mary Blount Christian** would tell stories to herself and her imaginary friends and make plays for the neighborhood children. She would roller skate to the library and read her way through the shelves, starting with the As. As an adult, Mrs. Christian has worked as a reporter, writer, and writing teacher for children, college students, and adults. Mrs. Christian has written over 80 children's books. She starts with real experiences and then mixes them with her imagination to create a story. Some of her books have even been translated into Japanese!

Nothing Much Happened Today   143

Literary Components

7 **The Language Comes Full Circle:** Stephen's line at the end echoes his line at the beginning. It reinforces his character, the story's theme, and the story's humorous premise.

Guiding the Reading

Literal

Q: How long did it take for all this to happen?
A: It took no more than twenty minutes.

Analytical

Q: Do you think the mother calmed down at the end of the story?
A: The mother probably did, especially since her kids were so nice and reasonable!

Nothing Much Happened Today

I Am Running in a Circle

Poem tie-in for

Nothing Much Happened Today

This poem is just for fun. But then, isn't running around inside a revolving door just for fun, too?

Here are some questions you can use to discuss *I Am Running in a Circle*.

Q: Do you like revolving doors?

Q: Have you ever felt "trapped" in a revolving door?

Q: Have you ever wondered why stores have revolving doors?

A: Our guess is that revolving doors allow less cold air into the building. They also control the flow of traffic in and out of the building.

Q: Listen to the rhythm. (Teacher: Read the poem with an emphasis on the rhythm.) What feeling does the rhythm give you?

A: The rhythm helps you feel you are spinning out of control. It seems to go faster and faster when the words are cut in half at the end.

I Am Running in a Circle
Jack Prelutsky

I am running in a circle
and my feet are getting sore,
and my head is
spinning
spinning
as it's never spun before,
I am
dizzy
dizzy
dizzy.
Oh! I cannot bear much more,
I am trapped in a revolving
. . . volving
. . . volving
. . . volving door!

Studying the Selection

FIRST IMPRESSIONS

Stephen provided the name for this story. What do you think Mother would have named it?

QUICK REVIEW

1. Where was Mrs. Maeberry when she first noticed the soap bubbles?
2. Why did they have to bathe the dog?
3. What happened to Mother's cake for the bake sale?
4. How long had Mother been gone?

FOCUS

5. How does the title of the story tell us something about Stephen's personality?
6. Draw a small chart on your paper with two columns and three rows. Label one column *cause* and one column *effect*. Under the column labeled *cause*, list three events. Write the effect for each cause on the row next to it in the *effect* column. Here is an example of a cause and its effect:

   cause: the children bathe the dog in soap
   effect: the soap suds make millions of bubbles

CREATING AND WRITING

7. Write two paragraphs about a chain reaction. Use one of the following topic sentences for your beginning:

   The waiter, who was holding a tray of drinks, heard a cry.

   The lights went out in the crowded room.

   Right where the horse was standing, someone set off a firecracker.

8. This story would make a good picture book. Your teacher will divide the class into groups and provide each group with arts and crafts materials. Each group will be assigned to draw one part of the story. Your group will draw a picture of the part assigned to you and write a description of what is happening in the picture at the bottom of the paper. When the groups have completed their pages, your teacher will collect them and bind them into a book.

Focus

5. The title is understated and calm. Stephen does not get excited or upset easily. We see that as he describes the events he is cool, calm, and collected.

6. Any three of the following can be used:

Cause	Effect
The robber	the policeman chases him
The police	ruins the cake
The ruined cake	they must bake a new cake
The new cake	makes the oven smoke
The smoke	makes them open a window
The open window	lets the cat in
The cat	is a magnet for the dog
The dog	knocks over the sugar bag
The sugar bag	gets on the dog causing him to need a bath
The bath	produces millions of bubbles

Creating and Writing

7. It will help your students to write an outline of their plot before beginning. Have them use a piece of scratch paper to list the chain of events they plan to write about. Then, tell them to write out the story in complete sentences.

8. It will be best to divide the class into eight groups. If this is not possible make adjustments accordingly. Give each group one of the following pictures to draw:

   - The robber running into the house
   - The policeman chasing the robber around the table
   - The policeman knocking over the cake
   - The oven smoking
   - The cat jumping through the open window
   - The dog chasing the cat
   - The sack of sugar falling on the dog
   - The bubbles coming out of the tub and through the door

   Collect the pictures and bind them with yarn or by putting them in a binder. If you have enough students, ask one or two to work on a cover for the book.

Studying the Selection

First Impressions

The mother in the story was overwhelmed by the events. She certainly would not have said nothing much happened. She would have used a title like, "How To Wreck a House in Twenty Minutes." Encourage your students to think creatively.

Quick Review

1. Mrs. Maeberry was on her way home from the grocery store.
2. The dog was covered with sugar.
3. It was ruined when the policeman knocked it over.
4. She had been gone for twenty minutes.

Food's on the Table

Lesson in Literature

How Is Setting for a Drama Different?
The Driving Test

1. The kitchen is the most important setting.

2. The letter from the BMV is the most important prop. A doll to represent the baby is the second most important prop. Any kitchen-related items—a mixer, a broom, a cookie jar—would help create the "kitchen" feeling.

3. The setting for Scene Two is the Bureau of Motor Vehicles. It would need a counter with some computers or telephones and a few chairs.

Selection Summary

The scene opens on a street in New York. The year is around 1940 and the streets are quiet and friendly. A group of children, five sisters and a brother, are walking along, looking for an address. They meet their teacher, who inquires why they are on the street at suppertime. They tell her that they've been invited to the new apartment of their aunt and uncle for supper.

They continue on and enter the apartment building they're looking for. They note that the apartment is on the third floor and walk up three flights of stairs. When they knock at the door of the apartment, they discover that no one is home, but the door has been left unlocked. Upon entering, they see a table set for three. On it is a note saying that the writer had to go out to do some shopping but to go ahead and eat without her. The children are not sure whether to eat or not, but are very hungry. They wonder why there are only three place settings, why there doesn't seem to be much food, and why they don't recognize the chairs and dishes. They come up with possible explanations for each of these anomalies and, being very hungry, decide to eat.

Midway through their meal, a woman, Mrs. Shiner, walks in and asks them why they are in her apartment! It turns out that they have walked up one extra flight of steps and are on the fourth floor, not the third. Chagrined and apologetic, the children don't know what to say. The children's Aunt Lena and Mama walk into the apartment in search of their lost brood. When they see that the children have eaten the Shiner family's entire supper, they join the children in their embarrassed apologies. Lena begins to laugh at the mishap and is joined by Mrs. Shiner. Lena tells Mama to see the humor in the situation and invites one and all to her apartment for supper.

T146   Unit 2

Lesson in Literature ...
THE DRIVING TEST

HOW IS SETTING FOR A DRAMA DIFFERENT?

- On a stage the setting is limited to whatever props and scenery are available.
- Often, one or two props will be used to suggest an entire setting. For example, a little sand and an artificial palm tree could be used to suggest a desert.
- Costumes and lighting are very helpful in creating a setting.
- Even background music helps create a setting.

THINK ABOUT IT!

1. In the stage directions for Scene One, several settings are mentioned. Outside the house, the living room, and the kitchen are all listed. If you were performing this play, which room would be the most important one to choose for your setting?

2. Props are a part of setting. List three props that are needed to set the stage for Scene One.

3. What is the setting for Scene Two?

Characters

JESSICA GREEN (age 14)	JILL GREEN (age 8)	THE BABY
JEFF GREEN (age 15)	BOBBY and SAM GREEN	BMV EMPLOYEE
JANET GREEN (their	(twins, age 6)	DAVID GREEN (their dad)
mom, just turned 45)		

Scene One

The home of the Greens. All of the children, except the baby, have just gotten home from school. As usual, Jessica gets the day's mail out of the mailbox as she walks into the house. Jeff is standing in the living room and hangs up his jacket on one of the hooks on the coat rack. As usual, Bobby and Sam drop their jackets on the floor and run into the kitchen for their snack. Jill shouts to them to pick them up. Mom sits at the kitchen table holding the baby.

JESSICA (*looking through the mail*): Hey, everybody! I got a notification from the Bureau of Motor Vehicles that it's time for me to register for my driver's test.

JEFF: That can't be for you. I'm the one who's older. Let me see it. (*He reaches out and grabs the letter out of her hand and pokes her.*)

JESSICA: Mom! It says *J. Green*.

MOM: That was very rude, Jeff. But he's probably right, Jessica. He *is* older. It just can't be helped, my dear. He *did* get here first!

JILL: Well, I guess it couldn't be for *me*. I'm too young! But Jessica, Jeff's name also begins with *J*.

146   Unit 2

Getting Started

Although this play is not a mystery, it has some of the elements of a mystery. It has clues that can be interpreted in more than one way. It has a surprise solution which reveals the true meaning of the clues. And it has a satisfying resolution. Like a mystery, the plot of this play depends on the audience and the characters misinterpreting clues. The author purposely plants ambiguous details so that they can be interpreted in more than one way. To drive this point home, we have written a scenario laden with ambiguous clues.

Read the paragraph below to your students and ask them to interpret the clues. The story is left open-ended. In question #7 of *Studying the Selection*, your students are asked to interpret the clues and write a conclusion to the story. Before they do this, reread the paragraph to them.

As they moved along the street, they heard a low rumbling sound. They turned around to see what was making it, but couldn't see anything. The day was foggy and it was hard to see. They shivered a little and

Target Skill:	Make and confirm predictions
Learning Strategy:	Questioning
Common Core Curriculum:	RL.3.3; RL.3.5
Genre:	Play

Related Vocabulary

dismayed (diss MAYD) *n.*: unhappily surprised	
dreadful (DRED ful) *adj.*: awful; terrible	
frankly (FRANK lee) *adv.*: truthfully and openly	
mystified (MISS tih fide) *v.*: puzzled	
outcome (OUT kum) *n.*: the way something turns out	
sibling (SIB ling) *n.*: a brother or sister	
stunned (STUND) *v.*: greatly surprised; shocked	
surveyed (sur VADE) *v.*: looked over in a general way	

Workbook

| Related Pages: | 50-55 |
| Answer Key Page: | 7 |

JESSICA: Yes, I know. (*She rolls her eyes and looks annoyed.*)

BOBBY: Maybe it's for *us*, me and Sammy. We may be young, but everybody thinks we're cute.

JEFF: Can't be for you two, they don't let you drive just because you're cute, and anyway your names don't begin with J.

Scene Two

The next day. At the Bureau of Motor Vehicles. After lots of begging and pleading in the morning with their dad, the children have been given permission to leave school early to go to the BMV to solve the mystery. Which J. Green was the letter for? The line for inquiries is very long. Everyone is growing impatient. Mom even let Jill, Bobby, and Sam come, because they didn't want to be left out. Even Dad shows up. Finally, the eight Greens are at the front of the line.

BMV EMPLOYEE: Next!

(*The Greens step up to the counter.*)

BMV EMPLOYEE: Are all of you here on one matter or let's see, 1-2-3-4-5-6-7 matters? Oops! I didn't count the baby! (*She laughs.*)

THE GREENS (*in one voice*): One matter!

BMV EMPLOYEE: Okay, what's this about?

DAD: Well, we received this notification, but it's not clear whom it's for. It is addressed to *J. Green*. Well, my wife is Janet, my oldest son is Jeff, and my older daughter is Jessica.

BMV EMPLOYEE: Golly, you *all* came in for *that*?

MOM: All the children were very excited about this. How could we leave them home? Besides, it was a family matter.

BMV EMPLOYEE: Let me see. (*She takes the postcard from Dad and types some information into her computer.*)

MOM (*sighing*): Well, I hope it's not for *me*. You know, maybe at 45 they make you take the tests all over again.

JESSICA: Oh Mom, don't be silly. You're not old. (*Jessica gives Mom a hug.*)

BABY: Wahh-hhh-hhh.

MOM: Time for me to change the little one!

JEFF (*he elbows his sister, Jessica*): You'll see. Of course it's for me.

JESSICA: Mom! Dad! Will you make him stop poking me?!

MOM: Jeff, this has got to stop!

JEFF: I didn't mean to be mean. Sorry.

BMV EMPLOYEE: Hey, anyone here named Julie Green?

THE GREENS (*in one voice*): Julie Green?!

BMV EMPLOYEE: Yeah. You got it. She's the one that's supposed to register for her test.

THE GREENS (*again, in one voice*): But Julie is just a baby!

JESSICA: Mom, show her Julie!

MOM (*holds out the baby, who is sound asleep*): This is the person to whom you sent the notice of registration.

BMV EMPLOYEE: Oh, wow. I'm so sorry for the mistake. And I'm sorry that you Greens had to suffer all of this red tape!

hurried along. Behind them, a bright light went on, creating a little pool of brightness in the fog. A siren began to wail. They moved faster. As they passed a doorway, a gust of warm air escaped and they smelled something. They paused, unsure of what to do next. Suddenly, they heard a voice calling to them.

Here are some questions to ask your class after you have read the paragraph to them. We have provided you with some possible answers, although your students may come up with better ones!

Who are they?

They may be children, adults, dogs, people in cars, aliens.

What is the low rumbling sound?

It could be thunder, a herd of elephants, a truck, a wheelbarrow.

What was the light?

It could be a car's headlights, a lighthouse, a lamp in a window, a searchlight.

Why was the siren wailing?

A police car was chasing a speeding car, a fire engine was racing to a fire, an ambulance was on the way to the hospital, the city was testing its sirens.

What was the warm air coming from?

It may have been coming from a bakery, a hothouse, an overheated apartment, a car's motor, a bear breathing heavily.

What was the smell?

They may have smelled bread baking, the flowers in the hothouse, cooking from the apartment, the gasoline fumes of the car, the bear's breath.

Whose voice was it, and what did it say?

It was the voice of: a policeman, fireman, dog barking at them, their friend asking where they'd been, park ranger …

Food's on the Table

In short, this story could be about some children passing a bakery on a rainy day, with the happy ending of everyone getting free doughnuts, or a frightening tale of some hunters running through the dark woods being chased by a bear—or any number of other funny, serious, or scary plots.

What have we learned from this exercise? We see that details alone do not tell the whole story. Even a "fact" can be interpreted in more than one way. To properly understand a situation, we must see a whole series of facts in context. Tell your students that to judge a situation, we need to gather as much information as possible. Sometimes, as in the story, the last piece of information will change the meaning of all the other facts. A good detective does not jump to conclusions!

Into . . . *Food's on the Table*

This play is a warm, friendly play adapted from the very popular book, *All-of-a-Kind Family*. In this particular story, the children make a mistake that leads to an uncomfortable situation. Thanks to the good nature of the parties involved, the discomfort is dispersed by a hearty laugh, and all ends well. Although, as we pointed out in the Student Edition, this is not a scary mystery, it does have some of the elements of a mystery. There are clues that point in one direction and there are misinterpretations made by the characters. Just like in a mystery, once the truth is revealed, the characters wonder how they could have missed the true meaning of the clues.

As you read and discuss the play, focus on two things. The first is "mistakes and mishaps." Everyone enjoys recounting funny mistakes that they have made and the embarrassing situations those mistakes put them in. The students will enjoy sharing some of those stories. Point out that in many cases, it is the person's attitude that can determine whether something will become a funny experience or an aggravating one. If everyone in this play had taken a scolding, resentful attitude, it would not have been a very enjoyable story. The second thing you can focus on is "clues." It is interesting how people make the facts "fit" their preconceived notions. Because the children were sure this was their aunt's apartment, they invented all kinds of reasons to explain things that were "wrong." Ask your students if they do this sometimes! A good detective would have looked at the reality and sensed that a mistake had been made. This is called being objective; it is a habit worth cultivating.

Blueprint for Reading

INTO . . . *Food's on the Table*

Six children are looking for an apartment on a lonely street. They arrive and knock on the door. No one is home, so they walk right in. The house is mysteriously empty. Things are not as they expected them to be. Why have their aunt and uncle disappeared? Suddenly, the door opens and ...

Does this sound like a scary mystery? Well, it could have been one, but as it happens, it's a play about some children who make a "delicious" mistake! As you read *Food's on the Table*, ask yourself how you would feel if you were in their shoes.

EYES ON *Drama*

Watching a play is different from reading a book in a number of ways. One way is that instead of having to imagine what the people, places, and objects in the story look like, we see them with our own eyes. Instead of having to imagine how the people in the story sound when they speak, we hear them with our own ears.

When the curtain rises on a play, the first thing the audience sees is the setting of the play. We look at the scenery and we begin to question. Is the setting inside a house? Is the house old-fashioned or modern? Based on what we see on the stage, we make predictions. If the stage is set to look like a palace, we may predict that the play is going to be about royal people in a foreign country. As we watch, we will find out if our predictions are right.

In *Food's on the Table*, the curtains open on a street in old New York, with six children walking along, looking for an address. Although we don't know enough to make many predictions, the setting tells us that we are in a neighborhood where friendly people live. As you read the play, see if this prediction proves to be true.

148 Unit 2

Eyes On: Drama

The literary element to be focused on in this selection is setting and how it influences plot. A play lends itself to the study of setting because setting is such a vital part of every play. Whereas in a book, the author can focus on a character's thoughts or personality in a way that is independent of setting, in a play, everything takes place on stage, within a setting. Before a word is spoken on stage, a message has been given to the audience via the setting. If music is part of the setting, an even stronger message is sent, depending on whether the music is happy or sad, fast, or slow, modern or classical. As the audience receives these messages, they make predictions about what the play will be about. The moment a character appears on stage, the audience predicts whether this character will be likeable or not, serious or funny, and so on. As the play unfolds, the audience adjusts its viewpoint and judgments. Sometimes, everything turns out as predicted. Other times—and who doesn't like surprises?—the audience find that they have been utterly

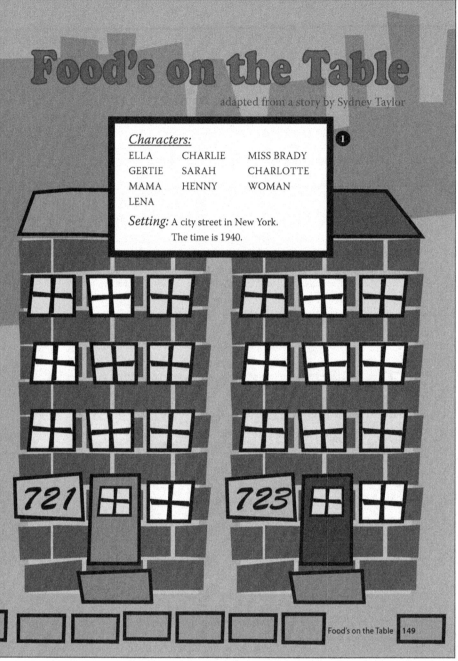

Food's on the Table

adapted from a story by Sydney Taylor

Characters:

ELLA	CHARLIE	MISS BRADY
GERTIE	SARAH	CHARLOTTE
MAMA	HENNY	WOMAN
LENA		

Setting: A city street in New York.
The time is 1940.

721   723

Food's on the Table 149

Literary Components

1 **Cast of Characters:** At the beginning of every play you will find a cast of characters that introduces you to every character in the play. As you read you will learn that all the children in the play are siblings.

wrong in their predictions, and that for example, that bumbling waiter was actually a daring fighter pilot!

The learning strategy your students will use as they read this play is *making predictions*, which is achieved by *questioning*. As we read (or watch) the play, we notice things and ask silent questions. Why is no one home in the apartment? Why is the table set only for three? Why don't the children recognize the chairs? Why is there only a little food when their aunt is known for serving lavishly? Having asked the questions, we make predictions, which is to say, we think of possible answers to our questions. We watch the play and see if our answers prove to be true. Authors who like surprise endings depend on the fact that audiences make predictions. If we didn't, the endings would fall flat. Good audiences, on the other hand, try to outwit the writer by figuring out which clues have been put there to mislead them. It's all part of the fun!

Food's on the Table

Literary Components

❷ **Exposition:** The storyline is introduced. Five sisters and their brother are invited to their aunt and uncle's new apartment for supper.

Guiding the Reading

Literal

Q: As the play opens, what are the children doing?

A: They are walking along the street, looking for an address.

Q: Who do they see walking along?

A: They see Miss Brady, Sarah's teacher.

Q: What time of day is it?

A: It's almost suppertime.

Q: Why are the children walking along the street at suppertime?

A: They are on their way to their aunt and uncle's apartment for supper.

Q: How many children are in the family?

A: There are five sisters and one brother.

Analytical

Q: How can you tell that the children are looking for an apartment building, not a house?

A: Charlotte says, "What is the number of their building again?"

As Curtain Rises: Children are walking along the street looking for their aunt's apartment.

ELLA: This is the school block, so the house can't be on this one.

CHARLOTTE: What is the number of their building again?

ELLA (*glancing at a slip of paper*): 725. It must be the next block.

(*At right an older woman appears.*)

SARAH: Look! There's my teacher, Miss Brady. It's almost suppertime, and she's just getting out of school.

GERTIE: I thought teachers were only supposed to work till three o'clock.

ELLA: Sometimes there are special things they have to do.

MISS BRADY: Hello, Sarah. What brings you here at this hour?

SARAH (*shyly*): Hello, Miss Brady. Our aunt and uncle just moved to the next block.

❷ They want us to see their new apartment, <u>so they invited us for supper.</u>

MISS BRADY: I didn't know you had so many sisters and brothers, Sarah.

SARAH (*grinning*): No, only one brother—little Charlie here. But we're five sisters. This is my oldest sister, Ella. She'll be graduating from high school next year, same time

150   Unit 2

as I graduate from here. Next comes Henny, then me, then Charlotte, and this is Gertie.

MISS BRADY: Quite a family. Are you all as good in history as Sarah?

HENNY: Not me! That's one subject I don't like.

MISS BRADY: Well, this is what I tell my class about that. "You don't like it because you won't like it, and you won't like it because you don't like it." Well, I won't keep you. Good-by and keep studying. (*exits*)

HENNY: History—ugh! Names and places and dates to remember. It's so boring.

SARAH: Oh, but it's not! Not the way Miss Brady teaches anyway. She makes you wish you lived in the olden days.

ELLA: Let's see. 721—723. Here it is—725. It's a nice-looking building. (*glances at paper*) Third floor, apartment 4.

GERTIE: Shouldn't we ring the buzzer?

ELLA: It's out of order. Lena said to go right up.

(*The children climb several flights of stairs and come to apartment number 4.*)

HENNY (*knocking*): There's no answer.

Food's on the Table **151**

Guiding the Reading

Literal

Q: What subject is Sarah good at that Henny is bad at?

A: Sarah is good at history, which Henny dislikes.

Q: Does Miss Brady make history boring?

A: No. She makes you wish you lived in the olden days.

Q: Why don't the girls ring the buzzer?

A: The buzzer is out of order.

Q: What happens when Henny knocks on the door?

A: There is no answer.

Analytical

Q: What does Miss Brady mean when she says, "You don't like it because you won't like it, and you won't like it because you don't like it"?

A: She means that the reason students may not like a certain subject is because they have decided beforehand that they won't like that subject. Once they have decided they won't like it, they don't work at it or let themselves get interested in it. The result is that they don't like it because they don't understand it. (Or vice versa, if they would come to the subject with an open mind, they would find it interesting and work at it. The more they worked at it, the more they would like it.)

Q: Can you give an example of something you didn't like because you decided ahead of time you wouldn't like it?

A: Answers will vary. Some people don't like certain foods because they refuse to even try them. Some people look at a math problem and say, "this is too confusing for me" so it remains confusing for them.

Food's on the Table

Literary Components

❸ Rising Action: This is the first "strange" thing noticed by the children.

❹ Characterization: These are well-behaved children. They have been taught good manners and try to use them.

❺ Foreshadowing: There are only three place settings. Does that mean anything?

Guiding the Reading

Literal

Q: What do the children do when there is no answer at the door?

A: They walk right in.

Q: What do they see on the table?

A: They see corned beef, potato salad, coleslaw, and a note.

Q: What does the note say?

A: It says that the writer went shopping and that they should go ahead and eat.

Q: How many settings were at the table?

A: The table is set for three.

Q: What do the children notice about the dishes and the chairs?

A: They are of good quality.

Q: What does Charlie want to do?

A: He wants to eat.

Analytical

Q: Why do you think only three places were set?

A: Answers will vary.

Q: Do you think the children should wait for Lena to come home before they eat?

A: Answers will vary. There is the note that says not to wait, but perhaps they should wait anyway.

Q: What makes them think that Uncle Hyman is doing well?

A: Since they don't recognize the dishes or the chairs, they assume they are new. In those days, new things were quite expensive, so the girls assume Uncle Hyman is doing well if he can afford to buy them.

❸ ELLA: <u>That's strange.</u> Aunt Lena is expecting us. (*turns doorknob*) Oh, the door is open.

HENNY: She must want us to come right in.

GERTIE: Maybe she's in the bedroom.

ELLA: Lena, Lena. We're here. Lena, Lena?

CHARLOTTE: Is anybody home?

HENNY: Well, anyway, the food's on the table. Mmmm. Homemade corned beef.

GERTIE: And potato salad! And cole slaw! Lena sure knows what we like.

SARAH: Look. She left a note on the table. (*Picking up note, she reads aloud.*) "I had to do some shopping. I'll be a little late. Don't wait for me. Go ahead and eat."

HENNY: Well, that's that. Let's eat.

❹ ELLA: <u>I don't think that would be polite. Let's wait a little while.</u>

SARAH: We could set the table in the meantime. Lena was in an awful hurry.

❺ <u>No plates—just three settings of silverware.</u>

HENNY (*opening door to cupboard*): Pretty dishes. Lena must have gotten a new set.

CHARLOTTE: And these kitchen chairs—they are pretty, too.

ELLA: Uncle Hyman must be doing well.

GERTIE: I'm glad Lena has moved near to us. Now we'll be able to see her more often.

CHARLIE: I'm hungry. I want to eat! ⑥

ELLA: We have to wait till Lena gets here, Charlie.

CHARLIE: But I'm hungry now.

HENNY: We're all hungry, Charlie. Can't you wait a little longer?

CHARLIE: I'm hunnnngry.

CHARLOTTE: So am I. Couldn't we at least get started? She said to in the note.

ELLA: Well, OK, but there isn't too much dinner, so let's be careful. (*Ella begins* ⑦ *to spoon out salad. Children begin to eat.*)

CHARLOTTE: Maybe Lena's not used to cooking for a big mob like us. There are only the two of them.

ELLA: That's true, but you know how they are about food. Usually their table groans with all the food they serve.

CHARLIE: I want another corned beef sandwich.

SARAH: It's a lucky thing corned beef comes in one big piece, or we wouldn't have enough of that, either.

ELLA: Well, take it easy. There's hardly anything left.

Literary Components

⑥ **Characterization:** Charlie is a little boy and, though he is well-behaved, he's not an angel!

⑦ **Foreshadowing:** Again, we have little hints and clues that something is not as it should be.

Guiding the Reading

Literal

Q: What does Ella notice about the amount of food available?

A: She says there's not too much food.

Q: How does Charlotte explain the small amount of food being served?

A: She thinks Lena is not used to cooking for such a lot of people.

Q: How much does she usually serve?

A: She usually has a lot of food for everyone.

Food's on the Table

Literary Components

8 **Suspense:** Suddenly, everything is unclear. Who is this lady? Why is she here?

9 **Humor:** For anyone who has guessed what is happening, the lady's understated comment is humorous.

10 **Humor:** Again, as the audience begins to realize what has happened, they find Ella's question humorous.

11 **Turning Point:** The woman has revealed that the supper—and apartment—are hers. It takes a little longer for the children to absorb this.

12 **Explanation:** The children and the audience are given the explanation for the mistake.

13 **Rising Tension:** We don't know how the woman will react. The children are mortified.

14 **Release of Tension:** We are relieved to see that the woman is good-natured and unflappable.

Guiding the Reading

Literal

Q: What does Ella say to the woman who walks in?
A: She tells her that her aunt isn't home.

Q: What does the lady say?
A: She asks the children who they are.

Q: What does the woman say when she sees that the food has all been eaten?
A: She says that the food was meant for her husband, her son, and herself.

Q: What surprising thing does she tell them, then?
A: She says that they are in her apartment.

Q: What mistake had the children made?
A: They thought they were on the third floor but they were really on the fourth floor.

Q: How did they make a mistake like that?
A: They thought you needed to walk up three flights to reach the third floor, but that's wrong. You count the floor on which you walked into the building as the first floor, then you walk up one flight, you've reached the second floor, and walk up another flight, and you've reached the third floor.

Q: What does Ella do when her mistake is explained?
A: She apologizes.

(Suddenly a woman comes in the door carrying a pile of boxes and bags. The children all turn and stare at the stranger.)

ELLA *(politely)*: My aunt isn't here yet.
WOMAN *(puzzled)*: You're expecting your aunt?
HENNY: Yes. Don't go away. She'll be here any minute. Let me help you with the packages.

8 WOMAN: Thank you, but ... *(sets down packages)* Now tell me, who are you, anyway?
ELLA: We're the nieces and this is the nephew, Charlie.

9 WOMAN: That's nice. I'm glad to meet you. *(Looking down at table, a look of dismay crosses her face.)* Oh my goodness! I see you ate up the whole supper!

10 ELLA: I'm awfully sorry. Were you invited, too?

11 WOMAN: Who's invited? The supper was for my husband and son.
HENNY: Good gracious. How many people were supposed to eat here tonight?
WOMAN: You don't understand. The supper was just for the three of us—my husband, my son, and me. After all, this *is* my apartment. *(a moment of stunned silence)*
ELLA *(shakily)*: Your apartment! This is your apartment?
WOMAN: Yes, darling.
SARAH: But isn't this apartment 4?
WOMAN: Yes.
ELLA: And isn't this the third floor?
WOMAN: No. The third floor is downstairs underneath my apartment. This is the fourth floor.
ELLA *(confused)*: But how could that be? We walked up three flights of stairs.

12 WOMAN *(nodding head)*: Oh, I see. You didn't realize that the ground floor is called the first floor. You should have walked up only two flights.

13 ELLA *(blushing)*: What a dreadful mistake. I'm terribly sorry. We thought we were in our aunt's apartment—then we read the note, and ...

14 WOMAN *(chuckling)*: Well, what's done is done. Don't worry. A mistake can happen.
HENNY: But we ate up all your food!
WOMAN *(laughing)*: Well, as long as you enjoyed it.
(The children begin to inch their way toward the door.)
SARAH: We just didn't know—
ELLA: We feel awful about it. And you've been so kind about it.

154   Unit 2

Q: What does the woman say?
A: She says that a mistake can happen and what's done is done.

Analytical

Q: Were you surprised that a woman just walked right in?
A: Answers will vary. (Some of the students will call out that they have guessed who she is, but caution them that we really don't know yet.)

Q: Were you surprised to hear that this was not the aunt's apartment, or had you guessed it? What were the clues?
A: There were lots of clues: No one was home, there were only three settings, there was not enough food, and they didn't recognize the dishes or furniture.

Q: Do you think the woman is nice?
A: The woman seems very kind. She has not screamed or fainted or pointed an accusing finger at the children. She has been polite to them and called Ella "darling."

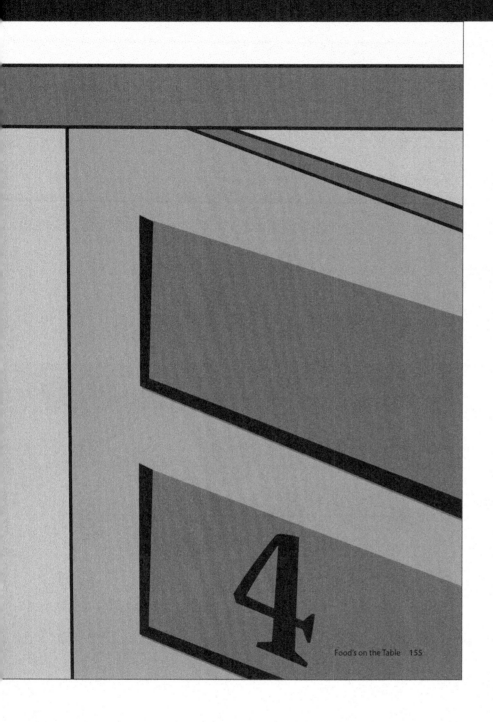

Food's on the Table

Literary Components

15 **Rising Tension:** The situation gets tense again as Mama arrives on the scene.

Guiding the Reading

Literal

Q: Who appear at the door?

A: Mother and Aunt Lena appear at the door, looking for the children.

Q: What questions does Mama ask the children?

A: She asks them what happened to their manners.

Analytical

Q: Do you think the children did anything wrong?

A: Not really. But if they had followed their best instincts, which were to wait for the host before they started, they would not have eaten up the family's dinner.

(*Mother and Aunt Lena appear at door.*)

15 MAMA (*demandingly*): What's the matter? <u>Where have you been?</u>

LENA: I was ready to call the police station. I kept opening the door to see if you were coming. Then we heard the voices and we came upstairs to see. <u>What are you doing here?</u>

ELLA: Oh, Mama.

HENNY: We made a mistake.

CHARLOTTE: We thought this was Lena's apartment.

CHARLIE: We ate the corned beef.

MAMA: One at a time. Ella, what happened?

ELLA (*embarrassed*): I know it sounds dreadful, but we went into this lady's apartment and ate her whole supper.

GERTIE: The whole supper. It was supposed to be for her husband and her son.

MAMA: How could you do such a thing? What happened to your manners? How could you sit down and eat with nobody there?

Dinner at our neighbor's house. <u>Downstairs.</u> Apartment 4!

CHARLOTTE: The note said we should.

MAMA: I must apologize for my children. They never did anything like this before.

WOMAN: Don't take it to heart. So they ate a supper in my house. What's wrong with that? <u>Believe me, it was a pleasure to see so many nice young</u> <u>faces around my table.</u>

MAMA: It was very wrong of them. They had no right—

LENA (*placing hand on mama's arm and laughing loudly*): Oh, you children. You ate up the lady's supper. Oh, Mama, they ate up the whole supper. Don't you see how funny it is? Oh! Oh! Oh!

(*Everyone begins to laugh.*)

WOMAN (*laughing*): Next—time— (*laughter*) next time—children, let me know—when you're coming—so I'll prepare enough.

LENA: Well, neighbor, what is your name?

WOMAN: It's Mrs. Shiner. Molly Shiner.

LENA: This certainly is a comical way for us to meet. Listen, Mrs. Shiner. I have plenty of food downstairs. Enough for twenty people! Leave another note on your table for your husband and son, and come downstairs with us. <u>Everyone is invited for supper!</u>

About the Author

Sydney Taylor grew up in a Jewish family in a crowded apartment on the Lower East Side of New York. Mrs. Taylor would tell her daughter, Joanne, bedtime stories about her fond memories sharing a small bedroom with four sisters. Mrs. Taylor wrote these stories down for her daughter, and as a surprise, her husband submitted them to a contest. The publishers running the contest liked Mrs. Taylor's book so much that they wanted to publish it! Children loved *All-of-a-Kind Family*, and its publication began Mrs. Taylor's writing career.

Literary Components

16 **Characterization:** Mrs. Shiner is a warm, good-natured, generous person.

17 **Resolution:** The good humor of Mrs. Shiner and Lena save the day.

Guiding the Reading

Literal

Q: Is the lady angry that the children ate up her supper?

A: No. She says it was a pleasure to see so many young faces at her table.

Q: What is the neighbor's name?

A: Her name is Mrs. Shiner.

Q: How does Lena solve the problem that has been created by the children?

A: She invites all the Shiners to her house for supper.

Analytical

Q: What had the children said about Lena that we now see was true?

A: They'd said that she always prepared a huge meal for her guests.

Analytical

Q: Do you think Mama forgave the children?

A: She probably did. She probably laughed about the story later on.

Food's on the Table

Breakfast

Poem tie-in for *Food's on the Table*

For the "texting" generation, this poem may not seem as unusual as it once did, but it is still a bit of a challenge to decipher. It's another of those "just for fun" poems and it would certainly be fun for your students to compose one of their own! You can help them by giving them a list of three or four topics to choose from, such as lunch, homework, or baseball, or any other simple topic.

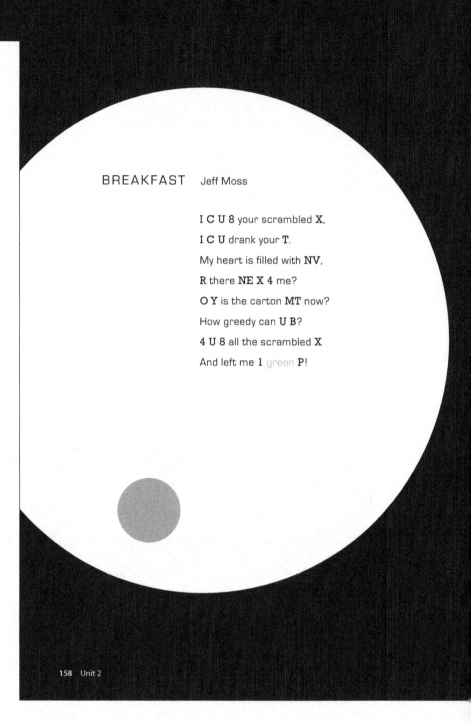

BREAKFAST   Jeff Moss

I C U 8 your scrambled **X**,

I C U drank your **T**.

My heart is filled with **NV**,

R there **NE X 4** me?

O Y is the carton **MT** now?

How greedy can **U B**?

4 U 8 all the scrambled **X**

And left me **1** green **P**!

158   Unit 2

Studying the Selection

Studying the Selection

QUICK REVIEW

1. For what were the children searching?
2. Why had they been invited to their aunt's and uncle's apartment?
3. What made them think the supper was for them?
4. What did Aunt Lena do at the end to make everyone feel good?

FOCUS

5. The children thought they were on the third floor, but they were on the fourth. Explain how they made this mistake.
6. There were a number of clues that told the children they were in the wrong apartment. What were three of those clues?

CREATING AND WRITING

7. In *Food's on the Table*, there are "facts" that could mean one thing, but really mean another. Your teacher is now going to read a story to you. The meaning of the story is not clear because the details can be explained in more than one way. Write a paragraph that gives your explanation of the story and makes everything clear. Then, since the story stops in the middle, write a good ending for it.
8. This play is about a family of children who make a big mistake. Your teacher will divide the class into groups. Each group will make a short play based on a mistake someone has made and present it to the class. Curtains up!

FIRST IMPRESSIONS

Have you ever had the feeling that something was not quite right, but couldn't figure out what it was?

First Impressions

Encourage the children to share their experiences. Make sure they explain why they thought something wasn't "right" and what the explanation was. Always come prepared with your own story, just in case the children don't have anything to contribute.

Quick Review

1. The children were searching for the apartment of their uncle and aunt.
2. They had been invited for supper.
3. They saw a note that said, "Don't wait for me. Go ahead and eat."
4. Aunt Lena invited everyone for supper.

Focus

5. They did not count the ground floor as floor one. They went up three flights of steps instead of two.
6. The clues were: no one was home; the table was only set for three; there wasn't enough food; they didn't recognize the chairs or dishes.

Creating and Writing

7. Reread the story fragment we provided in *Getting Started.* If you have not done so already, discuss how many possible interpretations lend themselves to the story. Have the students write one paragraph with their interpretation of the story and a second paragraph that gives a strong conclusion to the story.
8. Have each group spend a few minutes deciding on a plot. Ask one student in each group to write a little outline of the skit they are going to present. If you like, bring some props and costumes to lend some excitement to the skits. (One hat can make all the difference!) This exercise provides a lesson in creative writing, outlining, and speaking.

Across the Wide Dark Sea

Lesson in Literature

What Is the Main Idea?

Crossing America

1. The story's setting is the Overland Trail on which many Americans travelled westward to Oregon.

2. Some minor ideas in the story are:
   - Many women did not want to make the journey West.
   - The Indians were friendly and helpful.
   - Many men were suspicious of the Indians.
   - The women did a tremendous amount of the work along the trail.

3. The story is about the hardships of going West. Every detail and minor idea fit into that main one.

Selection Summary

This is the story of a young boy who is on a ship sailing for America. The members of his family are among the first colonists; when they reach the land it is almost uninhabited. The story is written in stark prose. Adding to the starkness of the story is the fact that no character is named, nor is the land they are going to referred to as "America." In the body of the story, we are presented with a universal tale of unnamed people leaving an unnamed country, seeking freedom of religion in an unnamed land at an unstated time. The one and only reason given for the group's journey to America is religious persecution.

The story is told from the point of view of the nameless boy who appears to be a solid, unemotional witness. Much of the story deals with the terrible journey over the ocean. The ship sets sail in the summer and arrives at its destination in the autumn. The crowding, storms, and illness that plague the passengers are horrific. When the ship finally reaches the new land, the passengers stay on the ship for weeks until the group of scouts they have sent ashore finds a suitable place to start their settlement. By the time the settlement is actually begun, half of the people have died! Winter comes as the houses are being built. More people sicken and die. At long last, there is a thaw in the weather. Hope is in the air, but it is mixed with trepidation, for signs of Indians have been sighted. But the settlers' anxiety turns out to have been for naught. The Indians are friendly and helpful.

Father and son work together to plant the fields. At home, the boy plants a garden of vegetables and herbs with seeds from the old country.

Lesson in Literature . . .
CROSSING AMERICA

WHAT IS THE MAIN IDEA?

- A story, play, poem, or an essay must all have a **main idea**.
- The less important (minor) ideas in the story should be connected to the main idea.
- In a well-written story, the characters, plot, and setting all contribute to the main idea.
- To discover the story's main idea, ask yourself: What is this story *about*?

THINK ABOUT IT!

1. The story's setting is very important to the main idea. What is the story's setting?

2. What are two less important ideas in the story that are linked to the main idea?

3. What is the main idea of this story?

We reached Vermillion Creek in the late afternoon and set up camp. There were the good smells of food cooking. Nothing special to eat but beans and bread and coffee, but it's nice to stop and rest and chat a little.

We are twenty wagons, and we are only at the beginning of our long journey. We just crossed the Missouri River. My Mama said we were seeing "the last of civilization." It has been hard to say goodbye to everything: my teacher, our fancy dresses, my best friend Emilia, and my pretty bedroom.

No one really knows what is ahead. We were told that when people first started crossing the Overland Trail they had bad maps. There were no settlers along the way to help them if they needed supplies. It is better now, Pa says, but it is hardly like living as we used to, in a city with shops and schools and neighbors. We sort of knew what to expect each day.

My Mama says that she, like many of the other women, really does not want to make this hard journey. She doesn't want to scare me, but she says it is important for me to know how difficult it will be. Yes, it will be an adventure. And if we all

The mother is comforted by the sight of new plants and expresses the belief that the settlers, too, will be able to strike roots in the new land. As the ship that brought these first settlers turns around and heads out to sea, leaving them with no means to return to their old lives, the narrator has a passing sense of regret and loneliness. But his father, firm and full of faith, turns him away from the sea to face the land, which is rich and green with the new plants. Together, father and son walk up the hill to their new home.

Getting Started

Read the story aloud until page 169 and the words, "And our ship sailed on." Then read the following questions to your students.

(For more information on how to use the aural exercises, see *Getting Started/The Story of the White Sombrero*.)

1. As the story opens, where is the narrator standing?
   a. On the shore of a wide dark sea   b. On a riverboat
   c. In a covered wagon, going West   **d. On a ship sailing across the ocean**

get there healthy, safe, and sound, and live in a good community, it will have been worth it. But I need to prepare myself to be very strong. Then she reminds me that I am only eight, and I'm still a young girl, so I can still come to her and complain!

Although the guidebooks say the trip takes three to four months, I know it is more like six to eight months. That means there will be some really bad weather. I know Mama will have a baby along the way. That will be very hard on her. I hope I can be a really big help to her.

Mama is not as afraid of the Indians as Pa is. She says that the Indians we have met were helpful. Pa calls them savages, even if they speak our language or are nice to us. Mama says they have made some good food trades with us, like those potatoes that we needed so badly. Pa just doesn't agree with that nice talk. Maybe he feels that way because getting along with Indians is new to him.

My Pa is a big man, tall and very strong, and stern. Actually, I don't call Pa, Pa. I call him Sir. He says no matter what, we have to get that free land in Oregon.

My Ma and all the other women and girls do all of the chores on the trail: They fix meals and sew; wash, dry, fold, and mend clothes; and care for the children. They figure out how to pack up the wagons. They drive the ox teams and collect buffalo chips as fuel for fires when there is no wood.

I don't know how the women and girls get it all done. The women on the trail also do all the caretaking of the sick or the injured or the dying. There have been times when epidemics of cholera have swept over the wagons of people going west. So far we have been spared.

We older children have been warned repeatedly that little children and even babies fall out of wagons. Children wander off and get lost. They can get lost with all the people, goats, and oxen milling around. Therefore, we are organizing teams to look out for the little ones.

Last night it poured. There was a huge rainstorm. Our wagons and tents were overturned. Mama, Pa, and I just tried to curl up and sleep. But all through the night we were wet, muddy, and cold. Today, the sun is shining and our clothes are drying out. On the road, we move through a forest that is so thick you almost can't see the sky. Pa says the trees are 300 feet high. Wow!

There's not a lot of time to write. Mama likes to write a little bit each day, too. I think it gives us a sense of security, when so much is happening that is new.

Target Skill:	Understanding the main idea and recounting details
Learning Strategy:	Inferring
Common Core Curriculum:	RL.3.1; RF.3.3
Genre:	Historical Fiction

Vocabulary

scarcely (SKAIRS lee) *adv.*: hardly
vast *adj.*: huge; covering a very great area
desperate (DESS prit) *adj.*: extremely needy
raging (RAY jing) *adj.*: angry and dangerous
miraculously (mih RAK yuh luss lee) *adv.*: as though through a miracle
hauling (HAWL ing) *v.*: pulling
plucked *v.*: pulled out with force
beams *n.*: thick, strong boards that go across the width of a ship
settlement (SET ul ment) *n.*: the beginnings of a town; a group of houses built in a new, unsettled area

Workbook

Related Pages:	56-61
Answer Key Pages:	7-8

2. What was the ship mainly used for?
   a. To carry people
   b. To carry cattle
   c. To carry guns
   d. To carry goods for trading

3. Why were the people going on this journey?
   a. To explore a new country.
   b. Fleeing a cruel king.
   c. To settle in a new land.
   d. Prove the world was round, not flat.

4. What were the conditions on the ship after the first few days?
   a. People were packed tight and it was cold and damp.
   b. The air was clear and the passengers felt strong and happy.
   c. Like being in a foreign country with strange food and language.
   d. It was exciting; most people wished they could become sailors.

5. How did the people react when the storm broke?
   a. They came on deck and helped the sailors fasten the sails.
   b. They ran below deck and howled in fear.
   c. They ran around throwing things overboard to lighten the ship.
   d. They cried and prayed and huddled together.

6. What was it like on the ship once the storm had passed?
   a. The people rejoiced that now all would be smooth sailing.
   b. The people cried and prayed that no storm would ever hit their ship again.
   c. One day was pretty much like the next, with storms coming and going.
   d. The ship was slowly sinking and the sailors were looking for an island where they could land and repair the leaks.

7. What happened when a man was swept overboard?
   a. He was rescued by the sailors.
   b. He was rescued by a passing ship.
   c. He clung to a board until he floated away, never to be seen again.
   d. He survived for three days in the water before he was found and rescued.

8. What did the sailors use the iron jack for?

   a. They used it to rescue the man who had fallen overboard.

   b. They used it to lift the beam that had cracked in the storm.

   c. They used it to grind wheat into flour.

   d. They melted it down and used the metal to patch a hole in the side of the ship.

Into . . . *Across the Wide Dark Sea*

How you lead into this story will depend, to some extent, on how much your students have learned about the Pilgrims. You can begin by describing what America looked like in the 1600s. In a very simple way, you can say that the Indians lived here, but they did not build cities. Much of the land was wild and unsettled. When settlers came from Europe, they found vast spaces where they could live and farm and build towns and cities. But nothing came easy. The journey from Europe, as described in the story, was difficult and often fatal. Sickness abounded and only the strong survived. Discuss with your students what the primitive conditions on the ship must have felt like. Imagine the amount of regret about leaving their safe homes many of the passengers must have felt. Ask them how, if they were on board, they could have helped and encouraged others to stay the course.

Once in the new land, the struggle for survival took on a new form. Not all the land was good for farming, bad weather, sickness, and hunger took their toll. But slowly, the settlements grew and took root. The Pilgrims learned what to farm and where to farm. Again, discuss with your students what it must have felt like to be the first people to live in a certain place. Imagine how lonely it must have been to be the only settlement for miles and miles. What would keep you going?

It is important to discuss the countries these people had left. What was bad about their lives there? Why did they come to America if it was so difficult? Do they think it was worth it? Mention at least some of the following:

- In Europe the people were not free to worship as they wished; here they were free to do so.
- In Europe, most people did not own land; here they could own huge portions of land.
- In Europe, many people were poor with no hope of escaping poverty; here, they could own land, earn money, and even become rich.
- In Europe, there was no democracy. Everyone had to obey the king or queen. In America, they were far away from the king or queen and much freer to do as they chose.

Blueprint for Reading

INTO . . . *Across the Wide Dark Sea*

Walk out into the street of any city in America. Horns are honking, buses are rumbling. Buildings, lights, signs, and people are everywhere you look. It's crowded and noisy and full of life. Now close your eyes and imagine these same cities when the first settlers came from Europe to America. Where there are streets and cars today, there are forests and wild animals. Any food or clothing or tools that you have were brought with you on a ship from the old country. If you want a house, you will have to build one. If you want vegetables, you will have to grow them. There is illness, cold, and Indians. But there is something else. There is the good, rich land. There is freedom to make a good life here. And there is your father's firm hand on your shoulder, telling you this is the place you want to be.

EYES ON *Main Idea*

In your imagination, picture a tree. It has a trunk and some branches. The branches have twigs and the twigs have leaves. A story is something like that. It has a **main idea** that can be compared to the tree trunk. Branching off of the main idea are some smaller ideas. These are connected to the main idea and help explain it. A story has many details, such as names and descriptions of how things look. These are like the twigs and leaves on the branches. Although they are important, they are not nearly as important as the main idea. When you read a story, you should be thinking about the following question: What is the author saying? Make sure you don't mistake a smaller idea or a detail for the main idea of the story.

As you read *Across the Wide Dark Sea*, try to identify the story's main idea, and then see if you can identify some of the smaller ideas and details, too.

- In Europe, many different types of people were persecuted. Here, everyone was considered equal.

The narrator of the story was fortunate to be young and strong. His strong, confident father made him feel safe. In spite of hardships, we feel certain that those watching the ship sail away from the New England harbor did not want to be on it. They embraced the new life they had toiled to create.

Eyes On: Main Idea

The target skill for this selection is *understanding the main idea.* How does one identify the main idea of a story? How does one distinguish between the story's main idea and other ideas that are presented along with it? In the Student Edition we compare a story to a tree. The trunk is the story's main idea and the branches are the subordinate ideas. The twigs and leaves are the details of the story. Like the trunk of a tree, the main idea is the one that all the other ideas grow from. Draw a simple picture of a tree on the board to help your students visualize the comparison.

Across the Wide Dark Sea
The Mayflower Journey

Jean Van Leeuwen

I stood close to my father as the anchor was pulled dripping from the sea. Above us, white sails rose against a bright blue sky. They fluttered, then filled with wind. <u>Our ship began to move.</u> ❶

My father was waving to friends on shore. <u>I looked back at their faces growing smaller and smaller, and ahead at the wide dark sea.</u> And I clung to my father's hand. ❷

<u>We were off on a journey to an unknown land.</u> ❸

Across the Wide Dark Sea   163

Literary Components
❶ **Exposition:** The setting for the next several pages is established. It is the ship on which the narrator and his family are sailing. Where they are going and why is not yet clear.

❷ **Contrast:** The contrast between the familiarity and safety of the old land and the emptiness and mystery of the sea sets the tone for the story.

❸ **Theme:** The theme of the story is the journey to an unknown land in search of religious freedom. Interestingly, the land is never named, nor are any of the characters.

Guiding the Reading
Literal
Q: Where is the narrator at the beginning of the story?
A: He is standing on the deck of a ship.
Q: Where were they sailing?
A: They were on a journey to an unknown land.

Analytical
Q: Can you guess where the ship was headed?
A: Since it says "an unknown land" it is probably America.

clearly right from the start. Whenever a selection like that is being read by your class, seize the opportunity to talk about main idea.

In some selections the main idea really is not stated until the middle or end of the story. Many subordinate ideas are presented first, and it is easy to confuse them with the main idea.

Let's take this story as an example. Here are a few of the story's ideas:

- Voyages on the ships of the 17th century were miserable.
- Many people in the days of the Pilgrims died of illness.
- America was a wilderness when the Pilgrims arrived.
- To survive a difficult journey one must have faith and be strong.
- The Indians turned out to be friendly and helpful, not warlike and destructive as the settlers feared.
- Cutting off all ties to the old homeland is frightening and lonely.
- America, the new land, was full of promise in both spiritual and material ways.

It is not always easy to identify the main idea of a story. Here are some steps that will help you.

- First, you must read the entire story to be sure what the main idea is.
- When you have read the story, stand back from it, as you would stand back from a picture to see it in its entirety. Ask yourself, what is the author trying to tell me? Try to go by instinct rather than logic.
- Think about some of the characters, the dialogue, and the description. What idea do they all seem to be building?
- If you are not sure which idea is the main one, ask yourself which one is dependent on the other. Which idea is absolutely necessary to the story? Which could be left out and leave the story about the same?

Needless to say, outside of the first point, these methods will at first be beyond the abilities of a third grader. We present them here to give you an idea of the direction you should be taking throughout the year. You will use these pointers in simplified form taught in small steps. Not every method will be used in every selection. Sometimes the main idea is stated

Across the Wide Dark Sea

Which of these is the main one? Although more time is spent on all of the previous points, in reality, the last point is the story's main idea. Why do we say that? Because the entire story leads up to that idea. The suffering on the voyage, faith of the father, the behavior of the Indians, and the returning of the ship—all these ideas contribute to the theme, which is: the suffering, the loneliness, the fear of Indians and wilderness—*all were worth the freedom and opportunity offered by the new land.* All the details and subordinate ideas are dependent on that one idea.

Again, identifying the main idea in this story is not an easy task. What you can do is ask the students to help you compile a list of ideas (such as the one above) presented in the story. With their help, get them to see that the last idea is the main one in the story. At this early stage, it is likely that you will be doing most of the work. As the year progresses, keep coming back to the discussion of main idea.

The learning strategy for this skill is *inferring.* In this story, in addition to inferring some basic facts, the reader is asked to infer the main idea throughout. As the story describes one difficulty after another, the reader infers that they are doing all this for a purpose. As the story unfolds, the promise of the new land becomes more evident and the main idea comes into focus. Because we are just getting started on main idea, it is probably best to keep discussion of inferring to a minimum at this point. Incorporate it where necessary, but save it for later in the year.

Literary Components

4 **Theme; Details:** The detailed list of what was brought along reinforces the theme of leaving the old and familiar and going to the new and unknown. It drives home how absolutely desolate the Pilgrims expected the new land to be.

Guiding the Reading

Literal

Q: How many people were on the ship?
A: Nearly a hundred people were on the ship.

Q: What was it like below deck?
A: It was very cramped. People could scarcely stretch out to sleep.

Q: What had they brought along on the ship?
A: They had brought tools, goods, guns, food, furniture, clothing, books—everything they would need in the new land.

The ship was packed tight with people—near a hundred, my father said. We were crowded below deck in a space so low that my father could barely stand upright, and so cramped that we could scarcely stretch out to sleep.

4 Packed in tight, too, was everything we would need in the new land: tools for building and planting, goods for trading, guns for hunting. Food, furniture, clothing, books. A few crates of chickens, two dogs, and a striped orange cat.

> WORD BANK
>
> **scarcely** (SKAIRS lee)
> *adv.*: hardly

164   Unit 2

Q: What animals had they brought?
A: They brought chickens, dogs, and a cat.

Analytical

Q: Can you guess when this story takes place? Explain why you think so.
A: It must take place long ago when ships had sails and people were crowded under the deck. Also, in modern times, people would not bring things along; they would buy food and clothing when they got to their new country.

Our family was luckier than most. We had a corner out of the damp and cold. Some had to sleep in the ship's small work boat.

The first days were fair, with a stiff wind.

My mother and brother were seasick down below. But I stood on deck and watched the sailors hauling on ropes, climbing in the rigging, and perched at the very top of the mast, looking out to sea.

What a fine life it must be, I thought, to be a sailor.

> ### WORD BANK
>
> **hauling** (HAWL ing)
> *v.*: pulling

Across the Wide Dark Sea **165**

Guiding the Reading

Literal

Q: How was the weather for the first few days?
A: The weather was fair but windy.

Q: Where did the narrator stand?
A: He stood on deck and watched the sailors.

Analytical

Q: At first, when the narrator watched the sailors, what were his thoughts?
A: He thinks a life at sea would be a fine thing.

Literary Components

5 **Imagery; Simile:** The mix of visual imagery and simile create a threatening atmosphere. The black wings of the birds and the choppy, "angry" seas are ominous.

6 **Sensory Images:** The howling and crashing sounds make it easy to imagine the storm.

7 **Simile:** To the people on board, the waves seemed like mountains.

8 **External Conflict:** The small ship surmounting the mountainous waves is both real and emblematic of the war the small band of Pilgrims will wage with the elements, illness, Indians, loneliness, and hunger before they will prevail.

9 **Humor:** There is a bit of wry humor here when the young boy learns to talk with the assurance of a seasoned sailor. It shows that he is less afraid now of the storms and that he is growing up.

Guiding the Reading

Literal

Q: What was it like when the storm broke?
A: Wind howled and waves crashed. The ship shuddered as it rose and fell.

Q: How did the people react to the storm?
A: They were terrified. They cried and prayed.

Q: What kind of weather did they generally have at this point?
A: It was usually stormy.

Analytical

Q: What do you think the people were thinking when the storm broke?
A: Many of them probably regretted ever having left home.

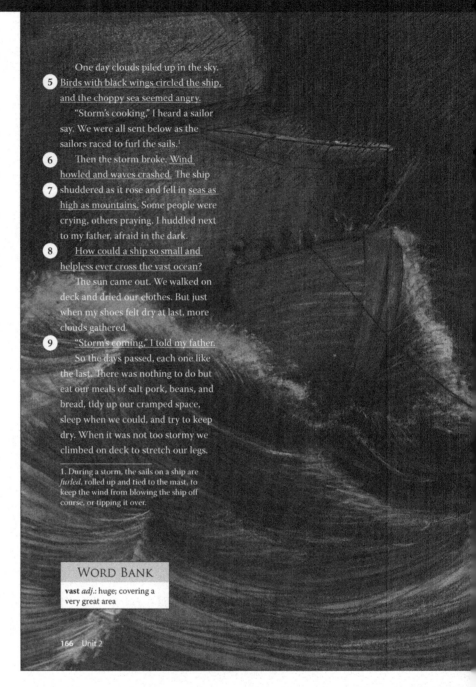

One day clouds piled up in the sky.
5 Birds with black wings circled the ship, and the choppy sea seemed angry.

"Storm's cooking," I heard a sailor say. We were all sent below as the sailors raced to furl the sails.[1]

6 Then the storm broke. Wind howled and waves crashed. The ship

7 shuddered as it rose and fell in seas as high as mountains. Some people were crying, others praying. I huddled next to my father, afraid in the dark.

8 How could a ship so small and helpless ever cross the vast ocean?

The sun came out. We walked on deck and dried our clothes. But just when my shoes felt dry at last, more clouds gathered.

9 "Storm's coming," I told my father.

So the days passed, each one like the last. There was nothing to do but eat our meals of salt pork, beans, and bread, tidy up our cramped space, sleep when we could, and try to keep dry. When it was not too stormy we climbed on deck to stretch our legs.

1. During a storm, the sails on a ship are *furled*, rolled up and tied to the mast, to keep the wind from blowing the ship off course, or tipping it over.

WORD BANK

vast *adj.*: huge; covering a very great area

166   Unit 2

But even then we had to keep out of the sailors' way.

How I longed to run and jump and climb!

Once during a storm a man was swept ⑩ overboard. Reaching out with desperate hands, he caught hold of a rope and clung to it.

Down he went under the raging foaming water.

Then, miraculously, up he came.

Sailors rushed to the side of the ship. Hauling on the rope, they brought him in close and with a boat hook plucked him out of the sea. And his life was saved.

> ### WORD BANK
>
> **desperate** (DESS prit) *adj.:* extremely needy
>
> **raging** (RAY jing) *adj.:* angry and dangerous
>
> **miraculously** (mih RAK yuh luss lee) *adv.:* as though through a miracle
>
> **plucked** *v.:* pulled out with force

Literary Components

⑩ **Rising Action:** The very real danger of the journey is described here. The life and death situations that the passengers faced continuously are illustrated.

Guiding the Reading

Literal

Q: What terrible thing happened once during a storm?

A: A man was swept overboard.

Q: What saved him?

A: He was able to cling to the ropes long enough for the sailors to haul him back on board.

Across the Wide Dark Sea

Guiding the Reading

Literal

Q: What was the weather at sea?
A: The weather seemed to be always stormy.

Q: What did the storm do to the ship?
A: It cracked one of the main beams and the ship began to leak.

Q: What did the men discuss?
A: They discussed whether to turn back.

Q: What is an iron jack?
A: It is a tool that is used to lift heavy weights off the ground.

Storm followed storm. The pounding of wind and waves caused one of the main beams to crack, and our ship began to leak.

Worried, the men gathered in the captain's cabin to talk of what to do. Could our ship survive another storm? Or must we turn back?

They talked for two days, but could not agree.

Then someone thought of the iron jack[2] for raising houses that they were taking to the new land.

---

2. A *jack* is a tool used to lift heavy objects. (Most cars carry jacks in their trunks so that the car can be raised if a tire needs changing.)

WORD BANK

beams *n.*: thick, strong boards that go across the width of a ship

168   Unit 2

Using it to lift the cracked beam, the sailors set a new post underneath, tight and firm, and patched all the leaks.

And our ship sailed on.

For six weeks we had traveled, and still there was no land in sight. Now we were always cold and wet. Water seeping in from above put out my mother's cooking fire, and there was nothing to eat but hard dry biscuits and cheese. My brother was sick, and many others too.

And some began to ask why we had left our safe homes to go on this endless journey to an unknown land.

Why? I also asked the question of my father that night.

"We are searching for a place to live where we can worship G-d in our own way," he said quietly. "It is this freedom we seek in a new land. And I have faith that we will find it."

Looking at my father, so calm and sure, suddenly I too had faith that we would find it.

Across the Wide Dark Sea   169

Literary Components

11 **Theme; Internal Conflict:** This is the underlying question and it will soon be answered. Although all of the passengers had left to seek freedom of religion in a new land, it took fortitude to remember this when the suffering was so great.

12 **Theme; Main Idea; Characterization:** Freedom of religion was the goal for these people. They were not seeking economic opportunity or fleeing bondage, they were looking for a place where they could worship as they pleased. That is the story's theme and main idea. The character of the father is strong, sure, and unwavering in his decision and in his faith.

13 **Turning Point:** Although perhaps we were not aware of the narrator's doubts, we now feel that he has turned a corner and is no longer afraid. He has ingested his father's calm faith and things will go easier for him, at least emotionally, from here on in.

Guiding the Reading

Literal

Q: After six weeks, what condition were the passengers in?
A: They were always cold and wet. Some were sick, too.

Q: What did the people begin to wonder?
A: They wondered why they had left their safe homes.

Q: Why were they going to a new land?
A: They were searching for a place where they could worship G-d as they wished.

Q: Was the father discouraged?
A: No, he was calm and sure.

Analytical

Q: When a person is in a situation like the one described here, what must he do to keep from getting discouraged?
A: He must remind himself why he came in the first place. He must remember that he is going to a good land and think about how much better life will be once he gets there. He should tell himself these difficulties are only temporary and they will end soon.

Across the Wide Dark Sea

Literary Components

14 **Turning Point:** If the narrator turned a spiritual corner previously, the passengers now turn a physical corner when land is spotted. This part of the journey is over and the next will soon begin.

15 **Theme:** How very appropriate that the first action taken by these seekers of religious freedom is to thank G-d for having brought them to the new land.

Guiding the Reading

Literal

Q: What did a sailor say one day?
A: He said, "Land's ahead."

Q: What signs of land did they begin to see?
A: They saw seaweed, a tree branch, and a feather from a land bird.

Q: How did the mother react when they saw land?
A: She wept.

Q: How did the father react?
A: He said a prayer of thanksgiving.

Analytical

Q: What have you learned about the country that the narrator was leaving?
A: In that country there was no freedom of religion.

Q: How would you have felt if you had been aboard that ship?
A: I would have felt happy/relieved/safe/worried about the new land/eager to start my new life.

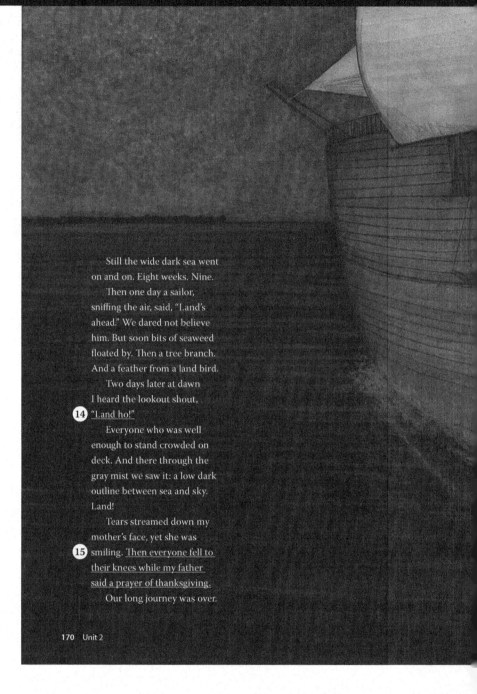

Still the wide dark sea went on and on. Eight weeks. Nine.
Then one day a sailor, sniffing the air, said, "Land's ahead." We dared not believe him. But soon bits of seaweed floated by. Then a tree branch. And a feather from a land bird.
Two days later at dawn I heard the lookout shout,
14 "Land ho!"
Everyone who was well enough to stand crowded on deck. And there through the gray mist we saw it: a low dark outline between sea and sky. Land!
Tears streamed down my mother's face, yet she was
15 smiling. Then everyone fell to their knees while my father said a prayer of thanksgiving.
Our long journey was over.

170   Unit 2

The ship dropped anchor in a quiet bay, circled by land. Pale yellow sand and dark hunched trees were all we saw. And all we heard was silence.

What lurked among those trees? Wild beasts? Wild men? Would **16** there be food and water, a place to take shelter?

What waited for us in this new land?

A small party of men in a small boat set off to find out. All day I watched on deck for their return.

When at last they rowed into sight, they brought armfuls of firewood and tales of what they had seen: forests of fine trees, rolling hills of sand, swamps and ponds and rich black earth. But no houses or wild beasts or wild men.

Across the Wide Dark Sea   **171**

Literary Components

16 Suspense: The silence of the wilderness may hold unknown terrors. The passengers wait and cautiously send out a small group of men to explore.

Guiding the Reading

Literal

Q: What were some of the questions the narrator has when he sees the dark trees all around?

A: He wonders whether they are hiding wild beasts or wild men, and whether there is food and water there.

Q: What did the men bring back from the land?

A: They brought firewood and tales of what they had seen.

Q: What did they say the land looked like?

A: They said it had forests, hills, swamps, and ponds. There were no houses or people there.

Analytical

Q: Do you think the worries the boy had were shared by the other people on the ship?

A: In all likelihood, they were. The people did not know much about the new land and did not know what they might encounter.

Q: From the description, do you think this was a good land?

A: Yes. The land sounds rich. Also, it's empty, so they can settle wherever they want.

Across the Wide Dark Sea

Guiding the Reading

Literal

Q: What was the first thing the mother did?

A: She washed their clothes.

Q: What did a small group from the ship do each day?

A: They explored the land, looking for the right place to build a settlement.

So all of us went ashore.

My mother washed the clothes we had worn for weeks beside a shallow pond, while my brother and I raced up and down the beach.

We watched whales spouting in the sparkling blue bay and helped search for firewood. And we found clams and mussels, the first fresh food we had tasted in two months. I ate so many I was sick.

Day after day the small party set out from the ship, looking for just the right place to build our settlement.

WORD BANK

settlement (SET ul ment) *n.:* the beginnings of a town; a group of houses built in a new, unsettled area

172   Unit 2

Literary Components

17 **Rising Tension:** The pressure of time weighs on the group. They must act soon or they will not last the winter.

18 **Idea:** It is interesting that they name the settlement for their hometown. This tells us that they did not hate the place they left and that they have at least some fond memories of it. Like so many immigrants, while they have warm recollections of their former countries, they have no desire to return to them. [If you like, you could pause and discuss how very many cities and streets are named for places in Europe. What does that say about our population?]

19 **External Conflict:** As mentioned before, the battle with the elements was a continuing factor in the lives of the Pilgrims.

The days grew cold. Snowflakes danced in the wind. The cold and damp made many sick again. Drawing his coat tightly around him, my father looked worried.

"We must find a place," he said, "before winter comes." **17**

One afternoon the weary men returned with good news. They had found the right spot at last.

When my father saw it, he smiled. It was high on a hill, with a safe harbor and fields cleared for planting and brooks running with sweet water. We named it after the town from which we had sailed, across **18** the sea.

It was December now, icy cold and stormy. The men went ashore **19** to build houses, while the rest of us stayed on board ship. Every fine day they worked. But as the houses of our settlement began to rise, more and more of our people fell sick. And some of them died.

It was a long and terrible winter.

Across the Wide Dark Sea   173

Guiding the Reading

Literal

Q: What season of the year was coming?
A: The winter was coming.

Q: What location did the people choose for their settlement?
A: They chose a spot high on a hill overlooking a harbor.

Q: What name did they give it?
A: They named it after the town from which they had sailed.

Q: What happened to many of the people on the ship during the winter?
A: Many fell sick and died.

Analytical

Q: What made the spot the settlers chose a good place for a town?
A: Building on a hill is good for a few reasons. Because water runs downhill, you avoid flooding if your town is at the top of a hill. Also, it is easier to spot an enemy from a hilltop and to defend your town from invaders. The place was near a harbor, which meant they could ship their produce to other places to sell, and allow people and merchants to travel easily. The area also had drinkable water and cleared fields.

Q: Why did so many people die during the winter?
A: In those days, there was very little effective medicine. The ship was cold and damp, and many people probably got the flu or pneumonia. Without good medicine, they weren't able to recover. Also, people didn't know about germs and bacteria, and they probably had very poor hygiene.

Across the Wide Dark Sea

Literary Components

20 **Tension:** The Indians are an unknown, which creates tension in the story.

21 **Characterization:** Another bit of the character of the father is revealed. He is caring and selfless. We can infer from what is being said that he is the spiritual leader of the group.

22 **Significant Fact:** The difficulty and sacrifice experienced by the first settlers is breathtaking. The fact that people came in droves despite the immense challenges tells us how strongly they wished to leave their countries of origin.

Guiding the Reading

Literal

Q: In addition to the sickness, what else worried the settlers?

A: They were worried about the Indians.

Q: When the settlers were all ready to leave the ship, how many people had survived the winter?

A: Only about half of the people had survived.

Q: What did the narrator hear one morning that told him spring was coming?

A: He heard birds singing.

Analytical

Q: How do you think the narrator felt when he heard the birds singing?

A: He felt hopeful. The terrible winter was over and maybe now things would get better. Almost everyone feels more lighthearted when the sun begins to shine.

We had houses now, small and rough. Yet the storms and sickness **20** went on. And outside the settlement, Indians waited, seldom seen but watching us.

21 My father and mother nursed the sick, and my father led prayers for them. But more and more died. Of all the people who had sailed for the **22** new land, only half were left.

One morning in March, as I was gathering firewood, I heard a strange sweet sound. Looking up, I saw birds singing in a white birch tree.

Could it be that spring had come at last?

All that day the sun shone warm, melting the snow. The sick rose from their beds. And once more the sound of axes and the smell of new-split wood filled the air.

"We have done it," my father said. "We have survived the winter."

But now the Indians came closer. We found their arrows, and traces of their old houses. We caught sight of them among the trees. Our men met to talk of this new danger. How could so small a settlement defend itself?

Cannons were mounted on top of the hill, and the men took turns standing guard. Then one day an Indian walked into the settlement. Speaking to us in our own language, he said, "Welcome."

Our Indian friend came back and brought his chief. We all agreed to live in peace.

And one of the Indians stayed with us, teaching us where to find fish in the bubbling brooks, and how to catch them in traps, and how to plant Indian corn so that next winter we would have enough to eat.

Across the Wide Dark Sea 175

Literary Components

23 Release of Tension: Finally, things seem to be turning around. Spring brings renewed hope.

24 Rising Tension: Just as things seem to be improving, a new threat appears.

25 Release of Tension: With one word, the Indian dispels months of apprehension on the part of the Pilgrims. It is interesting to note the sparse style of the author. Perhaps she wishes to evoke the bare-boned style of speech, dress, and behavior of the Puritans she is describing.

Guiding the Reading

Literal
Q: What new danger was growing?
A: The Indians came closer.

Q: What did the settlers do to protect themselves from the Indians?
A: They mounted cannons and stood guard.

Q: When an Indian finally did come, what did he say?
A: He said "Welcome."

Q: What did the Indians and settlers (Pilgrims) agree upon?
A: They agreed to live in peace.

Q: What did the Indians teach the settlers?
A: They taught them where to fish, how to trap the fish, and how to plant Indian corn.

Analytical
Q: How do you think the settlers felt when the Indian said "Welcome"?
A: They must have been surprised and relieved.

Q: How do you think the settlers felt about the Indians now?
A: They must have felt grateful to them for teaching them so much.

Across the Wide Dark Sea

Literary Components

26 **Theme:** The Pilgrims had come to build a home in the New World. At long last, that goal seems to be within their reach.

27 **Falling Action:** The last ties with the old country have been severed. The Pilgrims are on their own, alone in the wilderness. But we have already seen that the seeds they have planted are growing and will continue to grow and blossom.

Guiding the Reading

Literal

Q: What work did the narrator do with his father?

A: They worked together clearing the fields and planting the crops.

Q: What did the narrator plant in the garden next to his house?

A: He planted carrots, cabbage, onions, parsley, sage, chamomile, and mint.

Q: What made the mother feel more hopeful?

A: When she saw how everything grew, she felt that they could make a home in this new land.

Q: How did the narrator feel when he saw the ship disappearing on the horizon?

A: He felt sad and alone.

Analytical

Q: The mother liked herbs. What are chamomile and mint often used for?

A: They are used for tea.

Q: Have you ever tasted parsley or sage?

A: Answers will vary.

Q: What had changed now that the ship had sailed away?

A: Now there was no going back. The settlers did not have another ship, so, no matter how bad things got, they would have to stay in the new land.

My father and I worked side by side, clearing the fields, planting barley and peas and hills of corn.

Afterward I dug a garden next to our house. In it we planted the seeds we had brought from home: carrots and cabbages and onions and my mother's favorite herbs, parsley, sage, chamomile, and mint.

Each day I watched, until something green pushed up from the dark earth. My mother laughed when she saw it.

26 "Perhaps we may yet make a home in this new land," she said.

On a morning early in April our ship sailed back across the sea. We gathered on shore to watch it go. The great white sails filled with wind, then slowly the ship turned and headed out into the wide dark sea.

I watched it growing smaller and smaller, and suddenly there were

27 tears in my eyes. We were all alone now.

176   Unit 2

Then I felt a hand on my shoulder.

"Look," my father said, pointing up the hill.

Spread out above us in the soft spring sunshine was our settlement: the fields sprouting with green, the thatch-roofed houses and neatly fenced gardens, the streets laid out almost like a town.

"Come," my father said. "We have work to do." **28**

With his hand on my shoulder we walked back up the hill.

ABOUT THE AUTHOR

When **Jean Van Leeuwen** was growing up, she loved climbing trees, riding her bike, and playing baseball. Whenever she was indoors, she would read. In sixth grade, Jean tried to write her own book, but she soon gave up. Today, Mrs. Van Leeuwen has written over 40 books for children and young adults. Mrs. Van Leeuwen enjoys writing historical fiction because it combines her childhood career ambitions of detective and newspaper reporter. She searches for clues by researching the past and then reports her findings in her books.

Across the Wide Dark Sea | 177

Literary Components

28 **Theme:** These men and women have work to do. Far from the countries where men are persecuted for their religious beliefs, they will establish a land of liberty, where freedom rings.

Guiding the Reading

Literal

Q: What did the narrator see when his father pointed up the hill?

A: He saw the settlement with green fields, thatch-roofed houses, fenced gardens, and streets.

Analytical

Q: Why did the father make the narrator take a look at the settlement?

A: He wanted the boy to realize that their new home was real and was good. There would not be a need for a ship to take them back to the old country because what they had built here was better than what they had left behind.

Across the Wide Dark Sea

The World with its Countries

Poem tie-in for *Across the Wide Dark Sea*

The poet asks us to look around at the wonderful world we have been given. He asks us to express our gratitude for the "gift from above" by caring for it and striving to preserve nature for future generations.

Here are some questions you can use to discuss *The World with its Countries.*

Q: What are some of the different parts of nature that the poet names?
A: The poet names mountains, seas, flowers, trees, fish, etc.

Q: Do you ever stop and think about all the beautiful parts of the natural world?
Q: Have you ever seen a particularly beautiful or unusual sight that you would like to share with the class?
Q: What are some of the ways we can protect and preserve nature?

The World with its Countries

John Cotton

The world with its countries,
Mountains and seas,
People and creatures,
Flowers and trees,
The fish in the waters,
The birds in the air
Are calling to ask us
All to take care.

These are our treasures,
A gift from above,
We should say thank you
With a care that shows love
For the blue of the ocean,
The clearness of air,
The wonder of forests
And the valleys so fair.

The song of the skylark,
The warmth of the sun,
The rushing of clear streams
And new life begun
Are gifts we should cherish,
So join in the call
To strive to preserve them
For the future of all.

178   Unit 2

Studying the Selection

First Impressions

Some people are explorers and some are homebodies. Some people like dares and some like the tried and true. The "explorers" are excited by new experiences while the "homebodies" try to avoid them. There is no good or bad here, just different inclinations. The world needs both types of people. Take a survey among your students. Ask them which category they fall into. Although most people are a blend of personality traits, one trait or another will be dominant. Then, explain that even though people's natures may be one way, life sometimes places them in a situation that is contrary to their natural tendencies and they are forced to adapt.

In *Across the Wide Dark Sea*, a young boy finds himself in the role of explorer. Every experience he has is new. He is on a rickety ship on the high

Studying the Selection

QUICK REVIEW

1. Describe the conditions on the ship.
2. When the boy asked his father why they were going to a new land, what did his father answer?
3. About how many weeks had passed when they reached the new land?
4. When the group of men went to look over the new land, what did they report?

FOCUS

5. Why didn't the people all get off the ship as soon as they reached land?
6. Why did the boy's mother laugh when she saw the vegetables growing in her garden?

CREATING AND WRITING

7. Many people who journeyed to America kept a journal of their travels. Imagine that you were on the ship described in this story. Write four journal entries. The first should be for the day the ship set sail; the second should be for the day of the storm; the third should be the day you saw land; and the fourth should be in the springtime when the crops were beginning to grow.

8. The people on the ship had to bring along everything they would need to start their new lives. This included (a) clothing (b) building materials and tools (c) seeds and gardening tools and (d) food that could be used on the journey. Your teacher will divide your class into groups. Each group will "pack" what would be needed for one of these categories. Think about what would be absolutely necessary and make a list of what you will pack. Put these items (or pictures of them) into a suitcase, box, or bag and present them to your class, explaining why you packed each item. Remember two things: First, there is very little room on the ship so you can bring only what you need. Second, whatever you bring must be able to survive the trip.

seas during stormy weather. He is going to a land that is new not only to him but to all the adults on the ship. He will be part of a group who must forge a new life or perish. Whether he likes it or not, he must be a pioneer, a daring spirit, an adventurer. How does he take to this role? Ask your students to think about that question as they read the story.

Quick Review

1. The ship is crowded below deck. After the storm, it is damp and cold.
2. The father said that they were searching for a place where they could worship G-d in their own way.
3. About nine weeks had passed.
4. They had seen forests of fine trees, rolling hills of sand, swamps and ponds, and rich black earth. There had been no houses or wild beasts or wild men.

Focus

5. The people knew that it would be better to stay on the ship until they had found the right place to settle. Using the ship as their base, they could find a good place and prepare it for living. Once they had some shelter and water, they could leave the ship and begin the job of building and planting.

6. This question is open to interpretation. The boy's mother probably laughed from relief and happiness. Everything had been so difficult and strange until now. With the coming of spring, things got easier, and the herbs and vegetables that were coming up were familiar and reminded her of home.

Creating and Writing

7. It would be nice if the children drew a cover for their journal depicting something in the story. For that, you will have to give them paper and crayons and markers. In addition, give them four pieces of paper, one for each day they will be writing about. You can invent dates for each of the four days, basing them on the seasons implied by the story (winter and early spring). Don't forget that the whole journey took about nine weeks and that they stayed on the ship for a few weeks after they docked. Each of the four journal entries should reflect what is happening, or what the boy feels, at each stage of the journey. The children could add a little drawing on each page showing the change of weather, if they like. When the pages are complete, staple them together like a book.

8. This project can be done at home or in the classroom. If it is to be done at home, give the groups time during class to make a list of what they will bring and decide who will explain the purpose of each thing to the class. Tell them that they can use everyday objects from home to represent something the Pilgrims would have brought. If the project is done totally in the classroom, you might want to bring a lot of objects that the groups can choose from to put into their "suitcases." One additional point: Tell them that most people need more than just the necessities, so they may pack some favorite book, photograph, or memento. They will tell the class why they have brought this item.

Jill's Journal

Jill's Journal

Background Bytes

Why was the trip so difficult for the *Mayflower*? It is true that the north Atlantic Ocean has a changeable climate—calm one moment, stormy the next. But several factors made the trip worse than it need have been:

- the 180-ton, 100-foot *Mayflower* was badly overloaded;
- the *Mayflower* sailed at the wrong time of year;
- the *Mayflower* sailed *against* the strong Atlantic Gulf Stream current.

The first two factors have the same source. Originally, two ships were to make the journey: the *Speedwell* and the *Mayflower*. The settlers first got the *Speedwell* in Amsterdam. They then sailed to Southampton, England, where the *Mayflower*, the second ship, was leased for the voyage. In fact, in the summer of 1620, the two ships set sail. But the *Speedwell* leaked from the very first, and both vessels returned to England for repairs to the *Speedwell*. They made a second attempt to sail, with similar results.

Weeks were wasted. Finally, they realized that the *Speedwell* could not make the journey. (Although it is also true that some historians are convinced that nothing was wrong with the *Speedwell*, and that crew sabotage resulted in the stories of a leak.) Thus, not only did they leave too late, on September 16, but as many passengers as possible were crammed onto the tiny *Mayflower*.

Why was it too late? By the time they departed, they had lost all the fair winds. The weather was bad and the ocean was rougher, because it was simply the wrong time of year for a 2,700-mile voyage across the Atlantic. (Their late departure also meant that when they reached "the New World," winter would almost be upon them!)

The stormy weather they encountered also forced the passengers to remain below deck most of the time. Their quarters were cold, unlit, and had virtually no ventilation. These accommodations were a breeding ground for disease, which did little to strengthen the settlers for the hardship, toil, and freezing weather that awaited them on land.

What is the Atlantic Gulf Stream current? The Gulf Stream current begins off the coast of Florida, flows north, and turns towards Europe at Newfoundland. This current moves faster than the water that surrounds it. The Gulf Stream slows down any ship trying to sail against it. (In fact,

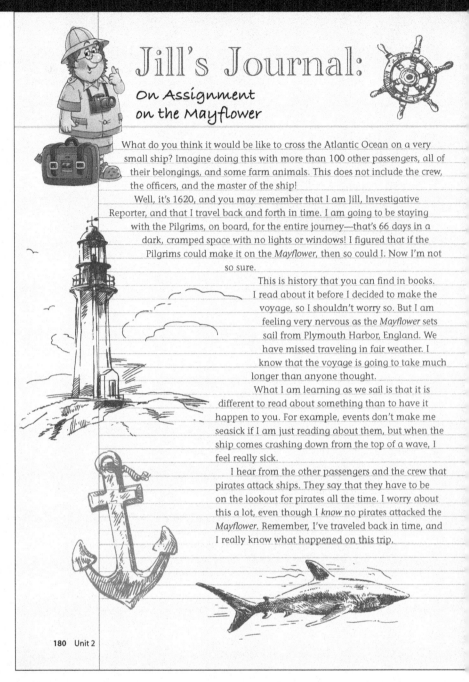

Jill's Journal:
On Assignment on the Mayflower

What do you think it would be like to cross the Atlantic Ocean on a very small ship? Imagine doing this with more than 100 other passengers, all of their belongings, and some farm animals. This does not include the crew, the officers, and the master of the ship!

Well, it's 1620, and you may remember that I am Jill, Investigative Reporter, and that I travel back and forth in time. I am going to be staying with the Pilgrims, on board, for the entire journey—that's 66 days in a dark, cramped space with no lights or windows! I figured that if the Pilgrims could make it on the *Mayflower*, then so could I. Now I'm not so sure.

This is history that you can find in books. I read about it before I decided to make the voyage, so I shouldn't worry so. But I am feeling very nervous as the *Mayflower* sets sail from Plymouth Harbor, England. We have missed traveling in fair weather. I know that the voyage is going to take much longer than anyone thought.

What I am learning as we sail is that it is different to read about something than to have it happen to you. For example, events don't make me seasick if I am just reading about them, but when the ship comes crashing down from the top of a wave, I feel really sick.

I hear from the other passengers and the crew that pirates attack ships. They say that they have to be on the lookout for pirates all the time. I worry about this a lot, even though I *know* no pirates attacked the *Mayflower*. Remember, I've traveled back in time, and I really know what happened on this trip.

the Pilgrims on the *Mayflower* traveled an average speed of two miles an hour.) It was not until 150 years later, that Benjamin Franklin identified the Gulf Stream current, which he named and mapped. He based his conclusions on his observations of whales. A transatlantic voyage was two weeks shorter, if mariners crossed the Gulf Stream rather than sailing against it.

During the first winter in the New World, the *Mayflower* colonists suffered greatly from diseases like scurvy, lack of shelter, and general conditions on board ship. Forty-five of the 102 emigrants died the first winter. Additional deaths during the first year meant that only 53 people were alive in November 1621 to celebrate the first Thanksgiving.

The autumn is a stormy time at sea. The storms frighten all of us and many get very sick from the rough movement of the water against the ship. Also, when it is stormy and the waves are huge, we cannot go up on deck and get fresh air. None of us has had a bath for several weeks. You can imagine that this is a place you might not want to be.

Forgive me for complaining so much, but I even find it hard to write in my journal. There is *so* little light down here, and we keep being knocked about by the ship's movement. (You should try writing with the feathers they use for pens!) However, my journal is the only thing that keeps my mind off of the difficulties. I try to be helpful to some of the mothers who aren't well, so that I will stop thinking constantly about myself. How can I be describing what the *Mayflower* voyage was like, if all I am doing is suffering?

I have just learned that the most recent storm is over, but it has cracked one of the big wooden beams. I'm pleased the crew has fixed it with something called a "great iron screw." I am not really interested in exactly how they fixed the ship, just as long as it's fixed and we get to America and I can go home!

Jill's Journal

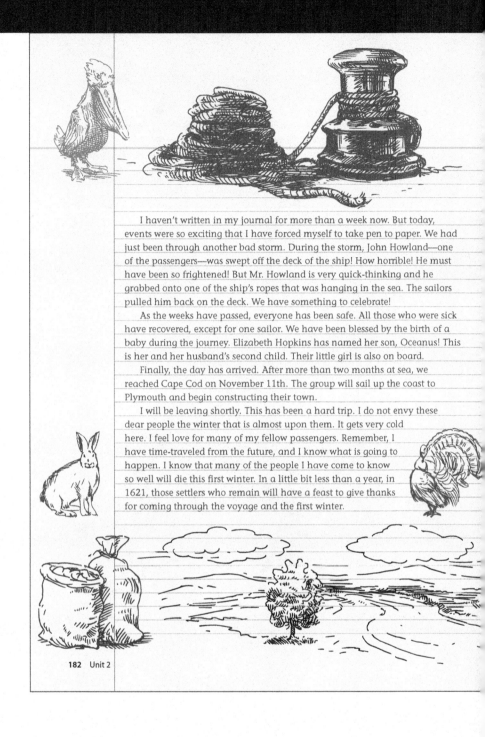

I haven't written in my journal for more than a week now. But today, events were so exciting that I have forced myself to take pen to paper. We had just been through another bad storm. During the storm, John Howland—one of the passengers—was swept off the deck of the ship! How horrible! He must have been so frightened! But Mr. Howland is very quick-thinking and he grabbed onto one of the ship's ropes that was hanging in the sea. The sailors pulled him back on the deck. We have something to celebrate!

As the weeks have passed, everyone has been safe. All those who were sick have recovered, except for one sailor. We have been blessed by the birth of a baby during the journey. Elizabeth Hopkins has named her son, Oceanus! This is her and her husband's second child. Their little girl is also on board.

Finally, the day has arrived. After more than two months at sea, we reached Cape Cod on November 11th. The group will sail up the coast to Plymouth and begin constructing their town.

I will be leaving shortly. This has been a hard trip. I do not envy these dear people the winter that is almost upon them. It gets very cold here. I feel love for many of my fellow passengers. Remember, I have time-traveled from the future, and I know what is going to happen. I know that many of the people I have come to know so well will die this first winter. In a little bit less than a year, in 1621, those settlers who remain will have a feast to give thanks for coming through the voyage and the first winter.

POWER SKILL:
Learning to Write About the Past

1. When writing a story that takes place long ago, an author has to be careful not to include objects that did not exist at that time. For example, if a writer described Abraham Lincoln turning on his radio to hear the news, the reader would laugh. The radio had not yet been invented when Abraham Lincoln was alive! In your notebook, make two columns. At the top of the first, write *Mayflower*, and at the top of the second, write *Modern*. Look at the list of objects below and put each of them into one of the columns.

Potatoes	Seeds for wheat
Blender	Captain's spyglass
Light bulbs	Down quilts
Spades	Electric blankets
Washing soap	A box of Cheerios
Calculator	Books

2. It's your turn to write a page in a journal. You are writing in the cabin that you and your fellow Pilgrims built after landing in Plymouth. Write about details such as what you're sitting on, what you're writing on, and what you're eating.

3. Draw a picture of the inside of the cabin.

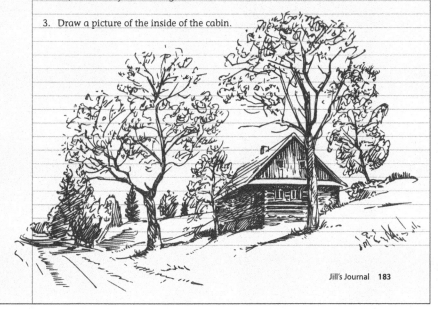

Power Skill

1. **Mayflower**
   Potatoes
   Spades
   Washing soap
   Seeds for wheat
   Captain's spyglass
   Down quilts
   Books

   Modern
   Blender
   Calculator
   Electric blankets
   A box of Cheerios
   Light bulbs

2 wrap-up

all about the plot!

In three of the stories in Unit Two, the main character travels from one place to another. A young boy sails on a ship from Europe to America in *Across the Wide Dark Sea*, Sybil rides her horse all through the Connecticut countryside in *Sybil Rides By Night*, and Jangmi flies on an airplane to America in *Good-Bye, 382 Shin Dang Dong*. In each story, the reader learns what the ride was like and how the character felt when the journey was over.

For the following exercise, choose one of the three main characters named in the paragraph above. Your teacher will provide you with two sheets of paper and some crayons or markers. One sheet of paper will be lined for writing. On it, you will write a six-line poem that doesn't rhyme. We have provided you with the first

Good-Bye, 382 Shin Dang Dong

Sybil Rides By Night

Nothing Much Happened Today

Food's on the Table

Across the Wide Dark Sea

two lines of the poem. Copy it onto the lined paper, and then write two lines which describe the character's journey. Write two more lines that describe how the character felt when the journey was over. You will now have a six-line poem. Take the crayons and the sheet of paper and draw a picture of your character on his or her journey.

Here are the first two lines for each of the poems:

1.

For the narrator of *Across the Wide Dark Sea*:

I sailed on a ship
Across the wide, dark sea

2.

For Sybil from *Sybil Rides By Night*:

I rode on a horse
Up and down the hills

3.

For Jangmi from *Good-Bye, 382 Shin Dang Dong*:

I flew on a plane
To a land that was strange and new

wrap-up continued

ACTIVITY TWO

Each of the selections in this unit takes place in a different place and at a different time. Choose a character from any one of the selections who is *not* a main character. With costumes provided by your teacher or brought from home, dress up as that character. Write a short paragraph about yourself and prepare to present it to the class.

Here's an example. You have chosen to be a sailor on board the ship in *Across the Wide Dark Sea*. Dress up as a sailor and prepare a little speech telling the class what your name is, what country you were born in, and what the life of a sailor is like.

186 Unit 2

ACTIVITY THREE

Although only one of the Unit Two selections is a drama, all of the selections could be *dramatized,* which means turned into a play. Your teacher will divide your class into five groups. Each group will be given one of the selections to dramatize. Each group should do the following:

1. Choose one scene of the story or play that you think is the most interesting.

2. Assign a part to each member of the group. If there are not enough parts, you may make up a character and some lines. For example, you could give Jangmi another friend or relative.

3. It's always fun to have some kind of costume or prop. Even a hat or scarf can be a costume. See what you can use to add some interest to your drama.

4. Decide what each actor is going to say.

5. Rehearse your scene.

6. Have a narrator tell the class what has happened in the play up until the part you are presenting.

7. Present the scene to the class.

ACTIVITY FOUR

Two of the selections in Unit Two are humorous. They are *Nothing Much Happened Today* and *Food's on the Table.* Are you a good comic writer? Let's see! Choose one of these selections and go over it in your mind. Then, think up a different ending for the story you chose, and write your idea down. Make sure your ending includes at least one new, exciting event that makes the story turn out differently. If you are writing an ending for *Food's on the Table,* don't forget to write your ending as a play.

Unit 2 Wrap-Up 187

CONCERN

STUBBORN

all about
characters!

The Printer

Lesson in Literature

What Are Character Traits?
A Different Kind of Hero

1. The mother's kindness is illustrated by her hiring of a sickly woman and helping her clean. Extra money was used for those in need.

2. The mother's generosity is illustrated by her providing a family with a refrigerator full of food and by feeding a homeless person.

3. The mother's sensitivity is illustrated by treating a homeless person like a respected guest, and by providing the homeless man with clean clothing to give him self-respect.

Selection Summary

This is a semi-fictional story about the author's father. The father was a printer who loved his work. Because he is deaf, the hearing printers largely ignore him. Although this saddens him, he doesn't seem overly burdened by the issue. He is friendly with a group of other deaf printers in the plant and is entirely devoted to his job. He is also a gentle and loving father. Each night, after work, he folds a page of the day's newspaper into a four-cornered printer's hat and puts it on his son's head. The son (the narrator) does not take it off until bedtime.

One day, a small fire breaks out in the plant. Only the father notices it, and realizes how dangerous it will soon be. He knows that his shouts will not be heard over the din of the presses, so he jumps on an ink drum and waves his arms until another deaf printer notices him. In sign language he conveys the urgency of the situation. The deaf printers rapidly spread the word to each other and run to alert the hearing printers. As the fire sweeps through the room, the men escape. The deaf printers do not leave until they know that everyone is out of danger. The father is the last of all to leave. Standing outside, the men see the entire plant engulfed in flames. They embrace one another, happy to be alive. Not one printer had been hurt.

When the plant reopens, the father happily returns to work. At the end of the day, the printers—hearing and deaf alike—gather around the father and present him with a hat of freshly printed newspaper. Then, silently, they sign: THANK YOU. That night, the father places the newspaper hat on his son's head. This time, the son wears it to bed, imagining himself standing next to his father before the printing presses, as real printers, working shoulder to shoulder.

Lesson in Literature...
A DIFFERENT KIND OF HERO

190 Unit 3

WHAT ARE CHARACTER TRAITS?

- **Character traits** determine the way a person thinks, feels, and behaves. Examples of character traits are honesty and dishonesty; generosity and stinginess; patience and impatience. Notice that character traits can be good or bad.

- You cannot always see a character trait, but you can feel one. You cannot always *see* whether a person is kind or cruel, but you can *feel* it.

- In real life, a person has many character traits.

- In a story, a character may appear to have only a few character traits. This is because the author wishes to focus on those few.

THINK ABOUT IT!

1. The mother had the character trait of kindness. What is one example of the mother's kindness?

2. The mother had the character trait of generosity. What is one example of the mother's generosity?

3. The mother had a third character trait. It was her ability to sense how a person was feeling and do something about it. If a person was feeling lonely, she might strike up a conversation. What example of the mother's sensitivity to another person's feelings can you find in the story?

Getting Started

A key component to understanding this story is knowing what a printing press is and being able to visualize a newspaper plant. Some schools take their students on a field trip to the local newspaper plant. That would be a wonderful way to introduce this story. If you can't do that, however, a short video showing the printing presses running would be helpful and educational. If that is not possible, then bring in some pictures of printing presses, including men setting type and newspapers coming "hot off the press."

You might like to tell your students about the "olden days" when people got all their news from newspapers, and most big cities published two or three papers a day. Add that there was usually a morning paper and an evening paper. Tell them about the paperboys standing at the corner shouting the headline of the day to the passersby, and about the boys and girls who rode their bicycles each morning or afternoon to deliver papers to the houses on their routes. You can explain that a newspaper plant is something like a factory. It is very important to understanding the story that

The Printer

When I was growing up, my father, my mother, my sister, and I lived in a house in Newark, New Jersey. It was not a big house, and the neighborhood was not a fancy one. But inside our house, we had many beautiful things and two grand pianos.

My mother loved to collect antiques. She was also a very good pianist and a fine piano teacher with many students. When I think about her these days, however, those are not the pictures that I see in my mind. Even though my mother had a great love of music and art, she was a person who never forgot those in need. Extra money was used first for those who needed it more than we did.

If I could write a letter to her today, I would say: *Dear Mommy: What I remember most about you is being loved by you. I loved knowing that you cared not just about us, but that you worried about people or animals who did not have enough.*

When my parents were able to afford cleaning help, they hired an older woman who was sickly. She was not very strong, so my mother cleaned right beside her, especially taking on the heavier, harder tasks. My sister asked my mom why she bothered to have a cleaning lady. My mother said, "Sarah comes because she needs the job." If there was a time when Sarah couldn't come—

let's say she was sick—my mom still paid her for the day.

I remember that my mom had been saving to buy a lovely old pitcher. Then she learned of a family with four children and a baby that had no place to stay. On our second floor, we had an extra bedroom with an attached kitchen. That is where the seven of them lived for several months. We all shared one bathroom. The day before the family arrived, my mom filled up their refrigerator with food. She never did buy that lovely old pitcher, for she had used the money for the family.

I recall a homeless person knocking on our front door looking for a meal. My mother set a little table for him on the front porch with a tablecloth and a cloth napkin. She made him a delicious sandwich, and gave him a glass of iced tea with an orange and a slice of cake. I had never seen anyone do that before. I have never seen anyone else do that to this day. When he left, he carried a bag with fruit, a loaf of bread, some cheese, some cookies, and a clean shirt.

There are different kinds of heroes. A person can save a spirit. My mother's heroic deeds were her kindnesses. She showed me how to pay attention to the lives of other people. Now my daughters show their children. Kindness starts with a little seed and grows into a tall and wondrous tree.

Target Skill: Ability to describe a character's physical traits, personality traits, and attributes

Learning Strategy: Visualizing

Common Core Curriculum: RL.3.3; RL.3.6

Genre: Realistic Fiction

Vocabulary

exchanged (ex CHANGED) *v.*: traded

fled *v.*: run away from

engulfed (en GULFD) *v.*: completely swallowed up

spewing (SPYOO ing) *v.*: throwing out with force

shafts *n.*: long columns

numb (NUM) *adj.*: without any feeling at all

image (IH muj) *n.*: picture in his mind

shuddered (SHUH derd) *v.*: shook slightly

midst *n.*: the middle of

Workbook

Related Pages: 62-67

Answer Key Page: 8

The Printer 191

they know the printing presses make a lot of noise. A newspaper plant is an exciting place; everything must be done quickly because as news happens it must be written about, sent to the printer (who, in those days, had to set the type), and the papers must be run through the press, collated, folded, loaded onto trucks, and gotten on the street all in a very short space of time.

Into . . . *The Printer*

This story can be called old-fashioned for two reasons. First, of course, is the way the newspaper is printed. The idea of movable type and huge presses is foreign to a generation raised on computers and copy machines. Second, and far more striking, is the absence of resentment on the part of the deaf father for being ignored by the other printers. As we read the story, we expect the usual anger, call to arms, lawsuits, and various other militant responses to the perceived prejudice. In this gentle story, the deaf father, far from being resentful, risks his life to save the others. He does not seem to be resentful in the first part of the story and, at the end, when

the printers reach out to him, he does not feel overly grateful. He appears to accept himself and others as they are. He lived at a time when people with handicaps were generally ignored, perhaps out of awkwardness, perhaps out of a mild, subtle prejudice against anyone who was different, but not usually out of any malice. The father seems to accept that and not be bothered by it. If anyone in the story *is* bothered, it is the son who only hints at how poor he considers the treatment the printers afforded his father.

It would not, therefore, be in the spirit of the story to launch a discussion about how unfeeling the printers were. The subject will probably come up, of course, but that is really not the focus of this story. The son wrote this story about his father's heroism, not his victimization. The boy is proud

The Printer   T191

The Printer

of his father's heroic feats of warning everyone about the fire and staying in the plant until the last person had been warned. The boy is proud of and intrigued by the fact that his father used his handicap in a way that could save people. This is probably the point to focus on. Everyone has flaws and weaknesses. The first step is to accept ourselves and be happy with the people we are. The second step is to use our weaknesses in creative ways that can benefit ourselves and others.

Eyes On: Character Attributes

In this selection, we return to a study of character. We don't stop at identifying who the characters are, as we did in Unit One; we begin the process of learning how to analyze them. The first stage of analysis is description, and that is what you should focus on. Have a discussion with your class that goes something like this:

- "Describe the father. Is he gentle or rough? How do you know?"
- "Is he kind or mean? Bring me some examples."
- "Is he a hard worker or is he lazy? What is your evidence?"

Then, a little more deeply:

- "Is he happy with his lot or is he discontented? What makes you think so? Don't tell us whether *you* would be happy, tell us about the father."
- "Does he complain about being deaf or does he accept it? What in the story points that way?"

And deeper yet:

- "Is he a good father or not a very good one? Why do you say so?"

As you ask your students questions about the character, a personality will emerge. You may wish to write a list of the character's attributes on the board. (At a later date, you may wish to compare characters from the same or different stories by writing two parallel lists of attributes.)

One of the goals of your questioning should be to teach the students to read the story closely. Don't accept opinions without proof from the story. They may, of course, have their own opinions about how the father *should* have felt or thought or acted, but that is not the point at this time. The first thing they must learn to do is to *know what the author has written.* Learning to notice and absorb what is actually *on the page* is a skill that is invaluable for all learning. One thing that is lacking in our multimedia-educated

Blueprint for Reading

INTO . . . *The Printer*

The Printer is based on a true story. A boy tells of his deaf father who works in a big building with a lot of other printers. Some of them are deaf, and others can hear. The hearing workers do not bother to talk to the deaf printers. However, the other deaf workers are his friends and they "talk" to each other in sign language. One day, something happens and all the printers have to be warned to leave the building. The warnings are drowned out by the noise of the big printing presses. Can anyone save these men? As you read *The Printer*, think about what advantages a deaf person might have in a noisy environment. Ask yourself, too, if the hearing printers had a lesson to learn.

EYES ON *Character Attributes*

Studying a character in a book or story is like putting together the pieces of a puzzle. We take all the information given to us by the author and piece together a picture. From the character's actions, words, and thoughts, we try to understand what sort of person the character is.

As you read *The Printer*, look for pieces of information that will help you understand the father. What makes him smile or frown? How does he feel about his son? How does his son feel about him? How does he react to danger? Readers love to get to know the characters about whom they are reading. It's almost like having a new friend!

192   Unit 3

student of today is the unwillingness to closely study the written word. If you start insisting at an early age that they read what is written and report what they have read, you are giving them a tremendous head start in learning almost any text-based subject.

The learning strategy for describing a character is *visualizing.* As the reader progresses through the story, he begins to picture not only the setting and how the characters look, but even their personalities and character traits. A mental image of the character is formed and added to as new events come to light. Encourage your students to picture the characters in this and every story they read. At this age, visualization can be helped along by asking the children to draw pictures of characters or settings. Visualizing should not be limited to the visual, though. It should include how people sound, their facial expressions, and their personalities.

The Printer

Myron Uhlberg

My father was a printer. He wore a printer's four-cornered newspaper hat. Every day after work, he brought home the next day's paper. After reading it, he always folded a page into a small hat and gently placed it on my head. **❶**

I would not take off my newspaper hat until bedtime. **❷**

My father was deaf. Though he could not hear, he felt through the soles of his shoes the pounding and rumbling of the giant printing presses that daily spat out the newspaper he helped create. **❸**

As a boy, my father learned how to speak with his hands. As a man, he learned how to turn lead-type letters[1] into words and sentences. My father loved being a printer. **❹**

Sometimes my father felt sad about the way he was treated by his fellow workers who could hear. Because they couldn't talk to him with their hands, they seemed to ignore him. Years went by as my father and the hearing printers worked side by side. They never once exchanged a single thought. **❻**

1. A printing press has wood or metal blocks with raised letters. The letters are placed so that they form words. Ink is put onto these raised *lead-type letters*, and the letters are pressed onto paper. This is how something is printed.

> **WORD BANK**
>
> **exchanged** (ex CHANGED) *v.*: traded

The Printer **193**

Guiding the Reading

Literal

Q: What did the father print?
A: He printed the newspaper.

Q: What did he do after reading the newspaper each day?
A: He folded one of the pages into a four-cornered hat and put it on the narrator's head.

Q: What disability did the boy's father have?
A: He was deaf.

Q: How did he know when the presses were running?
A: He felt the pounding and rumbling of the presses through his shoes.

Q: What language did the father use to speak?
A: He used sign language.

Literary Components

❶ Characterization: The father is an affectionate and gentle father.

❷ Characterization: The boy is an affectionate son. He obviously loves his father.

❸ Key Detail: The father's deafness will be a fundamental part of the story.

❹ Characterization: The father's personality is unfolding. Apart from being devoted to his son, he is devoted to his work.

❺ Characterization; Potential Conflict: The father's nature is revealed here. Although he is sad at being ignored, he is not angry. He doesn't dwell on it; rather, he socializes with the other deaf workers.

❻ Characterization: This time, it is the workers who are characterized. They don't seem mean in any way, just insensitive. It does not occur to them to try and communicate with the deaf workers.

Q: How did the hearing workers treat the boy's father?
A: They ignored him.

Analytical

Q: Why do you think the father made a little hat for the boy each day?
A: Answers will vary. Certainly the father was showing affection for the boy when he did this.

Q: Did the boy like this?
A: He did, and we know that because he didn't take the hat off until he had to go to sleep.

Q: What word is used to describe what the father felt through his shoes?
A: The word is vibration. He could probably also feel the vibrations of a train coming or someone running up the steps.

Q: Why do you think the other workers ignored the father?
A: Although some of the students will say they were mean, the fact is that they were just thoughtless. Because it was awkward for them to communicate with someone who couldn't hear, and it would take a lot of trouble and effort, it was just easier for them to ignore him.

The Printer

Literary Components

7 **Rising Action:** The plot begins to unfold. The action and the suspense rise.

8 **Rising Action; Characterization:** As the suspense rises, we see the character of the father develop. Ignored by his fellow workers, he feels a strong responsibility towards them.

9 **Theme; Characterization; Rising Suspense:** The story's theme is the heroism of the father. However, a sub-theme is that there is more than one way to communicate. The hearing printers know of only one way, and therefore ignore the father. The father knows how to talk with his hands, not only in sign language, but by gently putting a newspaper hat on his son. It is this skill that allows him to save all the printers.

Guiding the Reading

Literal

Q: Did the father have any friends?
A: There were other deaf printers at the plant who were his friends.

Q: Why didn't anyone hear the fire crackling?
A: The noise of the presses drowned everything out.

Q: What else would the presses have drowned out?
A: If someone had shouted a warning, no one would have been able to hear it.

Analytical

Q: Why do you think there were a lot of deaf people in the plant?
A: Printing was a profession where a person did not really have to hear. A printer could take the written copy and set the type without having to converse with anyone.

Q: What advantage did the father have over the other workers?
A: He could speak with his hands.

Q: Can you guess how the father will help the others?
A: He will be able to warn his friends with sign language. Then they will be able to warn everyone else.

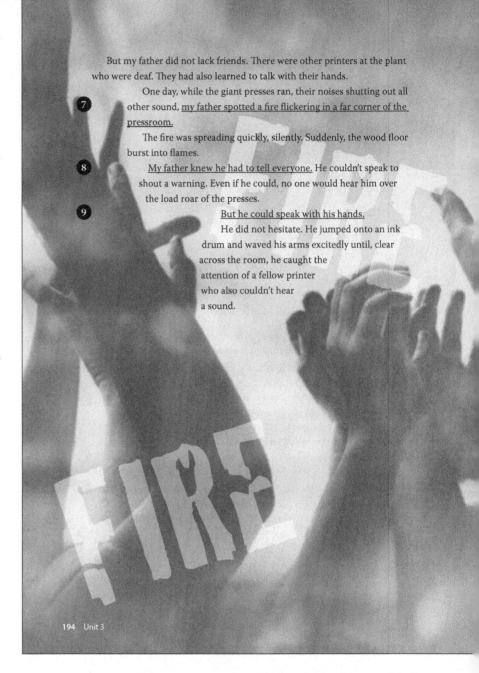

But my father did not lack friends. There were other printers at the plant who were deaf. They had also learned to talk with their hands.

7 One day, while the giant presses ran, their noises shutting out all other sound, <u>my father spotted a fire flickering in a far corner of the pressroom.</u>

The fire was spreading quickly, silently. Suddenly, the wood floor burst into flames.

8 <u>My father knew he had to tell everyone.</u> He couldn't speak to shout a warning. Even if he could, no one would hear him over the load roar of the presses.

9 <u>But he could speak with his hands.</u>

He did not hesitate. He jumped onto an ink drum and waved his arms excitedly until, clear across the room, he caught the attention of a fellow printer who also couldn't hear a sound.

The Printer

My father's hands shouted through the terrible noise of the printing presses,
FIRE! FIRE!
TELL EVERYONE TO GET OUT!
TELL THE HEARING ONES!

His friend climbed onto a huge roll of newsprint. His fingers screamed to the other deaf workers,
FIRE! FIRE!
TELL THE HEARING ONES!

All the printers who couldn't hear ran to fellow workers who could. They pointed to the fire, which had now spread to the wall next to the only exit.

Not one of my father's friends left until everyone knew of the danger. My father was the last to escape.

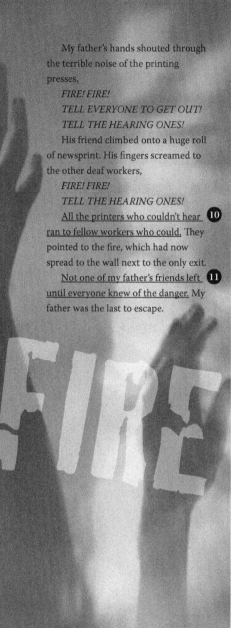

The Printer **195**

Literary Components

10 **Climax:** Will the deaf workers be able to warn the hearing ones in time?

11 **Characterization:** The deaf printers are heroic and feel a strong sense of responsibility to the others.

Guiding the Reading

Literal
Q: Who was the last to leave?
A: The father.

Analytical
Q: What does the author mean when he writes, "His fingers screamed to the other deaf workers"?
A: He means that the words were like a scream because of what they said. Also, the father probably motioned and had the facial expression of a person who is screaming.

Q: Based on what the father did, do you think he was angry at the other workers for always ignoring him?
A: The father does not seem to bear any grudge against the others. He sincerely wants to save them.

Q: Even more than the fact that the father warned the others, what did he do that makes him a real hero?
A: He stayed in the burning building until he knew that everyone had been told of the danger.

The Printer

Literary Components

12 **Release of Tension:** Now that everyone is safe, the tension diminishes and the story will proceed at a slower pace.

Guiding the Reading

Literal

Q: Why did the fire do so much damage?
A: There was enormous damage because the plant was full of paper.

Q: What happened to the giant presses?
A: They fell partly through the floor.

Q: How did the printers in the street feel?
A: They were happy to be alive.

Q: What was the father's reaction to seeing the plant destroyed?
A: He was numb. He was too shocked and saddened to feel too much.

Q: What wonderful thing happened thanks to the father?
A: No one was hurt in the fire.

Analytical

Q: When the author tells you that the father was numb when he saw the presses burning, what does that tell you about how the father felt about his job?
A: It tells you that he truly loved his job. He had a real sense of loss when he saw the presses burning.

By the time everyone had fled, the fire—feeding on huge quantities of paper—had engulfed the enormous plant. The giant presses, some still spewing out burning sheets of newspaper, had fallen partly through the floor. Great shafts of flame shot out of the bursting windows.

The printers stood in the street, broken glass at their feet. They embraced one another as the fire **12** engines arrived. They were happy to be alive.

My father stood alone, struck numb by the last image of the burning presses.

The fire destroyed the printing presses. The plant had to close for repairs. But not one printer had been hurt.

WORD BANK
fled *v.*: run away from
engulfed (en GULFD) *v.*: completely swallowed up
spewing (SPYOO ing) *v.*: throwing out with force
shafts *n.*: long columns
numb (NUM) *adj.*: without any feeling at all
image (IH muj) *n.*: picture in one's mind

The Printer

Literary Components

13 **Sensory Image:** The reader can feel the energy of the plant and begins to understand why the father is so devoted to his work.

14 **Characterization; Symbolism:** The hearing printers have finally awoken to the fact that the deaf printers are valued coworkers. They express their feelings by presenting the father with a hat, a symbol of belonging to the brotherhood of printers.

Guiding the Reading

Literal

Q: When the plant reopened, did the father return to work?

A: Yes, he went back to the work he loved.

Q: On the first day back, what did the workers do that they had never done before?

A: The workers gathered around the father and presented him with a newspaper hat.

Analytical

Q: As you read what happened, are you waiting for something to happen?

A: Answers will vary, but most readers will be waiting for the printers to thank the father.

When the printing press finally reopened, my father went back to the work he loved. The new presses were **13** switched on and roared into life.

When the day's newspaper had been printed, the presses shuddered to a stop. Now there was silence.

In the midst of the stillness, my father's co-workers **14** gathered around him. They presented him with a hat made of the freshly printed newspaper.

And as my father put the hat on his head, all the printers who could hear did something surprising.

WORD BANK

shuddered (SHUH derd) *v.*: shook slightly

midst *n.*: the middle of

They told him THANK YOU with their hands. **15**

That night, my father picked up the newspaper hat that his fellow printers had given him. After adjusting the four corners, he placed it gently on my head. I didn't **16** take off my hat, but wore it carefully to bed.

I imagined I was standing next to my father on a vast printing press floor, turning lead-type letters into words and sentences. We were wearing four-cornered newspaper hats.

We were printers.

About the Author

A hearing child of two deaf parents, **Myron Uhlberg**'s first language was American Sign Language. Myron learned spoken English by listening to the radio. From the age of six, he became his parents' ears and mouth. When Mr. Uhlberg was nine years old, he came with his parents to parent-teacher conferences to interpret between his parents and the teacher—and he was not always the easiest student! Mr. Uhlberg is a retired businessman who now writes children's books, some of which are based on his own experiences.

The Printer 199

Literary Components
- -

15 **Theme:** The hearing printers have learned that communication can take place in many ways. They have learned to reach out to someone who is different.

16 **Full Circle:** The story comes full circle when the father once again puts a newspaper hat on his son. This time, though, he is part of the group of printers, not a "deaf printer."

Guiding the Reading
- -

Literal

Q: After the father put on his hat, what did the other printers do?

A: They said "thank you" in sign language.

Q: What did the father put on the boy's head that night?

A: He put the hat the workers had given him on the boy's head.

Q: What did the boy imagine?

A: He imagined that he, too, was a printer, working side by side with his father.

Analytical

Q: Do you think that when the workers put a newspaper hat on the father it said the same thing as when the father put the hat on the boy?

A: Yes. Both are expressions of affection and caring.

Q: Do you think the boy admires his father?

A: Yes. The boy wants to do the same work as his father. He is very proud of his father for having saved all the workers.

NEWSPAPER PRINTER'S HAT

1. Take a full sheet of newspaper (4 printed pages with a fold in the center) and turn it sideways.

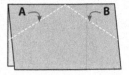

2. Fold down the corners A and B along the dotted lines.

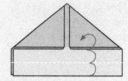

3. Fold up the top layer of the bottom edge twice.

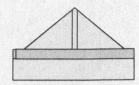

4. Turn the hat over.

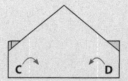

5. Fold the ends along the dotted lines C and D letting the edges of C and D meet in the center. (For larger heads, C and D are farther apart.)

6. Fold corners F and G inward.

200 Unit 3

Why a newspaper hat?

With printing presses running at speeds up to 20 miles per hour and 70,000 newspapers being printed, trimmed, folded, and bound into bundles every hour, a fine mist of paper dust and ink is thrown into the air. Pressmen often fashion a paper hat like the one shown here to keep the ink and dust out of their hair.

7. Fold the bottom flap up and over as shown, tucking MN in beneath HK.

8. Fold the tip P down and tuck it beneath RS.

9. Insert thumbs into the bottom opening. Open and flatten out the hat to create a new square, where R and S meet.

10. Fold in the tips X and Y and tuck them under R and S.

11. Then open out to form - - - - - - - - - - - - - - - - - ▸

Finished YOUR PRINTER'S HAT

The Printer

The Other Way to Listen

Poem tie-in for *The Printer*

The poet concretizes intuitiveness by calling it "hearing." A person who identifies very strongly with something and is very attuned to its existence and development is said by the poet to be "hearing" it. So, the old man who "hears the corn singing," is probably a farmer who has lived and breathed the planting, growing, and harvesting of corn for decades. But, besides being very experienced ("It takes a lot of practice"), the old man notices and connects with nature. He takes his time entering into its spell and allowing it to "speak" to him.

Here are some questions you can use to discuss *The Other Way to Listen.*

Q: Did the old man really hear the corn singing? What does he mean by that?

A: Corn is a living, growing thing that is constantly changing. Most people think of corn as just corn, a vegetable that appears on their plate in the summer. The old man sees corn as a living thing, moving from stage to stage, part of nature, and very beautiful. Although every reader will interpret the "singing" in a slightly different way, the general idea is that singing expresses the life force of the corn, its joy at being alive and part of the greater world. The man can hear the corn because he, too, is a growing, living part of nature. They are connected.

Q: Why is it so important not to be in a hurry when it comes to "hearing" the corn singing?

A: Getting in tune with the natural world takes time and thought. "Hearing" the voices of nature is done not with the ears, but with the heart and soul. When we want to reach our souls, we have to stop rushing around and be calm.

Q: City people are used to noise; even if the room is quiet, they can usually hear the hum of machines or clocks, horns honking outside, air conditioners going, and the like. Have you ever been in a place that was really quiet? Did you like the quiet? Do you think quiet helps people feel more deeply?

The Other Way to Listen

Byrd Baylor

I used to know
an old man
who could
walk
by any
cornfield
and hear
the corn
singing.

"Teach me,"
I'd say
when we'd
passed on by.
(I never said
a word
while he was
listening.)

"Just tell me
how
you learned
to hear
that
corn."

And he'd say,
"It takes
a lot of
practice.
You can't
be
in a hurry."

202   Unit 3

And I'd say,
"I have
the time."

He was so
good
at listening—
once
he heard
wildflower seeds
burst open,
beginning
to grow
underground.

That's hard to do.

He said
he was just
lucky
to have been
by himself
up there
in the canyon
after a rain.

The Printer   203

The Printer

He said
  it was the
    quietest place
      he'd ever been
        and he stayed there
        long enough to
          understand
          the quiet.

    I said,
    "I bet you were
    surprised
    when you heard
    those seeds."

But
he said,
"No,
I wasn't surprised at all.
It seemed like the most
  natural
    thing
      in the world."

      He just smiled,
      remembering.

Studying the Selection

FIRST IMPRESSIONS

If you were working alongside someone who was deaf, would you ignore him?

QUICK REVIEW

1. What did the father do each evening after reading the day's paper?
2. How did the father speak to others?
3. What was the first thing the father did to alert the other printers to the danger?
4. After the fire, what did the printers do to thank the father for warning them about the fire?

FOCUS

5. At the beginning of the story, the father put a four-cornered newspaper hat on his son's head. At the end of the story, the printers put one on the father's head. What is the meaning of putting a newspaper hat on someone's head?
6. We learn something about the father's personality from the story. Write down three personality traits that the father had. Next to each one, write down how you know that about the father. For example, the father is a hard worker. We know this because he has worked hard at his job for many years.

CREATING AND WRITING

7. Your assignment is to produce the front page of the newspaper on the day following the fire. Your teacher will divide your class into groups. Each group will write one article for the front page of the paper. One article will describe the fire. One will describe how the father and the other deaf printers alerted everyone else. One article will be about the newspaper company's plans for rebuilding the plant after the fire. The last group will write an article about fire prevention. In each group, one student may draw a "photograph" to illustrate the article.
8. Your teacher will provide your class with newspaper and you will make a four-cornered newspaper hat. Put it on and wear it for a while!

Studying the Selection

- -

First Impressions

Although not the focus of the story, the way the father is ignored by the hearing printers is commented on by the narrator. In the son's words, he "felt sad about the way he was treated ..." In this day and age of heightened sensitivity to the handicapped, the children will probably find the printers' behavior odd. You may explain to them that years ago people felt so uncomfortable around anyone who was a little different than they, that they would often just ignore the person. Today we know better. No one wants to be ignored, and there is no reason to feel uncomfortable around someone who is not exactly like you. Discuss with your students how the printers could have reached out to the father and the other deaf printers. Ask them for suggestions about how to communicate in non-verbal ways. Remind them that warmth is a universal language.

Quick Review

1. Each evening the father folded it into a four-cornered hat and put it on his son's head.
2. The father spoke in sign language.
3. The father jumped onto an ink drum and waved his arms excitedly until he caught the attention of a fellow deaf printer.
4. The printers presented him with a newspaper hat and said "thank you" in sign language.

Focus

5. The author sees this act as a gesture of warmth and affection. It says "I like you. You are one of us."
6. • The father is warm and gentle. We see this when he gently puts the newspaper hat on the boy's head.
   • The father is sensitive. He feels sad that he is ignored.
   • The father is not an angry person; he is not angry at the hearing printers.
   • The father is friendly. He has many deaf friends.
   • The father is responsible. He tries to tell everyone about the fire.
   • The father is creative. He figures out how to let everyone know about the fire.
   • The father is courageous. He stays in the building until everyone is alerted.
   • The father is devoted. He feels numb when the presses are burned.
     The father is steady. He goes right back to work when the plant is reopened.
   • The father is forgiving. He is gracious when the other printers finally pay attention to him.

Creating and Writing

7. Tell the students they may make up some details for their articles. For example, they can make up names, pretend they have interviewed someone, describe the weather that day, and so on. Each article should be two or three paragraphs long. They should also make up a headline for each article.
8. Instructions for making a four-cornered newspaper hat are in the Student Edition. Practice this at home first, so you can help the class with theirs.

Jill's Journal

Jill's Journal

Background Bytes

This is how you might want to use the information that follows with your class.

Start by asking whether any of your students have any friends or family members who are deaf. If any of your students raise their hands to speak in the affirmative, discuss their responses sensitively. Guide them, as well, to speak respectfully. What do your students think might be some of the problems for children and grownups who are deaf?

What would the situation be like for hearing children who have deaf parents? As you read the *Jill's Journal* be sure to discuss the dynamics that take place among the children and parents in the story.

You may want to review some facts with your class. Most of us would have no idea that there are more than 28 million deaf and hard of hearing people in the United States. If we ourselves know few or no deaf people, we would assume that the population of the deaf is small—except that at public ceremonies these days there is invariably a person present, standing out front, translating the words that are being spoken aloud into sign language for those in the audience who cannot hear. Twenty-eight million is a lot of people!

Have any of your students ever before thought about whether the children of deaf parents would be able to hear or not? More than 90% of deaf parents have children who can hear.

You may want to repeat to your class (if they have already read the *Jill's Journal*) that many people who are deaf use a special language that they make with their hands. In the United States, this form of hand-talking is called American Sign Language, or ASL. Remind your class that American Sign Language does not come from English. In fact, in each country, not only is sign language different from the language spoken in that country, it is also different from the sign language of every other country. Sign language varies from country to country, just as spoken language does. There are some 200 sign languages across the globe. Wherever communities of deaf people exist, sign languages develop.

It is useful to know that there is an organization called CODA (Children of Deaf Adults) that helps hearing children of deaf parents. The organization was begun in 1983, and includes people from widely different cultures and countries from all over the world. No matter where they live,

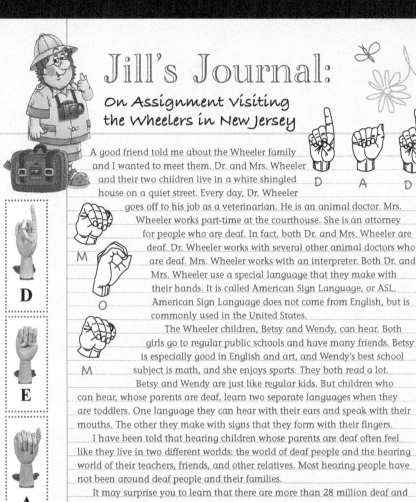

A good friend told me about the Wheeler family and I wanted to meet them. Dr. and Mrs. Wheeler and their two children live in a white shingled house on a quiet street. Every day, Dr. Wheeler goes off to his job as a veterinarian. He is an animal doctor. Mrs. Wheeler works part-time at the courthouse. She is an attorney for people who are deaf. In fact, both Dr. and Mrs. Wheeler are deaf. Dr. Wheeler works with several other animal doctors who are deaf. Mrs. Wheeler works with an interpreter. Both Dr. and Mrs. Wheeler use a special language that they make with their hands. It is called American Sign Language, or ASL. American Sign Language does not come from English, but is commonly used in the United States.

The Wheeler children, Betsy and Wendy, can hear. Both girls go to regular public schools and have many friends. Betsy is especially good in English and art, and Wendy's best school subject is math, and she enjoys sports. They both read a lot.

Betsy and Wendy are just like regular kids. But children who can hear, whose parents are deaf, learn two separate languages when they are toddlers. One language they can hear with their ears and speak with their mouths. The other they make with signs that they form with their fingers.

I have been told that hearing children whose parents are deaf often feel like they live in two different worlds: the world of deaf people and the hearing world of their teachers, friends, and other relatives. Most hearing people have not been around deaf people and their families.

It may surprise you to learn that there are more than 28 million deaf and hard of hearing people in the United States. I didn't know that. I also didn't know that more than 90% of deaf parents have children who can hear. I wanted to learn more about families with deaf parents and hearing children so I went to visit the Wheelers.

I have brought along an expert interpreter, Jane Wills, so that she can translate Dr. and Mrs. Wheeler's sign language for me. I did not want to use Betsy and Wendy as interpreters—even though they know ASL and English.

families of deaf adults with non-deaf children have many of the same problems and experiences that were described in the *Jill's Journal*. There are difficult feelings within the families. It can also be very hard to relate to the non-deaf society outside of the family. The children in such families develop a double identity—one for home and one for school. In many different ways, CODA helps both the children and the adults in these families. It also brings together families who have similar problems so that they can share their experiences with each other.

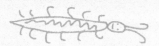

L

I

S

T

E

N

Lots of times people use children of deaf parents as interpreters. That may make the children feel very grown up, but children need to know that their mom is the mom and their dad is the dad. I don't want to be talking more with the girls than with their parents. After all, the mom and dad are the ones who make the rules and the decisions in this family.

I knock on their front door and I am greeted first by a barking golden retriever. Mrs. Wheeler opens the door and signs that one of the advantages of being deaf is that you can't hear the dog's barking!

Betsy and Wendy introduce themselves. When I follow Mrs. Wheeler into the kitchen, I see that Dr. Wheeler is on the phone—a special TTY phone that changes sound to printed words. He waves hello.

Betsy says, "It's an emergency call from the animal hospital. When he took the call, Dad said to tell you that he would try to make it short."

Mrs. Wheeler, Jane Wills, and the girls and I sit down at the large oak table. Mrs. Wheeler signs that the kitchen is the best place to meet, because then she can keep an eye on the food that is cooking on the stove. The doorbell rings and a light flashes on and off above the kitchen door.

The dog barks and Wendy says, "It must be the newspaper boy. He wants to get paid."

She jumps up, takes several dollars from a jar on the counter, and leaves the room.

D   O   G

Mrs. Wheeler signs, "With the dog—even though we can't hear him—we hardly need the flashing light!" Then she speaks more seriously through Jane. "It is hard for us—deaf people—to feel like we are part of the hearing world. People don't learn to sign, so we can't speak to just anyone. Even though my husband and I have good jobs, we cannot feel like hearing people."

Dr. Wheeler has finished his call and takes a chair at the table. Jane and I are introduced to him. He signs, "I remember when the girls were babies, and I worried how we would hear their cries. Sometimes we slept with a hand in the baby's crib to feel the vibrations when they awoke. You know, every sound makes a vibration that you can feel with your hands or feet. Now there are lots of devices that change sound to light."

Jill's Journal

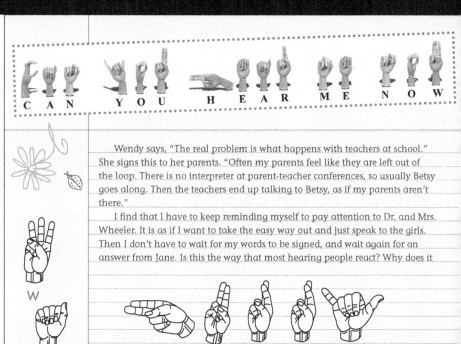

C A N   Y O U   H E A R   M E   N O W

Wendy says, "The real problem is what happens with teachers at school." She signs this to her parents. "Often my parents feel like they are left out of the loop. There is no interpreter at parent-teacher conferences, so usually Betsy goes along. Then the teachers end up talking to Betsy, as if my parents aren't there."

I find that I have to keep reminding myself to pay attention to Dr. and Mrs. Wheeler. It is as if I want to take the easy way out and just speak to the girls. Then I don't have to wait for my words to be signed, and wait again for an answer from Jane. Is this the way that most hearing people react? Why does it

H U R R Y

feel difficult to wait? I am in no hurry. After all, this is why I came here!

Betsy says, "Sometimes people shout loudly at my parents, as if they think they could hear them if they shout." Then, she signs her words.

"How does that make you feel?" I ask her.

"It makes me feel embarrassed. Then I try to understand why people might shout."

We continue talking until it is dark out. The signing and waiting has become easier for me. I am glad for this.

Mrs. Wheeler says, "Deaf parents should have honest discussions with their hearing children about what to do when people treat deaf people badly. We try to give them 'what to do' suggestions when those situations arise. Then, hopefully, they are less upset and less embarrassed."

I say that I have heard that deaf parents are caring and have excellent relationships with their hearing children. Then I add, "I know that it is late and we all have to be up early tomorrow for work and school. I am very grateful for your having me into your wonderful home and talking with me."

W
A
I
T

208 Unit 3

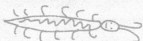

I leave the Wheelers knowing so much more about the lives of deaf parents with hearing children. What a fine family they are. I hope I have a chance to spend time with them again. I think I am going to work on learning ASL!

POWER SKILL:
Finger Spelling

W

H

I

S

P

E

American Sign Language Finger Spelling

A B C D E F G H I J K L M N O P Q R S T U V W X Y Z

1. Using the American Sign Language finger spelling chart, teach yourself how to finger spell your name.

2. Teach yourself to finger spell the following:
   How are you?
   I am fine.
   What is your name?

R

Lorenzo & Angelina

Lesson in Literature

What Is Point of View?

JoJo and Midnight

1. The two points of view are JoJo's and Midnight's.

2. Yes, JoJo does understand it, although he doesn't like it. He knows that Midnight is yawning to show how tired he is.

3. JoJo thinks he was floating peacefully when Midnight jumped in the water and would have drowned had JoJo not saved him. Midnight thinks JoJo was sinking in the water and would have drowned had Midnight not jumped in and saved him.

Selection Summary

This is a story about a girl and her donkey. They live on a farm in Mexico near a tall and beautiful mountain, El Padre Mountain. The story opens on a typical morning scene: Angelina, a young Mexican girl, is opening the barn to let out Lorenzo, her donkey. She begins to pack a barrel of milk and a crate of eggs onto his back and prepares to leave for the market. The story is told in small segments: first we hear Angelina's version of events and then we hear Lorenzo's version. Each time Angelina talks, the plot moves further ahead.

On this day, Angelina will stop at the village and sell her products to Señor Vives. What is different about today is that Angelina has decided to realize her long-held dream of climbing El Padre Mountain to its very top so that she can see the magnificent view of her country from there. As she guides Lorenzo to turn into the path that leads up the mountain, he stalls. Angelina attributes this to his native stubbornness, which she has complained about from the start of the story. Lorenzo, who shares his thoughts with the reader in his parts of the story, tells us that he has reasons for all of his stalling. He is not stubborn; he just has a different agenda from that of Angelina. In this case, he feels that the mountain path is an unknown and may be dangerous.

Angelina who, throughout the story, is portrayed as willful and single-minded, urges Lorenzo on, taking no heed of his silent warnings. She attributes all of his reluctance to stubbornness, and yells at him continuously. As they near the top of the mountain, Lorenzo becomes truly afraid of the danger and refuses to budge. As Angelina is launching into yet another tirade

Lesson in Literature . . .

JOJO AND MIDNIGHT

WHAT IS POINT OF VIEW?

- **Point of view** means the way *you* see things.

- The same events can be reported differently if two different people are reporting them from two different points of view.

- A story is usually told from the narrator's point of view. If there are two narrators, there will be two points of view.

- As people mature, they try to see things from another person's point of view as well as from their own.

THINK ABOUT IT!

1. What are the two points of view in the story?

2. Does JoJo understand Midnight's point of view about eating? Bring proof of your answer.

3. JoJo and Midnight report on a single event in two completely different ways. Write two sentences. In the first, describe Midnight's leap through the air from JoJo's point of view. In the second, describe Midnight's leap through the air from Midnight's point of view.

against him, her father and two policemen arrive on the spot. Angelina, truly blind to reality, complains even to them about Lorenzo's stubbornness. Not until they show her that she is only a few feet from a cliff does she fall silent. In typical emotional style, she completely reverses course and hugs Lorenzo passionately, thanking him for saving her life. Lorenzo, rather than being disgusted, is tickled by her praise.

Getting Started

Read the story aloud from the beginning until the words "However, this ..." on page 219. Then read the following questions to your students.

(For more information on aural exercises, see *Getting Started/The Story of the White Sombrero.*)

1. What is Angelina carrying with her to Lorenzo's stable?
   a. Shining jewels.   **b. Milk and eggs.**
   c. A wooden box.   d. A saddle.

JoJo's Story

It's a sunny, hot day today, just like I like it. Only Midnight, my wonderful black cat, does not like it hot. I want him to like what I like, so we can enjoy it together. What's worse is that he doesn't like water. Oh, he likes it to drink, but not to fool around in. I hope he is not going to spoil our fun this morning.

Midnight's Story

Well, meow. That is what I have to say. I love my JoJo. But he should know by now that I tire easily. After I have my delicious breakfast of Meaty Bittles, it is time for a nap. See JoJo, see how I am yawning and stretching my front legs out. It's the perfect position for rolling on my back in the dust and taking a rest.

JoJo's Story

Oh, that cat! I see right now he is giving me a big yawn and stretching a lot, to show how tired he is. After he eats he has to lick his paws and wash around his mouth. (Actually, I like how clean and shiny he is.) Let me tell you, every time he eats it's a great big deal. Then, of course, he has to rest. Sometimes he stands in the open doorway and takes a few minutes to decide whether he is going to go in or out. I find that irritating, but I am told it's a cat thing.

Midnight's Story

Yes, I'm a cat. You know I'm smarter than a dog, and dogs are pretty smart. I don't miss much. I can see that new pool the Señor and Señora bought for JoJo. I know he is excited to go swimming in there. He is going to want company, and cats hate water! He's going to say his friends are out of town. Now what does that mean— out of town? Do I ever get to go out of town? I wouldn't know if I were out of town, because I wouldn't know where I was! I yawn again, S-L-O-W-L-Y, so he can admire my wonderful cat fangs, and it's time for a rest under the lawn chair.

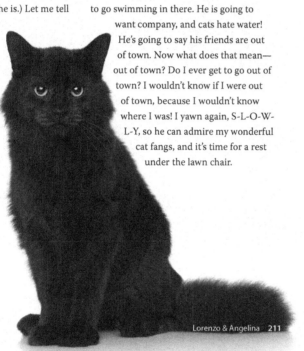

Lorenzo & Angelina 211

Target Skill: Identifying different points of view
Learning Strategy: Focusing on story structure
Common Core Curriculum: RL.3.3; RL.3.5
Genre: Fiction

Related Vocabulary

accuse (uh KYUZE) *v.*: to blame
budge (BUDJ) *v.*: to move slightly
craggy (KRAG ee) *adj.*: steep and rocky
eagerly (EE ger lee) *adv.*: enthusiastically
fatal (FAY tul) *adj.*: able to cause death
fortunately (FOR chuh nut lee) *adv.*: luckily
loyal (LOY ul) *adj.*: faithful; true to someone or something
thrilling (THRILL ing) *adj.*: very exciting

Workbook

Related Pages: 68-73
Answer Key Pages: 8-9

2. To let Lorenzo know she likes him, what does Angelina do?
   a. Gives him a fresh apple.
   c. Brings him fresh water.
   b. Sings their special song to him.
   d. Pats his back, gives him a hug.

3. What does Angelina usually do right after she greets Lorenzo?
   a. She tells him where they will be going on that day.
   b. She asks him to help her carry the milk and eggs.
   c. She begins to scold.
   d. She remembers something and runs back to the house.

4. When Angelina wants Lorenzo to start out, what does Lorenzo often do?
   a. Lorenzo looks around, chews the grass, and nibbles at the clover.
   b. Lorenzo shakes his head and stamps his feet.
   c. Lorenzo winks at her and looks mischievous.
   d. Lorenzo kneels down so she can load the packages on his back.

5. What does Angelina do when Lorenzo doesn't listen to her?
   a. She calls her father, who knows just how to handle Lorenzo.
   b. She loses her temper and shouts at him.
   c. She gives him candy and persuades him to do what she wants.
   d. She stalks away and rides her horse, instead.

6. Why isn't Lorenzo usually ready to leave when Angelina wants him to leave?
   a. Lorenzo just hates having to move.
   b. Lorenzo is very stubborn and won't follow any orders.
   c. Lorenzo dislikes Angelina and won't do anything she asks.
   d. Lorenzo has certain things he wants to do first, like smell the air and chew the grass.

7. Where does Angelina want to go this morning?
   a. She wants to go to the big city.
   b. She wants to visit her friend on the neighboring farm.
   c. She wants to go to the village.
   d. She wants to take Lorenzo out for exercise.

8. What was Angelina's mood when they finally set out for the village?
   a. Angelina was really angry at Lorenzo.
   b. Angelina was sad to be leaving home.
   c. Angelina was worried about the approaching storm.
   d. Angelina was happy and carefree.

Into . . . *Lorenzo & Angelina*

This simple story has several messages. The first is expressed through the character of Angelina. Angelina is willful and convinced that she knows best about everything. She is tone-deaf when it comes to the feelings or ideas of others. Although she is generous with her love and hugs, she doles out insults and epithets with equal generosity. Her overblown self-confidence nearly spells disaster for her and Lorenzo. At the end of the story, the reader almost wishes that her father were angrier with her.

Lorenzo represents a mixture of traits. At first, he seems more the easygoing sort, a foil to Angelina's nervous energy. He is a donkey who wants to stop and smell the flowers. But towards the end of the story, he represents the mature, wise type, who does not want to risk everything for a girl's whim. What Angelina and her father call stubbornness is simply the wisdom of experience. Is refusing to jump off a cliff called stubbornness?

Angelina has a few more faults. She loses her temper often. She is impatient and she screams at her faithful donkey. She is also lacking in the area of responsibility. She dreams up a need to go to the top of a mountain but does not ask her father's permission. She has never even thought about whether her parents would be worried if she was gone from home so long. On the plus side, Angelina is energetic, loving, and passionate about her dreams, persistent, and quick to relent when she is shown she is wrong. In short, she is a more complex character than we originally thought.

The story is told from two different points of view, that of Lorenzo and that of Angelina. The message is that the interpretation of every event

depends on the interpreter's point of view. Much discussion of this follows in the *Eyes On* section as well as in the questions at the end of the story. What we will add here is that this format highlights Angelina's obtuseness. Without hearing from Lorenzo, we would not see how very insensitive Angelina is to everything but her own will.

Eyes On: Point of View

The skill for this selection is *identifying different points of view*. The strategy for identifying points of view is to focus on the *story's structure*. In this selection, the story's structure is tailor-made for teaching this skill, as it is divided into paragraphs in which the characters alternate at expressing their points of view. A good way to begin would be to compare Angelina's story and Lorenzo's story on pages 214 and 215. From Angelina's point of view, she is being polite and Lorenzo is being stubborn. From Lorenzo's point of view, he is being reasonable and Angelina is being impatient.

Blueprint for Reading

INTO . . . *Lorenzo & Angelina*

Have you ever wondered what an animal was thinking? Do you go to the zoo and feel like the monkeys are making fun of you? Do you talk to your dog and imagine that he's talking back to you? Well, here is your chance to read a story that tells you just what an animal is thinking. Angelina is a girl who owns a donkey named Lorenzo. Although donkeys cannot talk, in this story we are told what Lorenzo is thinking. As you read the story, ask yourself: Who is wiser, the girl or the donkey?

EYES ON · Point of View

Sunny skies! Fluffy clouds! Warm weather! Fantastic—right? Not if you own a ski lodge and you need snow for your business. Thunder! Lightning! Rain! Miserable—right? Not if you're a farmer waiting for your fields to be watered. It all depends on your **point of view**, your individual way of seeing things. Lorenzo and Angelina have two different points of view and there is a constant struggle between them. Angelina expresses her opinion by shouting at Lorenzo and stamping her foot. Lorenzo, being a donkey, can only express his opinion by refusing to budge. It seems they will never agree! Until one day, something happens to change all that. As you read *Lorenzo & Angelina*, ask yourself what *your* point of view would be if you were there.

Lorenzo
&
Angelina

Eugene Fern

Lorenzo & Angelina   213

Understanding that the same event can be interpreted in drastically different ways depending on "where you are coming from," is an invaluable life lesson. Good literature teaches this lesson in story after story.

In an ordinary story, the points of view of the characters are not so easily identified. However, as you move through the year with your class, you can use this story as a touchstone for distinguishing the point of view of one character from another. You can ask your students to write parallel paragraphs in the style of this story with each character expressing a separate point of view.

Lorenzo & Angelina

Literary Components

① **Simile:** The dew is like shining jewels; this is a very basic, easy simile, one that will be easy for your class to picture.

② **Setting:** We begin to see that the story is set in a rural area.

③ **Characterization:** Angelina is a warm, affectionate girl.

Guiding the Reading

Literal

Q: Who is Angelina?

A: She is a girl who lives on a farm that is near a village.

Q: Who is Lorenzo?

A: He is some sort of animal that lives in a stable. He is an animal that carries small loads like eggs and milk, and the type you would want to hug. But it is not yet clear what animal he is.

Angelina's[1] Story

① **Every morning,** when the air is fresh and the dew lies like shining jewels over **②** the fields and trees, I go to Lorenzo's[2] stable. I carry with me the milk which Umberto[3] has put into a heavy wooden barrel and the eggs which Jacinta has carefully packed in a wooden box. I open the door and out comes Lorenzo. "Good **③** morning, my Lorenzo," I say. I pat his back, rub the top of his head, and give him a hug. Then I pack the barrel and box on him and I am ready to leave for the village. But not Lorenzo!

1. *Angelina* (AHN heh lee nuh)
2. *Lorenzo* (lohr REN zo)
3. *Umberto* (um BAIR toh)

Lorenzo's Story

4

Every morning, when Angelina comes to let me out of my house, she is glad to see me. She rubs my head, puts her face next to mine, gives me a squeeze, and says, "Good morning, my Lorenzo."

And every morning, to be sure, I am glad to see her too—that is, <u>until she starts to scold.</u>

5

Lorenzo & Angelina

Literary Components

4 **Story Structure:** Here we are introduced to the unusual story structure. The story will be told by both main characters. They will alternate in telling the story.

5 **Characterization:** Although you would not know it from Angelina's description of herself, we see that Angelina is more than the loving, hugging girl she portrays herself as being.

Guiding the Reading

Literal

Q: Lorenzo seems to like Angelina. Why does he like her?

A: He likes her because she is always glad to see him; she rubs his head and greets him each morning.

Analytical

Q: Just from reading the beginning of the story, can you tell what is unusual about the way it is being told?

A: Usually, only one person tells the story. Here, there seem to be two different narrators.

Q: How do Lorenzo and Angelina feel about each other?

A: Angelina likes Lorenzo, and Lorenzo feels loved. However, he does not like her scolding.

Lorenzo & Angelina

Literary Components

6 **Point of View:** From Angelina's perspective, Lorenzo is there to do her bidding. Lorenzo thinks differently.

7 **Characterization:** Lorenzo is stubborn as a mule.

Guiding the Reading

Literal

Q: What is Angelina's complaint against Lorenzo?

A: She complains that he does everything but what he is supposed to do.

Q: What does she do when he doesn't listen?

A: She loses her temper and begins to shout.

Analytical

Q: Angelina says that Lorenzo is very stubborn. What animal is known for being stubborn?

A: A mule is so stubborn that we have an expression, "as stubborn as a mule."

Angelina's Story

Every morning it is the same. I talk to him politely, but he looks this way and
6 that. He smells the air. He chews the grass. He nibbles at the clover. He does everything but what he is supposed to do!

I begin to lose my temper, of course. I shout at him. He pays no attention. He stands like a rock.

7 Though I love him dearly, there is no doubt that my Lorenzo is the most stubborn creature in the whole world.

216   Unit 3

Lorenzo's Story

Every morning, Angelina says, "Lorenzo, it is time for us to go to the village, so please begin to walk." But anyone should know I am not yet ready to go. I have to smell the morning air. I have to chew the grass under the eucalyptus tree.

"Lorenzo," she says, "let us go this very minute." But I am still too busy. "Move, you stubborn donkey!" she screams. "Move those stubborn feet!"

But of course I have to see if the house is in the right place, if the south fence has moved, if the sheep are where they're supposed to be. Naturally, I cannot leave yet.

It is only when she stamps her feet that I move. <u>I am very fond of Angelina and don't like to see her upset,</u> but is it not wrong for her to insult me this way? **8**

Literary Components

8 **Characterization:** Lorenzo and Angelina love each other through all the shouting and bickering.

Guiding the Reading

Literal

Q: Why doesn't Lorenzo want to leave when Angelina tells him to?

A: He has a lot he wants to do. He wants to smell the air, chew the grass, and see if the house is in the right place, and so on.

Q: When does he finally move?

A: He finally moves when Angelina stamps her feet.

Analytical

Q: Do you know what we call it when different people tell the same story, but each person tells it the way they think it happened?

A: When two people tell the same story, each will tell it from their point of view. In this story, Angelina is giving her point of view and Lorenzo is giving his point of view.

Q: Let's think about that. When Angelina asks Lorenzo to move, but he doesn't, what is Angelina's point of view about his dawdling?

A: She thinks he is being stubborn.

Q: What is Lorenzo's point of view?

A: He thinks he has several important things to do and that Angelina is being unreasonable.

Lorenzo & Angelina

Literary Components

⑨ **Exposition:** The story is finally getting underway. We have established characters and setting; it is now time for plot.

Guiding the Reading

Literal

Q: How could Angelina know that Lorenzo was happy to be going to the marketplace?

A: She could tell from the fact that his ears stood straight up and his quick movements.

Angelina's Story

⑨ <u>One morning,</u> <u>like all the other times, we finally set out for the village.</u> My stubborn Lorenzo had finished whatever it was he was doing, and I could tell by the way his ears stood straight up and by the quick movements of his feet that he was as pleased as I to leave for the marketplace at Cuzoroca.[4]

4. *Cuzoroca* (KOO zoh ROH kah)

Lorenzo's Story

One morning we finally set out for the village. Angelina had finished shouting and stamping. As always, she was happy once we started. <u>I could tell by the way she began to sing and laugh</u>—and every once in a while to skip along the road. She liked the little trip to the village, and, to tell the truth, so did I. **(10)**

Angelina's Story

However, this <u>day was to be different,</u> for I had decided to go to the top of El Padre[5] Mountain! Ever since I can remember, I had heard of the beauty and the glory to be seen from there. It is said that from the top of El Padre one can touch the sky. **(11)**

I was so excited about my great adventure that I hardly knew where I was going.

Lorenzo's Story

This day <u>was like all other days.</u> We went beside El Padre Mountain, through Quesada[6] Pass, across the flat meadows, through the forest, and into the village. **(12)**

5. *El Padre* (el PAHD ree)
6. *Quesada* (kay SAH dah)

Literary Components

(10) Characterization: Angelina has a lively, upbeat personality.

(11) Rising Action: We are told that something will be different. The action is about to begin.

(12) Contrast: Here is where man and animal part ways. Lorenzo has no idea what Angelina has in mind—how could he? The reader feels sympathetic towards Lorenzo who is innocent of Angelina's plans.

Guiding the Reading

Literal

Q: What did Angelina usually do on the way to the village?
A: She usually sang and laughed.

Q: Who liked the trip to the village?
A: Both Angelina and Lorenzo liked the trip.

Q: Why was this day going to be different?
A: Angelina had decided to go to the top of El Padre Mountain.

Q: Why did she want to go there?
A: She had heard that the view was glorious.

Analytical

Q: Did Lorenzo know of Angelina's plan to climb the mountain?
A: No. He says, "This day was like all other days." She has not told him of her plans.

Lorenzo & Angelina

Literary Components

13 **Foreshadowing:** We wonder along with Lorenzo what the strange land will hold. We see that Lorenzo's reaction to most things is to balk until he knows how to proceed.

Guiding the Reading

Literal

Q: Why had Angelina gone to the marketplace?
A: She'd gone to sell her eggs and milk.

Q: What happened when they came to the crossroads leading to the mountain?
A: The donkey refused to move.

Q: When Lorenzo would not turn onto the new road, what did Angelina think?
A: She thought he was being stubborn as usual.

Q: What was the first thing that was different that day, according to Lorenzo?
A: Angelina decided to go home a different way.

Q: When Lorenzo tells us why he wouldn't turn onto the new road, what reason does he give?
A: He says he is being cautious. He doesn't know what danger there may be in a strange land.

Q: What finally happens?
A: He finally gives in to her shouting and moves on.

Analytical

Q: Why won't Lorenzo move when they come to the crossroads?
A: He is a stubborn donkey and doesn't want to do something new. (That is how it appears right now.)

Q: Can you see how two different people can view the same event in two different ways? Again, each is telling the story from—what?
A: Each is telling the story from his or her point of view.

Angelina's Story

When we came to the marketplace, I quickly took care of my business with Señor Vives. He counted the eggs, weighed the milk, and paid me for them. I thanked him politely and then I climbed on Lorenzo's back. I could hardly wait to begin the trip to the top of El Padre Mountain!

As one might expect, when we came to the crossroads my stubborn donkey refused to move. Only after much shouting did he agree to take the right fork instead of the left.

Lorenzo's Story

Señor Vives was at his place, as usual. He took the milk and eggs from my back, counted the eggs, weighed the milk, and paid Angelina for them. As usual, he took the money from his strong little box under the counter. Then, as usual, we started for home.

But things no longer went as usual, for Angelina decided to go home a different way. Instead of taking the left turn after the road leaves the forest, she **13** decided to take the right. <u>At first I wouldn't budge. Who knows what might be in a strange land?</u> Finally, with all her shouting, I gave in and went where *she* wanted to go!

Lorenzo & Angelina

Angelina's Story

This road was different from the hard dirt road leading to our farm. It passed over rushing streams, between tall trees and huge rocks, always moving up—higher and higher. It was rough and rocky, and the higher we went, the rougher it got. Though I knew the sun would soon be sinking, I was determined to reach the top of El Padre Mountain. Lorenzo moved more and more slowly, but I urged him on.  **14**

15

Soon the road had almost disappeared. There was nothing ahead of us but a little rocky path. It was getting dark and Lorenzo stopped. Again I had to shout and scold until he moved on.

Lorenzo's Story

This road was not like the other. It was rough and rocky. It did not go through Quesada Pass but behind it, toward the top of El Padre Mountain. Higher and higher we climbed, and the higher we went, the harder it was to see the road. Soon there was no road at all, just a rocky path.

And still Angelina had to explore!

16

Once or twice I stopped, but she shouted so much that I kept moving. It was growing dark, and we were up so high I could hardly breathe. There were rocks on all sides, and every once in a while a poor little bush.

Lorenzo & Angelina   221

Literary Components

14 Setting: The mountain trail is perilous and deserted.

15 Characterization: Whereas most adults who depend on animals for their livelihood are very sensitive to the animals' "fifth sense," Angelina does not notice, let alone trust, Lorenzo's instincts.

16 Rising Tension: Although Angelina doesn't notice, the reader sees that this trail is very dangerous.

Guiding the Reading

Literal

Q: In what direction was the road going?
A: It was always moving up.

Q: Where was Angelina determined to go?
A: She was determined to reach the top of El Padre Mountain.

Q: What time of day was approaching?
A: Evening was approaching.

Q: What did Lorenzo keep doing?
A: He kept stopping.

Q: Why did Lorenzo keep moving even though he thought it was dangerous?
A: He kept moving because of Angelina's shouting.

Q: What happened to Lorenzo when they climbed very high?
A: He could hardly breathe. Mention to your students that the air at great heights does not contain as much oxygen as the air at lower heights.

Analytical

Q: Now that you have heard Lorenzo's point of view, can you explain why he keeps stopping?
A: Although Angelina thinks he is stopping out of stubbornness, he is really stopping out of caution. It is getting dark, the road is narrow, and he doesn't recognize the place.

Q: Who do you think is being wise, Angelina or Lorenzo?
A: Lorenzo is behaving in a mature way and Angelina is being irresponsible.

Lorenzo & Angelina

Literary Components

17 Suspense: The suspense increases when we see that Angelina trusts Lorenzo to protect her but Lorenzo himself feels the climb is extremely dangerous.

18 Theme: Lorenzo's stubbornness is actually wisdom. Angelina is too blind to see that he is saving her.

Guiding the Reading

Literal

Q: What was the weather like at this time of day?
A: The wind was stronger than before.

Q: Why wasn't Angelina frightened?
A: She trusted Lorenzo, who was as sure-footed as a mountain goat.

Q: What was Angelina waiting for?
A: She was waiting to see the glorious view from the top of the mountain.

Analytical

Q: Who was Angelina depending on to keep her safe?
A: She was depending on Lorenzo.

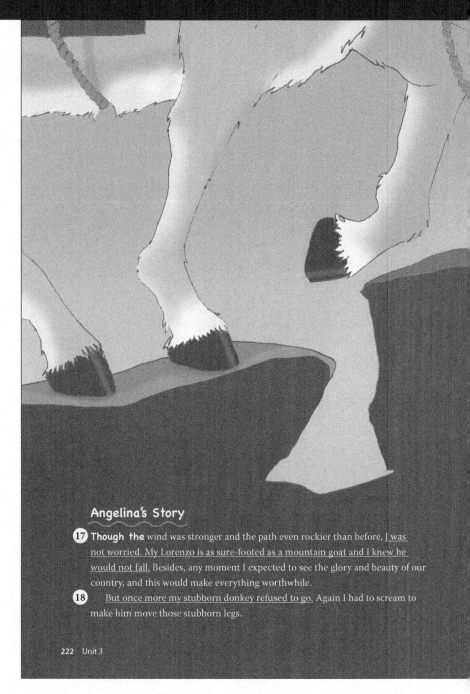

Angelina's Story

17 Though **the** wind was stronger and the path even rockier than before, <u>I was not worried. My Lorenzo is as sure-footed as a mountain goat and I knew he would not fall.</u> Besides, any moment I expected to see the glory and beauty of our country, and this would make everything worthwhile.

18 <u>But once more my stubborn donkey refused to go.</u> Again I had to scream to make him move those stubborn legs.

222   Unit 3

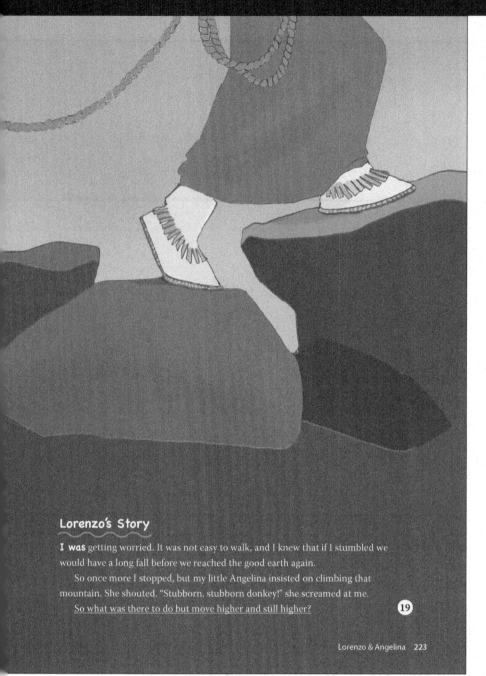

Lorenzo's Story

I was getting worried. It was not easy to walk, and I knew that if I stumbled we would have a long fall before we reached the good earth again.

So once more I stopped, but my little Angelina insisted on climbing that mountain. She shouted. "Stubborn, stubborn donkey!" she screamed at me. So what was there to do but move higher and still higher? **(19)**

Literary Components

(19) Rising Suspense: When will this donkey be stubborn enough to resist Angelina's yelling? We nervously wait to see what will happen.

Guiding the Reading

Analytical

Q: If Lorenzo could talk, what would he have said to her?

A: He would have told her not to depend on him because he was very frightened of stumbling. He would have explained that she did not understand how dangerous the climb was.

Lorenzo & Angelina

Literary Components

------

20 **Turning Point:** Lorenzo finally asserts himself and we know something has to change in the direction of the plot.

Guiding the Reading

Literal

Q: When did Lorenzo finally refuse to go a step further?

A: When they came to two huge rocks he sat down and wouldn't move.

Q: According to Lorenzo, why didn't he go any further?

A: The road ended at those rocks and he had no idea what was beyond them.

Q: What did Angelina do?

A: She yelled and screamed but Lorenzo wouldn't budge.

Analytical

Q: Do you think Lorenzo was right to refuse to go any further?

A: Answers will vary. Some may say that explorers always have to do daring things or nothing new would ever be discovered. Others will say Lorenzo was right.

Angelina's Story

It was when we came to two huge rocks that stood like sentinels[7] over the others that Lorenzo made up his mind not to move another inch. He sat down in front of the rocks in such a way that not even a tiny lizard could pass by.

Lorenzo's Story

Finally, what seemed to be the path went between two huge rocks. And then it ended! A bush grew between the rocks, and after that—who knows?

20 This time I decided the trip was over. Not another step would I take! I sat down.

Angelina's Story

I yelled at Lorenzo. I shouted. I pleaded. I screamed. I pulled at him. I pushed him from behind. He would not budge. He sat there looking like one more rock, among all the others.

Lorenzo's Story

The great explorer Angelina did not take to this kindly. Her shouts before were as nothing compared to the noise she now made. "Move!" she screamed. "We are almost at the top!" She pushed and pulled me. Tears of anger were in her eyes, but it did no good. This time I would not take another step.

------
7. A *sentinel* is a person who stands watch, like a guard. The two huge rocks *stood like sentinels*, guarding the path.

224   Unit 3

T224   Unit 3

Lorenzo & Angelina

226   Unit 3

T226   Unit 3

Angelina's Story

At this very moment I heard footsteps, and there behind us appeared my father, followed by Señor Vives and Señor Quiñones[8] of the police. Suddenly I realized how late it must be. I was sure Papá would be furious. Instead he picked me up and kissed me. All he said was:

"Little one, I am not angry because you took the right turn instead of the left. Children are always looking for new paths. This I understand. But why have you stayed so long? Didn't you know your mother and I would be worried? Everyone is looking for you."

I tried to explain how much I wanted to see the glory of the world from the top of El Padre Mountain and how much time I had wasted trying to get that stubborn Lorenzo to move.

Lorenzo's Story

Suddenly there were sounds behind us and who should appear but Señor Garcia, Señor Vives, and Señor Quiñones of the police! How happy they were to see us! Señor Garcia picked up little Angelina. He hugged her and whispered to her, while the other gentlemen, with big smiles, slapped him on the back.

Angelina looked ashamed and said, "I did so much want to see the top of the mountain, Papá, but that stubborn Lorenzo would not move. He simply refused to budge."

---

8. *Quiñones* (KEE nohn nais)

Guiding the Reading

Literal

Q: Who suddenly appeared behind Lorenzo and Angelina?

A: Angelina's father, Señor Vives, and Señor Quiñones suddenly appeared.

Q: What did Papá do to Angelina?

A: He picked her up and kissed her.

Q: What did Papá think was the reason they had climbed so high?

A: He thought they had made a wrong turn and gotten lost.

Q: What did Angelina explain?

A: She explained that she had purposely gone there to see the view from the top of El Padre. She added that Lorenzo was stubborn and wouldn't move.

Analytical

Q: Why had Papá come up the mountain with the police?

A: He was very worried when Angelina didn't come home from the market.

Q: Why wasn't Papá angry with Angelina?

A: He thought she had gotten lost. He did not know she went up the mountain on purpose.

Lorenzo & Angelina

Literary Components

21 **Suspense:** Angelina is about to get to the top of the mountain. What awaits her?

22 **Resolution:** Lorenzo is validated. The story must end soon, for what can Angelina do now?

23 **Characterization:** Lorenzo is not so stubborn; he is experienced. He knew instinctively that if bushes could not grow in a place, then it was dangerous for human beings (and donkeys). Had he been able to talk, perhaps he could have explained this to Angelina.

Guiding the Reading

Literal

Q: What does Papá show Angelina?

A: He shows her that the mountain ended just beyond the two rocks. Had Lorenzo taken another step, they would have toppled off the mountain.

Q: What did Angelina say?

A: She said nothing. She just stood there pale and trembling.

Analytical

Q: Is Lorenzo angry at Angelina?

A: No, he feels sorry for her.

Q: How do you think Papá feels about "stubborn" Lorenzo?

A: He probably feels very grateful to him.

Angelina's Story

21 **Papá said** nothing. He took my hand and led me between the two huge rocks. He pushed the little bush aside so I could see beyond it. I looked and my knees turned to water! Beyond the bush was the end of the path and also the end of the **22** mountain. Had Lorenzo and I taken but one step beyond the bush, we should never have taken a step again!

Lorenzo's Story

Señor Garcia did not say a word. He took Angelina by the hand and led her between the two rocks. Beyond the bush was nothing—no path, no rocks, just nothing.

It was, of course, as *I* suspected. What could one expect to find up here so **23** near the sky, where even the poorest bush finds it difficult to breathe?

Angelina said nothing. She just stood there, pale and trembling. My poor Angelina!

Lorenzo & Angelina

Angelina's Story

I do not remember too clearly what happened after that, for I was weak from fear and could hardly stand. But I do remember one thing. Seeing that dear, stubborn donkey standing there, I felt such a love for him that I kissed him gently and whispered, "Thank you, (24) my Lorenzo!"

Literary Components
- -
24 **Conclusion:** Angelina is repentant, although only, the reader suspects, for the moment. One can just picture her stamping her feet and yelling at Lorenzo on the morrow.

Guiding the Reading
- -
Literal

Q: What did Angelina do to Lorenzo and why?

A: She kissed him because she was so grateful to him for having saved her life.

Lorenzo & Angelina

Literary Components

25 **Characterization:** Poor Lorenzo! Beguiled by Angelina, he loves her still, regardless of how shrilly she has yelled, and will surely yell again, "stubborn, stubborn donkey" at him.

Guiding the Reading

Literal

Q: What did Papá do to Lorenzo and why?
A: He hugged him for saving Angelina's life.

Analytical

Q: In spite of all the yelling, how does Lorenzo feel about Angelina?
A: He loves her.

Studying the Selection

First Impressions

Angelina is one of those people who are very certain about everything. Not even the slightest doubt that she might be mistaken ever creeps into her mind. Angelina has the virtue of being energetic and decisive, but the fault of being shortsighted and stubborn. Lorenzo, older and wiser but unable to talk, tries to convey his views in his own way. While he looks slow and stubborn to Angelina, he is really methodical and logical. But Angelina cannot see beyond herself and what she wants. It never occurs to her that Lorenzo may have a reason for delaying or balking.

Many of us have had the experience of having to "eat our words" because we were so sure we were right. As we grow, we are supposed to become aware that there are many points of view. We are supposed to listen to what others have to say and consider their opinions before we make a final judgment. Had Angelina been less willful and more respectful of Lorenzo, she would have intuited that Lorenzo sensed danger and was protecting her. The story is told from the point of view of each of the two main characters. But being mature means being able to see something from another's point of view, as well as from your own. That is something Angelina cannot do, and it is why she nearly brings disaster upon herself and her beloved donkey.

Lorenzo's Story

Señor Garcia said, "You should be grateful to have such a stubborn donkey, my little flower. If not for him, I would have neither Angelina nor Lorenzo." He put his arms around my neck and gave me such a squeeze that I could hardly breathe.
25 When Angelina kissed me, my happiness was complete.

About the Author

Though **Eugene Fern** wrote children's books, he was primarily an artist. He illustrated his own books, and he worked for many years as a professor of art, artist, and illustrator. He also enlisted in the U.S. Air Force, in which he served in Alaska and became a sergeant. Mr. Fern enjoys anything artistic and creative, including music, dance, literature, and architecture.

230   Unit 3

Quick Review

1. Lorenzo is a donkey who belongs to Angelina, a farm girl.
2. Angelina's dream was to climb to the top of El Padre Mountain and see the glorious view.
3. Lorenzo saw that the path ended at the two rocks. He had seen that there were hardly any bushes there because the air was so thin. He concluded that it would be foolhardy to go beyond the rocks.
4. Angelina felt full of love and gratitude to Lorenzo.

Focus

5. Lorenzo may have been able to convince Angelina, but it is unlikely. Even if he could have told her that the path was dangerous even for a sure-footed donkey like him, she probably would have taunted him and called him a coward.
6. When a story has several characters, the characters usually talk to each other in dialogue. Sometimes the narrator tells us what the

Studying the Selection

FIRST IMPRESSIONS

Have you ever been *so* sure about something and then found out you were *so* wrong?

QUICK REVIEW

1. Who are Lorenzo and Angelina?
2. What was Angelina's dream?
3. When they reached the two rocks, why did Lorenzo refuse to go a step further?
4. How did Angelina feel about Lorenzo when she was shown how dangerous the mountain was?

FOCUS

5. If Lorenzo could have spoken, do you think he could have convinced Angelina not to climb the mountain? Why or why not?
6. Can you explain what is different and unusual about the way this story is written?

CREATING AND WRITING

7. Whenever policemen return from a call, they write out a report of what happened. Imagine that Señor Vives and Señor Quiñones of the police wrote a report about Angelina and Lorenzo and all that had happened. Write their report and include in it their opinion of Angelina and Lorenzo.
8. For this activity you will play a game that will show you how the same event can cause completely different reactions in different people. That is because we do not have the same point of view. Your teacher will tell you the rules and help you play "Who Am I?" Enjoy!

characters are thinking. In this story, two characters do all of the talking. Each tells a little story from his or her point of view and then the other character tells the same little story from a different point of view. So we hear each part of the story twice, told by two different characters.

Creating and Writing

7. Remember that the two policemen might have very different personalities from the father. They might have been cranky or angry or strict. Then again, they may have been like jovial uncles. Encourage your class to invent personalities for the two policemen and have their reports reflect those personalities. This exercise provides a third point of view for the story!

8. Below are four scenarios and the "characters" that react to each of them. For each scenario, write a list of its characters on the board. Call four students up to the front of the class and give each of them a card that has one of the identities written on it. After you read the

scenario, have each of the four students verbally respond with a reaction appropriate for their character. Ask the class to guess which of the characters each student is. Then, do the same for the next scenario.

Who Am I? Game

Scenario One

"Jackson warms up for the pitch. It's a fastball right over home plate. Valesco slams it! Bander in the outfield is running but ... THIS BALL IS GONE! HOME RUN!"

Characters:
- Jackson
- Valesco
- The man who left the ballgame a few minutes before the home run to beat the traffic
- The catcher

Scenario Two

There is a two-car crash out on Route 74. No one is hurt but both cars are pretty damaged. One car was driven by a teenager, Kelly. The other car was loaded with pastries, headed for a wedding.

Characters:
- Kelly's mom
- Kelly
- The bride and groom
- The mechanic who will fix the cars

Scenario Three

"Good evening, this is the six o'clock news. It is snowing heavily outside with no let-up in sight. Heavy snow squalls are expected overnight with an accumulation of eight to ten inches by morning."

Characters:
- Brian, a third grader
- Mr. Sanders, the principal of Brian's school
- Susan, whose birthday party is scheduled for seven o'clock tonight
- Joe, a cab driver

Scenario Four

Mrs. Davenport, the school cook, has burned the lunch, which was pizza and fries. The children will have to eat peanut butter sandwiches instead.

Characters:
- Mrs. Davenport
- Denise, a girl in the school
- Mr. Porter, who stocks the candy machines at school
- Mrs. Turner, the principal

A Day When Frogs Wear Shoes

Lesson in Literature

Relationships in a Story
When Snow Days Come, Dogs Have Beards

1. Mom never says anything to dampen Dad's enthusiasm, even when she thinks what he is saying is weird.
2. Will and Sarah feel sorry for the dog and want to help him.
3. The children seem to love their father. They like his humor and are happy he is so kind to animals.

Selection Summary

This is a charming story about a group of children with nothing to do on a hot summer's day. The story opens with the narrator, his little brother, Huey, and his friend, Gloria, sitting on the front steps grousing about the heat. Huey suggests they visit their father at work. The narrator explains that this would be "dangerous," as the one thing that gets their father angry is hearing that children are bored. Resolving to keep this bit of information from their father, they make the trek to his place of work, Ralph's Car Hospital, which is a garage owned by their father, a mechanic.

Dad welcomes them and gives them grown-up jobs to do. He sends them to buy lemonade and, while they are drinking it, asks the children what their plans for the day are. Fearful of saying they are bored, they invent an answer, saying they plan to go on a hike. Dad pretends to believe them and asks how they could think of hiking on such a hot day—a day so hot that "frogs wear shoes" to protect their feet. He finally extracts from them the secret that they are bored. After his initial objection to any boredom whatsoever, he admits that every once in a while, boredom happens. He offers to drive them down to the river in exchange for a little more help from them.

Dad buys the kids and himself ice cream cones, and they spend some delicious hours with Dad, wading, skipping stones, and watching minnows. They decide to look for frogs wearing shoes while their father naps. They have a good time catching frogs and throwing them back in the river. After a while, the kids come running to Dad to tell him he was wrong—frogs don't wear shoes, even on a day like today. To their surprise, Dad just shrugs and says he can't be right about everything. When the kids sit down to put on their shoes, they find frogs in every shoe. Frogs

Lesson in Literature . . .

WHEN SNOW DAYS COME, DOGS HAVE BEARDS

RELATIONSHIPS IN A STORY

- A **relationship** is the way two characters in a story connect with one another.
- A relationship may involve strong feelings such as love or hate.
- A relationship may remain the same throughout the story.
- Relationships between characters may change from the beginning to the end of the story.

THINK ABOUT IT!

1. What evidence can you find in the story that Mom is very considerate of Dad?
2. How do Will and Sarah relate to the dog with the beard?
3. What do you think is the relationship between the children and their father?

It is winter and we are watching an explosion of snow. My sister keeps saying, "Oh, how beautiful." And she is right. It is really beautiful. It looks like the sky is wearing a gown that grows closer and closer to the ground. But it bothers me when she says it many times. I guess I am not a patient person.

Hey, though, it's a snow day! Hurray! No school. Just fun. Maybe we'll go sledding! But I look outside and I see a dog shivering in the bushes with

232   Unit 3

are wearing shoes! And so, Dad, who is always right, turns out to be right about this, too!

Getting Started

A Day When Frogs Wear Shoes is one of those stories that have an indefinable charm. The source of that charm is the depiction of the father, a serious/humorous/stern/gentle/principled/flexible/reasonable/whimsical blend of a wonderful human being. The children love him and enjoy his company. The feeling is reciprocated by him. Any day spent with him would be a good day.

Although not every parent has the charm of "Dad," for many kids, spending a day with one or both parents can be a real treat. Ask your students if they have ever had the chance to spend a day with a parent or a favorite adult doing something special. The "something" might have been working, travelling, or just going on a walk. Try to steer the discussion towards the idea of connecting with a parent and away from descriptions icicles for a little beard. Am I really seeing what I think I am seeing? My father has a lot of strange expressions, and one of them is: *When snow days come, dogs have beards.*

When he uses one of his strange expressions, we look at him and wait for some of the others. We suspect that my mom thinks these sayings are silly, but she never says anything to dampen Dad's enthusiasm. My father is a joyful person.

We are all in the kitchen and we're making pancakes. So who's here? I'm Rosalie, the oldest (I'm twelve years old). My brother, Steve, is next at ten. Ella, who thinks the snow is so beautiful, is eight. Then comes a couple of younger ones, Will and Sarah, who have to do as they're told—and get very mad when I tease them with that.

My dad is here to help us make complicated snow forts after we're done making pancakes. (Also, he could not get the car out of the driveway.) He is looking out the picture window onto the backyard and scratching his head. He says to my mom, "You aren't going to believe this, but in addition to the squirrels and the birds and the deer who are eating the bread and seed you put out there, there is really a *dog with a beard*! And he doesn't look very happy."

"Yes, yes," I say quietly. "He looks so lonely."

Will and Sarah shout, "He must be very cold and shivery."

Ella runs to the window and cries, "Mom! We've got to do something for that dog. He looks like he's wearing a snow suit."

"Yes," says Steve. "You both taught us to care for all living things. And as Dad says, *Mice are twice as nice, but dogs are better than frogs.*"

Dad throws open the back door and tiptoes outside. "Come come, little dog," he utters softly.

The dog, one of those short dogs that already have a mustache, hops through the snow and leaps into Dad's outstretched arms.

Mom says, "Now don't everyone crowd around and scare the little guy."

We each approach the pooch as he curls up in my dad's arms. We pet it gently. Mom says, "Give it space so it can breathe!" We dry the dog with a thick towel. Dad asks, "Does he still have a beard, or did it melt?"

I put a little cooked hamburger down on a saucer. Dad sets the dog on the floor and it gobbles all of the food. Then Will brings over a bowl of water. Sarah pets the dog's head as it laps water. This really is a wonderful family event.

The dog has no collar or tags. Maybe we can keep it. Ella says the dog is much more pleasing than mice or frogs.

Target Skill: Studying the connection and relationships between characters	
Learning Strategy: Questioning	
Common Core Curriculum: RL.3.3; RL.3.6	
Genre: Realistic Fiction	

Related Vocabulary

arctic (ARK tik or AR tik) *adj.*: freezing cold	
clammy (KLAM mee) *adj.*: unpleasantly moist	
doze (DOZE) *v.*: to sleep lightly; nap	
explore (ex PLOR) *v.*: to look through something new	
locate (LO kate) *v.*: to find	
pastime (PASS time) *n.*: something done or played to avoid boredom	
puncture (PUNK chur) *v.*: to make a hole in something	
scalding (SKALL ding) *adj.*: burning hot	

Workbook

Related Pages: 74-79	
Answer Key Pages: 9-10	

---

of flashy amusement parks or the like. Tell your class that sometimes doing jobs with a parent is even more rewarding than doing "fun things." Maybe that's because when you do a job with a parent, you are feeling more like an adult, whereas when you have fun with your parents, they are feeling more like kids.

Into . . . *A Day When Frogs Wear Shoes*

This story beautifully evokes the "lazy, hazy, crazy days of summer" of a bygone era. Kids sit outside in the heat, because there is presumably no air conditioning inside. An ice cream cone and a trip to the river are sufficient to occupy the kids, who are just at an age when everything is new and exciting. Dad has a penchant for funny expressions, and the kids are never sure how literally to take him. When he says the day is hot enough for frogs to wear shoes, they take him at his word and look for some. Although they don't find them in the river, they do discover what they already knew, that Dad is always right.

In addition to the wonderful way in which the author makes us feel the heat of summer and experience the boredom of little kids with nothing to do, she creates a parent-child relationship that is both appealing and memorable. Dad is a fully grown-up adult who works hard and is an authority figure to his children. But he also treats the children with respect and affection, asking them for help and giving them adult jobs. His whimsical sense of humor keeps the children guessing; they can never quite figure out when he is being serious and when he is joking. The children not only love Dad; they love being around him. He has a gentle way about him that is also strong. When the children tell him he is wrong, he shrugs and says he can't always be right. When he turns out to be "right," it is only what the reader—and the kids—expect.

A Day When Frogs Wear Shoes

Eyes On: Connections and Relationships

The *Eyes On* section of the Student Edition starts out with the question "Who are you?" Discuss with your class the notion that we do not live isolated lives; rather, we are interconnected with all those around us. Our behavior at any given moment is a blend of who we are on the inside and the particular traits that are brought to the surface by the person we are with. Just as you can learn a lot about a person in real life by observing him in a variety of situations and relationships, you can learn a lot about a character in a story by thinking about how he relates to others and how others relate to him. A skilled author will reveal a character's many facets not by describing him to the reader, but by having other characters describe him or relate to him in ways that tell us what he is really like.

The literary skill for this selection is *studying the connections between characters*. *A Day When Frogs Wear Shoes* appears to be about a father, some children, and a trip to the riverside. But it is really about a relationship that goes two ways. It is about how three children think about their father (or their friends' father) and how the father relates to them.

The relationship is not easy to define. It is subtle; the love is there in a whisper, not a torrent of feeling. The story's humor is like a feather on the wind—here and there, right before your eyes but just out of reach. The mutual respect that is portrayed is like perfect weather—almost undetectable because everything is in just the right measure. We learn about the father by what the children say about him, what he says to the children, and what he does for the children.

How can we help our students define this relationship? Although they won't have the vocabulary to discuss subtleties, they will be able to label the fundamental traits of the father, the children, and the relationship. They will achieve this by the strategy of *questioning*.

Start by asking questions about the children in the story. What are their personality traits? Write a list of adjectives on the board and ask the class which words describe the children. Here is a sample list. (The correct answers are bolded.)

- **friendly** irresponsible **have a sense of humor**
- mean rude spoiled **curious cooperative** fearful
- rebellious cruel lazy disrespectful

Blueprint for Reading

INTO . . . *A Day When Frogs Wear Shoes*

It's a hot summer day and there's nothing to do. Have you ever had a day like that? If you have, then you know that the boredom is even worse than the heat. The kids think about going on a hike, but Dad says that the ground is so hot, even the frogs are wearing shoes. What should they do? In the days before people had air conditioned homes, the best way to escape the heat was to go down to the nearest ocean, lake, river, or creek, and jump in! In *A Day When Frogs Wear Shoes*, Dad takes the kids to the river to cool off. While he rests, they search for frogs wearing shoes. Do you think they'll find any?

EYES ON *Connections and Relationships*

Who are you? You are your mother's child, your friend's friend, your teacher's student—you are many things to many people. How you behave often depends on how you feel when you are near a particular person. You may be quiet near your teacher but loud near your friend. You may be respectful to your father but bossy to your little sister. One way we learn about characters in a story is by seeing how they connect with each other. As we read the story, we think about what the characters *say* to one another, what they *do* to one another, and how they *think* about one another. Some people consider the connections, or relationships, between characters to be the most interesting part of any story. As you read *A Day When Frogs Wear Shoes*, you will find that the father and children have a very special relationship. Can you describe it?

234 Unit 3

To sum up, the children could be described as friendly children with a good sense of humor. They are respectful and cooperative. We can add that they really enjoy their father's company and they "get" his kind of humor.

Now for the father. Another list:

- **kind** grumpy doesn't care what his kids do
- **understanding** lazy hates to see kids have a good time
- stubborn too serious **hard to tell exactly when he's joking**
- stingy irresponsible **fair**
- **generous good sense of humor**
- **likes kids** very bossy

In sum, the father is kind and understanding, a nice person who is not bossy, yet disciplines his kids. He has a good sense of humor, but sometimes the kids are not sure whether or not he is being serious.

Now for the *relationship*: The kind, understanding father clearly loves his children. He is firm about some things but there is a lot of room for

from *More Stories Julian Tells* by Ann Cameron

① My little brother, Huey, my best friend, Gloria, and I were sitting **②** on our front steps. It was one of those hot summer days when everything **③** stands still. We didn't know what to do. We were watching the grass grow. It didn't grow fast.

"You know something?" Gloria said. "This is a slow day."

④ "It's so slow the dogs don't bark," Huey said.

"It's so slow the flies don't fly," Gloria said.

"It's so slow the ice cream wouldn't melt," I said.

"If we had any ice cream," Huey said.

"But we don't," Gloria said. We watched the grass some more.

"We better do something," I said.

"Like what?" Gloria asked.

"We could go visit Dad," Huey said.

"That's a terrible idea," I said.

"Why?" Huey asked. "I like visiting Dad." **⑤**

Literary Components

① **Characters:** The three characters are introduced in the first line.

② **Setting:** The most important part of the setting—the heat—is introduced in the second line. We already know what the story is about: a few kids on a hot day. Some authors take a while to present the characters and setting; this author establishes the fundamentals right at the start.

③ **Main Idea; Conflict:** This is the story's conflict: children vs. boredom—who will win out?

④ **Imagery; Repetition; Humor:** Using language and humor to describe a situation is fun.

⑤ **Characterization:** We learn that Dad is likable.

Guiding the Reading

Literal

Q: Who were the three children sitting on the front steps?

A: They were Huey, the narrator's little brother; Gloria, his best friend; and the narrator, whose name we don't know.

Q: What type of day was it?

A: It was a very slow day.

Q: What was Huey's idea of something to do?

A: Huey wanted to visit Dad.

Analytical

Q: What does the narrator mean when he says, "we were watching the grass grow"?

A: It is a humorous expression that means they were just staring at the ground with nothing to do.

Q: Can you come up with a few other "slow day" expressions like "It's so slow the dogs don't bark"?

A: Answers will vary.

---

them to have a good time and express themselves as kids. He spends his hard-earned money on them and devotes an afternoon of his workday to helping them cool off. The children love their father and enjoy his company. They respect him and want to help him. They know he will appreciate their hard work, and not pick on the jobs they have done. They get a kick out of his humor and are beginning to adopt it themselves. When, at the end of the story the father proves to be "right," the kids are happy, because they want to feel their father knows best.

As you discuss the characters and the relationship, you should occasionally ask a student to quote a line from the story that supports what has been said. For example, to support the statement that the father is appreciative of the kids' work, we could quote what he says on page 239:

"Nice work, Huey and Julian and Gloria!"

For a more comprehensive exercise in backing up opinions with quotes from the story, see the workbook.

A Day When Frogs Wear Shoes

Literary Components

6 **Characterization:** We begin to learn why the kids like Dad. He treats them with respect and affection. He also buys them treats.

7 **Theme:** Dad insists that the world is too interesting for anyone to be bored. The rest of the story bears this out.

8 **Foreshadowing:** We just know he won't remember!

9 **Colorful Language:** The author loves to play with language and images. She especially likes to blend similes with humorous and exaggerated imagery. Here we have "hot shadows" (a contradiction of sorts) as one image. Then, the heat of the shadow is compared to the heat of a blanket.

Guiding the Reading

Literal

Q: What job did Huey's father do?
A: He fixed cars. He was a car mechanic.

Q: Was visiting Dad usually fun?
A: Yes. Sometimes he let them ride in cars on the lift and sometimes he bought the kids treats.

Q: Why won't it be fun today?
A: It won't be fun because the children will say they are bored and Dad hates it when people are bored.

Q: What was Huey's plan?
A: He wanted to visit Dad without telling him how bored they were.

Analytical

Q: Explain why Dad gets angry when people say they are bored. If someone's bored, is it his or her fault?
A: Dad feels that if someone is bored they are wasting their time. There is always something new to try or to learn about. If people are bored, it is because they are just too lazy to try something new.

Q: What does the narrator mean when he says that Huey was wearing his angel look?
A: He means that he looks as good and pure as an angel but he is probably planning some mischief.

My father has a shop about a mile from our house, where he fixes cars. <u>Usually it</u> **6** <u>is fun to visit him. If he has customers, he always introduces us as if we were important guests.</u> If he doesn't have company, sometimes he lets us ride in the cars he puts up on the lift. <u>Sometimes he buys us treats.</u>

"Huey," I said, "usually, visiting Dad is a good idea. Today, it's a dangerous idea."

"Why?" Gloria said.

"Because we're bored," I said. "My dad **7** hates it when people are bored. He says <u>the world is so interesting nobody should ever be bored.</u>"

"I see," Gloria said, as if she didn't.

"So we'll go see him," Huey said, "and we just won't tell him we're bored. We're bored, but we won't tell him."

"Just so you remember that!" I said.

8 <u>"Oh, I'll remember," Huey said.</u>

Huey was wearing his angel look. When he has that look, you know he'll never remember anything.

Huey and I put on sweat bands. Gloria put on dark glasses. We started out.

The sun shined up at us from the **9** sidewalks. <u>Even the shadows on the street were hot as blankets.</u>

Huey picked up a stick and scratched it along the sidewalk. "Oh, we're bored," he muttered. "Bored, bored, bored, bored, bored!"

A Day When Frogs Wear Shoes   237

Literary Components

10 **Characterization:** Dad has a whimsical sense of humor that the kids are beginning to imitate.

Guiding the Reading

Literal

Q: What were some of the things that Dad fixed on a car?

A: Dad fixed flat tires (punctures), rust, dents, brakes, and other things.

Q: What was Dad's name?

A: Dad's name was Ralph.

Q: Who was in the shop?

A: Only Dad was in the shop.

Analytical

Q: What does the sign mean when it says "bad brakes" and "bad breaks"?

A: It is part funny, part serious. "Bad brakes" refer to the brakes on a car that don't work properly, and "bad breaks" probably means that the body or something else on the car needs fixing.

"Huey!" I yelled. I wasn't bored anymore. I was nervous. Finally we reached a sign:

> **RALPH'S CAR HOSPITAL**
> **Punctures**
> **Rust**
> **Dents & Bashes**
> **Bad Brakes**
> **Bad Breaks**
> **Unusual Complaints**

10

That's my dad's sign. My dad is Ralph.

The parking lot had three cars in it. Dad was inside the shop, lifting the hood of another car. He didn't have any customers with him, so we didn't get to shake hands and feel like visiting mayors or congressmen.

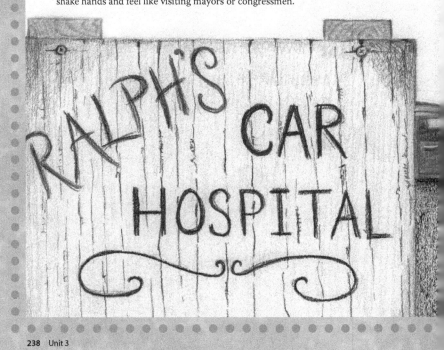

"Hi, Dad," I said.

"Hi!" my dad said.

"We're—" Huey said.

I didn't trust Huey. I stepped on his foot.

"We're on a hike," I said.

"Well, nice of you to stop by," my father said. <u>"If you want, you can stay awhile and help me."</u> **11**

"O.K.," we said.

So Huey sorted nuts and bolts. Gloria shined fenders with a rag. I held a new windshield wiper while my dad put it on a car window.

"Nice work, Huey and Julian and Gloria!" my dad said when we were done.

Literary Components

11 Characterization: Dad treats the kids with respect and teaches them to be capable. He asks them to help him in his real work and praises them when they do the job well.

Guiding the Reading

Literal

Q: How did the children help Dad?

A: Huey sorted nuts and bolts, Gloria shined fenders, and the narrator held a windshield wiper for his father.

A Day When Frogs Wear Shoes

Literary Components

12 Characterization: Dad is generous. Although he doesn't spoil the kids, he gets them simple treats as "payment" for their work. When he sits under the tree and drinks the lemonade with them he makes it clear that he enjoys their company.

13 Metaphor; Humor: Dad's good nature and whimsical way of viewing kids is expressed through his colorful way with words. He always hovers between the serious and the humorous, and the kids can't always tell which one he intends to be at that moment.

14 Characterization: Huey, the youngest child, is a perfect foil for Dad's humor. He is the one who takes Dad most literally.

15 Theme: The underlying theme of the story is the wonderful relationship between Dad and the children. When Gloria says they really came to visit Dad, and Dad looks pleased, we have the theme in a nutshell. The perfect mix of affection and respect the children have for Dad and the perfect mix of affection and authority that Dad extends to the children are immensely satisfying.

Guiding the Reading

Literal

Q: What treat did Dad buy the children?
A: He bought them lemonade.

Q: Why is Dad surprised that the kids want to hike?
A: He is surprised they would pick such a hot day to go hiking. The ground is too hot.

Q: What funny line does Dad use to express how very hot the day is?
A: He says that on a day like this, frogs wear shoes.

Q: What did Gloria admit to Dad?
A: She admitted that they weren't really planning to go on a hike; they had really come to see Dad.

Analytical

Q: Here are a few words that might describe Dad. Choose the words that are true, and explain your answer: strict; friendly; fun; angry; cold; generous.
A: Dad is not strict or angry or cold. He is friendly and fun and generous.

And then he sent us to the store across the street to buy paper cups and ice **12** cubes and a can of frozen <u>lemonade</u>.

We mixed the lemonade in the shop. Then we sat out under the one tree by the side of the driveway and drank all of it.

"Good lemonade!" my father said. "So what are you kids going to do now?"

"Oh, hike!" I said.

"You know," my father answered, "I'm surprised at you kids picking a hot day **13** like today for a hike. The ground is so hot. <u>On a day like this, frogs wear shoes!</u>"

14 <u>"They do?"</u> Huey said.

"Especially if they go hiking," my father said. "Of course, a lot of frogs, on a day like this, would stay home. So I wonder why you kids are hiking."

Sometimes my father notices too much. Then he gets yellow lights shining in his eyes, asking you to tell the whole truth. That's when I know to look at my feet.

"Oh," I said, "we *like* hiking."

But Gloria didn't know any better. She looked into my father's eyes. "Really," **15** she said, "this wasn't a real hike. <u>We came to see you.</u>"

"Oh, I see!" my father said, looking pleased.

"Because we were bored," Huey said.

My father jumped up so fast he tipped over his lemonade cup. "BORED!" my father yelled. "You were BORED?"

He picked up his cup and waved it in the air.

"And you think *I* don't get BORED?" my father roared, sprinkling out a few last drops of lemonade from his cup. "You think I don't get bored fixing cars when it's hot enough that frogs wear shoes?"

"'This is such an interesting world that nobody should ever be bored.' That's what you said," I reminded him.

"Last week," Huey added.

"Ummm," my father said. He got quiet.

He rubbed his hand over his mouth, the way he does when he's thinking.

"Why, of course," my father said, "I remember that. And it's the perfect, absolute truth. People absolutely SHOULD NOT get bored! However—" He paused. "It just happens that, sometimes, they do."

My father rubbed a line in the dirt with his shoe. <u>He was thinking so hard I</u> **16** <u>could see his thoughts standing by the tree and sitting on all the fenders of the cars.</u>

"You know, if you three would kindly help me some more, I could leave a half hour early, and we could drive down by the river."

"We'll help," I said.

"Yes, and then we can look for frogs!" Huey said. So we stayed. We learned how to make a signal light blink. And afterward, on the way to the river, my dad bought us all ice cream cones. The ice cream did melt. Huey's melted all down the front of his shirt. It took him ten paper napkins and the river to clean up.

Literary Components

16 **Metaphor; Humor:** Once again, the author treats us to her three-way use of images. First, the simile: "He was thinking so hard …," then the exaggerated metaphor: thoughts that stand by trees and sit on fenders.

Guiding the Reading

Literal

Q: What did Huey admit?
A: He said they were bored.

Q: How did Dad react to that?
A: He jumped up and yelled, "BORED!"

Q: What does Dad admit to the children?
A: Sometimes he gets bored, too.

Q: What funny description does the narrator use to tell us his father is thinking hard?
A: He says that he could see his thoughts standing by the tree and sitting on all the fenders of the cars.

Q: What deal does Dad make with the kids?
A: He tells them that if they will help him, they can leave work early and drive down to the river.

Q: What does Huey want to do at the river?
A: He wants to look for frogs.

Q: What treat did Dad get the kids?
A: He bought them ice cream cones.

Analytical

Q: What is Dad especially good at?
A: He is especially good at discovering the truth.

Q: Do you think Dad really knew why the children had come?
A: Answers will vary.

Q: Do you think adults are often bored?
A: Answers will vary. Ask the students to lend some support to their answers.

A Day When Frogs Wear Shoes

Literary Components

17 **Theme:** Dad's principle that the world is too exciting a place to ever be bored is proven here. The kids go down to the river and find endless things to observe and appreciate.

18 **Humor:** The kids are turning Dad's words against him, but all in a gentle, humorous way.

Guiding the Reading

Literal

Q: Where did Dad tell the kids to look for frogs?
A: He said they'd have to go down the bank a ways and look hard if they wanted to find frogs.

Q: What did Dad want to do?
A: He wanted to take a nap.

Q: Who was first to find a frog?
A: Huey was first.

Analytical

Q: What do you do with skipping stones?
A: You "skip" them over the water, meaning you throw them so that they sail very close to the water and touch the water as they skim along the top of it.

Q: What is the difference between grown-ups and kids when it comes to napping?
A: Most grown-ups enjoy a nap, but don't often have the chance to take one. Most kids hate the idea of having to take a nap, but can rarely get out of taking one.

After Huey's shirt was clean, we took our shoes and socks off and went wading.

17 We looked for special rocks under the water—the ones that are beautiful until you take them out of the water, when they get dry and not so bright.

We found skipping stones and tried to see who could get the most skips from a stone.

We saw a school of minnows going as fast as they could to get away from us.

But we didn't see any frogs.

"If you want to see frogs," my father said, "you'll have to walk down the bank a ways and look hard."

So we decided to do that.

"Fine!" my father said. "But I'll stay here. I think I'm ready for a little nap."

18 "Naps are boring!" we said.

"Sometimes it's nice to be bored," my father said.

We left him with his eyes closed, sitting under a tree.

Huey saw the first frog. He almost stepped on it. It jumped into the water, and we ran after it.

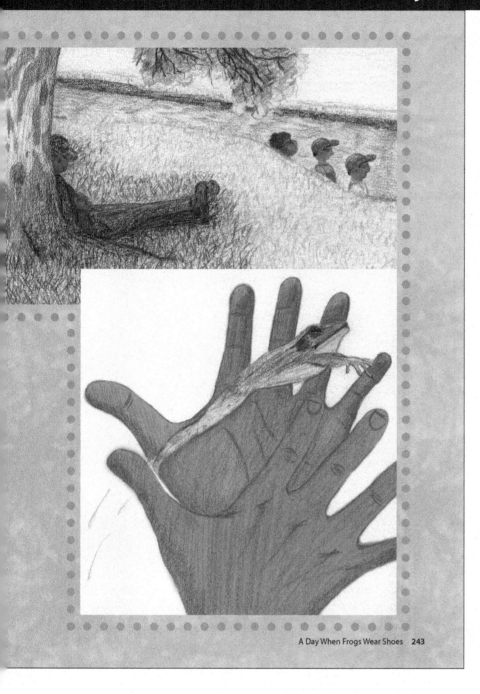

A Day When Frogs Wear Shoes **243**

A Day When Frogs Wear Shoes

Literary Components

19 **Characterization:** Little Huey is still trying to see if Dad is right about the frogs.

20 **Characterization:** Dad relates to the kids in his serious/humorous way. He expects the young reader to be in on the joke.

21 **Characterization:** Dad is never defensive. He is the authority and he and the kids know it. But he is fair, and not afraid to admit when he is wrong (as he did earlier about boredom).

Guiding the Reading

Literal

Q: How did the frogs feel to the children?
A: The frogs were cold and wriggly and they could feel their hearts beating.

Q: What did the children do with the frogs?
A: They threw them back into the river.

Q: What did Dad say when the children told him that frogs don't wear shoes?
A: He was surprised and said, "They don't?"

Analytical

Q: Have you ever held a frog? Would you want to?
A: Answers will vary.

Q: What was nice about the way Dad responded when the kids told him he was wrong about frogs wearing shoes?
A: He didn't try to defend himself or prove he was right. He just said, "I can't be right about everything."

Q: What was it that the children did not understand?
A: They didn't realize that their father was joking when he talked about frogs wearing shoes.

Huey caught it and picked it up, and then I saw another one. I grabbed it.

It was slippery and strong and its body was cold, just like it wasn't the middle of summer. Then Gloria caught one too. The frogs wriggled in our hands, and we felt their hearts beating. Huey looked at their funny webbed feet.

19 "Their feet are good for swimming," he said, "but Dad is wrong. They don't wear shoes!"

"No way," Gloria said. "They sure don't wear shoes."

"Let's go tell him," I said.

We threw our frogs back into the river. They made little trails swimming away from us. And then we went back to my father.

He was sitting under the tree with his eyes shut. It looked like he hadn't moved an inch.

"We found frogs," Huey said, "and we've got news for you. They don't wear shoes!"

20 My father's eyes opened. "They don't?" he said. "Well, I can't be right about
21 everything. Dry your feet. Put your shoes on. It's time to go."

We all sat down to put on our shoes.

I pulled out a sock and put it on.

I stuck my foot into my shoe. My foot wouldn't go in.

I picked up the shoe and looked inside.

"Oh no!" I yelled.

There were two little eyes inside my shoe, looking out at me. Huey and Gloria grabbed their socks. All our shoes had frogs in them, every one.

"What did I tell you," my father said.

"You were right," we said. "It's a day when frogs wear shoes!"

About the Author

When **Ann Cameron** was in third grade, she decided she wanted to be a writer. Today, children around the world have read her *Julian* books, originally inspired by stories that a friend, Julian DeWette, told her about his childhood. One time, Ms. Cameron wanted to write about Julian and Huey taking a river trip with their father. When she sat down to write, however, her idea suddenly seemed boring. It was a cold winter day, and Ms. Cameron began imagining how hot the hottest day would be. She ended up with *A Day When Frogs Wear Shoes*!

Literary Components

22 **Conclusion; Theme; Characterization; Humor:** Dad is right after all. The kids adopt his unique brand of humor and learn about nature in the process. Their initial boredom has evaporated and they have learned that doing something, whether it's work, visiting someone, or exploring nature, will banish boredom.

Guiding the Reading

Literal

Q: What was inside the children's shoes?

A: Frogs!

Q: How did Dad turn out to be right?

A: In a way, the frogs were wearing shoes!

A Day When Frogs Wear Shoes

Weather

Poem tie-in for *A Day When Frogs Wear Shoes*

The number one *reason* for the existence of weather is to provide mankind with an acceptable, neutral, and ever-changing topic of conversation. The number one *fact* about weather is that we cannot change it. And the number one *conclusion* that all people everywhere have come to is that we'll survive it.

Here are some questions you can use to discuss the poem *Weather*.

Q: What does the expression "to weather" something mean?

A: To weather something means to get through it, to survive it without any permanent damage.

Q: What message is the poem giving the reader?

A: The poem is telling us not to become upset when the weather is not to our liking because (a) we can't change it and (b) we'll survive it.

Whether the weather be fine,
Or whether the weather be not,
Whether the weather be cold,
Or whether the weather be hot,
We'll weather the weather
Whatever the weather,
Whether we like it or not!

Weather
Anonymous

Studying the Selection

FIRST IMPRESSIONS

What can you do to turn a hot, boring day into a day to remember?

QUICK REVIEW

1. Why were the three children sitting on the front steps?
2. Why was visiting Dad a "dangerous" idea?
3. What expression did Dad use to describe how hot it was?
4. What did the children find in their shoes at the end of the day?

FOCUS

5. The nice thing about Dad was that he let the kids feel both grown up and like kids. Which things did the children do that made them feel grown up? Which things did they do that let them feel like kids?
6. Dad was a very caring father. He wanted the kids to have confidence, so he gave them jobs and praised them when they did them well. A second trait he wanted them to have was to be able to relax and enjoy the world around them. What did Dad do to help the children develop this trait?

CREATING AND WRITING

7. Everyone has had a day with nothing to do. It might have been a rainy day in summer, or a cold day in winter. It might have been a day when you were sick, or a day when none of your friends could play. Write a short story about what you did to change a day from boring to fun. The story may be true or made up—just so long as it's interesting!
8. The English language is full of colorful expressions. Every generation has its own. Here are a few examples:
   - That name rings a bell.
   - Bite your tongue!
   - She's got a sunny smile.

   Do you know any? Choose an expression that you know or one from a list your teacher will provide and draw a picture of it. Under the picture, write the expression.

Studying the Selection

First Impressions

Ask the students what makes a day boring. Then ask what they do when they're bored. Do they ask an adult for help? How do their parents or other adults help them find something to do? What is the key to not being bored? For some, it is reading. For others, it's some kind of physical activity. Survey your students for their best boredom remedies.

Quick Review

1. The children were sitting on the steps because it was too hot to do anything.
2. Visiting Dad was dangerous, because he might find out that they were bored. More than anything else, Dad hated hearing that someone was bored. He felt that the world was so full of interesting things that no one should ever allow themselves to be bored.
3. Dad said it was a day so hot that frogs wear shoes (to protect their feet from the hot ground).
4. The children found frogs.

Focus

5. The "grown-up things" were the jobs Dad gave the kids to do at the garage. They sorted nuts and bolts, shined fenders, and helped install windshield wipers. The "kid things" were drinking lemonade, eating ice cream, and going to the riverside.
6. Dad wanted the kids to appreciate nature, and be able to relax and enjoy the world around them. He brought them to the riverside and encouraged them to notice all the living things in and around the water.

Creating and Writing

7. The story may be three or four paragraphs long. On the board, write a rudimentary outline for the first, middle, and end paragraphs. It should look like this:

   Opening paragraph: It should introduce the characters in the story and explain why the day is especially boring.

   Middle paragraph(s): It should tell what you wanted to do that was interesting and how you planned for it. Include the problems or difficulties that arose, or nice things that occurred while you were making your plans.

   Last paragraph: Describe how things turned out and how the characters felt at the end of the day.

8. Supply your students with a few more examples of colorful expressions and ask for suggestions from the class. Explain that now is not the time to make up new ones—we'll have that opportunity in the workbook. Then, give them art materials to draw their pictures. Make sure the expression they are depicting is written on the paper. A few more expressions:
   - It's hot as blazes out here.
   - You've let the cat out of the bag.
   - That money is burning a hole in my pocket.
   - That's a pipe dream.
   - She's got stars in her eyes.

The Burning of the Rice Fields

Lesson in Literature

Cause and Effect
The Grandmother

1. The people in the town liked Grandma and wanted to be like her. That was the *cause* of their being nice and not criticizing other people.
2. The *effect* of the War would be much suffering. People would be injured and killed.
3. The *effect* of Grandma's kindness was that the generals of both sides sent soldiers to guard Grandma's house for the remainder of the War.

Selection Summary

This simple, inspiring story has many of the elements of a Japanese folktale. It has a wise and beloved hero, a village, a natural disaster, and a marvelous and satisfying ending. The hero is Hamaguchi, a wealthy farmer who lives at the top of a hill surrounded by fertile rice fields. The village at the bottom of the hill is peopled by villagers who farm the fields. They are devoted to Hamaguchi who is, in turn, devoted to them. As the story opens, the harvest has just been completed. The villagers are down in the village celebrating the fine harvest, but Hamaguchi has stayed home with his grandson, Tada, in his farm at the top of the hill. He would have liked to join the revelers but he is hot and tired. He looks down at the village as the lights come on under the setting sun. As he gazes past the village out to sea, he is shaken by a terrifying sight. The sea, darker than usual, appears to be rolling away from the shore.

Hamaguchi calls to his grandson, demanding that he bring him a torch immediately. Tada complies and Hamaguchi runs to the rice fields and sets the stacks of harvested rice on fire. He runs from row to row, torching the harvested rice until the entire harvest is burning. The villagers, seeing the fire, run up the hill to try and put out the flames. Hamaguchi will not allow them to help. As the people gather at the top of the hill, mystified by Hamaguchi's strange behavior, they see a tidal wave crash onto the shore and devastate the entire village. Every single villager had escaped death because they had all come to help Hamaguchi.

"That is why I set fire to the rice" explains Hamaguchi. The villagers bow to the man whose quick thinking and selflessness have saved their lives.

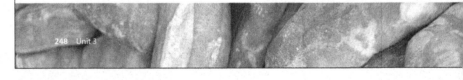

Lesson in Literature
THE GRANDMOTHER

CAUSE AND EFFECT

- A **cause** is something that makes another thing happen. (Joe *hit* the ball.)
- An **effect** is what happens due to a cause. (The window was *broken* by the ball.)
- In a story, sometimes the author will start with a cause and end with an effect.
- In a story, sometimes the author will start with an effect and end with a cause. (Mrs. Wilkins woke up to find her window broken. What had caused it to break?)

THINK ABOUT IT!

1. What caused the people in the town to try hard not to criticize others or say mean things about other people?
2. What would be the effect of the War on all the people?
3. What was the effect that Grandma's kindness had on the generals?

Not so long ago, there lived a grandmother in a town not far away. Her husband was no longer alive, but she had several grown-up children and many grandchildren. She was wise and kind, good to friends and strangers alike. It was almost as if she were everyone's grandmother. In fact, all of the people in the town called her Grandma.

Her children and grandchildren had learned from her. They each helped their neighbors whenever there was a need. They tried hard not to criticize others or to say mean things about other people. They had great respect for Grandma and wanted to be like her.

Then, war came to the land. The War was being fought between the Northerners and the Southerners. There were no newspapers or radios or telephones in the town, but eventually the townspeople got word of the conflict. Because the town was located mostly in the South, the townsfolk declared that they would stand with the Southerners.

Grandma said little about the War, except to shake her head sadly and say softly, "What a pity!" Although some of the reasons for the War were very important, the fighting would cause great suffering for many people. How much better it would have been if the struggle between the North and South had been solved peacefully!

Grandma was surprised to see that some of her own children and

Getting Started

This selection is about a man of outstanding character. It is a good vehicle for discussing what qualities make someone worthy of respect, as Hamaguchi was. Before you proceed, make sure that you are clear in your own mind about the definition of *character*. Character is the sum total of certain traits such as honesty, integrity, foresight, courage, selflessness, and kindheartedness. A person who possesses these traits in good measure is called a person *of character*. A person who is lacking in one or more of these areas is said to have *bad character* or *no character*. But this is too advanced for your students. What you should discuss with them is character *traits*. At a later date you, or a future teacher, can explain that good character traits add up to character.

Start the discussion by clarifying the difference between a *character* in a story and *character traits*. Explain that a character in a story is any person who appears in a story, as they have learned. Character traits are qualities that a person has. Ask your students to name some character traits. In

Target Skill: Recognizing that a character's actions influence the events of a story	
Learning Strategy: Questioning and making connections	
Common Core Curriculum: RL.3.3; W.3.1	
Genre: Folktale	

Related Vocabulary

abundant (uh BUN dunt) *adj.*: plentiful	
ancient (AIN shunt) *adj.*: extremely old	
boldly (BOLD lee) *adv.*: fearlessly	
decisive (dee SY siv) *adj.*: able to make decisions easily	
festive (FESS tive) *adj.*: happy; celebrating some happy occasion	
generosity (JEN uh ROSS ih tee) *n.*: the quality of giving	
panic (PAN ik) *n.*: sudden, extreme fear; *v.*: to feel sudden, extreme fear	
predict (prih DIKT) *v.*: suggest what will happen in the future	

Workbook

Related Pages: 80-85	
Answer Key Pages: 9-10	

grandchildren were excited by the War. Most of them were cheering for the South to win. Grandma said quietly to her oldest daughter, "Don't they know that even when you win a war, you still lose?" Nonetheless, several of her younger sons and her older grandsons went off to fight in the Southern Army.

Some of the townspeople thought that Grandma didn't take one side or the other because she was getting old and becoming less wise. Others thought it was because Grandma's cabin was located exactly halfway in the North and halfway in the South.

As the War went on, there was news that many young men had lost their lives in the fighting. As the fighting came closer to the town, people approached Grandma and declared, "Grandma, you have to take a side! You have to be for the South." Grandma remained silent.

That afternoon, Grandma called all of her daughters to her cabin. She told them that they needed to put all other chores aside. They must begin making loaves of bread, filling up available bottles with water from the well, and finally, tearing cloth for bandages. The daughters and grandchildren set to work right away.

When neighbors heard about this, they, too, baked bread, got water, and made bandages. Soon, the whole town was busy.

Six days later, the battle arrived nearly at Grandma's front door. In the field across the road, the soldiers fought. But stored in Grandma's cabin, there were more than a hundred loaves of bread, fifty bottles of water, and piles of bandages.

The fighting was terrible. It lasted for many hours. When it was over, hundreds of wounded soldiers from North and South lay about the field. They called for water. They called for their mothers. They called for their wives. The cries that came from the injured Northerners were no different from the cries that came from the injured Southerners.

Grandma gathered her children and grandchildren together. For once, she spoke very loudly. "It is time to go and give aid. You will not choose between North and South. We help every young man out there."

When word of Grandma's kindness reached the generals of the Northern and Southern armies, each side sent a regiment of soldiers to guard Grandma's house for the remainder of the War.

addition to the ones mentioned above, they may add wisdom, intelligence, patience, generosity, and such negative traits as stinginess, dishonesty, cruelty, and so on. Ask them if they consider some character traits more important than others. Ask them also if they consider some more difficult to acquire than others. It might be interesting to ask them to name one good trait that they think they have.

Finally, ask them which traits or qualities they think a hero would have. Write the list on the board and tell them that, when they have read the story, the class will take a look at the list and see if the hero of this story had those qualities.

Into . . . *The Burning of the Rice Fields*

Open the discussion by asking your class first, what a hero is, and second, if they can name any heroes. The natural response of a child is to picture a strong, brave person who has won some major battles in some arena or another. There are football heroes and war heroes. There are local heroes and national heroes. There are fictional heroes and historical heroes. Ask the children if they can find some single quality that every hero must have. That quality, as we state in the Student Edition, is selflessness.

A hero is someone (e.g. a firefighter, a rescue team, a Saint Bernard dog) who has put another person or idea (e.g. his country, freedom, the lives of others) before himself. A hero may be famous or unknown. We discuss famous heroes because they inspire us; they teach us to give our utmost to help another. But it is important to recognize that heroism can be very private and very individual, it can be something that each one of your students is capable of. Every time we do something that is selfless we are exercising our "hero" muscles and preparing for a time when we might be called upon for even greater heroism.

The Burning of the Rice Fields

A second quality associated with heroism is courage. Courage does not mean being unafraid, it means doing what you think is right even if you *are* afraid. In this story, the hero could have been afraid of the poverty into which he is throwing himself by burning his rice fields. But he doesn't allow that thought to deter him from his goal—saving the people of the village from the tidal wave.

A hero is someone who takes responsibility. That is to say, a hero doesn't wait for someone else to take care of a problem or find an excuse to do nothing. A hero sees a problem and makes it his own. Hamaguchi could easily have wrung his hands as the tidal wave swept over the villagers. No one would have blamed him or thought there was anything he could have done. Hamaguchi could have debated in his mind about what to do, whether it would be effective, and whether there was a way to save the village at less cost to himself and procrastinated until it was too late to do anything. The swiftness with which Hamaguchi came to a decision is part of his heroism. Because he is selfless he can come to a decision instantly. If saving the people is all that matters, deciding what to do is easy. It is only when you are weighing your own needs in the balance that things get murky. Every real hero can think quickly and clearly because he has a single goal.

Eyes On: Cause and Effect

The literary skill for this selection is *identifying cause and effect* by studying the thoughts and actions of the characters. The strategy for achieving an understanding of causes and their effects is *asking questions and making connections*. Adult readers do this automatically. As we read, we ask ourselves how a certain character's behavior will shape the outcome of the plot. We are curious about the effect the actions of one character will have on the other characters. Above all, we want to know the cause for every character's actions and the connection between these actions and the final outcome. A complex book will have layers of causes and effects that are ripe for analysis. A simple story such as this one is the best way to start off.

You can teach cause and effect as you move through the story. When you have read the opening of the story, you can start by listing some of the information given so far.

1. Hundreds of rice stacks lined Hamaguchi's fields.
2. Everyone was down in the village.
3. Hamaguchi stayed home.

Each of these facts has a cause. We can discover that cause by asking "why?" Why were there hundreds of rice stacks in the fields? Why was everyone down in the village? Why had Hamaguchi stayed home? The answers to the questions are the causes:

1. The harvest had been good.
2. The people wanted to celebrate the end of the harvest.
3. Hamaguchi was hot and tired.

As you progress through the year, your students will move from identifying very immediate, material causes to searching for psychological or emotional causes and motives. That is to say, they will become more sophisticated readers. In this story, you can ask a few "why" questions that don't have tangible answers:

1. Why did Hamaguchi run to burn the rice fields—why didn't he take a moment to think of a better plan, or to warn the people? (Hamaguchi's running is the effect—what was the cause?)

THE Burning OF THE Rice Fields

Lafcadio Hearn

FAR AWAY IN JAPAN, many years ago, lived good old Hamaguchi.[1] He was the wisest man of his village, and the people loved and honored him.

Hamaguchi was a wealthy farmer. His farmhouse stood on a hillside high above the seashore. Down by the shore, and scattered up the hill, were the houses of his neighbors. Around his own house the ground was flat, like the top of a huge step in the hillside, and all about him stretched his rice fields.

1. Hamaguchi (HA ma GOO chee)

1
2
3

Literary Components

❶ Setting: The place is Japan, the time is many years ago.

❷ Characterization: Hamaguchi's character is clearly presented: he is good, old, wise, beloved, and honored.

❸ Setting: We are given more details about the setting, and they will prove very important to the plot.

Guiding the Reading

Literal

Q: What country is the setting for this story?
A: The story is set in Japan.

Q: Describe Hamaguchi.
A: He is the wisest man of his village; he is loved and honored.

Q: Where was Hamaguchi's farm built?
A: His farm stood on a hillside high above the seashore.

Q: What stood between Hamaguchi's farm and the seashore?
A: The houses of his neighbors were built between the hill and the seashore.

Q: If Hamaguchi's farm was at the top of a hill, how did he have fields, which need flat land?
A: Around Hagamuchi's house the ground was flat.

Analytical

Q: Why did the people love Hamaguchi?
A: They loved him because he was wise and good.

2. Why did the people climb up the hill when they saw the fire? (The effect is their climbing the hill; what was the cause/motivation?)

3. Tada was really frightened (the effect). Why? What was the cause?

4. The people bowed to Hamaguchi (the effect). Why? What was the cause?

The causes in each case:

1. Hamaguchi ran because there was no time to be lost; the tidal wave would reach shore if he delayed at all.

2. The people climbed the hill because they were so devoted to Hamaguchi that they would do anything to help him, and they thought it was he who needed help.

3. Tada was frightened that his grandfather had gone mad, since his actions were those of a madman.

4. The people bowed to show how much they respected Hamaguchi's self-sacrifice.

The Burning of the Rice Fields

Literary Components

4 **Setting:** The fact that the harvest has just taken place, so important to the plot, is part of the setting of the story.

5 **Characterization:** Don't think Hamaguchi was above joining the villagers; no, he would have liked to join them.

6 **Rising Action:** The stage is now completely set for something to happen. We know the characters, the time, the place, the situation—we are waiting for action.

7 **Rising Action:** Here is the action we knew was coming. But what does it mean?

8 **Characterization:** Hamaguchi is experienced, calm, and wise. He is not easily frightened.

Guiding the Reading

Literal

Q: What was the season?
A: It was harvest time (usually autumn).

Q: Where was the harvested rice?
A: It was all stacked up in the fields on the hill.

Q: Why didn't Hamaguchi join the villagers in their celebration?
A: He was too tired to join them.

Q: What scene did Hamaguchi and his grandson see below them?
A: They saw the village all decorated with flags and paper lanterns, and the people getting ready for the dance.

Q: What suddenly happened?
A: Suddenly the hillside shook.

Q: What caused the hill to shake?
A: Hamaguchi assumed that the hill shook because of an earthquake.

Analytical

Q: Why does Hamaguchi think the earthquake is far away?
A: He thinks the earthquake is far away because the shaking is so gentle. If the earthquake were near, the shaking would have been much stronger.

4 It was the time of harvest. Hundreds of rice stacks lined Hamaguchi's fields. It had been a fine harvest, and tonight down in the village everyone was having a good time.

5 Hamaguchi sat outside his house and looked down into the village. He would have liked to join the other villagers, but he was too tired—the day had been very hot. So he stayed at home with his little grandson, Tada. They could see the flags and the paper lanterns that hung across the streets of the

6 village, and see the people getting ready for the dance. The low sun lighted up all the moving bits of color below.

It was still very hot, though a strong breeze was beginning to blow in

7 from the sea. Suddenly the hillside shook—just a little, as if a wave were rolling slowly under it. The house creaked and rocked gently for a moment. Then all became still again.

"An earthquake," thought Hamaguchi, "but not very near. The worst of it seems far away."

8 Hamaguchi was not frightened, for he had felt the earth quake many a time before. Yet he looked anxiously toward the village. Then, suddenly, he rose to his feet and looked out

The Burning of the Rice Fields

at the sea. The sea was very dark, and, strange to say, it seemed to be running away from the land.

Soon all the village had noticed how the water was rolling out. The people hurried down to the beach. Not one of them had ever seen such a thing before.

For a moment, on the hillside, Hamaguchi stood and looked. Then he called, "Tada! Quick—very quick! Light me a torch!"

Literary Components

9 **Rising Suspense:** Something has disturbed Hamaguchi and we know the main action of the story is approaching.

10 **Important Detail:** It is important to realize that the people had gone even closer to the danger at hand.

11 **Characterization; Conflict; Rising Suspense:** What is happening? Whatever it is that is alarming Hamaguchi is very important and frightening. What we see is that Hamaguchi is a man of action.

Guiding the Reading

Literal

Q: What did Hamaguchi notice about the sea that was very odd?

A: Hamaguchi noticed that the sea was very dark and seemed to be running away from the land.

Q: Did anyone else notice this?

A: Yes. Soon all the village had noticed and hurried down to the beach to see what was happening.

Q: What did Hamaguchi ask Tada to do?

A: He asked Tada to quickly light a torch for him.

The Burning of the Rice Fields

Literary Components

⓬ Approaching Climax; Rising Suspense: Something significant is happening but we still don't know why. Hamaguchi is setting fire to his own crops—to what purpose?

⓭ Powerful Visual Image: The towering flames against the dark sky create a strong visual image.

⓮ Rising Suspense: The author uses the character of Tada to echo our own thoughts and increase the suspense.

Guiding the Reading

Literal

Q: Where did Hamaguchi run with the lighted torch?
A: He ran to the rice fields.

Q: What did Hamaguchi do with the torch?
A: He set all the piles of rice on fire.

Q: Why did the rice burn so easily?
A: The rice was dry and the seabreeze was strong.

Analytical

Q: Why do you think Hamaguchi set fire to the rice fields?
A: Answers will vary. Keep reading for the true answer.

Q: By burning the rice, what was Hamaguchi destroying?
A: The rice was their food supply and all their wealth.

Tada ran into the house and picked up one of the torches that stood ready for use on stormy nights. He lighted it and ran back to his grandfather. Quickly the old man grabbed the torch and hurried to the rice fields. Tada ran with him, wondering what he was going to do.

⓬ When they reached the first row of rice stacks, Hamaguchi ran along the row, touching the torch to each stack as he passed. The rice was dry, and the fire caught quickly. The seabreeze, blowing stronger, began to drive the

⓭ flames ahead. Row after row, the stacks caught fire. Soon flames and smoke towered up against the sky.

⓮ Tada ran after his grandfather, crying, "Grandfather, why? Why?"

The Burning of the Rice Fields

Had his grandfather gone mad? Why was he burning the rice that was their food and all their wealth? But Hamaguchi went on from stack to stack, till he reached the end of the field. Then he threw down his torch and waited.

The bell-ringer in the tower on the hill saw the flames and set the big bell booming. And, down on the beach, the people turned and began to climb the hill. If Hamaguchi's rice fields were afire, nothing would keep them from helping him.

First up the hill came some of the young men, who wanted to fight the fire at once. But Hamaguchi stood in front of the fields and held out his hands to stop them.

"Let it burn," he ordered. "Let it burn."

Literary Components

15 **Important Fact:** In case the young reader hadn't realized what burning the rice would mean to Hamaguchi, the author spells it out.

16 **Turning Point:** When the people leave the seashore and begin to run up the hill, Hamaguchi's plan begins to work.

17 **Characterization; Theme:** The people are characterized as supremely loyal to Hamaguchi. (As we will see, Hamaguchi is equally loyal to them.) This is one part of the story's theme. The devotion the people felt to Hamaguchi saved their lives. Their act of giving gave them untold rewards.

Guiding the Reading

Literal

Q: What did the bell-ringer do when he saw the fire?

A: He rang the big bell.

Q: What did the people do when they heard the bell ringing?

A: They ran up the hill to fight the fire.

Q: What did Hamaguchi do when he saw the young men?

A: He stood in front of the fields and held out his hands to stop them.

Q: What did Hamaguchi say to the people who wanted to put out the fire?

A: He told them to let it burn.

Analytical

Q: What do you think was normally the job of the bell-ringer?

A: His job was to alert people to danger, or to call them together to help someone in danger.

The Burning of the Rice Fields

Guiding the Reading

Literal

Q: Why did everyone keep coming?

A: They all came to help put out the fire.

Q: What did Hamaguchi continue to do?

A: He continued to tell them not to extinguish the fire.

Q: What did Tada say when the people asked him why his grandfather wouldn't let them fight the fire?

A: He told them he didn't know. He told them that his grandfather had set the fire and he couldn't understand what was happening.

Q: Does Hamaguchi try to hide the fact that he was the one who set the fire?

A: No. He clearly says he set the fire.

Q: What does he ask the people?

A: He asks if everyone is there.

Analytical

Q: What do you think is happening—do you think Hamaguchi has lost his mind?

A: Answers will vary.

Q: Can you figure out, yet, why Hamaguchi set fire to the fields?

A: Answers will vary. If you want to give your class a hint, tell them to notice the line, "Are all the people here now?"

Soon the whole village was coming. Men and boys, women and girls, mothers with babies on their backs, and even little children came. Children could help pass buckets of water.

Still Hamaguchi stood in front of his burning fields and waited. Meanwhile the sun went down.

The people began to question Tada. What had happened? Why wouldn't his grandfather let them fight the fire? Was he mad?

"I don't know," cried Tada, for he was really frightened. "Grandfather set fire to the rice on purpose. I saw him do it!"

"Yes," cried Hamaguchi. "I set fire to the rice. Are all the people here now?"

The villagers looked about them. Then they answered, "All are here, but we do not understand—"

The Burning of the Rice Fields

Literary Components

18 Climax: As the people turn from the blazing rice fields to the thundering tidal wave, understanding dawns.

19 End of Climax: If the tidal wave slamming into the village was the first part of the climax, watching it recede and seeing the devastation it has left is the second part of the climax.

20 Resolution; Characterization: The mystery of Hamaguchi's behavior is solved and disaster, at least in terms of human life, has been averted. Hamaguchi's greatness is revealed.

21 Characterization; Resolution: Hamaguchi does not rest on his laurels for a moment. He has just saved everyone's life but, without pausing for a moment, he starts to worry about where they will stay until the village can be rebuilt. The reader feels confident that, with leadership like Hamaguchi's and cooperation like the villagers', the village will be rebuilt.

22 Characterization; Conclusion: The author repeats that Hamaguchi had impoverished himself without a thought in order to save the villagers. The story concludes satisfactorily by having the villagers recognize just how much Hamaguchi had sacrificed.

Guiding the Reading

Literal

Q: What did Hamaguchi then show the people?
A: He showed them the enormous wall of water that was headed for shore.

Q: What happened when the water hit the shore?
A: The noise was louder than thunder; the hillside shook; a sheet of foam dashed all the way up the hill.

Q: How did the village look when the sea went back?
A: Not a house was left on the hillside or along the shore.

Q: Can you explain now why Hamaguchi set his fields on fire?
A: Hamaguchi wanted everyone to run up the hillside to help put out the fire. This would take them away from the tidal wave that swept through the village.

"Look!" shouted Hamaguchi, as loud as he could. He was pointing to the sea. "Look! Now do you think I have gone mad?"

All turned and looked toward the sea. Far, far out, where the sea and sky seem to meet, stretched a cloudy line that came nearer and nearer. It was the sea coming back to the shore. But it towered like a great wall of rock. It rolled more swiftly than a kite could fly.

18 "The sea!" screamed the people. Hardly had they spoken, when the great wall of water struck the shore. The noise was louder than any thunder. The hillside shook. A sheet of foam was dashed far up to where the people stood.

19 When the sea went back, not a house was left below them on the hillside or along the shore. The whole village had been swept away.

The people stood silent, too frightened to speak. Then they heard
20 Hamaguchi saying gently, "That is why I set fire to the rice ... My house still
21 stands, and there is room for many. The tower on the hill still stands. There is shelter there for the rest."

Then the people woke, as if from a dream, and
22 understood. Hamaguchi had made himself poor to save them, and they realized how great a man he was.

About the Author

When **Lafcadio Hearn** was born in Greece in 1850, his parents named him Patricio Lafcadio Tessima Carlos Hearn. Mr. Hearn grew up in Ireland and went to school in England. When he was 19 years old, he came to America. In America, he worked in a library for a short time, but he was fired because he spent too much time reading instead of working. When Mr. Hearn was 40 years old, he moved to Japan, where he changed his name to Koizumi Yakumo and wrote many books about Japan.

258   Unit 3

Q: What kind offer did Hamaguchi make?
A: He offered to house the people until they could rebuild their homes.

Q: What had Hamaguchi sacrificed to save the people?
A: He had sacrificed his wealth by burning the rice fields.

Analytical

Q: Do you think the people still loved and respected Hamaguchi now that he was as poor as they were?
A: The people loved and respected him even more now because he had sacrificed his wealth to save them.

Q: What do you think will happen to Hamaguchi and the villagers?
A: Hopefully, they will be able to rebuild their village. But they will need outside help to replace their food supply.

The Burning of the Rice Fields

Until I Saw the Sea

Poem tie-in for *The Burning of the Rice Fields*

This poem uses language, verbs in particular, to make us see the sea a little differently. The poem speaks of wind that "wrinkles" the water, of sun that "splinters" the view of the sea, and of the waves being the sea's breath, inhaling and exhaling on the shore. It shows us how the poet sees things a little differently from the rest of us, and helps us see the world in a new light.

UNTIL I SAW THE SEA

Lilian Moore

Until I saw the sea
I did not know
that wind
could wrinkle water so.

I never knew
that sun
could splinter a whole sea of blue.

Nor
did I know before,
a sea breathes in and out
upon a shore.

Studying the Selection

FIRST IMPRESSIONS

Do you remember Tassai and her split-second decision? Here's someone else who must decide in one moment whether or not to give up all his wealth. Are you good at making big decisions? What about little ones?

QUICK REVIEW

1. Why was Hamaguchi a wealthy man?
2. Why were the villagers celebrating that night?
3. What did Hamaguchi see that shocked him?
4. Why did Hamaguchi set fire to the fields?

FOCUS

5. Hamaguchi showed that he was very smart; he knew just how to get the villagers to run from the village. Another trait Hamaguchi had was that he was decisive. He made decisions quickly and acted upon them. What important decision does Hamaguchi make and carry out?
6. Tada was so loyal to Hamaguchi, that he always obeyed him without questioning him. How did this trait help Hamaguchi's plan succeed?

CREATING AND WRITING

7. The author describes the huge wave that destroyed the village by comparing it to things with which we are familiar. He writes, *it towered like a great wall of rock. It rolled more swiftly than a kite could fly.* Close your eyes and picture a huge wave. If you were an author, how would *you* describe it? Write three sentences in which you compare the giant wave to something else that helps the reader feel its power.
8. The village below Hamaguchi's house would have to be rebuilt. What does a new village need? Your teacher will divide your class into groups and give each group a poster board. Each group will draw their idea of what the new village will look like. Before you begin drawing the village, write a list of the shops and buildings you will include.

Studying the Selection

- -

First Impressions

For some people, making decisions comes easily. For others, it is a painful process full of self-doubt and second-guessing. Ask your class for a show of hands: who here is a quick decision maker? Can you give us an example? Then ask the indecisive ones to raise their hands. Ask them to talk about choices that are hard for them to make. How do they react to questions like *chocolate or vanilla*? *Play inside or outside*? *Go with your Mom or stay home and play*? Ask your students if they have any suggestions for those who would like to make decisions more easily. Explain that decision-making is a very important skill, and that it is one that a person can work at improving.

Quick Review

1. Hamaguchi was wealthy because he owned many rice fields which produced a lot of rice.
2. The villagers were celebrating the conclusion of a very good rice harvest.
3. Hamaguchi saw that the sea was a very dark color and seemed to be rolling away from the land.
4. Hamaguchi hoped that when the villagers saw the fire they would run up the hill away from the village to his fields. They would thus be saved from the tidal wave that was about to roll over the village at the bottom of the hill.

Focus

5. Hamaguchi wasted no time in setting his fields on fire.
6. Tada's unquestioning obedience allowed Hamaguchi to put his plan into effect immediately. Had Tada delayed by asking a lot of questions, or being too lazy to run and bring the fire, the tidal wave could have struck before Hamaguchi could burn the fields.

Creating and Writing

7. Encourage your students to come up with inventive similes. To give them some practice, ask them to describe something else using similes. For example, *The silver cup shone like ...* a mirror/a jewel/a flashing sword ... *The wind howled outside like ...* a bear/an angry elephant/a train whistle ...
8. Distribute poster boards and drawing materials. If you choose, you could make the drawings three-dimensional by handing out little objects the students could glue onto the poster board.

   Make sure they make their list of buildings before beginning their drawings. The lists should include buildings like a schoolhouse, a fire station, and a hospital. Remind the students to put Hamaguchi's house at the top of the hill and rice fields on the hill. Remind them that this is a Japanese village, so they can include some nice touches like a tofu shop or a silk store. This exercise will develop their concept of what services a town needs to function.

Lesson in Literature

What Is Biography?

Betsy Brotman in Liberia

1. Betsy came to Liberia to research diseases. She was hired by an American drug company.

2. Betsy and her husband treated the chimps like children. They were kept in diapers and lived in the house. They were bottle-fed and later taught to eat with spoons and forks.

3. Betsy was kindhearted, inventive, courageous, smart, idealistic, and practical. Here is one example of each.

   - **Kindhearted:** She opened her home to all travelers.
   - **Inventive:** She thought of digging a deep canal between islands to separate the chimps.
   - **Courageous:** She stayed in Liberia during the wars.
   - **Idealistic:** She wanted to save the lives of "her" animals and worked very hard to do so.
   - **Practical:** She managed to live in very difficult circumstances and to do successful research against all odds.

Selection Summary

This is a biographical sketch of Helen Martini, the first woman zookeeper in the history of the Bronx Zoo. The narrative begins by asking the reader to imagine being a cold and hungry lion cub who is taken in, warmed, fed, and rocked to sleep by a wonderful, caring person. The person is Helen, and it is her husband, Fred, who has brought the baby lion home. Going back in time, the narrator explains that Helen and her husband had not started out with the intention of nursing sick animals. It was only after they lost their firstborn child and were told they would not be able to have any other children that they began to collect animals. Living in close proximity to the Bronx Zoo, Fred decided to take a job there. Soon, the birds and dogs in his house were displaced by lions and tiger cubs.

After successfully nursing the lion cub, MacArthur, back to health, Helen and Fred took on three tiny newborn Bengal tigers. In a short time, the scrawny babies were sleek, fat cubs, ready to go back to the zoo. They still needed bottles, however, and Helen set up a little room in the zoo where she could minister to them. From that experience grew the idea of opening a little nursery in an

Lesson in Literature...

BETSY BROTMAN IN LIBERIA

WHAT IS BIOGRAPHY?

- A **biography** is the true story of a person's life.
- A biography may take the form of a short story, a full-length book, or even a drama.
- A biography may cover the entire life of a person or may tell about only one part of the person's life.
- A good biography will tell only the facts about a person's life and allow the reader to form an opinion about that person.

THINK ABOUT IT!

1. What work did Betsy come to Liberia to do, and who had hired her to do it?

2. How did Betsy and her husband treat the chimps? Bring a few examples of the way they treated the chimps.

3. From a person's actions, one can learn about the character traits this person has. Name one character trait that Betsy had, and write down how you know that she had that trait.

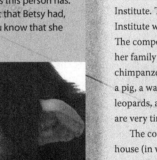

In 1974, Betsy Brotman arrived in Robertsfield, Liberia. She had come to the West African country from the United States. She was 32 and was going to do research on diseases.

Betsy was the director of the Liberian Biomedical Research Institute. The land set aside for the Institute was called a compound. The compound on which Betsy and her family lived became home to 150 chimpanzees, many cats, several dogs, a pig, a warthog, a mongoose, two baby leopards, and two dik-diks. Dik-diks are very tiny antelope.

The compound included the big house (in which Betsy, her daughter, and her husband, Brian, lived), a house

262 Unit 3

unused room at the zoo. Helen did that and her nursery became a revolving door, admitting sick, weak baby animals and turning out healthy bouncing young specimens. From volunteer nurse, Helen went to official zookeeper. Her loving care broke all records: in a zoo where no tiger born there had ever survived, she raised twenty-seven to adulthood. Helen continued to take baby animals home, too. The products of all these ministrations were sent to zoos all over the world.

Getting Started

Read the story aloud until page 268 and the words, "So he did." Then read the following questions to your students.

(For more information on how to use the aural exercises, see *Getting Started/The Story of the White Sombrero*.)

1. The author starts out by asking you to imagine you are a
   a. baby tiger.
   b. cold, hungry baby.
   c. man with a cage.
   d. sickly lion cub.

for the veterinarian, a large laboratory, many clean, spacious cages for the chimps, and many smaller guesthouses for visitors. The big house was set on stilts, because of the floods that occurred during the rainy season.

Betsy's home was like a hotel for people visiting Liberia. All of the pilots and flight attendants who flew on planes to Liberia from Europe and the United States visited Betsy. People who worked for foreign companies became good friends, as did the ambassadors from other countries.

Betsy worked very hard to organize the Institute and to do research that would help human beings. She loved the animals. Every chimp had a name and Betsy knew all 150 of them. The mongoose was called "Goosie," and lived in the big house. Of course the dogs and cats were allowed to sleep inside. The warthog came as a baby, and slept in the living room until he weighed 200 lbs.

Two of the chimps were babies. Fat Fanny Foo-Foo and Evelyn were kept in diapers and lived in the house. As infants, they were bottle-fed. As they got older, they wore little dresses and ate at the table with spoons and forks.

There were several bad wars in Liberia while Betsy lived there. During the wars, her daughter went to live with Betsy's parents in the United States. Betsy and Brian would not leave, because they wanted to protect the chimpanzees from the soldiers.

In the late 1980s, Betsy realized that the chimpanzees needed to be reintroduced to the wild. If a time came when they could no longer live on the compound, they would have to know how to take care of themselves. For a long time she tried to get the governments of other African countries interested in taking them. But in spite of many promises that were made, the chimps remained in Liberia on the compound. Finally, she persuaded some of the officials in Liberia to let her use two islands for the chimps' home.

She and her husband and their helpers took some of the chimps in boats to the islands. Every day, they took a boat full of mangoes, and went down the river to feed the chimps. The chimps were unable to learn how to find food after being cared for so many years.

One night, one of the big male chimps went over to the other island and killed another chimp. Betsy realized that they would have to dig a much deeper canal between the two islands. One of the drug companies for whom she was doing research agreed to pay for the digging.

While she was in Liberia, Betsy did not only adopt chimpanzees, a mongoose, and a warthog. She adopted four children, raised them, and they now live in the U.S. Sadly, her husband Brian died in 1993 during one of the wars.

Betsy left Liberia for good in 2009. She had spent a long time there, and she did not want to leave. The company that she had worked for all of those years no longer wanted to do medical research. She left behind the 63 chimpanzees that had somehow survived the many years of war.

Mother to Tigers

Target Skill: Understanding that a biography is usually a narrative about a famous or noteworthy person
Learning Strategy: Evaluating
Common Core Curriculum: RL.3.3; RL.3.5
Genre: Biography

Vocabulary

abandoned (uh BAN dund) *adj.*: left to manage on its own; deserted
roam (ROME) *v.*: to wander all around
pouncing (POWN sing) *v.*: swooping down on suddenly
strolled *v.*: walked in a casual way, without hurrying
grace *n.*: smooth and beautiful movement
pitiful (PIH tih FULL) *adj.*: causing one to feel pity
challenge (CHAL unj) *n.*: a test of one's abilities
sleek *adj.*: well-fed and looking fit
crouch *v.*: to bend low close to the ground preparing to leap
official (uh FISH ul) *adj.*: approved by the people in charge

Workbook

Related Pages: 86-91
Answer Key Page: 10

2. Which of these does the woman not do for you?
   a. bathe you
   b. sing to you
   c. warm your bottle
   d. put you on a pillow in her lap

3. Where would you go to sleep?
   a. in a box in the kitchen
   b. in a cage on the porch
   c. in the back seat of the car
   d. on the floor of a bedroom

4. Where would you go when you had grown bigger?
   a. to the veterinarian
   b. to the Cleveland zoo
   c. back to the jungle
   d. to the Bronx Zoo

5. Why did Helen and her husband take in baby animals?
   a. Helen had always planned to raise cubs.
   b. They wanted to raise animals because they had no children.
   c. They wanted to raise animals as pets for their children.
   d. They believed wild animals could be trained to live in houses.

6. What was Fred's job?
   a. Jeweler   b. Animal trainer   c. Scientist   d. Fred was retired

7. What was right down the street from Fred and Helen?
   a. an animal habitat
   b. the Bronx fire station
   c. a jewelry shop
   d. the Bronx Zoo

8. Why did Helen suggest that Fred work at the zoo?
   a. because he loved animals
   b. because they were both out of work and nearly broke
   c. because his good friend worked there
   d. because, as a scientist, he would be able to study the animals more closely

Mother to Tigers

Into . . . *Mother to Tigers*

By way of introduction, let us say that there are two tacks you may take here, depending both on you and on your class. If you and/or your class are the animal/outdoorsy/pet-owning types, gear your discussion towards animals and pets. If you and your class are city folk, and don't know a boxer from a beagle, you may focus more on the nurturing aspect of this story.

Almost every child has either cared for a small animal or imagined what it would be like to care for one. Nursing a sickly animal is a little different, but still in the realm of experience of many children. The author draws the reader in by asking the reader to imagine being hungry and cold only to be fed and warmed and comforted by a loving "mother." The picture is irresistible. You may ask the students if they've ever felt hungry or cold or sick and then taken care of by a loving parent. Most will enjoy sharing that experience and telling how they felt after they were comforted and put to bed. Once they have described *their* feelings, ask them for some words to describe their caregiver. They will come up with words like loving, caring, gentle, warm, and comforting. Make sure they include words that describe devotion, steadiness, and patience.

You may then wish to discuss the question of why someone nurtures another, especially if the other is not their own child. Perhaps the children will express, in their own way, the idea that many people just naturally want to give. Helping someone or something else makes the helper feel good and fulfilled. You might explain that it is a "win/win situation." Ask your students if there is some area in which they give of themselves without receiving any tangible reward. Students may tell you they help their grandfather or watch their baby brother. Another may help a lonely neighbor or a handicapped friend. Ultimately, all giving comes from the same source and is its own reward.

Eyes On: Biography

Mother to Tigers is a biographical story. Make sure your class knows the difference between a biography and a work of fiction. Assure them that in a biography, everything is true, unlike, for example, a piece of historical fiction where parts are true and parts are not, or a folktale, where all is fiction. Ask your students why an author may want to write the biography of a particular person. The answers should include the following:

a. This person was an important participant in events that affected many people. Examples: George Washington, Abraham Lincoln, Martin Luther King, Jr.

b. This person had a unique skill or talent. Examples: Ludwig van Beethoven, a great composer; Babe Ruth, a great baseball player; Dr. Seuss, a famous writer of children's books.

c. This person discovered something important. Examples: Thomas Edison, the light bulb; Alexander Graham Bell, the telephone; the Wright brothers, the airplane.

d. This person did something very good and inspiring. Examples: Florence Nightingale, Paul Revere, Clara Barton.

e. This person did something that the author is interested in. Examples: the author is interested in trees, so he writes about Johnny Appleseed; she's interested in birds, so she writes about James Audubon; and so on.

There are other reasons as well, some of which your students may suggest.

Mother to Tigers

GEORGE ELLA LYON

Suppose you were a lion cub—abandoned. ❶
Suppose you lay hungry and cold
in the straw at the back of the den,

and a man came in the cage ❷
and lifted you into a case

and put you in a car
to go home with him.

> **WORD BANK**
>
> **abandoned** (uh BAN dund)
> *adj.*: left to manage on its
> own; deserted

Mother to Tigers   265

Literary Components

❶ **Exposition:** The author draws you in by asking you to imagine what it feels like to be a sick, abandoned lion cub.

❷ **Rising Suspense:** The reader wonders who the man is, what his intentions are, and where they are going.

Guiding the Reading

Literal

Q: What does the author ask you to imagine?

A: He asks you to imagine you were a cold, hungry lion cub.

Q: What happens to the cold, hungry lion cub you have imagined?

A: A man comes and puts the cub into a case and takes him home with him.

Analytical

Q: Why would a lion cub be hungry and cold in a zoo?

A: Perhaps there were not enough zookeepers to care for a sick cub.

Are biographies written only about good people? Absolutely not. They may be about good, bad, or middling people. That is where our skill, *evaluating*, comes in. Evaluating means measuring and judging. Every time a homemaker goes shopping for tomatoes, she evaluates them. She picks up a tomato, looks at it, and thinks about its color. Then she feels it to see if it is too soft or too hard. She may even smell it to see if it is ripe and delicious. She looks at the price to see if it is expensive and weighs it to see how many tomatoes she will need. When we read a biography, we do the same. We read about the subject of the biography and arrive at an opinion about her. Is she good or evil or somewhere in between? Is she interesting or boring; unusual or ordinary; inspiring or depressing; someone we can relate to or totally different from us; and on and on. We dig deeper and ask why she did what she did. What in her background, her circumstances, and her character made her who she was? As we read, we are evaluating. When we have finished reading about this person, we have decided what our opinion of her is. We might be so fascinated or inspired by her life that we search for more books about her. On the other hand, we might feel we are just not very interested in this person. Finally, it would be interesting to ask by a show of hands whether the students prefer fiction or nonfiction, and why.

Mother to Tigers

Literary Components

3 **Release of Tension; Characterization:** The reader is no longer worried that harm will come to the baby lion. On the contrary, the reader conjures up memories of being sick and taken care of by a loving mother. The heroine, Helen, is being described through her actions. We are not *told* she is kind and caring, we observe that her *actions* are those of a kind and caring person.

4 **Language:** To characterize the lion and remind us that he is not a kitten, the author uses language specific to wild animals: "roam," "stalk," "pounce." There is also an element of gentle humor in the use of these words, because stalking a sofa is not traditionally a lion-like activity.

5 **Style:** The author skillfully makes the transition between the opening section, in which he speaks directly to the reader and asks the reader to "become" the baby lion, and the rest of the story, which he narrates in the usual third-person voice.

6 **Imagery:** Instead of saying "full of birds," the author only hints at birds by saying "song and feathers."

Guiding the Reading

Literal

Q: At home, what are some of the things the woman might do for you if you were the lion cub?

A: She might bathe you, warm your bottle, and put you on a pillow in her lap.

Q: Where would she put you to sleep?

A: She would put you in a box.

Q: Where would you go after you, the lion cub, got too big for the house?

A: I, the lion cub, would go to the Bronx Zoo.

Q: What is the name of the woman who is caring for the baby animals?

A: Helen Frances Theresa Delaney Martini.

Q: Why was Helen raising cubs?

A: She raised cubs because she had no children and wanted to care for something.

Analytical

Q: What are some of the ways that the woman treats the cub like a baby?

A: The woman bathes the cub, warms milk on the stove for him, gives him a bottle, and puts him on her lap—just as she would do for a baby.

3 Suppose a woman bathed you.
Suppose she warmed milk on the stove
and poured it in a bottle
and put you on a pillow in her lap
to drink till you were full and sleepy,

then put you in a box that would be your bed
in a kitchen that would be your home

4 till you got big enough to roam the apartment,
stalking the sofa, pouncing on the chairs,
till you outgrew a human's house
and went home to the Bronx Zoo.

5 Your name would be MacArthur,
and the woman who saved you,
Helen Frances Theresa Delaney Martini.

Helen never planned to raise cubs.
She and her husband, Fred, wanted children.
But their first baby died,
and doctors said she couldn't have more.

To ease their hurt hearts,
they collected pets: a parrot, a dog,
a starling,[1] and twelve canaries.

Before long, their little apartment
6 was full of song and feathers.

1. A *starling* is a shiny, black songbird.

WORD BANK

roam (ROME) *v*.: to wander all around

pouncing (POWN sing) *v*.: swooping down on suddenly

Mother to Tigers

Literary Components

7 **Poetic Language:** Although this is completely blank verse, the author does write poetically when he describes the movement of the animals.

8 **Parallelism:** Helen instructs Fred, and ends the paragraph with the words "So he did." Fred advises Helen, and the paragraph ends, "And she did." Not only does this give unity to the piece and add a touch of humor, it also establishes the wonderful, understanding relationship between husband and wife.

Guiding the Reading

Literal

Q: How far away from their house was the Bronx Zoo?

A: The zoo was just down the block from their house.

Q: Did Fred like animals as much as Helen did?

A: Yes. Fred loved watching the animals in the zoo.

Q: What did Helen suggest to Fred?

A: She suggested that he work at the zoo.

Q: Who was MacArthur?

A: MacArthur was a lion cub.

Q: How did Mrs. Martini know how to care for it?

A: Fred told her to do for the cub what she would do for a human baby.

Analytical

Q: What were both Fred and Helen interested in?

A: They both loved animals and were interested in being near them and helping them.

Q: How can you tell that Fred really wanted to do a good job of taking care of the animals?

A: When he came home at night, he tried to learn as much as he could about the animals.

On weekends, when Fred was free
from his job as a jeweler,
they strolled through the Bronx Zoo,
just down the street from their house.

Fred loved those times—
7 watching polar bears dive
and elephants amble,
studying the grace of giraffes.
Finally Helen said,
"Why don't you follow your heart
and work at the Zoo?"
8 So he did.

Each night he brought home questions
about animals he cared for,
and together he and Helen would read and learn.

When he brought MacArthur home
to the apartment on Old Kingsbridge Road,
the cub was a pitiful sight.
"Just do for him what you would do
for a human baby," Fred told Helen.
And she did.

> **WORD BANK**
>
> **strolled** *v.*: walked in a casual way, without hurrying
>
> **grace** *n.*: smooth and beautiful movements
>
> **pitiful** (PIH tih FULL) *adj.*: causing one to feel pity

Mother to Tigers 269

Mother to Tigers

270   Unit 3

After MacArthur
came Dacca,[2] Rajpur,[3] and Raniganj,[4]
a litter of Bengal tigers.

Rajpur was so cold and thin,
Helen thought he might die,
but she put him on a heating pad
and sat by him for hours
moistening his mouth with milk.
At last he gave a weak cry.
<u>Helen almost cried too.</u>

Feeding three was a challenge!
<u>Helen wished she were an octopus.</u>
But before long those scrawny babies
were sleek, fat cubs, ready to romp.

Once, washing clothes in the bath,
Helen heard Raniganj crying.
His head was caught behind a pipe.
While she ran to the rescue,

Rajpur and Dacca discovered the tub.
Crouch … leap … *splash*!
Tigers love water.

2. *Dacca* (DAHK KAH)
3. *Rajpur* (raj POOR)
4. *Raniganj* (rah NEE GUNJ)

WORD BANK

challenge (CHAL unj)
n.: a test of one's abilities

sleek *adj.*: well-fed and
looking fit

crouch *v.*: to bend low
close to the ground
preparing to leap

Mother to Tigers   271

Literary Components

❾ **Characterization:** Again, with no descriptive words used, we learn how intensely Helen cared about the tiger cubs.

---

❿ **Colorful Language:** The image of an octopus helps us understand how much help Helen could have used in taking care of three little tigers. It also lightens the somber mood of the previous paragraph. We experience the hard, round the clock, tension-filled work with the sick cubs opening up into the joy of watching playful tiger kittens romping.

Guiding the Reading

Literal

Q: Who were Dacca, Rajpur, and Raniganj?
A: They were baby Bengal tigers.

Q: How did Rajpur look when he came to Helen?
A: He was very thin and cold.

Q: What did Helen do for him?
A: She put him on a heating pad and sat by him for hours moistening his mouth with milk.

Q: What happened to the skinny little cubs?
A: They grew fat and sleek.

Q: Why did Raniganj cry?
A: He cried because his head was caught behind a pipe.

Q: What did Rajpur and Dacca especially like?
A: They loved water.

Analytical

Q: Why do you think Helen wished she were an octopus?
A: An octopus has eight arms. When you are taking care of three little tigers, two arms just aren't enough to hold them and feed them and soothe them.

Mother to Tigers

Literary Components

11 **Colorful Language:** The author likes to let the reader do some of the work. Instead of saying "the three cubs," he says the striped trio, and lets us figure out what he means.

12 **Characterization, Theme:** Not only Helen, but also Fred, are characterized as going beyond the call of duty in caring for the young animals. This quality of caring, giving, lovingkindness, devotedness, and so on is the story's theme.

13 **Rising Action:** Helen and Fred have a new project. Will it succeed?

Guiding the Reading

Literal

Q: Were the baby tigers completely healthy when they went back to the zoo?
A: No. They still needed their bottles.

Q: Where did Helen set up a little kitchen?
A: She set up a little kitchen in the sleeping room at the back of the baby tigers' cage.

Q: What idea did Helen have that would let her help zoo babies who needed special care?
A: She decided to start a nursery at the Zoo.

Analytical

Q: What does Helen do that is exactly what a mother would do for her baby?
A: She stays with the tigers until she knows they are fast asleep.

11 When <u>the striped trio</u>
had to go back to the Zoo,
they still needed their bottles,
so Helen brought a hot plate
and set up a little kitchen
in the sleeping room
at the back of their cage.

12 <u>The first night, she and Fred</u>
<u>ate their dinner there too.</u>
Helen didn't want to leave
till her cubs were fast asleep.

Come daybreak, she was back
and she was thinking:
These tigers will grow up,
but there will always be zoo babies
who need special care.
She couldn't take all of them home,
but she could bring home to them.
13 <u>She could start a nursery at the Zoo!</u>

272   Unit 3

Mother to Tigers

"Just give me a room," she said
to Mr. Crandall, the man in charge.
"I'll do all the work."
And she did.

She cleaned and plastered a storeroom,
which she painted pink and blue.

Then she begged, borrowed, and bought
everything she needed.

Starting out, she didn't get paid,
but that wasn't what mattered.
She was following her heart,
and her nursery filled up quickly.

Soon it was official:
She was the first woman keeper
in the history of the Bronx Zoo.

Before Helen arrived,
no tiger born at the Zoo had ever survived.
She raised twenty-seven,

WORD BANK

official (uh FISH ul) *adj.:*
approved by the people in
charge

Mother to Tigers   273

Literary Components

14 **Characterization:** Typically, Helen's qualities are expressed through actions. Her willingness to do all the work are characteristic of her and the reason behind her success.

15 **Characterization; Theme:** When you have a good heart, following it is a good idea.

16 **High Point:** Although it is hard to call this a climax, as the story doesn't have a real plot, it is certainly a high point in the story.

Guiding the Reading

Literal

Q: What room did she use for her nursery?
A: Mr. Crandall, the man in charge, gave her a storeroom to use.

Q: Did Helen have any "customers" for her nursery?
A: Yes. Her nursery soon filled up with sick little animals.

Q: What was Helen the first woman to do?
A: Helen was the first woman zookeeper in the history of the Bronx Zoo.

Q: How many tigers did Helen raise?
A: She raised twenty-seven.

Analytical

Q: Why was it especially meaningful that Helen raised twenty-seven tigers?
A: It had special meaning because until then not one single tiger born at the zoo had survived!

Q: Why do you think Helen was able to raise twenty-seven tigers when not even one had survived before?
A: Clearly, no one before Helen had put the time, effort, or know-how into taking care of the newborn tigers.

Q: Why do you think there had not been any women zookeepers until now?
A: In those days, many women did not work outside the home. Even those who did usually had only certain types of jobs, such as being a teacher, a secretary, or a nurse. People thought of many jobs as being only for men. Today, women work at almost every type of job.

Mother to Tigers

Literary Components

17 **Conclusion:** From the beginning of the story, Helen has grown from a woman who took a little lion cub and nursed him to health to an internationally known zookeeper who brought dozens of animals back to good health.

Guiding the Reading

Literal

Q: Can you name a few of the other animals Helen raised?

A: She raised yapoks and marmosets, gorillas and chimpanzees, and deer and ring-tailed lemurs. She took home baby lions, tigers, jaguars, and a black leopard.

Q: Did other people like the idea of a nursery for zoo animals?

A: Yes, the idea of the nursery spread.

Q: What does the story call Helen?

A: It calls her "mother to tigers."

Analytical

Q: What usually happens when someone has a good idea?

A: If someone has a good idea about how something should be done, people usually get excited about the idea and do the same thing.

Q: Do you think Helen deserved the title "mother to tigers"?

A: Yes. She loved and cared for the baby tigers just the way a mother would.

along with yapoks[5] and marmosets,[6]
gorillas and chimpanzees,
deer and ring-tailed lemurs.[7]

She still took cubs home, too:
lions, tigers,
jaguars, and a black leopard.

Helen's cubs had cubs
that were sent to zoos
all around the world.
The idea of the nursery spread too.

17 So, wherever you live,
when you go to the zoo,
look hard at the mighty cats.

Their grandparents
may have opened their eyes
on Old Kingsbridge Road,

may have learned to walk
in that apartment kitchen,

saved
by Helen Frances Theresa Delaney Martini,
mother to tigers.

---

5. A *yapok* (JAH pock), sometimes called a water opossum, is a gray opossum with dark bands on its fur. It lives on land and water.
6. *Marmosets* are monkeys that are about the size of squirrels.
7. *Lemurs* (LEE murs) are small, cat-like animals who have large eyes, fox-like faces, and long tails.

274   Unit 3

ABOUT THE AUTHOR

George Ella Lyon grew up in a house with a room just for books. She remembers building mazes out of books before she could read. Mrs. Lyon is named "George" after her mother's brother. As a child, she wanted to be a zookeeper. When she was 10 years old, she read a book by Helen Martini about her experiences raising lion and tiger cubs. This book sparked Mrs. Lyon's interest in big cats, particularly lions. Mrs. Lyon says that although she never became a zookeeper, she did end up marrying a Lyon.

Mother to Tigers   275

Mother to Tigers

Dreamer

Poem tie-in for *Mother to Tigers*

This poem is about dreams—not the ones you have when you're sleeping, but the ones you have when you're thinking about the future. It is about your hopes and your plans. Everyone's dreams are different. If you like, you may ask the students to share some of their dreams with the class. Tell them not to worry that their dream may sound unrealistic; that is exactly the point of having a dream.

The writer asks, "Do you understand my dreams?" He ends by saying, "Either way/It doesn't matter." Although it would be nice if others understood our dreams, it is not necessary. The important thing is to have dreams and to hold onto them, regardless of whether others understand them or not.

DREAMER
Langston Hughes

I take my dreams

And make of them a bronze vase,

And a wide round fountain

With a beautiful statue in its center,

And a song with a broken heart,

And I ask you:

Do you understand my dreams?

Sometimes you say you do

And sometimes you say you don't.

Either way

It doesn't matter.

I continue to dream.

276　Unit 3

Studying the Selection

FIRST IMPRESSIONS

When you hear the word "mother," what traits do you think of? When you hear that someone is called "Mother to Tigers," what do you think is her connection to tigers?

QUICK REVIEW

1. Why did Helen and her husband start to take care of pets?
2. How did Helen know what to do for the first sick cub Fred brought home?
3. What did Helen do so that she could continue to care for the animals she'd nursed back to health once they returned to the zoo?
4. What did Helen achieve that no one before her had?

FOCUS

5. What do you think was the hardest part of Helen's job?
6. Helen had many wonderful character traits. One of them was that she was a very hard worker. Another trait was that when something didn't go her way, she didn't give up; she tried something else. Write three sentences about someone you know who has one of these traits and how that person uses it.

CREATING AND WRITING

7. A zookeeper keeps logs of the progress of every animal in the zoo. Imagine that you are Helen and you have just taken home a baby tiger cub who is underweight, hardly moves, and has an eye infection. For the next seven days you will keep a log that records the cub's condition, what you fed it, what medicine you gave it, and what improvement you see. You will make up this information. Your teacher will give you instructions to help you make the chart.
8. Baby animals are magical! Together, your class will make a border they can put on the wall to liven up your classroom. If you can find pictures of baby animals at home, bring them in. Your teacher will supply you with some more pictures, and a cardboard border. Each student will cut out a picture of one baby animal and glue it to the border. When the border is complete, your teacher will hang it up.

4. Before Helen arrived at the zoo, no tiger born there had ever survived. She raised twenty-seven.

Focus

5. This is a matter of opinion. Our feeling is that sending the baby animal that you had nurtured back to the zoo is the hardest part of all.
6. Your students can find many people in their lives that possess at least one of these traits Helen exemplifies. Help them think of people they know who are hardworking and persevere. A simple example of a hard worker might be a parent or a sibling.

Creating and Writing

7. Distribute paper, rulers, and pencils. On the board, draw a diagram of how their papers should look. The front and back of the page should be divided into quarters (although the fourth quarter on the back of the page will not be used). Have them write the day of the week at the top of each quarter. Then have them write their three-sentence entry for each day. Remind them that the cub is making progress and that they should make note of that. Encourage them to name their cub and to write interesting details about the cub's behavior. Explain that as the cub recovers it will become more playful and active.
8. Make or buy a cardboard border that can go around the top of your classroom wall. Bring in pictures from magazines and other sources of all kinds of baby animals. Distribute scissors and glue and have each child cut out one or two animals and glue it to your border. Attach the border to the wall and enjoy!

Studying the Selection

- -

First Impressions

Mothering is almost synonymous with caring for, protecting, and nurturing. When we see the title *Mother to Tigers*, we most likely think the story is about a nurturing woman who raised tiger cubs as though they were her own babies.

Quick Review

1. When Helen and her husband lost their only child and were told they could not have any more children, they keep and take care of pets to ease the hurt they felt.
2. Fred told her to just do for the cub what she would do for a baby.
3. Helen took a storeroom at the zoo and painted it. She got equipment for it and used it as a little nursery for young animals who needed special care.

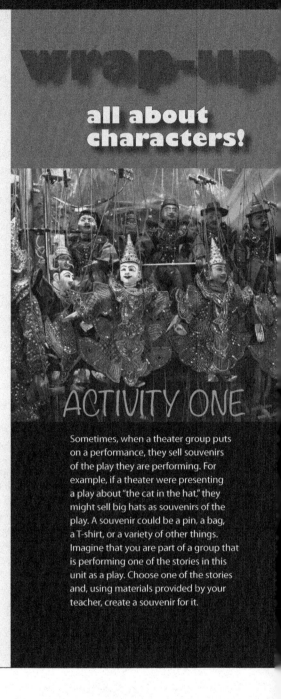

all about characters!

ACTIVITY ONE

Sometimes, when a theater group puts on a performance, they sell souvenirs of the play they are performing. For example, if a theater were presenting a play about "the cat in the hat," they might sell big hats as souvenirs of the play. A souvenir could be a pin, a bag, a T-shirt, or a variety of other things. Imagine that you are part of a group that is performing one of the stories in this unit as a play. Choose one of the stories and, using materials provided by your teacher, create a souvenir for it.

278 Unit 3

The Printer

Lorenzo & Angelina

A Day When Frogs Wear Shoes

The Burning of the Rice Fields

Mother to Tigers

ACTIVITY TWO

Your town is holding a contest to select a hero from amongst the townspeople. The hero is awarded a prize. They do this every year to show appreciation for the hero's good deeds and to inspire everyone else. This year, the choices have been narrowed down to two heroes. The first is the father from the story, *The Printer*, who saved the lives of all the printers by alerting them to the fire in the shop. The second is Hamaguchi from the story, *The Burning of the Rice Fields*, who saved the townspeople from being drowned by a tidal wave. Everyone in town has been asked to cast a vote for the hero of their choice. Decide who you would choose as the winner. Write a paragraph that you will read to the class in which you say why you think your choice of hero should win the prize.

280   Unit 3

ACTIVITY THREE

Let's play Memory! On cards that your teacher will give you, draw a picture of a scene or a character from one of the stories in this unit. Draw the same picture on a second card. After everyone has created two matching cards, your teacher will divide your class into groups of seven or eight. Each group will take the cards its members have drawn, mix them up, and spread them out face down. Following the rules of the game, Memory, take turns trying to find pairs. The student in each group who has the most pairs of cards is the winner.

ACTIVITY FOUR

It is a summer day and, once again, the three children in *A Day When Frogs Wear Shoes* are bored. This time, Ralph, the father of two of the children, has a plan. He is going to take them to the zoo. At the zoo, the group meets Helen the zookeeper (from *Mother to Tigers*), and she shows them her nursery of young, weak animals. The children immediately ask if they can take one of the tiger cubs home and nurse him back to health. Dad is not very eager to do this, and Helen is concerned that the children will not know what to do with the cub.

Write a conversation between the children (you can use their names: Huey, Gloria, and Julian, the narrator), Dad, and Helen in which they discuss whether or not the children should take home the cub. You will probably want to have Dad asking questions, the children insisting that they can do the job, and Helen giving warnings and instructions. The conversation, or dialogue, should be from six to eight lines long. To show who is speaking, write the speaker's name followed by a colon (:) and then the words that he or she says. Whenever a new character begins to speak, start another line.

Unit 3 Wrap-Up **281**

MOSDOS PRESS
Literature

- GLOSSARY
- ACKNOWLEDGMENTS
- INDEX OF AUTHORS AND TITLES

T282

glossary

A

abandoned (uh BAN dund) *adj.*: left to manage on its own; deserted

apothecary (uh PAH thuh keh ree) *n.*: a pharmacy

B

beams *n.*: thick, strong boards that go across the width of a ship

blacksmith *n.*: a person who makes horseshoes and puts them on the horses

blossomed (BLAH sumd) *v.*: grew and developed tremendously

brayed *v.*: sounded the harsh cry of the donkey

burro (BURR oh) *n.*: a small donkey used to carry loads

C

challenge (CHAL unj) *n.*: a test of one's abilities

coaxed (KOKST) *v.*: gently tried to get someone to do something

cooper *n.*: a person who makes or repairs barrels or tubs

crouch *v.*: to bend low close to the ground preparing to leap

D

desperate (DESS prit) *adj.*: extremely needy

E

engulfed (en GULFD) *v.*: completely swallowed up

enthusiastic (en THOOZ ee AS tik) *adj.*: excited and eager

exchanged (ex CHANGED) *v.*: traded

F

fled *v.*: run away from

furrows *n.*: narrow grooves made in the ground

G

grace *n.*: smooth and beautiful movements

H

hauling (HAWL ing) *v.*: pulling

I

image (IH muj) *n.*: picture in one's mind

independence (IN dih PEN dunce) *n.*: freedom; the right to think and act for oneself

glossary

J

jauntily (JAWN tih lee) *adv.*: worn easily, happily, and a tiny bit proudly

L

lariat (LARE ee ut) *n.*: lasso; a long, noosed rope used to catch horses, cattle, or other livestock

livery (LIH vuh ree) *n.*: a place where horses are cared for, fed, and stabled for pay

M

midst *n.*: the middle of

miller *n.*: a person who grinds grain into flour

miraculously (mih RAK yuh luss lee) *adv.*: as though through a miracle

N

numb (NUM) *adj.*: without any feeling at all

O

official (uh FISH ul) *adj.*: approved by the people in charge

P

pitiful (PIH tih FULL) *adj.*: causing one to feel pity

plucked *v.*: pulled out with force

poncho (PAHN cho) *n.*: a cloak that has an opening in the middle so that it can be pulled over the head and worn around the body

pouncing (POWN sing) *v.*: swooping down on suddenly

prospector (PROSS pek ter) *n.*: a person who searches and digs for gold in certain areas

R

radiator (RAY dee AY ter) *n.*: a room heater made of pipes through which steam or hot water passes

raging (RAY jing) *adj.*: angry and dangerous

roam (ROME) *v.*: to wander all around

S

scarcely (SKAIRS lee) *adv.*: hardly

settlement (SET ul ment) *n.*: the beginnings of a town; a group of houses built in a new, unsettled area

shafts *n.*: long columns

shuddered (SHUH derd) *v.*: shook slightly

skillet *n.*: frying pan

sleek *adj.*: well-fed and looking fit

glossary

spewing (SPYOO ing) *v.*: throwing out with force

stagecoach *n.*: a horse-drawn coach that carried passengers, mail, and packages

strained *v.*: tried to make them work even better than they usually did

strolled *v.*: walked in a casual way, without hurrying

T

tanner *n.*: a person who makes leather out of animal hides

thicket (THIK it) *n.*: a group of bushes or small trees growing closely together

V

vast *adj.*: huge; covering a very great area

acknowledgments

Illustrators

Sharon Bunting: Sybil Rides By Night

Eva Clair: A Cane in Her Hand; Boom Town; Across the Wide Dark Sea; Lorenzo & Angelina; The Burning of the Rice Fields; The Secret; The Other Way to Listen

Aviva Goldfarb: The Jar of Tassai

Lydia Martin: The Story of the White Sombrero; Taro and the Tofu

Julie Orelowitz: A Day When Frogs Wear Shoes

Across the Wide Dark Sea
From ACROSS THE WIDE DARK SEA: THE MAYFLOWER VOYAGE by Jean Van Leeuwen, copyright (c) 1995 by Jean Van Leeuwen. Used by permission of Dial Books for Young Readers, a division of Penguin Group (USA) Inc.

Boom Town
From BOOM TOWN by Sonia Levitin. Scholastic Inc./Orchard Books. Text copyright © 1998 by Sonia Levitin. Reprinted by permission.

Breakfast
"Breakfast", from THE OTHER SIDE OF THE DOOR by Jeff Moss, copyright © 1991 by Jeff Moss. Used by permission of Bantam Books, a division of Random House, Inc.

A Cane in Her Hand
Text © Ada B. Litchfield, 1977; illustrations © Eleanor Mill, 1977. Published by Albert Whitman & Company. Used by permission.

A Day When Frogs Wear Shoes
"A Day When Frogs Wear Shoes", from MORE STORIES JULIAN TELLS by Ann Cameron, copyright © 1986 by Ann Cameron. Used by permission of Alfred A. Knopf, an imprint of Random House Children's Books, a division of Random House, Inc.

Dreamer
"Dreamer" from THE COLLECTED POEMS OF LANGSTON HUGHES by Langston Hughes, edited by Arnold Rampersad with David Roessel, Associate Editor, copyright © 1994 by the Estate of Langston Hughes. Used by permission of Alfred A. Knopf, a division of Random House, Inc.

Food's on the Table
from ALL OF A KIND FAMILY UPTOWN by Sydney Taylor, copyright © 1958 by Sydney Taylor. No part of this excerpt may be reprinted in whole or in part without the express written permission of the Gersh Agency.

General Store
"General Store", copyright 1926 by Rachel Field, renewed 1953 by Arthur S. Pederson, from TAXIS AND TOADSTOOLS by Rachel Field. Used by permission of Doubleday, an imprint of Random House Children's Books, a division of Random House, Inc.

Good-Bye, 382 Shin Dang Dong
Reprinted by arrangement from the book *Good-Bye, 382 Shin Dang Dong,* by Frances Park and Ginger Park. Copyright © 2002 National Geographic Society.

I Am Running in a Circle
From THE NEW KID ON THE BLOCK by JACK PRELUTSKY. TEXT COPYRIGHT (C) 1984 BY JACK PRELUTSKY. Used by permission of HarperCollins Publishers.

I Go Forth to Move About the Earth
"I Go Forth to Move About the Earth" by Alonzo Lopez, from WHISPERING WIND by Terry Allen, copyright © 1972 by the Institute of American Indian Arts. Used by permission of Doubleday, a division of Random House, Inc.

Lorenzo & Angelina
Copyright © 1968 by Eugene Fern. Reprinted with permission of McIntosh & Otis, Inc.

Mother to Tigers
Reprinted with the permission of Atheneum Books for Young Readers, an imprint of Simon & Schuster Children's Publishing Division from MOTHER TO TIGERS by George Ella Lyon. Text copyright © 2003 George Ella Lyon.

New Kid at School
MESSING AROUND ON THE MONKEY BARS. Text copyright © 2009 Betsy Franco. Illustrations Copyright © 2009 Jessie Hartland. Reproduced by permission of the publisher, Candlewick Press, Somerville, MA.

Nothing Much Happened Today
Nothing Much Happened Today by Mary Blount Christian. Text copyright © 1973 by Mary Blount Christian. Reprinted by permission of the author.

The Other Way to Listen
Reprinted with the permission of Atheneum Books for Young Readers, an imprint of Simon & Schuster Children's Publishing Division from THE OTHER WAY TO LISTEN by Byrd Baylor. Text copyright (c) 1978 Byrd Baylor.

The Printer
First published in the United States under the title THE PRINTER by Myron Uhlberg, illustrated by Henri Sørensen. Text Copyright © 2003 by Myron Uhlberg, Illustrations Copyright © 2003 by Henri Sørensen. Published by arrangement with Peachtree Publishers.

Sybil Rides By Night
An excerpt from *Sybil Rides for Independence* by Drollene P. Brown. Copyright © 1985 by Drollene P. Brown. Reprinted by permission of the author.

Taro and the Tofu
From TARO AND THE TOFU by Masako Matsuno, copyright (c) 1962, 1990 by Masako Matsuno. Used by permission of G.P. Putnam's Sons, a division of Penguin Group (USA) Inc.

Until I Saw the Sea
From I FEEL THE SAME WAY by Lilian Moore. Copyright c 1966, 1967 Lilian Moore. All Rights Reserved. Used by permission of Marian Reiner.

The World with its Countries
The World with its Countries by John Cotton. Copyright © 1989 by John Cotton. Reprinted by permission of the author.

Note: We have expended much effort to contact all copyright holders to receive permission to reprint their works. We will correct any omissions brought to our attention in future editions.

286 Acknowledgments

index of authors and titles

Italics indicates selection.

Roman indicates author biographical information.

Workbook Answer Guide

Table of Contents

Workbook Answer Guide

To the Teacher:

Here are some suggestions regarding how to help your students best use the Activity Workbook.

Vocabulary—Activity One

1. Before assigning Activity One, review the vocabulary words with your students. Each student should be clear about the pronunciation and the meaning of every word.

2. Some Activity One exercises may use words that are new to the student that are *not* listed in the *Word Banks* of the textbook. These words are related to the selection thematically and are defined in the workbook glossary, not in the textbook glossary. Familiarize your students with the location of the workbook glossary.

3. Many vocabulary words may not be words your students use in ordinary discourse. Vocabulary lists derived from literature tend to be more advanced than the working vocabulary of the average American student. Please give your students practice using the selection vocabulary.

   The fine nuances of the new words they learn will help students think and express themselves with greater specificity. Moreover, if a student is often stumbling over selection words, reading will not be the pleasurable and informative experience it ought to be.

4. We all know that some words have several different meanings. We understand the meaning of such a word based upon the context within which the word is used. Vocabulary words that may have more than one meaning are used in the Activity One exercises *according to the definition given in the textbook Word Bank.* For the most part, the definition prompts given with each Activity One sentence use the very same words as the definition given in the textbook.

Vocabulary—Activity Two

Activity Two offers students the opportunity to think creatively and logically about the selection vocabulary. Students are called upon to categorize words, compare meanings, and manipulate the words in ways that develop both inferential reasoning skills and the ability to think deductively. Activity Two requires a solid understanding of the meanings of the words. It should *always follow* Activity One. Again, we suggest your reviewing all the vocabulary pronunciations and definitions before students proceed with Activity Two.

Language Arts Activity

This activity page offers practice with the language arts skill focused on in the selection. Activities are created to help students recognize the narrative elements, explore point of view, understand figurative language, and make predictions that will reinforce the skills taught in the textbook. These language arts skills and many others will give the student the opportunity to gain proficiency with the 3rd grade learning components that are an integral part of the Common Core Curriculum standards.

More About the Story

The More About the Story workbook page offers young writers a creative writing experience. A story-starter paragraph provides the student with a thoughtful prompt thematically linked to the selection.

Graphic Organizer

Graphic organizers help your students visually process information. Help students understand that a graphic organizer is a visual representation of the knowledge they have already acquired from working on questions and activities related to the selection. The graphic organizers are independent activities. Often the directions for a particular graphic organizer are multifaceted; make certain that students understand all of the steps in these directions.

UNIT ONE

The Jar of Tassai
(Textbook p. 4)

Vocabulary—Activity One (p. 2)

1. rural
2. compete
3. agriculture
4. feast
5. arid
6. craft
7. pottery
8. kiln

Vocabulary—Activity Two (p. 3)

1. Farming
2. Desert
3. Race
4. Woodworking
5. Food
6. Bake
7. Clay
8. Country

Language Arts Activity (p. 5)

1. c.
2. b.
3. a.
4. d.

Graphic Organizer (pp. 6-7)

Plot:

1. making a jar.
2. the people of the area to a feast.
3. Tassai
4. ran home to get it.
5. A little girl
6. a snake.
7. threw her jar onto its head to kill it.
8. saved the girl's life (and ruined her jar).
9. awarded Tassai a prize for her beautiful deed.

Characters:

1. Tassai
2. The Governor
3. The little girl
4. The girl's father

Settings:

1. The fields at the foot of the mesa
2. The secret place where Tassai makes her jar
3. The feast
4. Tassai's doorway, where the snake is killed

The Story of the White Sombrero
(Textbook p. 20)

Vocabulary—Activity One (p. 8)

1. pessimist
2. poncho
3. anxiously
4. burro
5. brayed
6. optimist
7. thicket
8. jauntily

Vocabulary—Activity Two (p. 9)

1. The burro
2. Bushes
3. In Mexico

4. When they are worried
5. Because he thinks the worst will happen
6. A hat
7. When you want to climb a mountain
8. A smile

Language Arts Activity (p. 11)

1. Underline: The problem was, she had read every one of the books in her house.
2. Circle: Maybe we can make a little library of our own.
3. The children got people to loan their books to the new schoolhouse library.

Graphic Organizer (pp. 12-13)

1. Andres said, "I am brave. I know we can make it all right."
   Francisco said, "I do not know, Mama, the way is long and many things can happen."
2. Francisco said, "Surely the wasps will sting our burros and something terrible will happen."
   Andres said, "If there are wasps flying around they will keep thieves from stealing our sombreros."
3. Francisco said, "We are in a hopeless state, let's go home."
   Andres said, "No, no."
4. Francisco said, "I told you it was hopeless."
   Andres said, "You give up too easily."
5. Francisco said, "Surely no one will want to buy them."
   Andres said, "We will try to sell them anyway."
6. Francisco said, "You had the courage to keep on trying. That is why our trip was a success."

A Cane in Her Hand
(Textbook p. 38)

Vocabulary—Activity One (p. 14)

1. active
2. avoid
3. stumble
4. obstacles
5. vision
6. physician's
7. enable
8. gradually

Vocabulary—Activity Two (p. 15)

1. A.
2. B.
3. A.
4. A.
5. B.
6. A.
7. A.
8. A.

Language Arts Activity (p. 17)

1. c
2. b
3. a
4. c

Graphic Organizer (pp. 18-19)

What was Valerie's biggest problem at this time?

1. Valerie could hardly see, and kept bumping into things.
2. Valerie was afraid her friends would reject her. She was afraid of being different.
3. Valerie hated when people did not realize how capable she was of doing everything.

Who helped Valerie the most at this time?

1. Valerie's parents and Dr. King helped her the most.
2. Miss Sousa helped her tremendously.
3. Miss Sousa, Valerie's friends, and understanding people helped Valerie.

How did Valerie solve her problem at this time?

1. Valerie went to Dr. King, who reassured her and encouraged her to talk to Mrs. Johnson.
2. Valerie tried to learn everything Miss Sousa could teach her. She accepted the cane and used it to help herself.
3. Valerie did not use the cane as an excuse to avoid doing things. She tried everything that other kids did and succeeded at most of them. She developed confidence in herself.

Boom Town
(Textbook p. 52)

Vocabulary—Activity One (p. 20)

1. furrows
2. blossomed

3. blacksmith
4. miller
5. tanner
6. apothecary
7. stagecoach
8. prospector

Language Arts Activity (p. 23)

1. where
2. time
3. when
4. season
5. where

Graphic Organizer (pp. 24-25)

Page 1

The sequence of events is:

1. 5
2. 2
3. 7
4. 1
5. 8
6. 4
7. 6
8. 3

Page 2

Have the students cut out the pictures of the different businesses that sprang up in *Boom Town*. Tell them to paste them on the page near the corresponding sign. Then have them color the pictures and add details to the overall picture of the town.

Taro and the Tofu
(Textbook p. 74)

Vocabulary—Activity One (p. 26)

1. responsible
2. dim
3. errands
4. lingering
5. respectfully
6. delicacy
7. struggled
8. triumph

Vocabulary—Activity Two (p. 27)

What would you do with …
1. B
2. A
3. B
4. A

What would you do if …
1. A
2. B
3. A
4. A

Language Arts Activity (p. 29)

First Story
1. poor
2. winter
3. sad
4. It had fallen through the hole in Eric's pocket.

Second Story
1. on a farm
2. a newborn lamb
3. a lamb had been born
4. Lynn would help take care of the newborn lamb.

Graphic Organizer (pp. 30-31)

1. *(2) Taro offers to run to the tofu shop for his mother*
   Taro says he is too tired to run to the tofu shop for his mother.

2. Taro doesn't stop to look at all the different shops along the way.
   (5) Taro stops at all the shops along the way.

3. *(3) Taro decides quickly which candy to buy so he could hurry home to his mother.*
   Taro spends a long time deciding, even though his mother was waiting.

4. *(7) Taro decides he must return the extra yen to the tofu man right away.*
   Taro decides to wait until tomorrow to return the extra yen to the tofu man.

5. *(1) The tofu man asks Taro if he's sure the extra money is the tofu man's and Taro says he's sure.*
   The tofu man asks Taro if he's sure the extra money is the tofu man's and Taro says he's not sure.

6. Taro gives some of his candy to the man for his sick grandson.
   (6) Taro does not share his candy with anyone.

7. *(4) Taro doesn't tell his parents that he gave his candy to the sick little boy.*
   Taro tells his parents about his good deed.

UNIT TWO

Good-Bye, 382 Shin Dang Dong
(Textbook p. 98)

Vocabulary—Activity One (p. 32)
1. foreign
2. despair
3. enthusiastic
4. radiator
5. farewell
6. correspond
7. suggest
8. aroma

Vocabulary—Activity Two (p. 33)
1. enthusiastic
2. foreign
3. farewell
4. suggest
5. correspond
6. despair
7. aroma
8. radiator

Language Arts Activity (p. 35)
The realistic paragraphs are 2, 3, 5.

Graphic Organizer (pp. 36-37)
1. 4
2. 5
3. 8
4. 1
5. 6
6. 3
7. 7
8. 2

Workbook Answer Guide

Sybil Rides By Night
(Textbook p. 120)

Vocabulary—Activity One (p. 38)

1. coaxed
2. independence
3. liberty
4. volunteered
5. route
6. alerted
7. strained
8. halted

Vocabulary—Activity Two (p. 39)

1. A
2. B
3. A
4. A
5. A
6. B
7. A
8. B

Language Arts Activity (p. 41)

1. b.
2. d.
3. c.
4. a.

Graphic Organizer (pp. 42-43)

6:00   At Sybil's home. Sybil mounts Star, salutes her father, and gallops off.

8:00   Sybil reaches the first farmhouse and shouts her message.

10:00 Sybil reaches Shaw's Pond. The people are asleep so she has to pound on their door with a stick.

11:00 Sybil arrives at Mahopec Pond, Star slips in the mud.

12:00 Sybil reaches Red Mills where Star stumbles and almost falls.

2:00   Sybil hears hoofbeats on the path. She fears they are either British soldiers or skinners.

4:00   Sybil reaches Stormville, but the people already know what her message will be.

6:00   Sybil and Star return home. It is sunrise and four hundred men have gathered.

Sybil goes to sleep.

Nothing Much Happened Today
(Textbook p. 134)

Vocabulary—Activity One (p. 44)

1. remarked
2. revived
3. intended
4. pandemonium
5. chaos
6. gasp
7. drifted
8. astounded

Vocabulary—Activity Two (p. 45)

First group of syllables spell out

- Astounded
- Chaos
- Drifting
- Gasped

Second group of syllables spell out

- Intended
- Pandemonium
- Remarked
- Revived

Language Arts Activity (p. 47)

1. Little Melissa dropped her lollipop
2. Father stepped on the lollipop
3. Coffee splashed out of Father's cup
4. Maxie jumped a foot in the air
5. Maxie knocked over the goldfish bowl
6. Dinah, the cat, ate the goldfish

Graphic Organizer (pp. 48-49)

Cause	Effect
The robber	the policeman chases him
The police	ruins the cake
The ruined cake	they must bake a new cake
The new cake	makes the oven smoke
The smoke	makes them open a window
The open window	lets the cat in
The cat	is a magnet for the dog
The dog	knocks over the sugar bag
The sugar bag	gets on the dog causing him to need a bath
The bath	produces millions of bubbles

Food's on the Table
(Textbook p. 148)

Vocabulary—Activity One (p. 50)

1. dismayed
2. mystified
3. dreadful
4. frankly
5. surveyed
6. siblings
7. outcome
8. stunned

Vocabulary—Activity Two (p. 51)

1. A
2. A
3. B
4. B
5. A
6. B
7. A
8. B

Language Arts Activity (p. 53)

1. C (If you want me to bake cookies for your lunch …)
2. B (No matter how carefully we watched him, he always …)

Graphic Organizer (pp. 54-55)

The Characters:
1. Ella
2. Charlotte
3. Sarah
4. Gertie
5. Miss Brady
6. Henny
7. Charlie
8. Woman (Mrs. Shiner)
9. Lena
10. Mama

The Settings:
1. The street
2. The apartment

The Facts That Just Don't Make Sense:
1. No one is home
2. The table isn't set
3. There is not enough silverware
4. There are new kitchen chairs
5. There is not enough food

The Mystery Guest:

The mystery guest is Mrs. Shiner. She is here because this is her apartment.

The Solution:

The reason for all the facts that don't make sense is that this is not Lena's apartment; it is Mrs. Shiner's. The reason the children arrived at Mrs. Shiner's apartment is that they did not realize that the ground floor is called the first floor, so they thought the third floor (where they were in Mrs. Shiner's apartment) was the fourth, where Aunt Lena lived.

Across the Wide Dark Sea
(Textbook p. 162)

Vocabulary—Activity One (p. 56)

1. scarcely
2. plucking
3. beams
4. raging
5. settlement
6. desperate
7. vast
8. hauling

Vocabulary—Activity Two (p. 57)

1. A
2. B
3. A
4. A
5. B
6. A
7. A
8. B

Language Arts Activity (p. 59)

Main idea: d

Graphic Organizer (pp. 60-61)

Ship One

Flag: We are searching for a place to live where we can worship G-d in our own way.

Sail one: At first we ate meat, beans, and bread; later, biscuits and cheese.

Sail two: We brought everything we would need in the new land: tools, goods, guns, food, furniture, clothing, books.

Sail three: Winds howled and waves crashed. The waves were as high as mountains.

Sail four: We were at sea for nine weeks.

Ship Two

Flag: It was a good idea. We had built a settlement and planted crops. Father wanted to be here and work.

Sail one: Half the people died of sickness.

Sail two: The Indians taught us where to fish and what to plant.

Sail three: My father and I cleared the fields and planted barley and peas and corn. I dug a garden for vegetables and herbs.

Sail four: The ship that brought us sailed away.

UNIT THREE

The Printer
(Textbook p. 192)

Vocabulary—Activity One (p. 62)

1. fled
2. spewing
3. shuddered
4. numb
5. engulfed
6. exchanged
7. images
8. midst

Vocabulary—Activity Two (p. 63)

1. burned
2. shocked, sad
3. ran, escaped
4. talked, conversed
5. picture
6. in the middle of

Language Arts Activity (p. 65)

1. C
2. B
3. D

Graphic Organizer (pp. 66-67)

1. My father was a printer.
2. My father gave me a newspaper hat every evening.
3. My father could not hear.
4. They did not speak to him.
5. My father spotted a fire.
6. Turning point
7. They alerted everyone to the danger.
8. Yes.
9. They were destroyed in the fire.
10. They gave my father a newspaper hat.
11. He gave me a newspaper hat.

Lorenzo & Angelina
(Textbook p. 212)

Vocabulary—Activity One (p. 68)

1. thrilling
2. eagerly
3. craggy
4. fortunately
5. budge
6. fatal
7. accused
8. loyal

Vocabulary—Activity Two (p. 69)

Answers may vary; here are some sample answers.

1. No, because the hill would be full of rocks that would make skiing impossible.
2. No, because healthy food cannot kill you, even if you don't like it.
3. Yes, because you should return your friend's kindness.
4. Yes, because I like scary rides. No, because I hate scary rides. No, because I'm so tough that roller coasters don't thrill me.
5. Yes, I could move a little bit. No, the rope would keep me from moving at all.
6. No, I would start it "unfortunately."
7. No, you should not accuse someone of wrongdoing unless you're sure the person is guilty.
8. Yes, my baby sister loves peas. No, my baby sister would throw them on the floor.

Language Arts Activity (p. 71)

a. The children

b. Mom

c. Mom

d. The children

Graphic Organizer (pp. 72-73)

1. Angelina: That stubborn donkey does everything but what he is supposed to do.

   Lorenzo: How can I hurry when I have so many important things to do before I go?

2. Angelina: My stubborn donkey refused to move.

   Lorenzo: Who knows what might be in a strange land?

3. Angelina: The road was rough and rocky, so naturally Lorenzo was going slower.

   Lorenzo: The road was rough and rocky and it was hard to see the road. Soon there was no road at all.

4. Angelina: I was not worried. My Lorenzo is as sure-footed as a mountain goat and I knew he would not fall.

   Lorenzo: It was not easy to walk and very dangerous. I was afraid I would stumble and fall off the mountain.

5. Angelina: Lorenzo was just lazy and stubborn. I was furious with him.

   Lorenzo: Who knows what lay beyond those rocks? It was too dangerous to experiment.

6. Angelina: I felt such a strong love for Lorenzo for saving my life that I kissed him.

   Lorenzo: I was so very happy to be appreciated, and when Angelina kissed me, my happiness was complete.

A Day When Frogs Wear Shoes
(Textbook p. 234)

Vocabulary—Activity One (p. 74)

1. explored
2. arctic
3. clammy
4. scalding
5. locate
6. punctured
7. pastime
8. doze

Vocabulary—Activity Two (p. 75)

1. C
2. C
3. A
4. B
5. B
6. B
7. C
8. B

Language Arts Activity (p. 77)

1. a
2. a
3. b
4. b
5. a
6. b
7. a

Graphic Organizer (pp. 78-79)

Rock 1: (Dad/excitable): 4.

Rock 2: (Huey): 1.

Rock 3: (Dad/treats everyone with respect): 2.

Rock 4: (Gloria): 7.

Rock 5: (Narrator/helpful): 5.

Rock 6: (Dad/generous): 3.

Rock 7: (The kids): 8.

Rock 8: (Narrator/good imagination): 6.

The Burning of the Rice Fields
(Textbook p. 250)

Vocabulary—Activity One (p. 80)

1. abundant
2. ancient
3. boldly
4. panic
5. predicted
6. decisive
7. generosity
8. festive

Workbook Answer Guide

Vocabulary—Activity Two (p. 81)

1. A
2. A
3. B
4. A
5. B
6. A
7. B
8. A

Language Arts Activity (p. 83)

1. B
2. C
3. A
4. B

Graphic Organizer (pp. 84-85)

1. Hamaguchi has hundreds of rice stacks. He will always be rich.

   All Hamaguchi's rice is burned. He is poor.
2. It's a shame Hamaguchi was too tired to join the villagers for the big celebration.

   It was very lucky Hamaguchi was not at the celebration when the big wave appeared.
3. When the hillside shook, it was probably just a small earthquake.

   When the hillside shook, it was the beginning of the disastrous wave.
4. How could Hamaguchi burn his own rice?

   Hamaguchi burned his rice to save the people.
5. The people ran up the hill to save Hamaguchi.

   When the people ran up the hill, they were saving themselves.
6. By not letting anyone put out the fire, Hamaguchi was hurting the people, who would have no rice.

   By not letting anyone put out the fire, Hamaguchi was making sure everyone ran up the hill away from the big wave.

Mother to Tigers
(Textbook p. 264)

Vocabulary—Activity One (p. 86)

1. abandoned
2. roam
3. strolled
4. pounce

5. pitiful
6. challenge
7. sleek
8. grace

Vocabulary—Activity Two (p. 87)

Cat: pounce, sleek
Movement: roam, strolled, grace
Sad: abandoned, pitiful

Language Arts Activity (p. 89)

1. fact
2. opinion
3. fact
4. fiction
5. opinion
6. fact
7. opinion
8. fact

Graphic Organizer (pp. 90-91)

1. MacArthur: 4
2. Dacca: 5
3. Twenty-seven tigers: 1
4. Rajpur: 2
5. Raniganj: 3

UNIT FOUR

The Town That Moved
(Textbook p. 4)

Vocabulary—Activity One (p. 2)

1. cyclones
2. transport
3. harsh
4. enable
5. ambition
6. briefly
7. primary
8. theory

Vocabulary—Activity Two (p. 3)

1. False
2. False
3. True

4. True

5. False

6. True

7. True

8. False

Language Arts Activity (p. 5)

1. <u>Mr. Jenkins pressed the elevator button</u>. (The elevator doors opened immediately,) and he stepped inside.

2. I was sound asleep <u>when that noisy alarm went off</u>. Why, (I almost jumped out of my skin!)

3. <u>The doe sensed danger</u>. She nudged her young fawn, and (the two fled into the woods.)

4. We were having a great time batting the balloons around when <u>one of the balloons hit a hot light bulb</u> (and burst with a bang.)

5. "What happened to you?" asked Helen. "Well," said Andrea, "<u>I fell down the steps</u> and (sprained my ankle.")

6. (Little Lonnie's mouth was bright purple.) <u>She was licking a purple popsicle</u> which was slowly melting onto her overalls.

Heartland
(Textbook p. 22)

Vocabulary—Activity One (p. 8)

1. fertile

2. hues

3. livestock

4. drought

5. weathered

6. toil

7. merged

8. define

Vocabulary—Activity Two (p. 9)

1. B

2. B

3. A

4. A

5. B

6. A

7. B

8. A

Language Arts Activity (p. 11)

1. top

2. fable

3. fixer

4. tradition

5. thicken

6. rarely

7. less

8. funny

No Laughing Matter
(Textbook p. 36)

Vocabulary—Activity One (p. 14)

1. debating

2. insistently

3. gawking

4. speculate

5. carousel

6. circumference

7. tufts

8. wafted

Vocabulary—Activity Two (p. 15)

1. A   5. A

2. B   6. B

3. A   7. A

4. B   8. A

Language Arts Activity (p. 17)

1. c   3. c

2. b   4. b

Graphic Organizer (pp. 18-19)

1. bored

2. frightened

3. irritated

4. worried

5. surprised

6. angry

7. happy

8. grateful

Workbook Answer Guide

Patrick and the Great Molasses Explosion
(Textbook p. 66)

Vocabulary—Activity One (p. 20)

1. enormous
2. rumbling
3. craving
4. rivets
5. molasses
6. cobblestones
7. clattered
8. chaos

Vocabulary—Activity Two (p. 21)

1. B
2. B
3. A
4. A
5. B
6. A
7. B
8. A

Language Arts Activity (p. 23)

1. 3
2. 5
3. 1
4. 2
5. 4

Graphic Organizer (pp. 24-25)

The Beginning

Patrick
molasses
Boston
harbor
Purity
molasses

The Middle

molasses
store
boom
wave
ran

picked
licking

The End

believe
bath
bed
truth
Papa
molasses
refused

Bear Mouse
(Textbook p. 96)

Vocabulary—Activity One (p. 26)

1. telltale
2. burrowed
3. skimmed
4. talons
5. darted
6. hibernation
7. intent
8. dodge

Vocabulary—Activity Two (p. 27)

1. Burrowed means living in a hole dug deep in the ground.
2. Telltale means something that reveals something that would be otherwise unknown.
3. Hibernation means the act of sleeping through the winter months.
4. Skimmed means passed over lightly.
5. Intent means determined.
6. Talons mean a bird's claws.
7. Darted means started suddenly to run from place to place.
8. Dodged means avoided.

Language Arts Activity (p. 29)

1. frightened
2. hot
3. interesting
4. sharp
5. damp
6. red

Graphic Organizer (pp. 30-31)

Left Hand Page

The meadow—a red berry

Turtle Pond—a covering of ice

The alder bush—a cocoon

The meadow—a hawk

Right Hand Page

The meadow—the cardinal

High in the pine tree—the snowy owl

The stone wall—the bobcat

The crack between the stones—a lot of seeds and acorns

UNIT FIVE

A Gift for Tía Rosa
(Textbook p. 134)

Vocabulary—Activity One (p. 32)

1. schedule
2. determination
3. confessed
4. flickered
5. fringe
6. frail
7. fierce
8. wisdom

Vocabulary—Activity Two (p. 33)

1. B
2. B
3. A
4. B
5. A
6. A
7. A
8. B

Language Arts Activity (p. 35)

1. B
2. C
3. A
4. A

Graphic Organizer (pp. 36-37)

Left Hand Page

Tío Juan to Carmela—he was a good listener

Tía Rosa to Carmela—she taught her to knit

Carmela to Tía Rosa—she showed her how much she loved her

Carmela to Tío Juan—she made him smile

Right Hand Page

Carmela to Tía Rosa—she visited her every day

Carmela's father to Carmela—he comforted Carmela

Tía Rosa to Carmela—she gave her a necklace

Carmela's mother to Carmela—she gave her good advice

Harlequin and the Gift of Many Colors
(Textbook p. 158)

Vocabulary—Activity One (p. 38)

1. swiftly
2. shabby
3. impoverished
4. sensitive
5. hardship
6. flexible
7. graceful
8. coward

Vocabulary—Activity Two (p. 39)

1. impoverished
2. swiftly
3. hardship
4. graceful
5. coward
6. sensitive
7. shabby

Language Arts Activity (p. 41)

The words that should be left out in a summary are italicized.

Jeff was a policeman. *He was six feet tall and had red hair.* Every day, he walked up and down the streets of his town to make sure everything was in order. He knew pretty much everyone in the town, *and greeted people with a cheerful "How's it going?"* He knew the little girls in *their school uniforms and the high school boys who always bounced a basketball on the way to and from school. He knew the little lady with the straw hat and the old man with the cane. He knew the garbage men and the mailmen.*

One day, he passed someone he did not know. The man was wearing a big yellow hat and walking a monkey on a leash. Jeff stopped in his tracks. "Who was that?" he thought to himself. That man was so familiar, yet he couldn't place him. *It was such a strange feeling, knowing someone and not knowing him at the same time.* Was the man dangerous? Should he be followed? *Jeff took off his policeman's hat and scratched his head. (Sometimes, that helped him remember things.) He pulled out his little notebook and looked through it to see if he'd ever made a note about a man in a yellow hat.*

When he got home, he told his wife and kids about the mysterious stranger. Guess what! They knew who he was! Do YOU?

Graphic Organizer (pp. 42-43)

Problem 1

Harlequin did not have a costume for the Carnival.

Setting: A dark room that is cold and bare except for a bed

Characters: Harlequin and his friends

Solution: The children decide to give Harlequin a bit of each of their costumes.

Problem 2

The bits and scraps that the children gave Harlequin looked like a bunch of rags.

Setting: Outside Harlequin's house on a sunny day.

Characters: Harlequin, his mother, and his friends

Theme: The children love and care about Harlequin.

Solution: Harlequin's mother sews the patches onto his suit to make a colorful costume.

Problem 3

The children could not find Harlequin at the Carnival.

Setting: The Carnival in the night full of music and delicious smells

Characters: Harlequin and his friends in costumes

Solution: The friends recognize the pieces of their own costumes that are now part of Harlequin's costume.

Claw Foot
(Textbook p. 174)

Vocabulary—Activity One (p. 44)

1. uselessness
2. captives
3. addressed
4. dismounted
5. rigid
6. gnarled
7. disguise
8. awkwardly

Vocabulary—Activity Two (p. 45)

1. B
2. A
3. A
4. A
5. B
6. A
7. B
8. B

Language Arts Activity (p. 47)

1. b
2. c
3. a

Graphic Organizer (pp. 48-49)

Under Claw Foot

1. Sioux
2. A boy of about twelve years old.
3. His tribe needs food, especially many buffalo.

Under Claw Foot and Broken Wing

1. Claw Foot has a twisted, deformed foot and Broken Wing has a twisted, useless arm.
2. Claw Foot's name and Broken Wing's name both reflect their physical injuries.
3. Both want to help their people more than anything else.
4. Both agree that Claw Foot will keep whatever land a buffalo hide can cover.
5. Each has respect and admiration for the other.

Under Broken Wing

1. Crow
2. Broken Wing is an adult.
3. He offers only one buffalo.

Beatrice's Goat
(Textbook p. 194)

Vocabulary—Activity One (p. 50)

1. sturdy
2. coarse
3. kindhearted
4. yearned
5. declared
6. produce
7. lashed
8. disbelief

Vocabulary—Activity Two (p. 51)

Answers may vary.

Language Arts Activity (p. 53)

1. F
2. O
3. F
4. F
5. O
6. O
7. F
8. O
9. O
10. F
11. F
12. O
13. O
14. F

Graphic Organizer (pp. 54-55)

First Page
Before Mugisa
1. 3.
2. 4.
3. 1.
4. 2.

After Mugisa
1. 4.
2. 1.
3. 3.
4. 2.

Second Page
Before Mugisa
1. 4.
2. 2.
3. 3.
4. 1.

After Mugisa
1. 2.
2. 1.
3. 3
4. 4.

The Gardener
(Textbook p. 212)

Vocabulary—Activity One (p. 56)

1. efficiently, efficiently, efficiently
2. gravely
3. sprouting
4. nurtured
5. vessels
6. employed
7. survive
8. corresponded

Vocabulary—Activity Two (p. 57)

1. A
2. B
3. A
4. B
5. B
6. A
7. A
8. B

Language Arts Activity (p. 59)

The Kittens are Similar

1. They are both two months old.
2. They love playing hide and seek.

The Kittens are Different

1. One is ginger and one is black.
2. One's green eyes glow like jewels and the other's green eyes look friendly and warm.

Jen and Ben are Different

1. Jen is a girl and Ben is a boy.
2. Jen has red hair and Ben has blond hair.
3. Jen likes books and clothes and Ben likes trucks and balls.

Jen and Ben are Alike

1. Both dislike going to sleep on time.
2. Both are sleepy in the morning.
3. Both hate soft-boiled eggs.
4. Both love apples and chocolate.
5. They have the same birthday.

Graphic Organizer (pp. 60-61)

First Page

1. Sample
2. 1.
3. 3.
4. 2.

Second Page

5. 4.
6. 1.
7. 2.
8. 3.

UNIT SIX

Rocks in His Head
(Textbook p. 262)

Vocabulary—Activity One (p. 62)

1. quarries
2. mineralogist
3. garnet
4. lift
5. confidence
6. solemnly
7. hesitation
8. admiration

Vocabulary—Activity Two (p. 63)

1. Lift
2. Quarries
3. Gar*net*

4. Solemnly
5. Conf**idence** (dents!)
6. Admi**ra**tion (ray)
7. He**sit**ation (sit)
8. **Mineral**ogist

Language Arts Activity (p. 65)

1. The kids on Maxy's block are nice, friendly, and caring.
2. a. The cousins are musical/like music/good at playing instruments.

   b. The cousins are good at/enjoy sports.

Graphic Organizer (pp. 66-67)

1. An old house—5
2. A lady riding in a Packard—7
3. A chess board—2
4. A sign saying Curator of Mineralogy—8
5. A pile of spare parts—4
6. A janitor's broom—6
7. Shelves with rocks on them—3
8. A sign that says "Antler Filling Station"—1

The Naming of Olga da Polga
(Textbook p. 274)

Vocabulary—Activity One (p. 68)

1. unaccustomed
2. delicacy
3. vanished
4. inhabitants
5. withdrawn
6. reassuring
7. temptingly
8. considered

Vocabulary—Activity Two (p. 69)

1. A
2. A
3. B
4. A
5. A
6. B
7. A
8. A

Language Arts Activity (p. 71)

1. F
2. R
3. F
4. F
5. R

Graphic Organizer (pp. 72-73)

Answers will vary.

A Toad for Tuesday—Part One
(Textbook p. 290)

Vocabulary—Activity One (p. 74)

1. sturdy
2. countless
3. glistening
4. gratitude
5. cautiously
6. snooze
7. sputtering
8. dazzled

Vocabulary—Activity Two (p. 75)

1. sputtered
2. cautiously
3. dazzling
4. gratitude
5. snooze
6. countless
7. glistened

Language Arts Activity (p. 77)

1. Character
2. Setting
3. Plot
4. Character
5. Main idea

Graphic Organizer (pp. 78-79)

First Page

Answers counterclockwise:

Eyes that blink: Warton
Calm nature: Warton
Clean table: Warton

Laundered tablecloth: Warton
Beetle Brittle: Morton
Antimacassar: Warton
Very Helpful: Morton
Clover blossom tea: Morton
Well-cared-for plant: Morton

Second Page

Some lunches: the knapsack
3 sweaters: Warton's back
Furry slippers: the knapsack
Warm cap: Warton's head
2 pairs of mittens: Warton's hands
4 coats: Warton
Skis: Warton's feet
An extra pair of mittens: knapsack
Beetle brittle: knapsack

A Toad for Tuesday—Part Two
(Textbook p. 304)

Vocabulary—Activity One (p. 80)

1. flustered
2. dreary
3. astonished
4. refreshing
5. unravel
6. snarled
7. talons
8. flabbergasted

Vocabulary—Activity Two (p. 81)

1. A
2. B
3. A
4. A
5. A

Language Arts Activity (p. 83)

1. The air was hot and *humid*. Gramps and Gram sat on their front porch and fanned themselves as they rocked back and forth in their *creaky,* squeaky rocking chairs.
2. The alligator slithered through the thick, *slimy* mud. He was the longest, ugliest, and *meanest*-looking alligator I'd ever seen.

Workbook Answer Guide

3. Pop, pop, pop went the popcorn. Little Jessica had taken the lid off of the popcorn maker, and popcorn was *snowing* down all over Mom's spotlessly *clean* kitchen floor like flakes of pure white.

4. Silently the Indian scout walked through the dark woods. He found his way by the light of the gleaming *silvery* moon that shone *brightly* through the leaves.

5. Mr. Clark, who owned the candy store, was a *grouchy,* short-tempered man. The kids were a little afraid of him and asked for candy in soft, *frightened* voices.

6. New York City is full of *tall* buildings. The people hurry along the streets, always looking busy and *rushed*. The horns toot loudly, and the subways *rattle* and roar beneath the ground.

Graphic Organizer (pp. 84-85)

First Page

The owl doesn't have a name/The owl chooses George for his name.

The owl doesn't have a friend/George now has Warton as a friend.

George says he doesn't want any tea/George asks Warton to make some tea.

George has never laughed/George laughs at Warton's story.

George never said "goodnight"/George says "goodnight" to Warton.

George usually stayed out late/George starts to come home earlier.

George had no one to tell his troubles to/George tells Warton what a bad day he had.

Second Page

The nest was dark and dreary the first night. *Candles*

Warton was cold and uncomfortable the first night. *Furry slippers and robe*

Warton was cold and tired and needed something hot and refreshing. *Pot of tea*

The nest was a mess. *Broom and dustpan*

Warton enjoyed good conversation. *Toad and owl talking over tea*

The owl's nest was so high that there was no way to escape from it. *Sweater partially unraveled*

George kept reminding Warton that he would eat him. *Heart with word "hope" in it*

A Toad for Tuesday—Part Three
(Textbook p. 322)

Vocabulary—Activity One (p. 86)

1. gaped
2. tattered
3. stirring
4. bewilderment
5. exasperated
6. wooded
7. passageway
8. immensely

Vocabulary—Activity Two (p. 87)

Answers will vary.

Language Arts Activity (p. 89)

The story's mood is cozy.

The fire in the fireplace tells us it's cold outside.

The clock on the wall tells us it's a little after seven. We do not know whether it is morning or evening just by looking at the picture. (We learn that it is evening in the first paragraph of the text.)

Characters

1. Warton is smiling pleasantly in the picture.
2. Morton is pouring the tea.
3. The picture creates a sense of friendship and warmth. The brothers are sitting together looking happy and peaceful, one is serving the other, they are conversing, and the atmosphere is congenial.

Graphic Organizer (pp. 90-91)

WHO...?

... *came to rescue Warton?* Sy

... *did Warton think would miss him the most if the owl ate him?* Morton

... *did Warton see in the distance as he and the mice skied over the snow?* George

... *was attacking George?* A fox

... *had told George how good juniper-berry tea was?* Warton

... *did George really want as a friend?* George

... *did Warton really want as a friend?* Warton

... *gave Warton a ride to Aunt Toolia's?* George

... *probably enjoyed the beetle brittle to the very last drop?* Aunt Toolia